The Art of InterGroup Peace

by George C. Halvorson

© George C. Halvorson. All rights reserved. 2017 edition.
ISBN 978-0996499460

Dedication

This book is dedicated to Sun Tzu, who pioneered taking strategic directions to intergroup interactions on the field of war in his book *Art of War* — and to Nelson Mandela who personified, exemplified, and demonstrated in very real ways the things we need to do to achieve InterGroup Peace.

Acknowledgments

My deepest gratitude and my deepest appreciation to my family for all the time that I spent away from family functions and activities in the past couple of years writing this set of books and for giving me often spirited and always insightful feedback on the concepts, contentions, beliefs, thought processes and paradigms that are the anchor for this work. This set of books is not perfect, but it is significantly closer to being perfect as a result of that process and that much appreciated and sometimes challenging and invariably thought provoking feedback. Special thanks to Gina whose support and assistance kept the process on track and made all of the books possible.

Contents

PREFACE
We Need a Strategy and a Commitment to Help Create and Maintain
InterGroup Peace in America 1

INTRODUCTION
The Art of InterGroup Peace 17

CHAPTER ONE
We Need to Be Skilled at The Art of InterGroup Peace 75

CHAPTER TWO
Our Us/Them Instincts Can Make Peace Both Very Difficult and Possible 95

CHAPTER THREE
We Need to Avoid Having Any Part of Us Be Them 123

CHAPTER FOUR
Turf, Traitor, Riot, and Alpha Instincts Can All Have Huge Impact on
InterGroup Interactions 139

CHAPTER FIVE
Our Cultures Can Be Used as Anchors for Peace or as Triggers for Conflict 175

CHAPTER SIX
We Can Build and Shape Our Cultures to Meet Our Needs 207

CHAPTER SEVEN
Learning About Peace and Conflict from Other Multi-Ethnic Countries 223

CHAPTER EIGHT
Six Steps and Key Triggers to Use to Create Instinct Supported Alignment 257

CHAPTER NINE
Basic Organizational Models for InterGroup Interactions 301

CHAPTER TEN
We Need Win/Win Commitments for All Groups to Sustain InterGroup Peace
in America 347

CHAPTER ELEVEN
We Need to Support Every Child and Improve Our Health Together 373

CHAPTER TWELVE
Our Us/Them Instincts Have Created Much of Our History 419

CHAPTER THIRTEEN
Our History Included Inventing "White" and Using "White" to Discriminate 445

CHAPTER FOURTEEN
The Art of InterGroup Peace for America Needs to Turn Our Instincts into Assets
and Give Us the Tools We Need to Defeat Our Common Foes 477

CHAPTER FIFTEEN
Threats, Challenges, and Risks to Peace. 503

CHAPTER SIXTEEN
Multiple Issues Create the Stress and Anger That Triggers the Explosions 533

CHAPTER SEVENTEEN
The American Dream and Our Core Values Can and Should Unite Us All
and Create Peace. 565

PREFACE

We Need a Strategy and a Commitment to Help Create and Maintain InterGroup Peace in America

WE LIVE IN hard times. We have groups of people in our country who are angry with other groups of people at some very basic levels. People are angry with other people at a clearly inter group level, and people are doing negative things to one another individually and in groups in the context of that anger.

We need to take that whole situation extremely seriously and we need to understand exactly what is happening because we can be permanently damaged as a nation if we do not get this right.

We are at risk of having key parts of what we do, and key parts of who we are badly damaged by basic levels of inter group anger, inter group conflict, negative inter group ethics, dysfunctional and divisive inter group beliefs, and deeply dangerous and too often intentionally destructive inter group values that will allow people in this country to do damaging things to one another and to feel right and justified in doing them.

That is the future we will face if we don't intervene and very intentionally keep our worst sets of inter group instincts from steering us as a nation to truly dangerous inter group interactions.

We have fallen under the influence and control of some very dangerous instinctive behavior packages. We are going through an array of negative inter group interactions that are deeply embedded in a context of instinct driven behaviors, emotions, thought processes, and basic beliefs.

Our instincts are shaping our thought processes and our beliefs — and we are not even aware (most of the time) that we are under their influence and control. We are angry and distrustful with one another and we generally do not know or even suspect why we have the levels of anger and division that we are feeling.

We feel divided and angry, and that anger feels justified in every angry person because it is instinctive in ways that cause us each to feel justification for those feelings. The sense of division that affects too many of us today in multiple ways seems absolutely right and emotionally normal and correct to us, because our instincts skew our thinking and emotions, and our instincts make us feel entirely right when we do the things that our instincts guide and steer us to do.

Knowledge is power. We need knowledge about the power of instincts over our lives — and we need that knowledge about the impact and the role of instincts now.

We need to understand those specific sets of instincts that do the most damage to us in order to overcome their most negative impacts, and to very intentionally and deliberately create and maintain inter group Peace in America.

We all need to know what our most relevant group related instincts are — and we each need to know how they influence what we feel, think, believe, and do relative to each other and to people from other groups.

"Us/Them" Instincts Cap the Danger List

We are most heavily impacted at this point in our history by our instincts that divide the world into "Us" and "Them," and then have us act very differently toward people based on our perception of whether people are "Us" or "Them."

We do kind, caring and protective things to our "Us" — but we do bad, damaging and even evil things to "Them." Dangerously, the way the actual process works, we too often feel no guilt, and we too often do not trigger any sense of conscience or remorse in doing damaging things to "Them."

We, in fact, often celebrate damaging them, and it often feels entirely right and good to us when we keep them from succeeding.

In political campaigns, when those sets of instincts are activated, we tell lies and we feel no ethical relevance or remorse about the falsehoods we tell, because our basic instinct structured value set, embedded in our minds, forgives and even encourages any sets of behaviors that do damage to whoever we perceive to be "Them."

When those instincts are activated, we not only forgive our leaders for not telling us the truth — we too often actually want our leaders to use false information if we believe that false information will damage the enemy that we perceive to exist in those situations.

Those thought processes clearly lead us very quickly to very dangerous and dysfunctional interactions — and we need to know them for what they are and chose in personally accountable ways to use a different set of values to guide our thinking about other people in those settings.

We need our political leaders to stop getting their guidance and moral compass from our most negative instincts, and we need our leaders to replace Art of War thinking with Art of Peace thinking.

Those deeply negative ways of thinking about the other group in conflicted settings actually anchored a famous book called *The Art of War*, which was the direct and linear inspiration for this book about inter group Peace.

The Art of War was written roughly two thousand years ago to advise leaders in that highly conflicted and dangerous era about how to win wars. The author of that book taught leaders how to survive and defeat enemies who wanted to destroy and defeat their own group of people. It is a powerful and useful book — and it has clear instinctive linkages at several levels.

Very clear and basic inter group instincts that encourage unethical and damaging inter group and interpersonal behaviors are clearly embedded in that book. Sun Tzu, the author of *The Art of War*, not only allowed for lies and falsehoods as part of his strategic approach — he strongly recommended using them and he actually built lists of lies to tell and suggested a number of specific ways to deceive and betray the enemy that you face.

American politics today are increasingly under the influence of similar sets of our most negative instinct guided inter group values. Our political environment in this country has changed from our political interactions being perceived to be differences between two opposing but basically mutually respectful political parties who each shared a core sense of being a kind of American "Us," into being a set of confrontations between good and evil where we now too often perceive the other side in American politics to be a "Them" at an instinct triggering level.

When those particular sets of inter group instincts are activated, we all tend to believe that the current "They" in our political settings are actually a clear and intentionally damaging Enemy and not just the incorrect Opposition.

Being the incorrect and misguided opposition is very different from being the viscerally evil enemy who must be defeated and crushed in order for good to prevail.

That sounds like extreme language, but sadly, we do now have political parties who both demonize and dehumanize the other party, and who do actually see the other party and its leaders as being evil — not just wrong.

That is a very dangerous way for us to conduct our political interactions. We do very bad things to people in far too many ways when we perceive them to be both enemies and "Them."

We need to change the way we think about that entire set of issues and interactions.

The good news is — we do not need to stay on this dysfunctional and damaging trajectory as a country. We can rise above this level of negative and dysfunctional interactions. We can actually choose to bring our political interactions back to a higher and more civil and more civilized level.

To do that, we will need to make the conscious decision to see and understand both how we think and what we actually just did — and we will need to make the conscious and intellectually informed decision to return our perception of the other party in our political environment to being the opposition instead of being the enemy.

When we as a people understand what just happened to us in very dysfunctional ways in this extremely divisive political campaign, we can and should change what we are doing. We can and should collectively make the enlightened and accountable decision to call our leaders and key elements of our news media to a higher standard for the next set of elections.

We can and should each choose to look at our own thought processes and recognize how much we have each allowed our "Us/Them" instincts to skew and even control our thoughts and emotions in the current political environment. We can decide to go forward into the next round of elections pushing hard for our own sides to prevail politically — but with a sense of our shared values as Americans as core to that process, and not with an obsessive focus on our most divisive differences.

We need to bring Peace to our political settings — and we need to bring Peace to all of our other inter group settings as communities and as a country.

We have more than just current political anger in our country. This book reaches far beyond the political differences we have into the vary basic inter group issues we have as a country.

When we look honestly at where we are today, we need to recognize and understand that we, as a country, also have inter group anger with deep racial, ethnic, economic, and cultural roots. We need to deal with each of those sets of issues in order for us to have a successful future as groups and as a country.

The intense political division we face today as a country is exacerbated by a number of basic and significant inter group angers and inter group divisions that have very clear racial, ethnic, and economic underpinnings. We have a Black Lives Matters group, for example, that has a clearly stated belief system that says there are evil things being done to Black people in this country for racial reasons. Those concerns about inter group damage are being felt and expressed along clearly racial lines for many people.

We have had protests and even riots in a number of our communities. We need to look clearly at what is actually going on in each of those settings. We need to be extremely honest with ourselves about the inter group situation we are in, and we need to build on that honesty to give all groups the best chance of success going forward into our future

We need to extend the American Dream to every group.

The American Dream is a wonderful, powerful, and effective dream that has allowed many Americans to do really well with their lives.

We have created barriers for too many people to that dream — and we need to make those barriers for all of those groups of people to go away.

We are actually trying to do exactly that as a country. We have made a number of very enlightened changes in our laws in the last half century or so to improve inclusion in that dream and to make explicit discrimination by group illegal. We have much to be proud of in a wide range of inter group discrimination areas.

But even with an extensive set of very positive and directionally correct new laws and regulations, there are key sets of numbers that show us today that we have a long way to go as a country relative to inter group equity and inter group alignment.

There are clear differences in average economic status in many communities by group that we need to both understand and address in intentional ways.

The inter group numbers are painful and some of the basic data points prove how far we have to go. Graduation rates from both high school and college are much lower for our minority Americans, for example. We have much lower graduation rates and school proficiency levels for minority Americans in too many of our schools.

Economic issues are also painfully obvious. We cannot deny the cold, hard economic fact that minority Americans have an average net worth of less than a third of the average net worth of White Americans.

That lower average economic status is true for Black Americans, Hispanic Americans, and Native Americans. Every group of Americans has some very wealthy and successful people, but the overall group data points us to issues that must be addressed.

No one can deny the numbers. Differences exist. Minority Americans are much more likely to drop out of school, and minority Americans are much more likely to be imprisoned.

We actually have more African American males in jail or on probation in this country today than the total number of African American males who were enslaved at the beginning of the civil war.

The slaves who were in this country before the Civil War could not vote — and people who are convicted of felonies in this country today also can not vote — so there are some people who believe we are actually using our prison systems in a very expensive, but very intentional way to deny a huge percentage of minority Americans the ballot box.

Those are a complex set of issues — but they are very real and it is clear that there are some very real issues that need to be addressed if we want inter group Peace and prosperity in our country.

Our inter group issues in this country tend to be racial, ethnic, cultural, and economic — but they do not tend to be religious. That is a blessing. We have a relatively low level of discrimination and actual internal conflict in our country today that is based on religion.

However, we need to know and clearly see that the rest of the world does have multiple religious conflicts, religious stress points, and even religious wars going on — with Shia, Sunnis, Kurds, Syrian Alawites, Israeli Jews, and other tribe linked religious alignments for groups of people in various settings, that too often cause people to kill each other in huge numbers with no sense of guilt in each of the areas where those particular sets of issues are creating inter group conflicts.

Tribes and religions tend to create unholy alignments around damaging inter group behavior. The Middle East, much of Africa, much of Asia, Indonesia, and major portions of Sri Lanka have hundreds of thousands, and even millions of people in open conflicts and killing each other based on the religious alignment of their tribes. More than 50 million people are in exile in the world today today — and various kinds of ethnic cleansing with religious links are forcing many people in far too many settings to be exiled from their tribal and ethnic homeland.

We have more than 200 ethnic conflicts going on in the world today. They exist in almost every inter ethnic setting.

Russia, China, and India each have groups of people in their countries doing battle and seeking autonomy from the nation they are in. Religion has very clear linkages to most of those conflicts. The people seeking autonomy in each of those settings generally have a different religion alignment and religious identity than the people around them.

We have not faced those purely religious conflicts to a large degree in our country, but we do have had a growing number of places where damage is being done to Americans along religious lines as a spillover from those religious conflicts in those other settings. Killings, bombings, and mass murders in Boston, Florida, and Southern California are direct spillovers from those Middle Eastern and European religion anchored conflicts.

We need to be very sure that we minimize the damage levels that exist here in our country as local spillovers from those sets of conflicts.

We do not have religious wars in this country, but we do have very serious and significant sets of political, ethnic, racial, and economic inter group issues, angers, and even open inter group conflicts to deal with.

We can make a huge difference and we can change the trajectories of those inter group conflicts if we are honest about what they are and why they exist — and if we deal with them directly in the interest of truly achieving inter group Peace in America.

The four InterGroup books all deal directly and explicitly with those sets of issues.

In our own country, we need to understand what we are doing and what we have done relative to our inter group angers and behaviors, and we need to take steps that will lead us to a future of inter group Peace — not to a future of perpetual inter group conflict and inter group damage.

Again — we need to start by being extremely honest with ourselves. This is not a time for magical thinking, wishful thinking, or dogmatic and ideological politically correct thinking. We need to look at facts of each situation. We need to know both who we are today, and what we are becoming.

Honesty needs to anchor that process. We have to tell the truth to each other about who we are and what we have done.

We Are on an Irreversible Path to Diversity — with a Majority of Births in Our Country This Year to our Minority Mothers

To anchor that entire process, we all need to recognize that we are on an absolutely irreversible path to being an extremely diverse country. That is our future. That extreme diversity for this country is a new reality and it is beyond dispute or debate.

We have changed. We have been a country that was run by a very sizable White majority group for a couple of centuries. That White majority group created an instinct supported sense of "Us" for itself, and that majority group then discriminated in many intentional and sometimes creative ways as an "Us" against each of the minority groups in this country.

The books *Cusp of Chaos*, *Primal Pathways*, and *Peace In Our Time* all describe that discrimination and the negative impact it has had on all of the minority groups that make up the fabric of America.

Slavery, Jim Crow Laws, land purchase exclusions, denials of voting rights, denial of inter group marriages, and multiple other levels of negative inter group behaviors that were channeled and fueled by the "Us/Them" instincts of the White majority are described and explained in those books.

Our challenge today is not to go back and try to change that old reality — because that old reality is about to become irrelevant. We don't need to fix the past. We now need to steer the future.

We all now need to recognize the fact that America is becoming much more diverse — and the reality that we will need to address and will need to deal with to create Peace in America will be a reality of several groups working together without having a single group as the overwhelming majority.

We need to become very good at being diverse — and we need to turn our diversity into the strength that it must be for us to succeed and survive as a nation — because we have crossed the line into our future of irrevocable diversity and we can never go back.

Look at who is being born here to be absolutely clear about what our future will be.

We very definitively crossed that line into our future this year when half of our births in this country were to our minority populations. We no longer have White births as the majority of births in America. Those days are gone and they will never return.

We also have reached the point this year where the majority of children in our public schools are minority children.

Our children are our future. That is an obvious fact. Our future is clear. Our future is Brown, Black, Asian and White — with White clearly being a major group, but not the majority group in all settings.

Hawaii, Detroit and Los Angeles today each look a lot like the entire country will look tomorrow.

So we are on an irreversible path to diversity — and we need to recognize that path and channel ourselves into the best possible future. That can and should be done.

We can turn that highly diverse future for this country into a wonderful tomorrow — where we extend the American Dream successfully to all Americans — where we all do well and prosper.

Or we can tribalize — we can divide — and we can let our worst "Us/Them" instincts steer us into behaviors in our communities that will cause us to be economically weak, educationally deficient, and collectively unsafe.

If we unite around our shared values, we truly can continue being great as a nation as we unite. We can be stronger and we can be better than we ever were if we turn our diversity into the strength it should be.

This set of InterGroup books and the overall Art of Peace strategy calls for us to unite around our shared values. This set of books calls for us to turn our diversity into a strength and major asset for the country.

This set of books also calls for us to avoid, reject, and overcome the seductive slippery slope into parochial inter group conflict, and to align with each other based on our shared and collective commitment to win/win outcomes for us all.

We need to collectively and individually turn our instincts into our servants, and have our instincts be our tools rather than having our instincts steering us blindly to damaging behaviors and destructive places.

In our usual historical approach to running our lives and our communities, our core instincts set our goals and we then build cultures in each setting and in each group to help us achieve those instinctive goals. We have hierarchical instincts, for example, so we have hierarchies everywhere and every culture invents the rules and the expectations of its hierarchy.

We feel right at a core level when our behaviors are aligned with our instincts — and we feel right at a core level when or behaviors are aligned with our cultures. We all have strong instincts to align with our culture and to be loyal to our culture — and we generally achieve our instinctive goals in each culture in the context and expectations that the culture builds to guide us in achieving our instinctive goals.

Our intellect generally helps us achieve both those instinctive goals and those cultural goals.

In that model, our intellect serves as the tool of both the culture and the instinct to guide our lives.

That is the normal process — but we now know that is not the most enlightened approach to use for guiding our lives. We can do better — and at this point in our history, we need to do better to prosper, to thrive and to even survive.

We need to flip that overall process over, and we need to very intentionally and explicitly reverse it. We need to add enlightened thinking to the process as a core for what we do.

We need our intellect to build a set of shared values and enlightened goals, and we then need to very intentionally and deliberately structure our cultures in each setting to help us achieve those enlightened goals in ways that still meet the core and best needs of our instincts.

We need to be accountable. We need to be ethically, morally, and intellectually accountable.

We need to be accountable at a higher level for our lives and for our individual and group behaviors.

We need accountability as individuals for enlightened behaviors, and we need explicit accountability as groups to functionally achieve those enlightened values in each of our settings.

The InterGroup books are intended to help directly with that process. Becoming accountable is the goal of the InterGroup process — and the books are intended to help us be accountable.

Each book offers a piece of the pathway to more enlightened and accountable behaviors. Each book has its role and function for the inter group Peace process.

Primal Pathways explains our instinctive inter group behavior and how it affects our lives.

Cusp of Chaos explains what a mess we are in today because of those instinctive behaviors.

Peace In Our Time explains how various settings have dealt successfully with that mess, using instinctive behaviors as part of the tool kit for solving them.

Three Key Years explains the science and the process of brain development in kids and explains what we need to do for each child from every group in the first months and years of life to give every child strong brains and a best start in life. We can't achieve inter group Peace in America until we help children succeed from every group.

This book — *The Art of InterGroup Peace* — is a very intentional explicit, and carefully field tested counter balance to the old Sun Tzu *Art of War* book. This book was written to create a sense of context and to give us tools we can use in every setting to create alignment, understanding, and Peace.

The Art of War preaches deceit, deception, and teaches and promotes the goal of crushing and destroying the other side. The basic Art of Peace strategy that is embedded in this book teaches honesty, transparency, and the clear shared and warmly embraced goal of having us all succeed.

Win/Win in *The Art of InterGroup Peace* replaces Win/Lose or even Lose/Lose in *The Art of War*.

We do need to be good today at the Art of Peace. We really don't have a good alternative.

We should not have anyone lose. We should have everyone win.

That can be done when we understand the tool kits, approaches, and commitments that can create win/win outcomes in any settings.

Use the InterGroup books to set up conversations and thought processes about this entire range and set of issues — and then make the process you chose to use in various settings even better than the one described in these books.

We Need Continuous Improvement for InterGroup Peace

The very best organizations today in both business and health care use a very well engineered and extremely intentional process of continuous improvement to create great products and great care. Organizations who use those continuous improvement tools well tend to excel in what they do. That approach to continuous improvement is both a tool kit and a commitment, and it has great power to create both group alignment and inspire and channel creative thinking on any topic it addresses.

Continuous improvement assumes we do more than just set performance goals in any given area. Continuous improvement assumes we figure out the explicit process that helped us achieve the goals and then figure out ways of continuously making that process better so that the outcome gets continuously better.

The author of this book saw continuous improvement processes and tools cut the HIV death rate in half for a very large population — and cut the hospital pressure ulcer rate drop from 5 percent of patients to less than 1 percent of patients in a large and complex care system, by continuously improving care and by doing it in a culture that made the patient the focus of everything the care team did.

Diversity was a key part of that organization's success. The organization that achieved those very high quality improvement goals for millions of people was 51 percent diverse in its patient base, and more than 59 percent diverse in its work force.

That organization had only two of its eight Regional Presidents as white males, and they actually ran smaller Regions. It was diverse at every level. It was excellent, and performed well as an overall organization because of how inclusive it was at every level.

Diversity can create excellence when it is anchored in inclusion and when people work together for common goals in a shared value based culture, and when people anchor their thinking in the tools and practices of Continuous Improvement.

Both the book *Peace In Our Time* and the book *KP Inside* explain how to turn inclusion into performance excellence.

We need to take a similar process-based look at our diversity as a nation — and we need our shared commitment to both win/win outcomes and continuous improvement to cause us to all help each other succeed.

The alternatives to inter group Peace for us as a nation are truly grim. We have ample proof of how ugly those alternatives are. We have anger and inter group damage in too many settings today. Let's change the worst parts of our current trajectory and let's do it in ways that will give us long-term success and real Peace for us as a nation and a people.

Let's give our grandchildren the best world we can give them, and let's have our grand children look back at us and thank us for our wisdom, our skill, and our commitment and for our obvious love for them and for their future.

Enjoy the books and have fun with all of the inter group tools.

Peace.

It can be done — and we really can't afford the alternative.

INTRODUCTION

The Art of InterGroup Peace

WE NEED TO be skilled at creating Peace.

We live in a deeply conflicted world. There are more than 200 current ethnic conflicts today in countries around the world — settings where people are damaging each other and killing one another in purely inter group conflicts.

In our own country, we are not killing each other in groups, but we have deep and long-standing levels of inter group anger and inter group division — and we are seeing that anger and division manifest itself in a number of settings when flashpoint events in those settings unleash and uncover layers of underlying inter group distrust, inter group unhappiness, inter group resentment, and deep seated inter group anger.

We have had protests, demonstrations, and even riots in a number of settings that tell us clearly that there are inter group angers and inter group stress points that are very real and very relevant to people in those settings.

This book was written to help deal with those issues. This is a book from the Instititute for InterGroup Understanding about creating and protecting inter group Peace. It is a "how to" for creating inter group Peace in America — with some advice offered as well about how to create and maintain inter group Peace in other settings in the world.

This book is intended to help key people, and key groups of people in each relevant setting, be successful and effective at achieving what this book calls The Art of InterGroup Peace. This book is based on the belief that we need to be very good in our country at The Art of InterGroup Peace, or we will face a future of growing inter group conflict and of sadly inevitable and extensive inter group damage that will significantly undermine our future success as a nation and as a people.

We are not a nation at Peace with itself today. We have done well on a range of inter group issues in a significant number of areas of our society, but we have other areas where we have ongoing currents of inter group anger and division that need resolution.

We Have Been a Beacon of Enlightenment and Evil

We have been a beacon of enlightenment to the world in a number of key ways. There are a number of ways where we are the most enlightened country on the planet. But there are also far too many areas where our inter group behaviors and our group interactions have been divisive, damaging, dysfunctional, and, far too often, intentionally and deliberately destructive. There are too many instances where those interactions have been cruel, and even — in the worst sense of that word — clearly evil.

It is a very bad thing when we do evil things to one another. It is particularly bad when we do evil things to each other as groups and when we do evil things to groups for long periods of time. Sadly — we have a history as a nation of doing exactly that in a number of undeniable and irrefutable ways for very long periods of time.

We have done some things well. We have done some things very well. We have been making significant progress as a nation in a number of important inter group areas — and we should recognize, understand, honor, defend, protect, and even celebrate that progress — but we very clearly also have continuing streams, currents, and ongoing patterns of inter group distrust, anger, and division that have the potential to take us to some very dysfunctional, dangerous, damaging, and destructive outcomes in our future as a country if we don't change specific inter group and interpersonal behaviors in some key areas.

The inter group problems we see as a country have deep historic roots and those deeply rooted problems are being exacerbated in many settings by our rapidly growing diversity. Our growing diversity is changing the inter group realities for our communities and for our country and changing them much more rapidly than most people either know or understand.

We are becoming much more diverse as a country. We all need to recognize and understand that reality because if we handle it badly, we will be badly damaged and the future for all sets of people in this country will be challenged and grim.

We Are Becoming More Diverse at a Rapid Rate

Our diversity as a country is increasing at a rapid and powerful level and pace that significantly exceeds most peoples' awareness level about those group relevant population composition realities. We are changing from being a country that has had White Americans as our single very large majority group that has functioned as our defining and controlling majority ethnic group for literally hundreds of years, and we are becoming a country with several very large minority populations whose growing collective size will soon erase forever that long-standing majority group status for that old White majority.

We all need to see and understand both that reality and what it will mean for us as a country going forward into our future as a people and a nation.

The path we are on to our new and permanent levels of diversity is beyond debate, and it is a path we cannot and will not change.

Look at the actual situation today.

More Than Half Our Births Last Year Were Born to Minority Americans

A basic logistical fact of life is that our future population as a country comes overwhelmingly from the babies who are born to our people. We have some immigration — but actual births in this country are the key and largest determinant of who our future population will be.

More than half of the actual births in this country last year were to our minority populations.

That is an historic change. After several centuries of White Americans having the largest number of births in America, we have now reached a reality where White Americans no longer make up a majority of our births. Most births are now to our minority mothers.

More than half of the students in our public school system this year are already from our minority populations. The diversity of our schools has also reached an historic group composition tipping point and our school diversity has already moved beyond it.

White Americans continue to make up the majority group for the entire country, but we now have many counties and a growing number of major cities that no longer have a majority ethnic or racial group of any kind.

All groups in those highly diverse cities now share varying levels of minority status. If there is a majority group in an American city today, there is a good chance that the current majority group is one of our former minority groups for that city. More often than not, no group is currently in a pure majority status in our largest cities.

We all need to recognize the fact that our pathway to extremely high levels of diversity as a nation is inevitable, inexorable, indisputable, irreversible, and highly imminent — effectively, immediate.

That increasing level of diversity is happening now and it will continue to happen for the foreseeable future.

We Need Our Diversity to Be a Strength – Not a Risk or a Danger

What does that set of demographic realities tell us?

It tells us that we are today at a point in our history where we need to make our growing diversity a strength, a benefit, an asset, and even a blessing — rather than having our diversity be a source of division and the cause of internal inter group conflict in our various workplaces, schools and community settings.

That can be done. We can, in fact, make our growing diversity into a strength and an asset. That is very possible to do. This book and its sister books point out how to do exactly that.

We do not need to go down the road of having our diversity divide and weaken us. We can have our diversity make us better, stronger, and more successful as a people and a nation.

We can turn our growing diversity into an asset, if we very intentionally create alignment in the right ways for all of the groups that make up the rich fabric of our nation's population, and then work together in very intentional and explicit ways to make America great into the foreseeable future.

We can have our growing diversity be an asset in each setting if we create alignment about our core beliefs and our core values and if we create that alignment in meaningful and effective ways for people in each of our work settings, communities, and schools.

Creating that alignment is the core strategy of *The Art of InterGroup Peace*. This book was written to help us understand, support, and functionally achieve that goal.

We will either be just another multi tribal nation at war with itself — and we will clearly suffer both internal and external damage for all of our people from every group if we choose to go down that path — or we can choose to align around our best values, expand access to the mutually beneficial achievement of the American Dream for all Americans—and have a future that creates safety, prosperity and success for people from every American Group.

The clear and immediate reality is that we can hurt ourselves — or we can help ourselves — and helping ourselves is clearly better.

It will not be easy. We will need to do the work of helping ourselves very intentionally and in mutually enlightened ways — but we can do that if we recognize both intellectually and emotionally exactly who we are today and if we collectively understand what we need to do to have a future where we make each other successful rather than being at war with each other and doing damage to people from the other groups who make up the rich fabric of the people of America.

We need a plan.

A successful future will not appear of its own accord. We need to both design and build it. An enlightened and intellectually grounded strategy of intentional and effective inter group and interpersonal alignment needs to be both our plan and our explicit collective goal at this point in our history.

This book was written to explain where we are today and to outline both that strategy and its underpinnings. This book was also written to very directly help support that process of alignment.

This book is anchored in the belief that we need to be a nation, and a people united and mutually supported and reinforced by our enlightened and heartfelt-shared beliefs — not a nation divided by race, ethnicity, economic status, religious belief, or by any other category or grouping that divides us.

This book is anchored in the belief that we will can and will succeed, thrive, prosper, and even jointly and individually win when we go intentionally and collectively down those enlightened and intellectually grounded paths together.

This book is supported by three sister books about instinctive behaviors — *Primal Pathways*, *Cusp of Chaos*, and *Peace In Our Time* — that each explain in some detail who we are now and outline ways we can use our high levels of diversity to make us hugely successful as a nation and a people.

This book is also very directly supported by *Three Key Years* — a book that explains how we can eliminate the learning gaps and reduce the significant differences in education attainment, health care status, economic status and incarceration rates that exist today in this country by doing the right things for every child from every group in the first three years of life for each child.

Those five books work as a package to describe the inter group situations we face, and have faced and to describe what we need to do next to understand our own behaviors and to do what we need to do to personally and collectively succeed as a people and a nation.

This particular book explains how we can work together as a nation and a people to create and protect inter group Peace for America.

The Art of InterGroup Peace strategy and approach outlined in this book to create inter group Peace for America is very directly and intentionally anchored in, and built on the foundation of a set of carefully

chosen, clearly articulated, very explicit shared values, and mutually supported, collectively enlightened, and fully aligned beliefs we can use to become an American "Us."

The final chapter of this book describes those foundational values and explains how we can use them to align us in the future because those values actually now serve as an anchor and a direct guide for the best parts of who we are today as a nation and a people.

If we want to turn our growing diversity into the strength and the asset that it should and can be — we need to very deliberately come together now as a nation that is literally and clearly aligned as a people based on that shared, clearly understood, explicit, and very intentionally inclusive system and set of core values and enlightened beliefs.

Alignment at those levels is our only hope. We need to be aligned around our shared beliefs or we will tribalize, and we will each be aligned in separate subsets around our more primal, divided and divisive sets of "Us." Falling now into purely tribalized conflict is actually a very tempting pathway for us to go down. The last election cycle pointed us in some dangerous directions and we need to be sure not to damage ourselves by going down some of those divisive paths.

Some of our most negative thought processes are emotionally reinforced and rewarded by triggering inter group anger — and that anger is far too easy to trigger in ways that directly affect and guide our emotions, behaviors and beliefs. We cannot allow that basic and primal set of instinctive emotional rewards that are too easily triggered by doing negative things to shape our future as a country.

We will collectively fail and we will be damaged as groups, as individuals, and as a nation if we allow ourselves to fall victim to the slippery slope that exists in the direction of those seductive and self reinforcing highly negative and extremely dangerous inter group interactions and emotions.

We need all of us to understand that reality. We are at risk of finding inter group conflict to be an emotionally attractive path for us to follow. Our growing diversity can activate that kind of conflict.

We need to choose with solid intellectual and ethical underpinnings to go in the exact opposite direction — and we need at this point in our history to make our diversity a strength and an asset rather than a pathway to conflict and anger.

We need people in each diverse setting to celebrate, appreciate, understand and utilize our diversity and we need to have our diversity function as a benefit and a strength — not a risk or a liability in each setting.

That can be done. These InterGroup books outline, describe and explain specific ways that approach has already been done successfully in very diverse settings.

We know from settings where that strategy has been used that being diverse can create synergy, creativity, innovation, collaboration, shared learning, mutual defense and shared security, collective growth, and mutual support in ways that let us all embark on a journey of continuous improvement to outcomes where we all benefit and where our future will be more secure because we share it with one another.

We need to be both diverse and united in order to have our diversity be a strength rather than a weakness.

Being united in an important and anchoring way is a core strength of the strategy for having diversity be an asset. As a core strategy for inter group Peace and mutual success, we need to be a people united by our actions and united by our shared core beliefs.

We need to be mutually committed to a set of core values that defines both who we are and how we will interact with one another.

The alternative we face to alignment our diverse people by those shared core value levels is ugly and grim. If we don't come together as a nation unified by our beliefs, then we will far too easily divide by group, and we will face the grim, damaging, collectively dangerous, and highly dysfunctional future of being just another tribalized nation at war with itself.

There are more than 200 significant ethnic conflicts going on in the world today — and we will become just another nation at war with itself if we don't choose, instead, to accept our own growing diversity as a strength rather than a threat.

If we don't decide to create that alignment around the values we share in the face of our growing diversity, we will find ourselves with diverse work places, diverse schools, and diverse communities that are divided against themselves, and we will find ourselves in a state of inter group stress and inter group conflict that will do damage to each of us and to all of us in each of those settings.

Nations Are Now at War with Themselves

We would not be alone if we achieve that situation and that tribalized and conflicted status for ourselves as a nation.

The world is full of nations who are at war with themselves. World history is on a new path. War in the old world used to be between separate nation states. That was the pattern for wars for centuries. It has changed. Wars between nations are now rare.

We are still a world at war — but the wars that define and damage us today are civil wars. Civil wars exist in many settings today. The new model of internal wars that happen entirely inside nations is everywhere. War is now an internal phenomenon. Wars within nations and inter group conflicts that exist entirely inside nations are now happening all over the world.

There are literally more than 200 active ethnic conflicts going on in various settings in the world today, and people are damaging other people in each of those settings.

There are clear historic reasons for the emergence of those inter group conflicts in all of those other countries. *Cusp of Chaos* outlines those realities in those other internally conflicted countries in some detail. The tides of history are now creating a significant number of newly independent nation-states that currently actual do battle with themselves and who often do things that significantly damage their own people.

Both colonial powers and the Soviet Union dominated major areas of the world for a long time — and those overarching powers each used their armies and their police forces to keep the traditional and historical ethnic conflicts that existed in many settings from being relevant and doing damage to people in those settings while they were under either Soviet or colonial control.

The colonial powers and the Soviet Union had clear economic and functional reasons to suppress local ethnic conflict — and they did that conflict suppression very consistently and very effectively for a very long period of time in many settings.

They often played one ethnic group against another in the local settings as part of their control strategy — and that part of their strategy kept temporary local Peace but it often exacerbated long term inter group hatreds and tribal and ethnic resentments in the areas they ruled that often turned into angry, bloody and damaging inter group revenge behaviors after each of those internally conflicted nations became independent.

All of those overarching macro power structure elements are now gone from those settings. The end of colonialism and the equally dramatic collapse of the Soviet Union have each created a plethora of newly independent, and almost haphazardly structured, non-sensically multi-ethnic and inadvertently multi tribal nations that tend to have groups of people who hate other groups of people in each artificial national setting.

A large percentage of those new, nonsensical multi tribal nations tend to have groups of people who are, in a state of ongoing, dysfunctional, debilitating and often intentionally damaging, cruel, and even evil, local and direct conflict with the other tribal groups who have been forcibly locked into their shared national boundaries with them.

Iraq, Syria, The Congo, The Sudan, Pakistan, Nigeria, Yemen, and Ruanda all clearly have those patterns of inter group behavior with fighting tribes at their core. More than six million people have died just in Congo related inter tribal wars.

We need to understand who is killing whom in each of those settings in order to have a sense of why there is so much conflict inside of those national boundaries and in order to have any sense of future approaches that might reduce those levels of conflict. The patterns of conflict in each of those settings are clear and obvious.

People have been historically aligned in all of those settings as ethnic groups and as tribes. People in those settings identify themselves by their tribal birthright and not by the name of their local country.

Their personal loyalty and group loyalty from their day of birth has been to their tribe and not to their country or nation. People align with their tribe — have loyalty and allegiance to their tribe — and defend their tribe against the enemies of their tribe and only deal with their nation in the context of being required by law to recognize the existence and function of that national name and structure.

Our news media has been carefully trained to never see or acknowledge the existence or roles of tribes in those conflicts — but the people in each setting who are actually killing each other know exactly who they are killing and the people doing the killing know why they are doing what they do as tribes to the people in those settings who are not from their tribes.

Their enemies are — in each setting — other tribes.

Syria is a perfect example. The Alawites of Syria are clearly killing people from several other local tribes. The Kurds of Syria are fully and tightly aligned with their own Kurdish tribe and they defend their tribe and its turf against each of the other tribes in that setting. The Kurds in Syria are clearly and consistently shooting people who are not from their tribe.

The outside world writes and talks about Syria as though it had a political set of divisions. There actually is no political division in Syria. That revolution and that supposed civil war is entirely tribal and the people from Syria who have been forced into exile from that country have been part of a very intentional and well executed process of ethnic cleansing that designed to make key parts of the country safe for the Alawite tribe.

The refugees from Syria have fled to both other Sunni Muslim countries and to Europe and those refugees are both unhappy and largely unwelcome in those other settings. Ethnic cleansing has been a functional success for the Alawites and their Shia allies from Iran — who enjoy seeing local Sunni countries having to deal with those refugees. That purely tribal war has been a disaster at several levels for multiple other countries that have to deal with the ethnic cleansing refugees.

Syria is far from unique in having those patterns of tribal divisions for their local conflict. The clear functional reality we can very easily see in Iraq, Nigeria, Kuwait, Sri Lanka, The Sudan, Kosovo, Chechnya, Tibet, and even The Ukraine is that tribes tend to kill tribes in setting after setting.

Almost all of the new internal wars in all of those settings are interethnic and intertribal conflicts. Only a very few of the new wars that we are seeing today in any of those countries are actually ideological or political in any traditionally political or ideological ways.

The groups in conflict in those settings often do have either political or ideological names or labels. But when you drill down to see who belongs to each political party or who are the members of each ideological group in each of those conflicted settings, the actual direct alignments of the people who are shooting other people in each setting tend to be almost purely tribal.

Ethnic wars, ethnic cleansing, and "Us/Them" instincts activated by ethnic triggers in those multi ethnic countries define major sections of the world today.

That whole process that was done by the colonial powers of creating those multi tribal new nations could have not been more disrespectful of the underlying right for groups of people to determine and achieve their own group self governance. Local groups in all of those settings were not respected in any way relative to their natural desires to become tribal, self-governed countries based on their actual history and identities as groups — and the attempts of many local ethnic groups to achieve self-governance and independence as a legacy culture and group are often suppressed in bloody ways by the largest or most powerful tribes in each setting.

The worse sets of inter group instincts are being activated in places like Kosovo and Aleppo as the result of groups holding power in each setting being able and willing to damage people from other groups with those instincts in full gear.

The book *Cusp of Chaos* describes that situation of activated inter group instincts for countries on every continent.

Some of the inter group wars that are happening today in some settings are labeled as religious wars. That label is both accurate and misleading. Religion is clearly a major factor in multiple inter group conflict settings, but again — when you carefully look very directly at who is actually shooting each other even in those purportedly religious wars — the religious wars that we see in so many places also all very clearly actually have very clearly defined tribes of people at their core who are actually killing one another in those settings as tribes.

That pattern is clear. Our instincts and the basic patterns of history and the most common human interactions that our instincts tend to create — favor creating tribes that give the people born into them a sense of being "Us." We have powerful instinctive needs to be part of an "Us." People in many settings have their instinctive need to be an "Us" met by being in their tribe.

In each of those settings, our instincts then create cultures that follow a normal pattern in most historical settings of having people choose and acquire their religious alignments as tribes. That alignment and linkage between tribal identity and religious alignment is true for American Indians, Tibetans, The Sikhs of India, the Jews of Israel, and the Kurds and Alawites of Syria.

People in multiple settings end up in religions as Tribes. Tribes tend to take on their religion as an entire tribe, and then the tribes fly the banners of their religion and speak the rhetoric of their religion while killing each other as tribes in what are clearly tribal groupings and tribal conflicts.

India and Pakistan followed those patterns with a very high level of consistency for the inter group wars that killed over a million people there after Great Britain gave up colonial control over that area of the world. Bangladesh then killed another million people in what was also clearly and purely tribal warfare in that country.

Aleppo is clearly ethnic cleansing.

In the Middle East, The Shia, The Sunni, and the Kurds all have various tribal groups at their functional core — and people whose tribe has chosen one of those religious alignments fight other people under the banner of their tribe.

There are no individual and personal religious converts in those wars. The people with guns are each born into the group that is giving them their gun. Conversions at an individual level to another religion are actually forbidden by law in a wide range of Middle East settings and our very powerful and very clear instincts to detest, hate and punish traitors are triggered in some harsh and cruel ways when people try to convert from one religion to another in those countries.

Those conflicts and loyalty levels in all of those settings are extremely tribal. There are no Jews flying planes in the Jordanian air force and there are no Palestinians flying warplanes or driving tanks for Israel. You don't see that diversity in those conflicted settings because people fight for their tribe in all of those settings and their primary loyalty for almost all of those fighters is to their tribe and not their nation.

The reality we face today is that people are killing each other along tribal lines in countries throughout the Middle East, Asia, Africa, and Eastern Europe.

Indonesia and Sri Lanka are also clearly awash in tribal conflicts.

Russia, India, and China all have significant internal separatist movements with people with different ethnic histories and identities and clearly tribal alignments killing each other in each setting in each of those countries in the cause of inter-ethnic hatred and intertribal division.

Tribes killing tribes is the standard model for conflict and it is happening in almost every former colony and former satellite nation.

Europe Is Awash in Immigrant Groups

To further complicate the inter group conflict situations that we face in the world today, Europe is now awash in immigrant groups who are forming what tend to be highly divisive local ethnic communities in each country. "Us/Them" instincts are also very clearly activated in all of the European countries.

Large percentages of people in new immigrant groups who are now living in European countries are choosing not to assimilate at any level into the traditional ethnic populations or cultures of those countries.

Europe has always been very tribal. Each of the countries of Europe has traditionally had their own tribe — with a tribal language, tribal history, tribal turf, and tribal identity. The Swedish tribe lived in Sweden. The French tribe lived in France. The Norwegian Tribe made it very clear to the world and to each other that they were not part of the Danish Tribe or the Swedish tribe.

The Norwegian tribe actually celebrates their separation from Sweden every year as a day of collective achievement, and shared, and remembered joy. Not unlike the American Fourth of July Independence Day celebration.

The historic behavior pattern we have seen for centuries has been that very few people immigrated between those extremely tribal European countries. They had some internal tribal diversity with small minority groups living in a couple of the countries — but the Europeans tended to have a long history of having the culture of their tribe dominate their interactions and their direct self governance as a tribe in each setting.

Today, however, Europe has many millions of immigrants — and the new residents in those countries are from Africa, the Middle East, Asia, and other non-European ethnic and tribal origins.

The major European communities are very different today than they were even a decade ago. The new immigrants in those countries are generally forming their own communities, continuing to practice their old religion, and creating very clearly instinct triggered internal division in each country along ethnic, tribal, and racial lines.

More than 10,000 cars were burned in Paris a few years ago in what was a very clear explosion of open inter-ethnic conflict in that city. Those cars were burned in pure inter group anger — with people who are choosing not to assimilate into the French legacy culture feeling deep division and intense anger relative to the people from that legacy culture.

The original French people of Paris were confused, dismayed, angered, and even a bit frightened by the level of anger that their new minority populations clearly were feeling toward the legacy culture and legacy tribal population of their country. Because they did not understand instinctive behaviors — and because they were not thinking in any systematic and non ideological way about how to deal effectively and directly with their new levels of diversity — the French government allowed the inter group situation in that country to get worse in a number of significant ways.

The French are not alone in not dealing well or in not dealing directly with any level of intellectual awareness, understanding or enlightenment about those instinct linked inter group issues. Everyone in leadership roles in those countries has just hoped that their new inter group problems would some how, run out of steam, go away and or simply end of their own accord.

That did not happen. People are people — and people from each group in each setting are doing the kinds of things that people do with other people in each setting. The normal packages of instinctive inter group behaviors that we all have embedded in us are now creating major divisions and stress point in many places in Europe.

All European countries now face similar problems and challenges and all of the countries are facing both internal divisions and growing inter group anger.

A number of cities on that continent now have significant neighborhood areas where crime rates are high, and where people are literally at risk if you are from the wrong tribal group. Paris, Brussels, and Zurich all have had areas where even the police have hesitated to enter.

The immigrant groups in all of those increasingly diverse settings have generally been very unhappy — and they have been taking to the streets in protests and functioning in mobs in many settings to show how much inter group anger they have, and to demonstrate how much they resent, dislike and even hate the dominant and historic legacy culture and group in their setting.

London, Copenhagen, Brussels, Amsterdam, and a number of German cities have each had their own inter group anger and inter group protests and divisions.

Instinctive behavior is at the heart of each of those conflicts — and the people who run those countries will now need to deal in intellectually informed ways with the relevant sets of instincts in order to have any chance of creating long-term Peace in those settings.

We Americans can clearly see the pure inter group anger that exists today in each of those settings.

We can see the suicide bombings, mass shootings, and the use of large vehicles as weapons to kill groups of people in European settings clearly from our country through the international news media, which tends to cover each of those events in some detail.

The news media describes each individual event — but the media tends to be almost stunningly unaware of the overall patterns of inter group behavior as a functional reality, and they seem to have almost no sense of the underlying inter group issues that exist in each of those areas.

Because the news media is highly focused on each incident, event, and occurrence, they do give us extensive coverage of the activities that are relevant to each story, so we know those events are happening.

Our news media — and our news commentators, analysts, and basic sets of pundits — generally do not have any sense that instinctive inter group behavior is relevant, and even central, to those conflicts and events — but the media tends to do a good job of describing each event in its own situational context.

That level of superficial reporting about relevant inter group issues will probably change with time, because the patterns are so extremely clear and the inter group facts are so obvious once you learn to see them — but the media is still focused on incidents and occurrences, and not seeing or understanding patterns for all of those terrorist events.

We had extensive and highly situational coverage of the recent shooting in Paris where the staff of a French newspaper was coldly murdered by extremist immigrants to that country. That very clear inter group-anger event was widely publicized around the world.

Mass shootings by terrorists at a French rock concert also recently killed large numbers of people at that concert. That particular inter group-anger event was also widely publicized.

The underlying levels of division and inter group anger that exist in all of those increasingly divided countries are becoming more visible to all of us and knowing that those problems exist in those settings should tell us that we need to be very sure as Americans that we need to minimize the likelihood of that kind of damage being done in our cities and communities.

The issues in each of those inter group setting are basic and primal. Because we are becoming more enlightened about the impact of instinctive inter group behaviors, we now know exactly what they are doing in each setting and we know why they are doing it.

Those behaviors and thought processes all have clear and deep roots in the basic inter group instincts that are explained several times in a variety of ways in each of the four basic the InterGroup institute text books.

Even the recent "Brexit" vote — where the majority of people in Great Britain voted to leave the European Union — had an array of very clear instinctive behavior thought processes embedded in that election result and those Brexit results make great sense when you recognize the "Us/Them" issues embedded in that election.

So the reality we all need to face for both our country and the world is that we human beings have clearly not moved beyond instinct guided and instinct structured behavior as modern people. It is increasingly clear to all of us that modern people in modern settings too often do very primal and negative things to one another, and feel very justified in doing those damaging primal things to other people when the wrong sets of inter group interactions, the wrong sets of inter group values, and the more damaging levels of inter group beliefs and emotions are activated and shaped by our basic sets of inter group instincts in those settings.

Our Inter Group "Us/Them" Instincts Trigger and Shape Inter Group Conflicts in Those Settings

We can only make that inter group situation better in any setting if we understand it clearly. We all need to understand how much our inter group behaviors and our inter group beliefs and emotions are influenced, shaped, and guided by our basic sets of instincts that are activated by inter group situations and realities.

The basic set of underlying instincts that generates the most significant problems in all of those settings are the instincts we have to divide the world into "Us" and "Them" and then act very differently toward whomever we perceive and define to be "Us" and "Them."

We each instinctively need to be part of an "Us." We all feel a strong need to be aligned with an "Us" that is relevant to our lives in each setting. We each need at a purely instinctive emotional level to be part of an "Us" and we will often do very significant things to make that sense of being "Us" a part of our lives.

We each feel security and comfort when we are part of an "Us," We instinctively hate being in a setting where other people are "Them" — and we feel instinct triggered stress, anxiety, and unhappiness when we are surrounded by "Them" or when we are in settings where some category of "Them" is in control of relevant aspects of our lives.

We react as individuals and groups, and we react in very consistent and predictable ways as communities, groups, organizations, and even nations to the pull and the power of those instincts. We very consistently and very instinctively build cultures for ourselves in every setting, and our cultures tend to create expectations about our inter group behaviors.

Our cultures in each of our settings serve both to channel our instincts and to guide what we do both collectively and individually to help us achieve our instinctive goals.

The book *Primal Pathways* explains our culture building processes and our use of cultures in significant detail.

Our cultures are much easier to understand when we understand their links to instinctive behaviors. We all feel very right acting in alignment with our instincts, and we feel equally right acting in alignment with our cultures. That ability of our cultures to cause particular behaviors to feel right when we do them is a core functionality that is used to anchor and underpin the Peace strategies that are outlined in this book.

Instincts use our cultures in every setting as a key tool to achieve their goals. They influence us by having what we do either feel wrong or feel right.

We each tend to feel right when our behaviors fit both our instincts and our cultures.

We also feel wrong, and we tend to experience anxiety, discomfort, stress and even some levels of situational anger when our behaviors are out of alignment with either our instincts or our cultures.

Because we now know that linkage between our cultures and our instincts to be true, we need to make intellectual decisions to very intentionally align and structure our cultures to guide and steer us in enlightened ways. For maximum positive impact, we need our cultures to be reinforced in direct ways in that steering process by our most positive instincts.

We can't change or eliminate instincts. Instincts are forever.

We will all have our full set of instincts until the day we die — and there is no way for any of us to cause any instinct to disappear.

We can, however, each individually choose to use our instincts in enlightened ways, and we can each clearly very intentionally and very directly use our intellect to design and support cultures that achieve enlightened goals and enlightened behaviors.

All of those approaches are key strategies and basic functional components for *The Art of InterGroup Peace*. This book and the *Primal Pathways* sister book both explain the various ways we can choose to shape our cultures in each setting to have our cultures shape and support Peace.

The book *Cusp of Chaos* explains what happens in too many settings in this country and other parts of the world when we don't embed Peace as a core value into our cultures and our chosen beliefs about what is right.

We Need American Leaders Skilled at the Art of Peace

To create and maintain inter group Peace in America, we need both our leaders and informed groups of relevant people to have that basic knowledge about those kinds of instinctive behavior patterns. We all need to understand the extremely damaging and dangerous kinds of behaviors that originate far too easily and far too often from our basic instincts — and we need to use that knowledge in both intentional and enlightened ways to make choices and to create realities that will protect us as a country from their worst and most damaging impacts.

We need to have enough knowledge about those issues and those behaviors to make sure that the most damaging kinds of inter group behaviors are not shaping our primary interactions and our basic inter group realities here, and we need to make sure the kinds of inter group hatreds that define behaviors in the

200 settings in the world, where ethnic conflict is driving behavior and affecting lives, do not structure who we are as Americans and do not define us collectively as a nation going forward.

We need leaders who are focused on the strategies of Peace and who are skilled at creating Peace in the settings they lead.

We need to have the people who lead our schools, our communities, and our various organizations and work places to have the skills necessary to create inter group Peace in each setting.

We need that skill set and that commitment today. The problems we face in a wide range of inter group settings in this country today are very real and they are immediate. We all need to understand exactly what kinds of inter group tensions, angers, and levels of division we face today, and we need to choose to focus our future on inter group Peace rather than accept our future as a negative and dysfunctional extension of our current inter group divisions.

It is very easy to see evidence of our current inter group divisions. We have had confrontations between groups of people in multiple settings, which all tell us clearly that there are underlying inter group tensions and angers in each setting.

The Minneapolis schools systems, for example, recently had student-inter group, physically violent, and riot related events that functionally paralleled and echoed — at a much smaller scale — some of the inter group riots that have happened in the last several years in London and Paris.

The inter group angers in Minneapolis stemmed from the same well of primal inter group conflict, and from the same inter group instinctive behavior patterns that created those inter group behaviors in England and France.

We need to understand why the various groups of students in those Minneapolis schools — White, Black, Hispanic, American Indian, Hmong, and Somalian-American students — felt so much anger toward other sets of students in those schools.

When we understand the relevant sets of instincts that have been activated in that setting, we need to take immediate action to bring inter group Peace to those schools.

In a similar and much more visible vein — the inter group conflicts and anger levels in Ferguson, Missouri, dominated our news for several months. The Ferguson protests and demonstrations were clear proof points that there are very real and deep-seated inter group angers, divisions, and conflicts in that community.

The cover photo for *Cusp of Chaos*, one of the sister books to this book, looks like military tanks of some kind putting down a protest in Syria or Iraq. But that photo on the cover of that book is actually a Ferguson, Missouri police tank. The authorities in that town were using approaches to respond to their citizens at that moment in time that told us basic and primal "Us/Them" inter group instincts were being activated for far too many people in that setting.

Ferguson has been far from alone in demonstrating the existence of significant inter group protests and anger in our communities. There have been a number of other American cities where we have had protests that have told us clearly that inter group anger is an underlying reality for those cities. Detroit, Chicago, Milwaukee, Cleveland, Baltimore, Oakland, and a number of other cities have had people going into the streets to make it very clear that underlying levels of anger exist in each of those settings. People are very angry with other people in each of those communities.

We can see those deep-seated angers in those communities revealed by various inter group events, incidents, and actions where people feel another group has damaged their own group.

The actual incidents that occur in those settings do not actually create the anger. The incidents trigger responses, and the responses unveil the fact that the anger exists. The incidents are often primarily a catalyst for expressing existing anger levels between those groups in those settings rather than an incident that generated waves of anger entirely on its own merit.

Police are often involved in the triggering event. There have been a number of incidents in a number of communities where police actions of some kind have triggered inter group anger at significant levels.

The most common anger trigger that creates community backlash events often involves a police officer — usually, but not always a white officer — shooting and killing an unarmed minority male, without apparent justification for deadly use of force.

A combination of 24-hour public media news cycles, wide use of social media connections, and the ability of citizens to use their cell phones to record problematic inter group events all work together to create a new reality for our inter group energy and anger levels.

Each of those events sends a message to the relevant communities that inter group anger exists, and the level of anger has been exacerbated by the event. Those kinds of damaging inter group events have always occurred in our country, but they generally occurred in the past, and in much less visible ways — or much more visible — to the community.

Negative inter group events that were most visible in earlier times — like public lynchings — were often done in highly visible and public ways and targeted toward the local minority populations.

We don't have that particular set of highly visible and egregiously negative events today — but we do have a high level of visibility for a wide range of also very visible triggers and events.

The Black Lives Matter movement and a number of other related civil rights and discrimination-focused organizations now exist, and those organizations and movements can make each trigger-event very visible.

Those organizations all clearly invoke those sets of instinctive thought processes, emotions, values and behaviors in a wide range of American settings.

The collective group-anger about those trigger events should not surprise us — because we have a long historic foundation of inter group anger in a number of settings, and that anger is highly susceptible to symbolic trigger events.

Anyone understanding the history of our inter group interactions explained in this book, and in both *Cusp of Chaos* and *Peace In Our Time* can get a sense of why those movements have generated such strong support with so many people, and why those trigger events create the energy and support they create in our cities today.

Each of the core InterGroup books has long sections explaining the history of racism, the legacy of inter group damage, the patterns of inter group discrimination, and the overwhelming evidence and history of negative and damaging inter group behaviors, which have been a major part of our history as a country.

The currents sets of protests in America by these new movements have been basically Peaceful, but violence has been triggered in a number of settings. In fact, there has now been more than one instance where we have seen an angry Black American, who has been listening to the angry inter group rhetoric, actually then shooting and killing White American police officers.

Each of those highly visible instances of someone from a group being killed by a person from the other group, causes the people who already believe negative things are intentionally being done to their group to be reinforced, and confirmed in that belief.

We will need to deal directly with those sets of issues and those basic beliefs as we go forward to create inter group Peace in America.

We Also Now Need to Fear Jihadist Inspired Attacks and Damage in Our Settings

We will also now need to deal with a new set of inter group issues that are being triggered by inter group angers in foreign settings that have the potential to cause people in our country to hurt and even kill other people here.

In addition to our purely internal sets of inter group stress points and issues, we also have a growing number of examples of people who are now living in this country who feel alignment and allegiance to groups of people in other countries who hate America.

There are a number of groups of people in the world who hate America. Those behaviors and beliefs are beginning to have an impact on us in this country.

We have American armed forces in several other countries where there are groups of people who feel damaged by our military. Jihadist groups in a number of countries hate us for doing things they feel impair their ability to function and succeed as jihadist groups, and some of those groups have a clear and highly intentional practice of doing violent and damaging things against people they target from other groups.

Those hate inspired inter group behavior patterns are clear, and some things that happen are almost impossible to believe. The basic packages of "Us/them" instincts are activated at the most primal and negative levels for those people.

There are literally suicide bombers killing themselves every day with the intent to kill other people in a number of settings in the world — and the suicide bombers in each of those settings are always killing people they define at a core instinctive level to be "Them." Jihadist groups teach those killers both to hate their target "Them" and to sacrifice themselves to kill the "Them" they hate.

Jihadist groups in the Middle East who are trying to gain control in several Middle Eastern and African settings often make hating America and doing things to damage America a key part of their beliefs and core behaviors.

That is relevant to us relative to achieving and protecting Peace in our own country, because there are some people in our country today who share that hatred, and who personally share and feel that Jihadist activated and Jihadist defined inter group anger.

There are a number of people in our country who feel alienated from everyone else, and who do not feel like they are members of the standard "American Us" — and those people who feel that alienation look for other categories of "Us" to align with to meet their personal core need to be part of an "Us."

Some people find their need to be an "Us" at a meaningful level with terrorist Jihadist groups who commit acts of terror against other Americans they perceive to be "Them."

People with those belief systems and purely instinctive values in place have committed both shootings and bombings in several American settings, which fit the basic patterns of pure instinct guided inter group behaviors they exhibit in the home countries of the terrorist organizations that they align with.

The Boston Marathon bombings and the mass shootings of Americans committed by Jihadist killers in California and Florida have made it clear that our oceans do not protect us from people who now actually live here in our country, and who have their worst "Us/Them" instincts activated against other Americans.

Real people with those alignments to those Jihadist groups in their heads and hearts see Americans as a "Them" and want to hurt, damage, and even kill "Them."

What we know from all of those highly visible terrorist inspired damaging interactions is that inter group anger and division about the jihadist sets of issues is very real. We now know we need to deal with those issues and that anger, or we will face major problems in many settings that will both damage people, and undermine our quality of life and sense of personal security in a wide range of settings.

We need to identify those with Jihadist based hatred and anger activated in their hearts who live here now, and work hard to prevent them from doing damage.

We also need to convert those people, when possible, to a mindset that is not anchored in inter group hate and anger, and that has America and Americans perceived to be a category of "Us" and not just a "Them."

We also need to do what we need to do to have as few people as possible from our own internal groups feel the levels of inter group division and alienation that cause those people to align in their own minds and belief systems as Jihadists, instead of aligning as Americans.

We need to win the fight for the hearts and minds of the people at risk for being converted to those beliefs and commitments to evil behavior, by doing things that cause the people facing that future to feel that they can be an "American Us" — with us — instead of being forced to be a "Them."

Those issues are highly visible because those shootings and bombings are, themselves, highly visible. But those issues are not, actually, *the* most important "Us/Them" issues we need to deal with as a nation.

The issues that caused protests and riots in Milwaukee, Ferguson, and North Minneapolis affect many more people, and will have a bigger impact on our future as a country than any Jihadist converts and their terrorist activities.

To deal effectively with our traditional inter group anger and inter group division sets of issues, we need to understand both our history and our patterns of instinctive behavior. We need to look at our own history and at our basic sets of values, and we then need to collectively decide what kind of future we want to have as a country.

Again — we need to create a sense of "Us" for all groups that will allow us to align, rather than fight in our cities, schools, and community settings.

We need people from every group in America to look in intellectually grounded ways at those issues, those behavior patterns, and those opportunities, and then we need people to make the fully informed decision together to become a country anchored in an enlightened way on our shared values and on a shared commitment and desire to build and protect inter group Peace.

The truth we need to face is that we need to do very intentional and well grounded things together, collectively, to make Peace happen here, or we will be increasingly divided, and people from all groups will damage people from other groups and will feel right, at instinctive levels, for doing the damage they do.

Damaging and hating each other is clearly the wrong future for us to create as a country. We need to create a future of inter group Peace. To be successful, Peace strategies for our own country need to be real and they need to be anchored in our instinctive behavior patterns and focused on the actual situation existing in each setting.

We need Peace — piece by piece.

We need to build and support Peace in all places — our communities, schools, neighborhoods, work sites, and in each of the settings where we get together and interact as individuals and interact as groups.

We need each work place, school and community to have its own very intentional and supported processes for bringing people into alignment, inclusion, and inter group and interpersonal trust.

Leaders are key to that Peace process in every setting. We need leaders in all settings who believe in inter group Peace and who understand our inter group instincts, and who are committed to achieving and protecting inter group Peace in the settings they lead. This book is intended to help leaders in our country at all levels do the right things in planned and systematic ways to achieve inter group Peace for the people they lead.

We are faced right now with just having gone through a Presidential election where significant parties in the electoral process did things that were clearly designed and intended to activate and empower some of our most primal and damaging sets of inter group instincts and thought processes.

Anyone who wonders how easily we Americans can be led down the emotional path to instinct reinforced inter group conflict and instinct supported inter group anger only has to look at how easy it was to frame this election in those terms for many of the participants.

Groups of people ended up with a sense of anger relative to other groups of people — and both conscience and ethics were suspended for many people as the result of those packages of instincts structuring both our thought processes and our emotions.

That is a dangerous set of events.

It is actually very tempting at an emotional level for us to simply continue down the trajectory set up by that election, and down the same paths of inter group division that activated too many people emotionally in the campaign.

That would be a huge mistake. That path will lead us to failure as a country and it will lead us to failure as a people — and it will cause us to put in motion actions, reactions, and interactions that will damage both who we are and what we need to accomplish together to be a nation at Peace with itself for the foreseeable future.

We need to rise above that temptation now and we need to make the conscious and collective choice to act in ways that achieve and maintain inter group Peace.

With the goal of preserving and extending the best parts of whom we are today, this book is intended to help with that process.

Sun Tzu Wrote *The Art of War* to Win Wars

This book was inspired by a very old book written by Sun Tzu about leadership in times of conflict and war called *The Art of War*. *The Art of War* is being used today in some very real ways by people who are seeking to divide America and who aspire and plan to have subsets of our population win at the expense of the rest of the population.

This book is modeled after *The Art of War*. It is intended to help people aspiring to help America become a nation at Peace with itself.

Sun Tzu believed wars were the natural and normal interaction between groups of people, and he stated clearly that any leader who deserved to be a leader should have real and practical skills in The Art of War.

Tzu believed war was both a science and an art. He believed war needed to be addressed with skill, knowledge, insight, and wisdom at multiple levels in order for wartime leaders to succeed and in order for nations to survive war.

Sun Tzu was a pioneer of for both systematic process analysis and continuous improvement in his thought processes. He believed in both processes and patterns. He did not believe in using simple circumstantial, incidental and individual event triggered responses to war situations. Sun Tzu believed war followed patterns, and he believed parties in times of war faced very predictable types, sets and categories of behavioral and functional realities.

He believed good leaders should know how best to respond to each war situation and to each war setting in the context of those larger patterns.

In *The Art of War*, he wrote a book of insight, strategies, and tactics that leaders could use to cause their own groups to at least survive their wars and, when possible, to win their wars.

Sun Tzu advised leaders about how they could avoid the defeat, and the destruction that would be the consequence of not leading their people well and effectively in times of war.

This book — *The Art of InterGroup Peace* — was inspired, influenced, and partially shaped by that very useful book about war. It was actually originally simply titled, *The Art of Peace* — but it became clear during the writing process that it would be more accurate and directionally useful to add the word InterGroup to the title, to identify exactly what kinds of Peace the book is intended to create.

The Art of InterGroup Peace has a number of echoes, reflections, and parallel influences and guidance approaches that originate from *The Art of War*.

Sun Tzu wrote his users guide to war — a how-to book and an instruction manual — because he believed that wars were inevitable and he believed strongly that the basic skill set for winning wars was needed by leaders for the actual preservation of each state he served.

I believe we definitely need a similar book for creating Peace at this point in our history. We are also at risk today in very significant ways, and that means we now need to be good at Peace for the preservation and the protection of our own people and our own American state.

This Peace book contains very specific patterns and behavioral expectations that can be very useful at this point in time to help our leaders both create and preserve Peace.

The truth is that even our most well intentioned leaders today too often do not have a skill set and knowledge base that is highly likely to create and protect Peace in the face of challenging inter group divisions and conflicts.

Our leaders tend to be very well intentioned, but they too often do not understand either the factors that keep us from Peace, or the factors that can be utilized to create and protect Peace.

We need leader insight and knowledge — in addition to clearly needing good leader intentions.

We need leaders to understand both their own group's behavior patterns and their own thoughts, feelings, beliefs, and approaches to inter group interactions.

We very much need leaders who personally want Peace for their people and for the world.

Too many of our leaders have the unfortunate tendency, and even the actual intentions, to deliberately lead us into conflicted and damaging inter group situations with the clear goal of somehow helping their own groups win or prevail in those divided and conflicted settings.

Too many leaders love — and can even become addicted to — the basic emotional and neurochemical rewards that can come from having Alpha status with their groups in times of conflict — and too many leaders with those neurochemicals activated are willing to lead their groups into war-like behaviors and emotions in order to increase their own power and support in their groups.

Both *Primal Pathways* and *Cusp of Chaos* discuss those problems and those basic functional and motivational challenges and risks relative to Alpha status and Alpha behaviors.

Those levels of leader behavior are both dangerous and damaging relative to creating Peace.

We need leaders who want Peace — not war — and we need leaders who know how to create and maintain Peace. That means we need leaders who understand and use instinctive behaviors for both individuals and groups, and who know their own group will ultimately be damaged if they try to have their group win and triumph over other groups.

We need leaders who understand and believe in win/win outcomes and interactions, and who are not committed to win/lose interactions for their groups.

Our world is too complex — and our country today is too intertwined and too inter related — for us to have any kind of successful future where one group wins while the other groups lose.

Any attempt to create a win/lose set of outcomes for any group today will result in damage done to all groups, and will result in ongoing weakness, vulnerability, and damage to the group that tries to win in a win/lose set of interactions.

We need to understand the power, positive impact, direct benefit, value, and ongoing success that can happen for all groups if we actually achieve win/win outcomes for all groups.

We also need to clearly understand and fear the damage that will be done to each group and to all of us in a group if any group attempts to create win/lose outcomes in our extremely intertwined society and nation.

We need leaders for all groups who are committed to achieving win/win outcomes, and who understand all of the instinct influenced inter group behavior patterns that affect how we think and what we do, and who have the clear ability to use that knowledge to help guide their own groups to inter group Peace rather than inter group conflict.

Both Books Rely on Lists of Situations, Relevant Factors, and Strategies

The two guidance books for group leaders resemble one another in several key ways. Both books are full of lists. Sun Tzu wrote a book that heavily used lists of both likely and common situations, and optional tactics and strategies to tee up thought processes and to create a sense of mental context to win battles and wars.

He wanted leaders facing all war situations to be able to think about those situations in a relevant context, so he enabled and empowered thinking about context by creating several sets of lists that create a continuum of information about each key issue.

He was an expert compiler of lists. For *The Art of War*, Tzu included lists of terrain, lists of tactics, lists of situations, lists of strategies, lists of structures, and lists of relevant circumstances.

Tzu believed leaders in each setting needed to know all relevant options for actions and responses, and he believed leaders needed to study both situations and their opponents very carefully to see which options should be used in each setting.

Tzu is a major advocate for understanding the other party. He advised war leaders in war situations to understand the other party in their conflict very clearly because he believed strongly that deep understanding of the other relevant party in a war setting could help assure the other parties defeat.

The Art of InterGroup Peace also advises leaders to understand the other party in each setting very clearly — but with the very different goal of Peace focused leaders using that knowledge in practical and functional ways to help assure the other parties success. It is much easier to help the other side in a Peace building situation succeed if you have studied them closely and if you know in clear and useful ways what an actual success would be for them.

The Art of InterGroup Peace is targeted for win/win outcomes for several very functional and practical reasons.

The first reason to work for win/win outcomes in a setting is that if both sides win, by definition, your own side wins. We all want our side to succeed, thrive, and to win—and that goal can be met in a win/win situation by the simple fact of winning.

We also want our side to have a future where the other relevant groups and other relevant people are not constantly trying to damage or defeat us. Winning alone generally creates vulnerability for the winner, because the side that doesn't win in any setting generally doesn't disappear. They continue to exist and a major motivation for them going into the future is to do damage to your side so that you ultimately lose.

Winning alone creates an inherent and very real vulnerability that does not exist when the other side wins as well.

The third reason why win/win makes sense as the preferred strategy for group interaction is that you have natural allies when both sides win, and you have natural enemies when either side loses. It is almost always far better to have allies and friends rather than enemies.

Allies are good. Enemies are bad. Win/win creates a better outcome, and win/lose has inherent flaws and risks even when you win.

So this book preaches and advocates win/win interactions for all of us in a setting, and both this book and *Primal Pathways* teach how to make win/win happen.

The Art of War Preaches Deceit — *The Art of InterGroup Peace* Preaches Honesty and Openness

As a result of those huge differences in both the ultimate and primary goals of the interactions and the major differences in the core strategies for the leaders in each setting, the two books take exactly opposite positions on the relevance and the appropriateness of ethical behaviors relative to the other group.

Sun Tzu preached that ethics and morality were not a relevant factor or an expectation or even an aspiration at any level for interactions with the other side in a war setting. His thinking on that issue of ethical behavior clearly follows and echoes primal and standard "Us/Them" instinct guided thought processes.

Our "Us/Them" instincts create very clear patterns of ethical and unethical behavior when they are each activated and Sun Tzu advocated using the negative sets of ethics we invoke when we perceive the other party to be a "Them."

People with their "Us/Them" instincts fully activated in negative ways tend to suspend ethics and tend to eliminate or ignore moral standards in dealing with people perceived to be "Them." The negative behaviors and the clear and complete lack of ethics and morality for interactions with a "Them" can be extreme when those particular instinctive values are shaping people's thoughts and behaviors.

Lying to the other side happens with great frequency and ease in "Us/Them" situations — and that set of behaviors makes it much harder to create inter group Peace and interpersonal trust when those are our goals in any setting.

The "Us/Them" instinct packages are very powerful instincts when they are fully activated. Sun Tzu clearly had those instincts activated in his own mind for *The Art of War* strategic agenda he built into his book.

He strongly advocated using deception, dishonesty, and deceit as tools of war. He, in fact, advised leaders to very intentionally and skillfully mislead the enemy at all times to undermine the enemy's strategies, confuse their thinkers, and help ensure their defeat. He offered lists of effective deceptions and described clearly when to use many of them.

That book has survived for 2,000 years because it has been a useful tool for a number of leaders in a range of competitive and conflicted situations, and because those behaviors feel right when those sets of instincts are activated to help leaders win in any setting.

The Art of InterGroup Peace believes that long-term Peace between any sets of people should be grounded in positive, clear, and explicit ethical values and behaviors that stem from, facilitate, and support having a broad and shared sense of "Them."

The Peace core strategy believes Peacemakers should avoid both deception, and even the perception of deceit, in order to build and maintain the levels of trust between both individuals and groups that is necessary to build and maintain Peace.

Trust is needed for several important functional reasons to maintain Peace between groups of people who will continue to function and to interact with each other over time as groups of people.

Trust can only be earned and maintained in settings through honesty, transparency, and a very intentional, deliberate, and visible lack of deceit.

Any inter group relationship that has anchors in deceit or dishonesty has flaws in the foundation of the relationship that put the groups at risk of future problems and of future setbacks when the deceit comes to light and when unintended consequences of the deceit become realities.

Both Books Create a Context of Terrain — Physical for War and Instinctive for Peace

Both books believe in context.

The Art of War describes an array of relevant physical and logistical options and terrains, and explains how to deal with each physical setting and context to improve the chances of success in war.

The Art of InterGroup Peace describes and outlines a clear and powerful array of mental terrains, and explains how to deal with each of those mental terrains and mental settings in ways that can abet, support, create, defend, and perpetuate Peace.

That mental terrain is the context where instincts play a major role in *The Art of InterGroup Peace*. The primary and most important mental terrain issues and realities that are described and outlined and used strategically in *The Art of InterGroup Peace* are our basic instinctive behaviors. When we study those levels of behavior closely, it is clear our instincts create a kind of extremely relevant terrain that gives us a working context for our inter group interactions.

Instincts are key. Instincts create many of our goals and they shape our thought processes, our values, our emotions, and both our core patterns and behaviors. We need to understand our instincts in order to understand how groups of people interact with one another and so that we can guide and influence what relevant groups do.

The initial sister book, *Primal Pathways*, is directly, explicitly and overwhelmingly focused on our instinctive behaviors. The second sister book, *Cusp of Chaos*, explains how those basic sets of inter group instincts have created both the 200 ethnic wars we see in the world today, and the centuries of discriminatory and damaging inter group behaviors and belief systems that have damaged so many people in our country and in the world around us for so long.

The fourth InterGroup Understanding sister book, *Peace In Our Time*, is a case study — and has some anecdotal history and real-world experience components that explain how some of the instinct-linked strategies outlined in this set of books have been both learned and used in various relevant inter group settings.

The fifth book — *Three Key Years* — is included with the other Peace books because it will be extremely difficult to create inter group Peace in America if we continue to imprison roughly 1-in-3 African American males and incarcerate hugely disproportionate numbers of other minority Americans. We need to change that reality — and both *Three Key Years* and Chapter Eleven of this book explain how that reality can be changed by helping children from every group in the first months and years of life.

All five of the InterGroup books are intended to help people understand very clearly how extensively we tend to be influenced at significant and powerful levels by our instincts in multiple areas of our behaviors and thought processes.

That influence created by our instincts is particularly relevant to our inter group behaviors. We tend to build our cultures and our inter group strategies and even our perceptions of reality around our basic sets of instinctive realities and thought processes, and those perceptions guide both our thoughts and our behaviors.

We have instincts to be territorial, hierarchical, and tribal. We have instincts to detest and punish traitors. We have instincts to celebrate and reinforce group loyalties.

We have instincts to be loyal to our leaders and to our teams.

We have instincts to build cultures and to create rule sets in every setting and we clearly build those cultures and rule sets in every setting in ways that reinforce and support our basic sets of instincts.

We Build Cultures to Achieve Our Instinctive Goals

The role of our cultures very much needs to be understood as we plan for our future behaviors and interactions. Our cultures, in setting after setting, function as tools of our instincts.

We have instincts to be hierarchical, for example, so every culture builds its own rule sets and its own approaches to hierarchies. All cultures build hierarchies and the rules set by each culture create specific hierarchies that achieve the goals of hierarchical instincts in that setting.

We have strong turf instincts — both for group turf and individual turf — so every culture builds its basic rule sets to define turf in that setting. We have property rules and property expectations of various kinds everywhere, and those rules are invented to help us achieve our turf instincts in each setting.

We have strong instincts to function in families — so all cultures create family designs, family structures, family behaviors, and family expectations. When we understand the role and function of cultures in each and every setting it gives us the ability to shape our cultures, and use them as tools to promote and perpetuate inter group Peace.

Three of the InterGroup books have chapters on how to build and manage cultures as tools for Peace.

Alpha, Beta, and Theta Instincts All Guide Behaviors

Hierarchical instincts also shape many of our behaviors. We have strong Alpha instincts, for example, which guide us to very clear patterns of Alpha behaviors when they are activated.

People who have their Alpha instincts activated tend to react and behave in very predictable ways relative to issues like turf protection, inter group positioning, and inter group conflict. Alphas do Alpha things relative to other Alphas and to each groups positioning relative to other groups.

In worst case settings, we have Alpha leaders who combine narcissism with sociopathy and manipulate the groups they lead into some dysfunctional and damaging behaviors in order to maintain the surge of reinforcing neurochemicals that Alpha status triggers in their own brain.

So we need to be aware of the impact of those instincts.

We also need to understand the fact that we have strong instincts that outline patterns of behavior and expectations for people in Beta roles in each setting, and we even have sets of instincts that guide us in various Theta roles in our hierarchies. The sister book *Primal Pathways* explains the relevance of all of those behaviors to inter group Peace more fully.

For this Art of InterGroup Peace text book, the key point to make is those instinctive behavior packages that we all have and cannot eliminate, actually, very clearly and directly, affect inter group behaviors, inter group interactions, and multiple areas of interpersonal behaviors and interpersonal interaction.

Our Most Challenging Instincts Divide the World into "Us" and "Them"

The most important sets of instincts that we need to understand and utilize effectively relative to The Art of InterGroup Peace are our instincts to divide the world into "Us" and "Them" and then to act and react very differently based on whether other people are an "Us" or a "Them."

Those instincts were mentioned earlier in this introduction, and they are mentioned again now because those are the single most important sets of instincts for us all to understand in order to have any chance of creating inter group Peace in each inter group setting.

Those very specific sets of instincts shape most of our inter group interactions. They have great power and major influence over our thoughts, our emotions, our values, and our behaviors. We react very differently to people based on whether we perceive the people to be an "Us" or a "Them."

Those same basic patterns of "Us/Them" thinking and "Us/Them" behaviors exist all over the world and they affect how people interact and think in every setting.

The "Us/Them" patterns are clear, powerful, and — when we learn to see them — obvious. But we too often have them guide our emotions, thoughts, behaviors and values without being aware in any conscious way that they are massively and directly influencing our lives.

We think that our behaviors and our thoughts on a given set of issues are simply "normal" and are not aware of their influence and steering power because those instincts feel so natural and so normal even when they are actually controlling and shaping what we do and how we think.

Knowledge is power — and we need explicit knowledge about those behavior patterns and instinctive thought processes in order to have power over them.

We Support "Us" and We Distrust "Them"

The patterns created for both individuals and groups by those packages of instincts are, in fact, both extremely clear and highly consistent. When someone is an "Us," we are supportive, protective, nurturing, accepting, forgiving, and inclusive. We tend to trust us and we tend to feel comfort and some level of safety when we are surrounded by people we perceive to be "Us."

When someone is a "Them," we tend to be suspicious, distrustful, and basically antagonistic. We tend to feel stress or a sense of threat when we are surrounded by "Them." We tend to fear that we will be damaged by "Them."

That is a universal set of feelings that we need to understand and deal with when it is relevant to our lives. People in all settings tend to feel discomfort and even anxiety whenever we find ourselves surrounded by any category of "Them." We often do not know why we feel either anxiety or stress in those circumstances, but those feelings influence what we do and how we react when those feelings are in play in our mind.

When our "Them" instincts are fully activated, we tend to feel anger, dislike, distrust, and even hatred for "Them." The patterns of instinct- influenced behavior that exist relative to "Them" are often ugly and very intentionally cruel.

People Damage Them with No Sense of Guilt

Guilt far too often disappears entirely when someone is clearly perceived to be "Them." That is a painful thing to say or write — but it is so often true that we all need to understand how powerful that ability to feel no guilt is to shape our behavior in terrible and clearly evil ways.

People do evil things to "Them" with no sense of regret, remorse, or shame when those instincts are fully activated. Ethics are suspended when someone is perceived to be "Them." People who take great personal pride in being intentionally and very deliberately ethical relative to the "Us" in their life will often suspend ethics entirely relative to "Them" and they will not even notice they are no longer acting in ethical ways because their unethical behavior relative to "Them" feels so normal and so right.

People in settings all over the world today are doing very negative things to "Them," with no regret, and with high levels of collective negative energy. The mass shootings we are seeing today in multiple settings clearly involve people who have the ethics level of a "Them" activated for the people they are killing.

People are being forced into exile in many settings today for being "Them" to someone with the power to expel them. Ethnic cleansing is deeply rooted in "Us/Them" instinctive thought processes. There are more than 50 million people in exile today, because this set of instincts has been activated in a wide range of settings and because the people who were exiled from each setting had been perceived by someone with the power to expel them to be "Them."

Those kinds of unethical "Them" linked instinctive behaviors are happening right now, and they are happening in far too many settings. Entire villages and communities are being destroyed by armed soldiers, and people are being killed because the people in those settings are perceived by the weapon holders to be "Them."

Ethnic cleansing based on those sets of instincts is a reality in too many settings today. Ethnic cleansing is clearly and purely an "Us/Them" instinct driven set of behaviors.

People ethnically purge "Them" from "Our" settings. People in too many settings very intentionally expel "Them" from settings that people perceive to belong to "Us," and feel joy instead of guilt as the people are being expelled.

Syria, The Sudan, parts of Nigeria, sections of Kosovo — and multiple other settings are currently practicing their own levels of local genocide — and the mass murderers feel no guilt because the people they are expelling or killing are perceived to be "Them."

Those inter group behaviors rooted in "Us/Them" instincts have existed throughout history and they are very real and far too prevalent in the world we live in today.

Those are not hypothetical or theoretical issues. There are actually more than 50 million people in the world today who have been ethnically displaced and forced into exile by other people who perceived them to be "Them," in a wide range of settings.

The InterGroup sister book, *Primal Pathways*, explains those instinctive behaviors in significantly more detail, and the sister book, *Cusp of Chaos*, describes many of the problems created today by those instincts in settings across the planet.

Those very primal behaviors can happen anywhere. They do not just happen in war zones. In any inter group setting — school, community, and workplaces

— those instincts and those perceptions can be activated, and they can steer the way people think and act. When that activation happens, people tend to distrust and dislike whoever is perceived to be "Them" in that setting.

Our history as a nation has been largely defined by those sets of instinctive inter group behaviors. It is impossible to understand our history as a country without having a clear sense of how those instincts have shaped our thoughts, behaviors and values as a nation.

Every Minority Group Has Faced Discrimination

Slavery was truly the epitome of "Us/Them" thinking and behaviors for our country.

We actually enslaved people in this country for centuries. The direct activation of those specific sets of instincts allowed people not to feel guilt when doing an extremely, obviously, and clearly evil thing to other people for very long periods of time.

Slavery in this country finally ended, but slavery was followed by other levels of clear and intentional inter group discrimination and damage. Slavery was far from our only inter group sin as a nation and our history as a nation of doing multiple levels of intentional inter group damage with those sets of instincts clearly activated is painful to acknowledge and describe.

Anyone who reads this book and then walks through the new African American Museum in Washington D.C., will find irrefutable proof points on every floor for every claim about how badly people act and behave when those instincts are the context for our thought processes, values, ethics, and emotions.

In this country we have committed multiple levels of inter group sins against many people who have been perceived (by the people in power) to be "Them." After slavery was abolished, our country created evil and damaging Jim Crow Laws and constructed other legal barriers, voting rights barriers, and a wide range of functional and economic restrictions and limitations to very intentionally continue to damage whomever the majority group in this country perceived to be "Them."

The overarching inter group behavior patterns have been painfully clear. Our instinctive behavior patterns have created very consistent damage to people who have been perceived to be "Them" by the majority group in this country. All minority groups in our country have faced similar, very negative, instinctive inter group responses.

The history we need to understand could not be clearer about those behaviors. Our country has had a pattern of very clearly discriminating, very intentionally and very deliberately, against each of the minority ethnic groups in this country — Native Americans, African Americans, Hispanic Americans, Asian Americans, and every other set of people who trigger a perception of being "Them" to the people who run the country.

The patterns for us as a nation could not be more obvious, transparent, and consistent. Those highly consistent sets of inter group thought processes, behaviors, and inter group interactions have had a massive impact on our history as a nation.

All of those minority groups affected have been functionally perceived, by the White majority who made the laws in various settings, to be some category of "Them" and each of the minority groups were treated with the ethical standards and the damaging inter group thought processes and dehumanizing values that are triggered by that set of instinctive behaviors.

Every one of those groups has a clear and undisputed history of direct discrimination, and all of those groups have suffered both collective and individual damage as a consequence of those instinct shaped behaviors and those instinct-guided thought processes.

To create inter group Peace going forward from where we are today, we need to recognize the reality that every minority ethnic and racial group in this country has faced major discrimination, economic barriers, education shortcomings, and it is clear beyond any challenge that people from every minority group have had a harder time achieving the American Dream than White Americans.

The American Dream is a wonderful thing. It is a beautiful way of approaching the world. The American Dream has created some of the very best sets of opportunities, and some of the most enlightened values available for any set of people anywhere at any time in history.

The American Dream is a shining component of our very best and our most enlightened legacies, and it is one of the most valuable assets embedded in our history as a nation. We need to cherish, protect, defend, and extend the American Dream to all of us if we hope to succeed and survive as a nation in the complex and extremely diverse years that lie directly before us.

We now need all Americans to have a full opportunity to benefit directly from that dream.

We need to continue to honor and utilize that Dream, and we need to extend it to a growing number of people, because the Dream is extremely useful and it creates massive economic, functional, and structural benefits to us when people make the dream a reality. We now need to extend the benefits of the Dream to as many people as possible to maximize the positive overall impact of the Dream on us as a country.

A painful and accurate reality we need to recognize and accept at this point in our history is that primary and direct access to that dream has actually been limited for a couple of centuries primarily to White males.

Women and minorities have all been able to have some access to the dream, but the barriers to that Dream have been consistent and real for almost all people who were not White males.

Those barriers are now lower—but they have not disappeared. We still face challenges in achieving those goals in the most inclusive ways for many of our people. We are clearly on a path to achieve that goal of removing barriers to the Dream, but multiple group-related economic reports about the relative income levels and financial asset levels by different groups of people show us we have not achieved that goal of economic opportunity fully for all people yet.

We still have significant economic and educational disparities we need to address successfully for more people going forward to the America we all aspire to be part of. We still have people in multiple settings who discriminate in their hiring practices, promotions, economic opportunity creation, and in their direct interactions with other people in ways that are negatively influenced by those sets of instincts.

We have multiple levels of unconscious bias that still drive some negative decisions, and we have layers of conscious bias that drive other negative decisions. We clearly have not moved past bias as a guide for various behaviors.

So we need to use our rule sets and our regulations to create cultural expectations that make the most egregious of those kinds of biased behaviors and actions illegal.

We also need to use peer pressure from enlightened peers to discourage and prevent many of the worst sets of discriminatory behaviors.

Rules are extremely important tools in that process. We tend to build our rule sets into our cultures. We need to create the right sets of rules, and we need to both enforce and reinforce the right rules we create.

We need to both celebrate and protect the gains we have made.

Protection of progress is a valid concern. Wherever we have achieved real progress on a key behavioral issue, we are always at risk of losing ground on our achievements if we don't understand exactly what we did and explicitly remember what those achievements are and then take very intentional steps to protect them.

We can revert and return to unenlightened behaviors and negative beliefs with amazing and painful speed when the opportunity presents itself.

Sexual harassment is a good example of the kinds of behavior that are always at high risk for fast regression. When rules and cultural expectations make harassment illegal, and when harassment is both punishable and punished, it tends to stop. But when the rules and laws that relate to sexual harassment are not both clear and enforced, regression to ugly behavior happens in far too many settings far too quickly.

The books *Primal Pathways* and *Peace In Our Time* both explain some of those issues and behavior patterns in more detail.

We are always at some level of risk for those sets of negative issues after progress has been made because the functional reality is that we have changed our culture — but not our instincts.

We Feel Right Acting in Accord with Our Instincts

We will never be free of our instincts or their ability to shape our emotions and our thoughts.

Our instincts shape our behaviors in large part by manipulating our emotions and by activating or deactivating our sense of internal alignment.

We tend to feel stress when our behaviors are out of alignment with our instincts and our cultures, and we tend to feel both justified and "right" when we act in accord with our instincts and our cultures. The ability to make behaviors feel right or feel wrong gives our cultures much of their power.

Those feelings guide and influence our decisions and our behaviors with great consistency — and they need to be understood and responded to with a clear intellectual knowledge of what they are and how they function.

It is important to recognize the fact that we tend to "feel right" when we act in accord with our instincts.

It feels right to follow a leader who activates our follow instincts. It feels right to protect our turf when our protective behaviors are aligned with our turf instincts.

When our children are threatened, it can feel extremely right to act in ways that protect our children from the threat.

We can feel rage at that threat to our children and we can feel rage at a threat to our personal or group turf, and our behaviors in response to that rage can feel very right.

It can also feel right to reject a traitor and to even damage a traitor.

It can even feel right to be in a mob and to damage other people in the emotional context that is often created by being in a mob. Every police department in every major city of the world has mob resistance gear and mob control training because that set of ugly and damaging mob-linked instincts exist in all of us and those instincts create very similar sets of behaviors that feel right — or even imperative — to people whenever they are explicitly and situationally activated.

The Art of InterGroup Peace strategy directly uses those sets of instincts to guide us in the path of Peace rather than simply continuing to have us dangerously descending instinctively to the slippery, seductive, and sometimes even addictive slope of emotionally reinforced inter group conflict and collectively achieved and mutually reinforced and activated inter group hatred and damage.

Hatred can be seductive and instinct reinforced hatred can generate its own collective instinctive power to coalesce, focus, define and energize group behaviors. People can feel very right in doing collective angry things that are actually very wrong and even deliberately evil when those most negative instinct packages are activated.

We saw some of those behaviors in our last Presidential election cycle — where a significant number of people had their personal "Us/Them" instincts activated at a very high level and actually perceived the other side in that election to be a primal enemy rather than simply their Political opposition.

Evil replaced wrong as the perception of the other side in that election for many people. Too many people perceived the other side in that political process to literally be intentionally evil — not just simply politically wrong. That is a dangerous, damaging, and highly dysfunctional way of approaching our electoral politics. We need to move beyond those primal instinct structured thought processes, and we need to bring people together as a values driven and mutually enlightened; mutually supportive "American Us."

We need to call to our better angels to align us — and then we need to have our future political battles in the context of political differences, and not in a context where people perceive people to be the personification of sin and evil.

We need to avoid doing things that will divide us in ways that damage us all.

For us to succeed as a nation, we will now need to move away from the dangerous and full extension of our worst instinct grounded thought processes into our political process, and we need to think of the election as being a competition between political foes who are all part of the great American "Us."

We need to not think of the next set of elections as being a battle between Good and Evil — in ways that dehumanize the opposition rather than just oppose them — but rather as a disagreement within our family by two sets of people who all inherently share positive feelings toward one another and who want everyone to succeed.

We need to think of Peace for all of us from all groups as a goal for us as a nation and we need to create inter group Peace and inter group inclusion and synergy in all of the settings and communities we have in this country, with the goal of having us all thrive.

We need schools that function effectively and well in a context of major and growing inter group diversity.

We need worksites that pull together and create group success and inter group inclusions and acceptance. We need our worksites and our communities to benefit from the creativity and synergy that diversity can create in any setting.

Six Alignment Triggers Can Bring People Together

The Art of InterGroup Peace is a tool kit and includes time-tested approach for bringing people together. The book explains six very effective ways we can get people in almost any setting to be aligned with one another. *Primal Pathways* also describes that six trigger group alignment tool kit in some detail.

Leaders and group members in all settings should know how to use each of those six very useful alignment triggers because Peace is far more possible when alignment is in place.

Leaders in all settings can use those triggers to create alignment and to create a context of Peace by understanding clearly when those tools fit the specific situation that exists in each setting.

Those six alignment triggers range from having a sense of shared danger that triggers alignment to having a sense of shared mission and vision that also triggers alignment. Each of those triggers is explained in *The Art of InterGroup Peace* chapter that describes how to use that particular tool kit.

Those triggers are outlined in chapter eight of this book and explained and illustrated with real world examples of their use in the sister book *Peace In Our Time.*

We Need to Be Accountable – and We Need Our Intellects to Be in Control

As we look at the world we live in, it is clear we will not succeed in creating a future of inter group Peace in our country, or in any other conflicted country, if we just continue blindly down the paths we are on.

Our instincts to divide the world into "Us" and "Them" and then to create cultures, strategies, behaviors, and belief systems that reinforce and exacerbate the impact of the negative impacts of those instincts are extremely powerful, and we need to use our intellect and our enlightened sets of values now to take those instincts out of the driver's seat for our thought processes. It is time to finally put our intellect in charge and to have our intellect use enlightened values in personally accountable ways as the core for our inter group behaviors and interactions.

When we understand how our instincts and cultures actually work, we know that we finally have actual choices relative to what drives our most important behaviors. We have real choices. We can simply act instinctively or we can act intellectually. Knowing how those processes work means we can actually have our intellect steer, guide, and channel our instincts, if we choose that approach.

That is actually the only path we have to full accountability.

To be fully accountable at an ethical level, we need to use our intellect to make enlightened and positive decisions about the way we want to behave and we then need to use our intellect to make key decisions about how we want to interact with other people, both as individuals and as groups. We need to create very specific values at an intellectual level to guide our thoughts, behaviors, and interactions.

Then we need to use our intellect very intentionally and skillfully to embed those desired behaviors and values in our cultures in ways that cause those behaviors to be aligned with out most enlightened and most ethical sets of instinctive behaviors.

We Need to Be Ethically and Intellectually Enlightened, Values Based, and Individually and Collectively Accountable

So what values should we use to guide our lives? Some are obvious.

We need a culture of inclusion. We need a culture of shared opportunity. We need a culture of enlightened intellectual and religious freedom. And we need a culture of InterGroup Peace.

If we allow our instincts to continue to prevail as they have in the past at this point in our history — knowing what we now know about those instinctive influences and instinctive behaviors — we should be deeply ashamed of ourselves. We should be truly disgusted with ourselves if we don't deliberately and intentionally embed explicit Peaceful values into our cultures now and for the future at every level.

Knowledge is power. We need to understand and comprehend, and we need to care. Caring is important. We need to care deeply about each other, and we need to care about the fact that we very much want us all to do well and succeed.

We Also Need to Care About One Another in Enlightened Ways

We need to care about one another in enlightened ways as we go forward and we need to make that caring about one another in positive and effective ways a functional reality for the world we build for ourselves.

We need to show that we care about one another by explicitly committing to win/win values, win/win outcomes, and win/win thought processes for all groups, and then we need to clearly celebrate and feel good collectively and individually when all groups win. This book and *Peace In Our Time* explain the importance of us making win/win a strategy, goal, and skill set.

Caring about one another and helping each other win is the goal, the message, and the core commitment about who we are and who we need to be that is embedded in *The Art of InterGroup Peace*.

We should not mislead ourselves about how much damage has been done to our minority populations in the past, and we should not mislead ourselves to believe we don't need to do things now to keep that damage from extending itself in angry ways to more people and to more settings.

We should celebrate the progress that we have made, but we need to recognize that there are still major negative economic consequences for groups of people in our country that have resulted from our discriminatory behaviors in our collective past.

We need to make our children a major focus for us as a nation, and we need to begin today to help children from all groups do well in the first weeks, months, and years of life when neuron connectivity levels determine lifetime learning ability levels for each child.

Every community leader in America should know the basic science and the basic child brain development processes that are explicitly outlined in the *Three Key Years* book and in Chapter Eleven of this book.

We need to take the right steps in all settings to create inter group Peace in each setting that is anchored in win/win beliefs and behaviors.

We Need to Create Peace Piece by Piece

We need to create Peace very intentionally in each community and setting. That can be done. We just need to be very intentional in doing what we need to do to achieve those outcomes in all settings. To create Peace in America, we need to recognize how much anger and conflict exists today in a wide range of settings as the result of centuries of inter group discrimination and inter group prejudice.

We need to acknowledge how driven our history has been by "Us/Them" instincts that have caused our majority population to discriminate in very deliberate and often damaging ways against large segments of our minority populations in various settings.

To come together now as an increasingly diverse nation at this point in our history, we need to make a fully informed commitment to inter group Peace in America in a context that is anchored on a shared desire to have people from all groups prosper and do well. We need to very explicitly build a win/win future — with win/win functioning as a goal, a process, a belief system and a strategy.

For America to win, we need all of the groups that constitute America to win. That is possible to do, and we need to make the explicit and shared commitment to do it if we want any groups to win in our increasingly diverse future.

We need to anchor that strategy on a clear understanding of our best and worst instinctive behaviors and we all need to understand how both our history and our future are already anchored on those realities.

We Need to Commit to and Be Guided by Our Core Beliefs

The final chapter of this book deals with the core beliefs that anchor us today as a people and a country. Those are extremely important beliefs. We cannot succeed without them.

We all need to understand those beliefs, and we all need to commit to supporting those beliefs in each community and setting.

We need to be a people united and aligned by our core beliefs. We need a set of enlightened beliefs that guide our thoughts and our interactions, and we need to be so clearly committed to those explicit beliefs that we can use them together and collectively as the foundation for a new American "Us."

We need to be an American "Us" so all the positive feelings, ethical standards, feelings of mutual support, and feelings of mutual protection that are instinctively triggered by being "Us" extend to us as a nation in ways that allow us to overcome and transcend the other factions, factors and grouping approaches that otherwise divide us.

The final chapter of this book very carefully outlines a dozen key and foundational beliefs that are intended to serve as a reflection and articulation of our best values that have guided us in our most enlightened ways to be an American "Us." We need to be explicit, clear, and undeniably committed to that set of values and those beliefs.

The final chapter of this book outlines those values and explains their meaning to us as a guide to our commitments to one another as an American "Us."

We need to use those values and we need to use our sense of inclusion to create Peace, piece by piece, for all of us — and we need to do that work very directly in each inter group setting.

We need to use the basic Art of InterGroup Peace strategies outlined in this book situationally, tactically, functionally, operationally, and very strategically when and where they are relevant to our schools, communities, places of work, and our various governmental settings.

Those strategies are anchored on us doing important and very specific things to help children from every group succeed. We cannot succeed as a country unless we deal with the issues that relate to our children from every group.

We need to begin the Peace process with absolute honesty. This is the right time for us to be brutally honest with ourselves. We should be honest with ourselves about the fact that we just went through a divisive Presidential election — but we should be even more honest about the fact that we went into that election process as a nation with some high risk areas of division and those areas needed to be addressed and healed regardless of what we did in that particular electoral process.

We should not mislead ourselves about how much risk we face as a nation going forward. We have a very long history of inter group damage and we will be facing an extremely high level of highly conflicted inter group diversity if we don't understand and accept who we now are, and if we do not choose to turn who and what we are into an asset for Peace. We will hurt ourselves and each other, and we will fail as a nation and a people if we don't do this right.

The alternative to choosing Peace and to choosing alignment around key values and beliefs is grim.

The alternative to inter group Peace is a slippery, steep, and grim slope to inter group anger and conflict. We are on the *Cusp of Chaos* if we do not get this right.

We will fail as a nation and we will turn into a multi-tribal nation at war with itself if we don't do what we need to do to turn our growing diversity into a major asset that will make us safe, secure, and prosperous for the next millennium.

Major areas of the world are clearly at war today with themselves. People in each of those areas who are at war with themselves today will need to deal very explicitly with those same behaviors and conflicts if they hope to create Peace in their settings.

Each of those multi tribal and conflicted settings will need to look at their problems in the context of these sets of instincts being activated in very damaging ways.

We can't let the failures and difficulties faced by those other countries affect us. We need to create Peace and we need to do that by understanding the issues involved, and then making the intellectual choice to resolve those issues in the context of having us all thrive and win.

There is no possible future scenario where any part of us can win by going our own way and being triumphant rather than mutually supportive. Any short-term gains will be erased by long-term inter group anger, division, conflict, and decisions by groups of "Us" to damage other groups of "Us."

That would be the wrong future—and no one would win. We need, instead, to be a nation anchored in our core values and committed to the success of us all in a world of safety and Peace.

We each need to make the very clear commitment to each other to know, understand, believe in, use, celebrate, and honor those core values, and we each need to use them to achieve Peace.

We need to make continuous learning about creating Peace a guideline, a mantra, and a skill set, and we need to be collectively smarter tomorrow about making and preserving Peace than we are today.

The Art of InterGroup Peace is intended to be more than a general compass pointing in that direction. It is intended to be a road map for major parts of the journey — and everyone who is part of the American "Us" is welcome to join us on that journey.

Enjoy the ride. It will be worth the trip — and the alternatives are too painful to consider.

As a basic plan of action, take the lessons of this book, use them, test them, learn from using them, and make them better. This is a step in the right direction. It is a step we need to take and one that we need to continuously improve once we start down this road.

We need Peace to be both a commitment and a process of continuous improvement — and we can't continuously improve this Peace process until we start down that path.

So check out the best and most useful parts of this strategy for Peace — and then make the whole process better by enhancing those strategies in the context of the situations you are in.

This book is a primer — not a final architectural drawing or design. Enjoy it for what it is and also turn it into something better.

Peace.

In our time.

Peace — because the alternatives are too painful, and because we owe it to our children and our grandchildren to get this right.

CHAPTER ONE

We Need to Be Skilled at The Art of InterGroup Peace

Sun Tzu, in *The Art of War,* declared that the study of war and the skills needed to conduct and win a war were of "vital interest" to the state and should be a top priority for leaders in every conflicted setting.

"Vital interest" is a very high priority. Sun Tzu was probably right at the time he wrote that book that leaders in times of war needed to be skilled in the Arts of War.

Today, 2,000 years later, what we need are leaders in every relevant setting who are highly skilled at the Art of InterGroup Peace. Peace ought to be a vital interest to us as a country today — and we need our leaders today in every setting to be highly skilled at creating Peace, protecting Peace, and sustaining Peace into the future.

This book is intended to help our leaders be as skilled at the Art of InterGroup Peace as Sun Tzu wanted his readers to be skilled at the Art of War centuries ago.

The stakes have never been higher. Intergroup conflict dominates the focus of people across the planet. There are more than 200 ethnic wars going on in the world today — with more than 50 million people displaced by ethnic conflict.

In our own country, as we become much more diverse very quickly, we need to create a future that turns our diversity into a national asset, rather than having our diversity put us on a slippery slide into the kinds of intergroup conflicts that diversity can create if we let our most negative and damaging intergroup instincts guide our thinking and our behaviors.

We need intergroup Peace in America. Intergroup Peace ought to be our commitment and our goal. We need to have this country be at Peace with itself.

We also need the people in each setting in this country working together in inclusive and aligned ways — to keep us from having internal intergroup flash points and intergroup conflicts in all of our various settings.

We need the people who make up all of the diverse groups who make up the fabric of this country to be supportive of each other's success.

Peace for us would mean that the very diverse groups of people who make up the fabric of our country will not be in a state of intergroup anger, conflict, animosity, anxiety, dislike, distrust, and are not ready, prepared, and eager to do very intentional intergroup damage to one other.

To succeed at The Art of InterGroup Peace at the highest and best level — we need all of the groups of people who make up the complex diversity of America to be unified by shared beliefs and aligned by shared values. We need people from all groups to want the success of their own group and to also want simultaneous success for all other groups. We need a shared and universal commitment to win/win outcomes for all groups as a country.

We have very inconsistent levels of success in too many areas today. We are not a country that is living in a state of internal intergroup Peace in all settings today.

At multiple levels in multiple settings, we have intergroup distrust, stress, anger, and various degrees of intergroup conflict.

We are not killing each other in large numbers by groups in the ways that so many other countries have people killing one another. We don't have the armed intergroup conflict of Syria or Iraq, or Nigeria or Sri Lanka, Chechnya or The Sudan.

We don't even have the pure tribal separation and the pure intergroup division that we see in Barcelona or Glasgow.

But we do have significant intergroup issues that are moving us toward division and increasingly negative intergroup intentions in many parts of our country.

We have major learning gaps that exist for children from various groups. We have significant differences in average economic levels for our various groups that are causing people to be economically damaged and increasingly angry about the economic disparities in their lives.

We have significantly higher incarceration rates for our minority American populations. Hispanic males are three times more likely to be imprisoned and African American males are six times more likely to go to jail than White Americans.

High school dropouts from all groups have the highest rate of incarcerations. More than half of the African American males in their 30s who are high school dropouts are in prison today.

So we have some overarching areas where we clearly have not achieved equivalent wins for people from every group. We have a number of areas in our work places, schools, and communities where people dislike one another, distrust one another, and are divided in clearly group-linked ways from one another.

We have made massive progress in a number of areas relative to issues like voting rights, equal access to schools and public facilities, and in making direct discrimination in hiring clearly illegal. We are far better off on almost every single civil rights issue than we were just a couple of decades ago.

That gives us a good foundation to build on for intergroup Peace.

We have Americans from every group who are doing well and who are individually achieving the American Dream. Some of the wealthiest and most influential Americans are women and minority Americans.

We still have communities, however, where significant portions of the population do not trust the police, and we have education systems where the learning gaps that exist for groups of people are damaging significant numbers of people for their entire lives.

We Need to Move from Division to InterGroup Peace

We need to create better results and outcomes in all areas.

We need to move away from the areas of growing division in this country to a clear commitment to intergroup Peace. That commitment to intergroup Peace will not happen on its own.

We will need to work very intentionally across all groups to make intergroup Peace happen. To achieve long standing intergroup Peace, we need to work both intentionally and skillfully to create a state of optimal Peace and intergroup trust in each setting in our country. We need to make that state of Peace both our conscious commitment and our deliberate goal in each setting.

When we do achieve a state of intergroup Peace, we can be in a situation where groups of people understand, appreciate, and support the existence of other groups of people. That should be our explicit goal.

We need to be in a situation where the groups of people who make up the fabric of America are each committed to a functional reality of win/win outcomes for all people — with wins expected and wins achieved for everyone from all groups.

Optimal Peace is a win/win situation where all groups can achieve wins for their own group and where each group both celebrates and supports other groups in their functionality, their prosperity, and their own group wins and group success.

In a best situation for our own internal overall realities as a nation, Peace means that the various ethnic, racial, cultural, and religious groups that comprise the basic fabric of America act in enlightened ways to create both collective success as a country and individual successes for their own groups, and where all groups fully endorse, respect, and support the successes for each of the other groups who are part of the overall and overarching American Us.

That inclusive and collaborative commitment to win/win results for all of us is a key strategic component embedded in *The Art of InterGroup Peace*.

We Need a Broad and Inclusive Sense of Us

We need to anchor that strategy on creating a broader and more inclusive sense of "Us." We need to achieve a collective sense of being an American Us at a very functional level in order to achieve and sustain overall and on-going Peace for this country.

That overarching and collectively aligning sense of us that we need to create for us overall doesn't need to eliminate or erase any of the other sets of group identities that make up the fabric of America today. We need to build on our current diversity — not eliminate it or erase it.

The overarching sense of us that can align us all with all of us needs to be inclusive — creating an overall and very direct sense of "Us" for all groups and celebrating our ability to bring all of our groups together in key and relevant ways to create and protect both a vision and a clear, mission focused, belief system driven sense of us.

This book explains the key components of that overarching strategy in more detail in each of the 16 chapters. At a very basic level, we need to achieve a state where win/win thinking replaces win/lose and lose/lose thinking for groups of people in America. Win/win outcomes can give us a safe and sustainable anchor for intergroup Peace.

When we are in a state of intergroup alignment and Peace, then the instinctive reactions we have to divide the world into us and them and to distrust, dislike, and do damage to "Them" can be mitigated and defused in those key and important places where those instincts damage us and impede us most significantly today as a country and as a people.

As the introduction said — this book was written to help us achieve very basic levels of Intergroup Peace, and was inspired very directly by one of the most widely read books on the planet – *The Art of War*, by Sun Tzu.

The Art of War has survived and has been read by strategists for centuries because it offers very functional, practical, tactical, operational, and deeply strategic advice about conducting and winning a war. That particular book is absolutely clear about defining multiple key points on multiple issues and multiple factors that are relevant to the practical aspects of conducting and winning a war.

Sun Tzu wrote his book in a time of constant War. He focused entirely on war as a topic and his book outlines various techniques that can be used to help win a war.

Defeating the other army and not being defeated are the twin goals of his agenda.

He wrote the book because he believed that being successful at war is absolutely "essential for the survival of the state." Sun Tzu believed that survival for the state and success in conducting war can best be achieved by using the right sets of strategies, and the right combination of skills and situationally appropriate tactics to defeat your enemy.

He believed that any tactics that worked to win the war should be used to win the war — regardless of their ethical or moral content, or their ethical or moral consequences.

Ethical standards, ethical behaviors, and morality guidelines he believed, both could not and should not apply in war. Sun Tzu, in fact, strongly and clearly endorsed explicitly unethical behavior.

The Art of War uses very different approaches than the Art of InterGroup Peace in those areas of both strategy and behavior.

Deception and Deceit Help Win Wars

Sun Tzu wrote that deception and deceit were essential for winning a war. He celebrated, encouraged, recommended, and endorsed deception. His book advocates using a wide variety of deceptive strategies and tactics to achieve an enemies' defeat.

He also endorsed both finding and creating weakness in the other army that would cause the enemy to be easier to defeat — and he advocated doing explicit and effective damage to the other party in the war settings when that damage was needed to win a war.

The reality of war that Sun Tzu wrote about was basically centered on armed conflict — with one set of soldiers attacking, damaging, and killing the other set of soldiers whenever killing, destruction, and damaging tactics and strategies were necessary to win the war.

Strategic Direction Can Be a Major Asset

He was, at his core, a very clear strategist.

He strongly believed in the power of strategy as an essential and highly effective tool for winning wars. He thought of strategy as being the premier part of a leader's tool kit.

He actually preached that truly skilled and excellent warriors could sometimes prevail in war by having strategies so sound and so excellent that the enemy would be defeated before any battle actually began.

In some key ways, putting in place a very similar proactive strategic approach to achieve wins without combat can be used for the Peace process. If we have fully skilled leaders who are putting in place strategies that are so sound and so well designed that Peace is highly likely to happen before any intergroup interactions begin, then Peace is more likely to happen in settings where those leaders lead.

In a number of ways, the Peace strategies we need are the exact opposite of the war-linked strategies. In other ways, the strategies themselves are almost identical — but with an entirely different goal in mind.

Damaging the other side in a conflict was a major tool used in the process of war. In direct contrast, strengthening the other side in a conflict can be a major tool that is used to help achieve Peace.

The Art of War preaches win/lose outcomes. *The Art of InterGroup Peace* advocates win/win outcomes. *The Art of War* celebrates deceit and deception. *The Art of InterGroup Peace* believes that Peace is dependent on honesty, transparency, and candor and advocates intergroup honesty as a key way of building that Peace.

Getting the other side to surrender and to be assimilated by force of arms was a goal of Sun Tzu's strategic thinking in *The Art of War*.

Getting the other side to stop fighting and then getting the other side to create appropriate and functional Peaceful intergroup interactions that can include agreements, assimilation, and voluntary alignments as key interaction choices are a key part of the goal set and the strategic direction for the Art of InterGroup Peace.

Understanding the Other Side for Defeat or Support?

Both books recommend knowing the other side in a situation well.

Sun Tzu preached achieving a deep and detailed understanding of the other party in each setting. Sun Tzu strongly recommended understanding the enemy well in order to maximize damage, minimize risk, and to undermine the enemy's ability to win the war.

As part of the deep understanding process, Sun Tzu advised generals to study their enemies very carefully and in depth. He advocated completely understanding the enemy at very intense and detailed levels in order to assure the enemies' defeat.

He even strongly recommended placing spies in the enemies' forces to give the leader of an army the very best and most current information about the enemies' situation, status, and intentions.

Sun Tzu recommended having a deep understanding of the other group — but he only advocated that deep understanding as a tool that can be used against the other side in the context of the conflict to move effectively, and more completely defeat the other side.

The Art of InterGroup Peace also preaches understanding of each side in a setting by all parties in the setting — but not to cause the other group's defeat.

The Art of InterGroup Peace believes we need to achieve understanding of other groups of people so we can help people help each other win — and so that we can create the level of intergroup interactions that can functionally anchor Peace.

We have people across our planet today following Art of War-based patterns of behavior for intergroup conflict and intergroup interaction. We have people in multiple settings across the planet who are working to do damage to other groups of people and who are willing to do highly unethical and destructive things with no sense of guilt to inflict damage on the groups of people they see as their enemies in each setting.

We have people who are following the Sun Tzu guidelines for understanding the other groups and who are then damaging other groups of people using that understanding as a weapon of war.

We need to change those damaging and destructive Art of War behaviors in our country into the strategies that are needed to achieve Peace. We need each party in each setting to understand the other party clearly in order to help the other party achieve its legitimate goals and to create win/win outcomes for all parties.

Understanding the other group in any setting can help define what an actual win can be for the group, and then it can help make that win a reality. Win/win outcomes give us the foundation we need for lasting Peace.

Those are not the outcomes that are being pursued in those 200 ethnic conflicts. To win at Peace in our own country, we need to understand — at a very basic level — why so many people are at war today and why *The Art of War* is so relevant to people in so many settings.

Us/Them Instincts Create War, Conflict, and Stress Today

We clearly have to deal with some basic patterns of instinctive behaviors to get groups to work together and to avoid intergroup conflict.

The absolute consistency of those damaging intergroup behaviors in so many places on this planet tells us that our very basic instincts to divide the world into us and them, and then do damage without guilt to "Them," are at play in far too many intergroup settings.

Those instincts are described in more detail later in this chapter and again in the next three chapters of this book. Those packages of us/them instincts are influencing intergroup behaviors in very negative and damaging ways all across the planet.

There are actually well over 200 settings today where groups of people are in conflict with one another. People are being killed in large numbers and people are being damaged in all of those settings.

We need to understand what we need to do to keep those sets of instincts from triggering that same kind of intense conflict and intergroup damage in our country. We need to understand those very basic instinctive behaviors very clearly. We then need to use our basic packages of intergroup instincts to help us avoid war and create Peace instead of allowing those instinctive behaviors to cause people in this country to hurt other groups of people and feel right in doing the damage.

The skill set and the strategies that are embedded in *The Art of InterGroup Peace* guidebook are badly needed today because we have too much war. There is far too much intergroup conflict happening now in the world around us. This guidebook for Peace was written with the belief that what we very much need now are the key skills needed to achieve Peace… not the skills needed to win a war.

We Need an Appreciation for Peace

War and conflict are very seductive. When we separate into groups and believe that another group is a "Them," it is easy to fall into a persuasive emotional mind set that calls for us to do damage to "Them."

Group energy can create both negative intergroup team behavior and intergroup mob behavior — with "Us" feeling both justified and empowered in our negative behaviors toward "Them."

We need to avoid going down that instinct-reinforced slippery slope into conflicted behaviors. We need to deliberately choose Peace as our intergroup goal and strategy.

We Need a Shared Commitment to Achieve Peace

We need to move collectively at this point in our history to an appreciation of Peace and to a commitment to achieve Peace. Peace needs to be understood and Peace needs to be valued.

We need to collectively appreciate the value of Peace and we need to make a collective commitment to actually achieving Peace.

We need to call our leaders to be central to that Peace process. Leaders who do not want Peace can easily destroy Peace. We need leaders to understand the value and benefits of Peace.

The Art of InterGroup Peace is intended to help leaders of each relevant group understand the value of Peace so the leaders can safely set their own sights on ending conflict and achieving intergroup Peace, instead of being focused in each setting on protecting their own people and on creating damage in that setting for the other group in order to ensure the other groups defeat.

Our leaders need to understand that the best outcome for their own group in this country is to be included in collective, win/win based, long-term Peace — and our leaders need to know and understand that there are very explicit things they can do as leaders to help us all achieve and protect that Peace.

The strategies outlined in the Art of InterGroup Peace are intended to help leaders and everyone else understand that approach and do that work.

For the Art of InterGroup Peace to succeed, we need leaders who understand that the best functional goal of the Peace process is to create win/win outcomes for all parties — not to create outcomes where one side is defeated.

Working to achieve win/win outcomes can be difficult to achieve for leaders who are personally vested and embedded in current conflicts and in thinking today about winning at the expense of other parties.

We need leaders who are comfortable with the other party doing well instead of leaders who feel the need to create outcomes where the other side is functionally damaged or even destroyed.

Lose/Lose Outcomes, by Definition, Hurt Everyone

We also need leaders who understand that lose/lose outcomes are particularly bad for us all. The worst option for winning and losing is for both sides to lose. Win/win, win/lose, and lose/lose are the only three options we have for our goals.

It seems illogical for lose/lose strategies to be a deliberate chance by anyone, but the unfortunate truth is that some leaders are so angry today about their own sets of intergroup issues that they are willing to select both tactics and strategies that are directly based on achieving lose/lose outcomes for the groups in their setting.

We need leaders to recognize and know that lose/lose outcomes do not actually meet the needs of any group of people. The needs of your people are not met when lose/lose outcomes result because inevitably, in any lose/lose situation, by definition, your group loses — and that loss is not a win for your group.

We have some leaders in the world — and some leaders even in our own country today — who are so full of intergroup hatred that their number one priority is to do damage to the other group, even at the expense of their own group. We either need to replace those leaders or we need to convert them to a different set of outcomes.

We need leaders in all settings who understand that winning should be the goal for each group and we need leaders who understand why win/win results — with collective winning for all groups — is functionally, operationally, and strategically better than individual wins for separate groups and much better than lose/lose outcomes. Chapter Seven of this book is focused on how to achieve win/win outcomes and how to avoid both lose/lose and win/lose outcomes.

Prosperity for all parties is also a very basic and key goal for The Art of InterGroup Peace.

Each group of people in a time of real Peace can individually and mutually prosper and each group can thrive. Win/win thinking and win/win commitments replace both win/lose and lose/lose strategies as the context for intergroup behavior in a time of Peace.

Chapter Seven explains in more detail why we need to set win/win goals and why we need to all believe in win/win outcomes to achieve Peace.

Honesty, Clear Intentions, Ethical Behaviors, and Mutual Respect Are Key to Peace

That win/win approach to intergroup interactions needs to be consciously, intentionally, and deliberately done. It also needs to be done in a behavioral context that makes it possible to do. Having multiple parties winning simultaneously in win/win settings requires honesty, clear intentions, solid understanding, and mutual respect.

The practical and functional reality that needs to be understood is that Peace cannot be achieved using unethical behaviors. Deceit may win wars, but deceit does not work as a foundation for Peace.

Win/win consequences require ethical behaviors relative to all parties who are at Peace in any setting. Ethical behaviors need to be a key part of our skill set and our tool kit if we want to create and sustain Peace.

We need ethical behaviors to create trust and we need ethical behaviors to sustain the agreements and to maintain the understandings between groups that keep Peace in place.

Peace depends on ethical behaviors both happening and being clearly perceived to be happening. Deceit puts Peace at risk.

The Art of InterGroup Peace Relies on Achieving the Common Good

We need to understand very clearly that basically unethical tools cannot be used to achieve Peace. Treachery is not a path to Peace. We cannot use the same skill sets and values that are needed to win a war to win a Peace.

That is a very basic and practical point that needs to be understood. Peace cannot be achieved or maintained using treachery, duplicity, or dishonesty because those behaviors contain the seeds for their own ultimate failure relative to Peace.

There is a very practical and functional reason for making that statement. Those tools based on deceit cannot be used for Peace because we want Peace to survive over time. That is a major part of our goal set. We want stability for Peace. We want Peace that lasts. We don't simply want momentary or temporary Peace. We don't want just to create truces. We want permanent Peace.

Any Peace that is created by deception begins with an unstable and fragile underpinning and that underpinning fragility makes it much more likely to fail in the future.

Peace Needs to Be a Belief System, a Strategy, and a Commitment

Peace needs to be a belief system and it needs to be anchored on a clear commitment by all parties that make duplicity both unnecessary and dangerous.

Peace needs to be a value and a strategy as well as a state of being. Peace needs to be anchored on a belief that it is legitimate and good for the other group to win, while your own group also benefits directly from winning.

If you build a Peace with supposed win/win underpinnings and if you actually really do want the other side in that setting to lose and to not share in a mutual win — then future behaviors on your part with that goal in mind are likely to cause that hidden goal to be seen and understood to be your real goal.

That intent triggers a visible violation of your agreement to create Peace. When that happens, the people who discover they have been misled, in any

Peace setting, will feel deeply betrayed. A sense of betrayal can be deeply destructive in an intergroup setting and creates real anger.

The anger that can result from that deception being exposed can be very volatile and damaging. When people feel deceived, revenge can be extremely costly for everyone involved. Behavior values can be so negatively distorted when people have that motivation as their focus for intergroup thinking and intergroup behavior.

Revenge isn't sweet. It is painful and it can be incredibly expensive.

We need people to understand that win/win is the right commitment to make — and we need people to understand and recognize that we need that commitment to win/win outcomes to be real and to be honestly embedded in behaviors, decisions, and interactions for each of the groups.

We need to do more than just ending current violence and bloodshed to achieve real Peace. We need to resolve real issues that are creating intergroup conflicts. Real issues can and do exist.

For our own country, we also need to deal honestly and openly with the legacy layers of existing intergroup tensions and conflicts that exist in too many of our settings today. We need to understand our real current issues.

We also need to avoid the intergroup flash points — the anger and even mob behavior that can spring up far too easily with relatively little provocation in any stress-laden intergroup setting. We need to understand those angers and we need to avoid those flash points.

A key to The Art of InterGroup Peace is not to have intergroup explosions that damage intergroup trust — and not to have people in any intergroup setting perceiving other people in that setting to be "Them." That particular perception can do great damage in any setting where people aspire to Peace.

When flash points do happen in any setting, we need to take steps immediately to defuse the crisis situations. We need honest and trusted leaders who can defuse the crisis situations. We need leaders who can defuse each relevant crisis.

We need to understand that our leaders will need to trust one another to do that work well. We need leaders who we trust who also have the ability to reach out to create alliances and create trust with other leaders as leaders.

Too often, our key group leaders today do not know or do not trust the leaders of other groups. We need to have our leaders each make a commitment to us that they will reach out and get to know the relevant leaders from other groups on a personal basis.

We need leaders who know leaders to make intergroup Peace real.

We need to end basic distrust between people and between our leaders to create, and then stabilize Peace in any setting.

Ending distrust is important. Honesty is a key part of that process. We can't use deception to end distrust. We need to move away from intergroup animosity and we need to reduce and eliminate intergroup stress and distrust.

Peace requires intergroup trust and interpersonal trust — at a very basic level. We need alignment for Peace, and that alignment will only happen when people trust one another.

We need to create functional settings where people inherent in mutually beneficial ways and we need to create a context where the relevant groups of people are actually aligned in key and Peaceful ways. We need to set up processes where all groups in a setting know that other groups in that setting are also aligned and can be trusted in their alignment.

We Do Not Have InterGroup Alignment Today

We obviously cannot say that we have achieved that particular state of intergroup alignment, intergroup trust, and intergroup Peace in our country today. That's why we need to be very good at *The Art of InterGroup Peace* at this point in our history.

We are not in active intergroup conflict. Blood isn't being shed very often — although there are incidents of intergroup bloodshed that do trigger significant levels of intergroup anger when they happen. We are in a state of partial alignment and we are making progress at an intergroup level in a number of ways.

We Have Options and Tools We Can Use for Alignment and Peace

The steps that lead from conflict to Peace are listed in Chapter Five. We need to move from truces to treaties, and we need to move from treaties to trust and alignment in order to end up with intergroup Peace. This book describes each of those steps and interaction-options in more detail below.

There is also a list of nine very specific and very possible intergroup interaction levels that are described as intergroup alignment options in Chapter Eight of this book. Chapter Seven explains six very powerful and effective key tools we can use to create alignment as groups. Those tools can trigger alignment in multiple settings when they are used well.

Chapter Five outlines seven key steps we can take to create a culture in any setting, and explains how we can use those same basic steps to build and support a culture of Peace for our country and for any setting.

Chapters Two, Three, and Four identify the 12 sets of instincts that we need to channel and use to end conflict and promote Peace. We will need to use all of those tools in the interest of Peace in this country because we are not at Peace today, and those tools can be used to help us move collectively toward that goal.

We have multiple settings in this country today where we have groups of people who are currently in a state of conflict and situational stress relative to other groups of people.

Our major cities tend to have ethnic and racial divisions that are clearly basic intergroup angers at multiple levels in multiple settings in our country. The intensity of those divisions and the extent, scope, and scale of those intergroup divisions are increasing in a number of settings.

We Need to Focus on the Common Good

Peace, for the definition of this book, involves achieving levels of community interaction where the various ethnic and racial groups in any given setting end up working together in important ways for the common good, rather than having the groups in each setting being angry, conflicted, confrontational, distrustful, and divided by the emotions and the behaviors of any or all groups in each setting, who feel the need to be in conflicted situations with each other.

We need people to be united in real ways doing meaningful things together to achieve the common good in key areas. The common good is a unifying concept and approach. Achieving the common good in very significant and obvious ways can help bring people in any setting into alignment.

We need to explicitly figure out what is involved and what should be included in the common good for us as a country. We need to figure out what can collectively be achieved for the common good. Then we need to work together collectively in each setting to achieve the common good for all groups of people in each setting.

We also need to understand the various options and strategies we have to achieve Peace in each setting.

In advising Generals about how to win a war, Sun Tzu pointed out the five fundamental factors that are needed to win a war. He pointed out 14 ways of deceiving the enemy. He pointed out six important situations that can exist in wartime, and he suggested strategies for dealing with each relevant situation.

In addition, Sun Tzu pointed out six strategies that can be used for dealing with an enemy — with each option on that list based on the relative strength of the enemy.

He identified six strategic mistakes to avoid, and he explained three ways that a ruler could bring misfortune and defeat to his army.

Sun Tzu also listed "five circumstances in which victory may be predicted," and he outlined the five elements that a general needed to consider before entering into combat.

And — as Chapter Two of this book pointed out — he outlined the six kinds of terrain that a general needed to understand to make victory in battle more likely in each geographic setting.

Some of the advice that is written into *The Art of War* is highly specific. All of the advice is clearly embedded with a blend of common sense that is seasoned and enhanced by the actual and functional wartime experience of Sun Tzu.

"When an advancing enemy crosses water," Sun Tzu said, "do not meet him at the waters edge. It is advantageous to allow half his force to cross — and then strike."

The Art of InterGroup Peace Uses Multiple Lists As Well

The Art of InterGroup Peace, in a similar vein — and inspired very directly by Sun Tzu's example and *The Art of War* teaching format — also includes lists of situations, opportunities, challenges, difficulties, tactics, and strategic options that are relevant to Peace. *The Art of InterGroup Peace* and the book *Primal Pathways* both identify the 12 key categories of instinctive behaviors that create the context and "terrain" for intergroup interactions.

The Art of InterGroup Peace focuses on the 12 most relevant packages of instincts that we need to deal with effectively in order to actually achieve Peace.

The Art of InterGroup Peace also outlines the six key response options we have for dealing with the potential or current negative activation of instincts centered on "Them", in any setting.

Those instincts, when adversely activated in any setting, can create significant damage and can set back the cause of Peace in that setting. *The Art of InterGroup Peace* outlines six functional options we have for dealing with — or preventing — that very damaging instinct activation.

The Art of InterGroup Peace also describes the seven options we have for putting in place structural intergroup interactions that can lead us both to situational Peace and to functional alignment between groups.

That set of seven structural options for intergroup interactions ranges from complete separation at one end of the intergroup continuum, to full melding and complete assimilation of the groups at the other end of that continuum.

One of the final chapters of *The Art of InterGroup Peace* outlines the 10 primary threats and challenges that exist relative to Peace, and outlines ways of addressing each of those 10 challenges. Those challenges need to be addressed, or Peace can be lost once it has been attained.

The Art of InterGroup Peace is anchored — at its core — on a key foundational strategy of getting people in this country to be inclusive, mutually supportive, and proactive in creating a new American "Us" that will bring our people together under the behavioral umbrella and the functional safety of triggering our "Us" instincts for all of us.

CHAPTER TWO

Our Us/Them Instincts Can Make Peace Both Very Difficult and Possible

To CREATE INTERGROUP Peace in America and to protect, maintain, and perpetuate intergroup Peace in America, we need to understand and make skillful and strategic use of the basic sets of instincts that we have to divide the world into Us and Them, and then to act in very different ways toward people depending on the category of Us or Them that we perceive people to be in.

Those instincts have great power. They influence our intergroup behavior constantly. Those instincts can both cause us to do good and they can cause us to do evil things to other people. It is extremely important for us all to recognize the fact that those instincts can cause us to feel right and to feel justified in doing both good and evil.

We need to use those instincts as a tool. We need to have those instincts cause us to help, protect, and defend other people in inclusive ways. We also need to avoid having those very powerful instincts activated in dysfunctional ways that can create intergroup division and intergroup damage.

We need to understand that set of instincts so well that we can mitigate or avoid the damages that those instincts create and so that we can benefit from the positive behaviors that can flow from those instincts when they are triggered in positive ways.

When we understand those instincts and their consequences, we can have control over their impact on our lives.

Those instincts trigger a very basic set of intergroup functions and they create very consistent patterns of behaviors.

At their most basic level, we tend to define the people around us as being either "Us" or "Them." We can do that in fairly flexible ways. There can be multiple possible definitions of both us and them for each of us. But the reality is that the people in any situation or any setting tend to know who they align with in that situation and setting as an us, and who they define in that setting to be Them.

The Divisions into Us and Them Directly Affect Beliefs and Behaviors

Those divisions into us and them have influenced human behavior throughout the entire history of mankind. It has been a universal differentiation approach that has affected behaviors wherever groups of people have existed. Behaviors, values, structures, thought processes, and emotions have all very consistently resulted from those us/them delineations.

Our us/them instincts have shaped human history. They have very clearly shaped American history. Those instincts shape human behaviors and they are clearly creating history today.

The Art of InterGroup Peace depends entirely on dealing effectively with those packages of instincts. To make Peace possible, we each need to understand how those instincts work and we each need to know how they affect our thoughts, emotions, values, and behaviors.

We need that knowledge so that we can both trigger and defuse those instincts when necessary and appropriate, and so that we can activate them and utilize them intentionally, skillfully, and strategically as tools to bring us together in the pursuit and achievement of Peace.

The most relevant instinctive thought and behavior patterns created by those instincts are fairly simple, and those patterns are easy to detect and describe.

We Protect Us — and Distrust and Dislike Them

The core reality is that we instinctively divide the world into us and them. We tend to feel protective, supportive, and nurturing for whomever we define to be an "Us."

We tend to be suspicious, antagonistic, and territorial relative to whomever we define to be a "Them."

We tend to distrust "Them." We fear, dislike, and avoid "Them." We tend to feel uncomfortable and unhappy when we are surrounded by "Them" — and we tend to be much more comfortable and safe when we are surrounded by our "Us."

We tend to treat us and them very differently. When our "Them" behavior patterns, values, and emotions are fully activated, we tend to discriminate against "Them." In far too many settings, we can do negative things to them and we generally feel no guilt for those negative behaviors that are done to "Them."

Feeling no guilt for what we do to "Them" has a massive impact on intergroup behaviors and thinking.

We Suspend Conscience in Harming "Them"

Us/Them behaviors have been extreme in too many settings.

In some settings, we enslave them. In others, we ethnically cleanse them. We often purge and displace them from our communities.

We can do very negative things to them in a wide variety of ways, and we far too often actually suspend conscience and feel no guilt for our actions when we are dealing with "Them."

Those guilt free damaging behaviors are a particularly important, highly relevant and very negative impact that results too often when those us/them instincts are fully activated in any setting.

Those patterns of us/them behavior and values have been seen throughout history. In World War II, we fire bombed the city of Dresden, killing men, women and children, and we awarded medals to the people who dropped the bombs. The Germans were a "Them" to America at that moment in history — so we actually killed a great many people with fire, and did it with no sense of guilt for the deaths of "Them."

In that same war, we dropped an atomic bomb on Hiroshima. One of the reasons the City of Hiroshima was selected as the site of that first bomb, was that the city had no prisoner of war camps with Americans in them. We were willing to incinerate and obliterate "Them" — but we felt reluctant to drop that same horrific bomb on any group of "Us."

Suicide Bombers Kill "Them"

Slavery — wherever and whenever it occurs — is an absolute us/them behavior. So is ethnic cleansing. So are the terrorist bombs that are going off in multiple cities in multiple countries today. In each of these cases, the target is "Them." Us/Them values and Us/Them behaviors are the clear consequence of perceiving people as "Us" and "Them." The terrorists do not set off their bombs where their own family, clan, or tribe happens to live.

Terrorist bombs are almost always intertribal — killing whomever the terrorists perceive to collectively be "Them." The bombs tend to be aimed at groups of people — not at individual targets. When we are thinking in us/them terms, we tend to lump "Them" together and we feel that any action taken against any one of "Them" is a legitimate thing to do to "Them." We tend to "depersonalize" whoever we perceive to be a "Them."

Unfortunately — sometimes tragically — we can categorically depersonalize, and stereotype entire sets of people by tribe, race, ethnic group or nationality in very negative and dehumanizing ways. We then kill "Them" with no sense of guilt or remorse.

In too many cases, the intergroup anger that is felt is so great that the people who personally become bomb deliverers with their own bodies are willing to die in order to kill numbers of Them... and there are settings in the world where people with guns and weapons massacre groups of "Them" with no sense of guilt at any level for killing those people.

There are some exceptions to the intertribal and intergroup killings by those kinds of terrorist attacks today — where people do kill people from their own group — but those exceptions to intergroup killing are relatively rare. In those rare exceptions to intertribal killing where people kill people from their own group or tribe, the mass murderers doing those bombings or those shootings generally manage to somehow depersonalize the people they are killing. Even those non-intertribal mass murderers generally manage to achieve a mental model for themselves where they see the people they are killing through the cold and distancing lens of full us/them depersonalization, or through some level of complete collective dehumanization for the people who they decide to kill.

In the intergroup Us/Them conflict settings that we see in so many places in the world, those killings are not aimed at individual people in order to punish each of the individual people for their own personal behavior or their own personal sins.

Those killings in those settings are aimed at groups of people in a depersonalized way as collective retribution for some level of perceived collectivized group sins. That is a sad and pathetic, tragically dehumanizing way of thinking about people and treating people — and it happens all the time in far too many settings because one set of our us/them package of instincts causes us to have those behaviors and those collective perceptions, and to feel and embed those values as guides for our behavior.

People have their us/them instincts activated and behave in damaging and sometimes purely evil ways relative to who ever they perceive to be "Them." The behaviors that result from those activated instincts create a history of intergroup damages that is used to reinforce future intergroup behaviors.

The history of those damaging intergroup behaviors in each setting becomes the history of each group in the setting — and future interactions between the groups are heavily influenced by the power of that history to trigger intergroup anger, distrust, and hatred.

It is a very self-reinforcing cycle and a self-perpetuating legacy.

Our instincts create our intergroup behaviors. Our behaviors create our intergroup history. The history strongly influences future intergroup behaviors.

It is a very damaging and very powerful cycle — particularly when we don't recognize the instinctive triggers.

Exiles, Purges, and Jim Crow Laws Resulted from Those Instincts

Our own history as a nation has been highly and heavily influenced by our us/them instincts. The history section of this book explains that intergroup situation in our country in far more detail. We can only understand our own history as a nation clearly when we clearly understand those instincts and see their impact and influence on us all.

To successfully achieve the intergroup Peace strategies that are outlined in *The Art of InterGroup Peace,* we need to understand that intergroup history and we need to deal, today, very honestly and directly with the residual and relevant consequences of that history.

Slavery, Tribal Exiles, and Evil Behaviors Stem from Those Instincts

Us/Them instinctive behaviors are obviously very powerful and they have a huge impact on our collective legacy as a country. As the sister books to *The Art of InterGroup Peace,* both *Cusp of Chaos* and *Primal Pathways* describe how those instinctive behaviors have created centuries of discriminatory, and far too often cruel, damaging, and even evil behaviors for people in our own country at multiple levels. Slavery, tribal exiles, forced dislocations for Native Americans, Jim Crow laws, and various instances of intergroup evil, and destructive and damaging economic, physical, and political intergroup actions, all stem from that same basic pattern of us/them values and behaviors — and from that same set of "Us/Them" instincts.

Those patterns of behaviors and those intergroup values are clearly part of our American national history. We have done some very damaging things to one another in our past in the context of those instinctive behaviors.

It is also very clear that various levels of us/them behaviors and values continue to be part of our current reality and our current set of behaviors — even though we have made major progress toward more enlightened behaviors in a wide range of areas.

The progress we have made toward more enlightened behavior in a number of intergroup areas needs to be both celebrated and protected. That progress we have made in several areas is very real — and it deserves our support and understanding.

We need to recognize that we are never free of our instincts. It is very true that our packages of us/them instincts continue to define our interactions at various levels today. Those basic sets of intergroup instincts will continue to trigger a sense of InterGroup distrust across our country. That intergroup distrust is reinforced by an array of InterGroup concerns and intergroup issues that exist — today — in a number of settings in this country.

We have very real sets of economic differences between groups of people in this country. We have health disparities and we have education level disparities that need to be addressed.

We have made great progress on our relative legal status for women and minorities in this country, but we still have a number of other areas where there are very real issues that need to be addressed.

We Can't Afford to Trigger Us/Them Instincts Between Groups

We need to be very open about the sets of issues that still exist. We need to address all of those issues in the context of creating a sense of "Us" in each of our communities and settings.

We also need, at this point in our history, to avoid the activation of "Them" instincts in all of our intergroup settings. We need to avoid us/them language and we need to avoid us/them trigger points and interactions. Wherever we have a sense in any setting that those packages of instincts are being triggered or activated, we need to take responsible steps to defuse and deactivate them.

The consequences of activation for those sets of instincts can be major in any setting. People can get angry and do things that leave scars on other people's levels of acceptance and trust. Even angry us/them rhetoric can cause people to trigger their own us/them instinct-guided responses — and escalation can be rapid and damaging at multiple levels.

Most of the negative things that people have been doing to each other as groups have their origins in our us/them instincts. We need to keep those sets of instincts from doing that damage wherever we can keep them from having that negative impact.

In each of our communities, schools, and work settings, we need to be constantly aware of the dangers of having those sets of instincts activated in a negative way. We need to be aware of those issues at a very conscious level and we need to take steps to deactivate, defuse, or counter those sets of instincts in each of our settings.

We also need to be constantly aware of the opportunities we have to activate our "Us" instincts in an inclusive and positive way. We can very intentionally do things to bring people in each setting to have a sense of "Us." Chapter Four explains six basic triggers we can use to create a sense of us and functioning levels of intergroup alignments in various multi-group settings. We need to use all six triggers regularly and well — getting people to see the advantages and benefits of aligned, Peace centered agendas and behaviors.

We need groups of people to perceive the common danger created by our common enemies — the people who do not want us to succeed as a nation — and we need to share a common set of beliefs that can band us together as an American "Us."

We have been trying to become more enlightened and more inclusive as a country. We have had some successes that can help band us together across multiple groups — and those successes have been very real. Our laws that extend the vote to women and to non-White Americans have been a major step in that direction. The repeal of the evil and discriminatory Jim Crow Laws and their replacement with laws that make functional discrimination that is based on race, ethnicity, or gender both illegal and unacceptable all point us in good directions.

Our entire history is described in more detail in other chapters of this book. We have done some horrible things to one another — but we also have a growing number of areas where real progress has been made. We need to build on that progress and have it reinforce our sense that we are a nation of values we all can untie behind. We are far from perfect, but we are moving in good directions on many issues, and we can go even further when we get to know one another as people, and when we articulate and commit to a shared set of key values to guide our lives.

We Can't Simply Sweep the Slate Clean Today

Groups do not have a high level of intergroup trust in a number of key areas today. Groups have done evil things to one another. Prejudice and discrimination has been painful, deliberate, and entirely intentional at multiple levels.

Even where behaviors today are significantly better, memories of the old behaviors are painful and fresh.

We have had too many years of American functional reality where those packages of instinctive behaviors have created significant prejudice and very direct discrimination against too many of our people.

Both intergroup deception and absolute intergroup bias have been part of that instinctive behavior package in very visible ways for massive numbers of people. This book looks at that history in more detail in Chapter Five.

We clearly need to recognize the intergroup reality and beliefs that have been created by those years of duplicity, prejudice, and discrimination and we now need to deal with its implications directly if we want intergroup Peace today. As we build the strategies for The Art of InterGroup Peace for America, we need to recognize that we have too many years of really unfortunate intergroup behavior in our past as a country to simply sweep the slate clean today and start over — even with good intentions and lofty goals.

We also can not simply wipe the slate clean today and start over as a single group, because we actually are a nation of multiple groupings — multiple races, ethnicities, and cultures — and there is no way for us not to have intergroup instincts activated in various ways in the face of our obvious intergroup reality.

We Are Not Molding into a Single Group

We may have passed enlightened laws on multiple points, but we still wake up every morning in the context of a wide array of groups who each will continue to trigger basic and primal instinctive group alignments for each group's members.

The basic array of instinct triggering differentiation factors — how we look, how we sound, and who we each affiliate with at the most primal level — will not be erased. We are not melding into a new single group.

Because we are not melding, we will always be in the position where certain sets of instinctive triggers can be relevant. Even if we ignore all division factors relating to our history and to our legacy behaviors — we still have key differentiations that exist and are relevant now.

So we can't start over. But we can begin now to work with what we have and who we are to do what we now need to do.

We Are Increasingly Diverse

Our us/them instincts are going to be increasingly relevant to us, right now, at this point in our history because we are clearly becoming increasingly diverse as a country. Our diversity is inevitable and it is growing daily.

Intergroup diversity — as we know from experience and history — can trigger those sets of us/them instincts easily.

We used to be a country that had one very large majority group with relatively few sizable minority groups. That is changing.

In many of our cities, there is no majority group in place today. In a number of American settings where a local majority group does exist, the local majority group in that city is often a former minority group that is still a minority group in the overall context of its entire state or our entire country, but is now the local majority group in specific settings.

Our urban settings are now highly multi-ethnic and multi-racial. The entire country is becoming more diverse at a very rapid pace. Our younger Americans tend to be significantly more diverse than our older Americans in almost every setting.

That increasing diversity is changing our work forces, our schools, and our political demographics.

The number of people who are entering our work force from our minority populations will be a majority of all new workers in a relatively few years. Minority Americans are a majority of our new and existing workers in many urban settings now.

The Majority of Our Births Are Now from Minority Groups

Probably the most significant piece of information about our growing diversity is that a majority of all births in this country last year were from our minority populations. More than half of all births in this country last year came from our overall array of minority populations.

The future is clear. Diversity is our future. We all need to be very aware that our us/them instincts are very easily triggered by group differentiations. Our differentiations are growing.

The truth that we all need to recognize is that our diversity can either lead us to conflict, or we can turn it into a major asset that benefits us all. It is entirely possible to have our diversity be a great source of strength to us as a country.

We can be the most productive and safest country on the planet and we can choose to celebrate our diversity in the process.

Intergroup Peace needs to be our conscious commitment, strategy, and our national focus to make that happen.

We know now that major on-going diversity in so many other parts of the world leads almost inevitably in every site to constant intertribal and intergroup stress, intergroup conflict, and even civil war. There are more than 200 ethnic conflicts going on in other multi-ethnic settings in the world. It would be a huge tragedy to allow that kind of interethnic future to happen here.

It does not need to happen here.

We Need to Make Our Diversity a Great Strength

We need to recognize and celebrate our growing diversity — and we need to align our diversity into a common agenda and a shared set of behaviors and values that will benefit all of us. It is far better to make our diversity a great strength.

Making our diversity into strength will require a context of InterGroup Peace. We need to be skilled at the Art of InterGroup Peace to achieve those goals. This is the time for us to make a commitment to Peace and to do the work needed to achieve Peace. Everyone will benefit if everyone has the benefits of Peace.

To achieve that Peace we need to recognize the fact and the reality that our basic us/them instincts have the obvious and very real potential to turn our growing Diversity into increasing levels of stress, and into serious and damaging InterGroup division.

If we don't take appropriate steps to keep those instincts from defining the future of this country in an increasingly negative way, then the more negative aspects of those packages of instincts will have a high likelihood of prevailing, and they will then define both who we are and how we function as a country in very dysfunctional, divisive, and destructive ways.

We need to keep that from happening. We need to create intergroup Peace and we need to create that Peace now. We need to begin with the places that we live.

We need to work hard to create a sense of "Us" for each community. We need to eliminate the factors in each community that divide us. We need to have people in each setting who believe in and trust the court system, and who believe the processes that govern each community actually function as an extension of "Us" rather than being perceived as "Them."

So how can we create that sense of community us? We need to make some choices and we need to use some of the tools we have available to us. We need to use those tools as a nation and we need to use them in each community that we are a part of.

We Need the Right Strategic Choices

This book, like *The Art of War*, is a book of lists. *The Art of InterGroup Peace* has lists of alignment triggers, lists of interaction structures, lists of culture enhancement tools, and lists of ways that we can make life better for us all. The book has lists of core beliefs that we all can share, and lists of behaviors to avoid if we want to function collectively as an "Us."

The Art of InterGroup Peace has lists of key instinct packages that create the functional terrain for our intergroup interactions. All of those lists can help us achieve intergroup Peace in America.

All Instincts Can Be Used for Good Or Evil

The lists of instincts are particularly important.

We need to be very clear about the fact that all of our instincts can be used for good — and that all of our instincts can also be used for evil. The underlying terrain reality that we face is that we all have the potential to be saints — and we all also have the potential to be sinners.

Saints or sinners. We get to choose. *The Art of InterGroup Peace* calls for us to make the right choices, and the Peace strategies help outline exactly what the right choices are.

We do need to make the right choices. We need to select the right alignment motivators, and we need to use the right organizational model for our intergroup interactions.

Knowledge is power — in a very direct way. We collectively need to understand the terrain we are facing, and we need to build our strategies in ways that address the sets of situational realities that are created by each relevant terrain.

Being situationally relevant is equally true for war and Peace.

Underlying that entire set of strategies and tactics is a core belief that we will succeed when we merge to come together as a values-based American "Us." Instead of being divided by race, or group or ethnicity, we need to be a nation unified around our values and our beliefs.

To support that process, this book also describes, explains, offers, and endorses one dozen key beliefs and functional values that we can use to create a collective commitment to Peace.

Having a set of shared values can be extremely important to our future. If we don't have agreement on our basic and core values, the likelihood of successfully achieving Peace will be significantly lower.

We need to be a people united by our shared values and united by our shared beliefs. The last chapter of this book identifies a basic, fundamental list of those unifying values and recommends that we commit to using them.

The first part of the Peace strategy is to understand the role of instincts and to understand that we can use our instincts rather than simply being used by them. Our instinct packages influence us to a very high level.

Our instincts will be key to our success.

Creating Peace and achieving intergroup alignment for our country, for our communities, for our schools, and even for our work sites can be done more easily if we use our basic sets of instinctive behaviors as tools rather than having our instincts functionally triggering our problems and creating most of our challenges.

The Art of InterGroup Peace strategy is anchored on the reality that our basic intergroup behaviors are heavily influenced by several packages of instincts that we all share.

Those sets of instincts all interconnect and interact with the instincts we have to divide the world into us and them.

We have instincts, for example, to identify with and protect turf. We activate our turf instincts as individuals and we activate them as groups.

We also have instincts to create hierarchies. We have hierarches everywhere — and they all tend to have Alpha leaders with Alpha instincts at the top of each hierarchy and people with equally clear Beta instincts embedded inside each hierarchy.

We have instincts to build cultures. We build cultures in every setting and we use them to give us the rule sets and the expected behaviors we use for each setting.

We have very strong instincts to detest traitors — and we have equally strong instincts never to personally be a traitor. Those traitor-related instincts can strongly influence our interpersonal behavior relative to interactions with other people and with other groups of people.

We Act Most of the Time in Alignment with Our Instincts

We need the personal humility and the personal wisdom to recognize that we tend to act, most of the time, in the direct context of behavior patterns that have been sculpted and influenced for each of us and for all of us by our basic packages of instincts.

Sun Tzu wrote about the physical and geographic terrain that was relevant to the Art of War. *The Art of InterGroup Peace* involves psychological and behavioral pattern terrain that is even more relevant to Peace.

Our instincts-structured behavior tendencies create a kind of situational terrain that gives us some very clear and predictable behavior patterns to work with relative to intergroup interactions.

We need to build Peace in the context of those patterns.

We also need to use that knowledge to create internal alignment and functional Peace in our workplaces, organizations, and communities.

We have the same behavioral tendencies in all of those settings, and this same set of insights and instincts can be highly useful at a very immediate level in any group that we form.

The sister book, *Primal Pathways,* is a book that is almost entirely about instinctive behavior. *Primal Pathways* deals in some detail with 12 basic packages of instinctive behaviors that are most relevant to intergroup interactions and to the Peace process.

This section of *The Art of InterGroup Peace* deals more directly with roughly half of those relevant behavior packages. The sets of main instinct-linked behavior patterns that are described below in the next four chapters of this book are important for us to understand in order to succeed at *The Art of InterGroup Peace.* If we understand those sets of instincts and use or manage them well, we are significantly more likely to succeed in creating intergroup Peace.

Instincts Tend to Make Behaviors "Feel Right"

Those instincts are important to The Art of InterGroup Peace because each of those instincts make particular sets of behaviors and particular ways of thinking feel right to people. Instincts have the very significant and useful power of making behaviors feel right.

"Feeling Right" is often a very good sign that an instinctive behavior has been triggered in our minds. That is an important point to understand that is highly relevant to *The Art of InterGroup Peace,* as well as to *Primal Pathways* and *Cusp of Chaos.* Any time any behavior feels entirely and extremely "right," there is a high likelihood that the behavior that feels so right has instinctive roots, and there is a very high likelihood that the specific behavior that feels so right is also getting direct instinctive reinforcement at some level.

Many examples are obvious. Protecting our home "feels right." That feeling is basically instinctive. Protecting our homes is very instinctive behavior. Protecting our family turf "feels right" as well.

The fierce level of energy and the intense emotions that can be triggered when we need to protect our children clearly has very deep-seated instinctual roots.

It clearly feels very right to do things to protect both our children and our turf.

Four Useful Tests of Instinctive Behavior

We obviously share those particular packages of instincts to protect both our offspring and our nest with a myriad of other species. Those specific behaviors also seem to feel very right to the other species who we can see are exhibiting those same sets of basic and fundamental instinctive behaviors.

Feeling right is one of the four basic tests and guidelines we can use to figure out whether that particular behavior is either instinctive or highly influenced by our instincts.

We can use those four basic criteria in looking at any set of consistent behaviors to see if the behaviors we see are each being created independently in their own intellectual and situational context, or to see if it is highly likely that those particular consistent behaviors have an instinct at their core.

1. Universal Behaviors Tend to Be Instinctive

Universality is a very useful screening factor for determining whether or not a behavior has instinctive roots. Look for "universal," examples of the behavior as a useful sign that behavior is instinctive.

If the behavior you are thinking about is everywhere, there is a high likelihood that it is everywhere because our instincts trigger it everywhere.

One of the best ways of identifying the fact that any specific behavior is instinctive is that we see the same behavior pattern in all cultures and in all human settings. Universal behaviors tend to be instinctive.

Instincts are functionally the only mechanism that exists that can actually create behaviors that are basically identical everywhere. The book, *Primal Pathways,* explains that process in more detail, and explains the sets of tools that are used by our instincts to have their universal impact on our lives in all of our relevant settings.

2. History Is a Reflection of Instinctive Behaviors

History is also useful. The second best way of recognizing that a specific behavior is instinctive is that we can see that same basic behavior in obvious long-standing patterns of human history.

When history books tell us we have done the same pattern of behavior for a very long time, then we can safely look for instinctive origins for the behavior.

Behaviors we have always done and that have created major patterns and clear patterns in our historical record tend to be instinctive at their core.

History repeats itself, in very large part, because the patterns we follow for many behaviors have universal instincts at their core that have not changed over time.

Our history books tend to be the situational and fact-based reporting of how our instincts have been manifested for groups of people in each time and in each setting.

Historians tend to tell us about the incidents and events that have occurred, and historians tend to name the people who have been important to what was done in each setting. Historians tend to not focus on, acknowledge, or even discuss the underlying patterns of instinctive triggers and behaviors that have been the primary architecture for major portions of our historical record.

History is easier to understand when the impact of those instinctive behaviors is more clear. Economic theory linked directly to behavioral theory can be very useful for describing and explaining much of our history.

The missing link that sometimes overpowers the impact of economics-grounded explanations of history is the actual highly consistent influence of those sets of instincts on our lives.

3. The Behavior Triggers Instinctive Emotions

Emotions tend to be very useful tools for our instincts and they give us a clue that a behavior might have instinctive roots.

Several basic emotions tend to be used in both detectable and discernable ways by our instincts to steer our behaviors.

A good way of identifying that a behavior is instinctive at some level is that the behavior triggers, activates, and stimulates similar sets of emotions in people in all settings.

Emotions are one of the most effective tools of instincts. Our instincts use emotions very consistently to guide us to and from relevant behaviors.

"Feeling right" was mentioned above. Any behavior that feels very right when we do it probably has an instinct at its core. It often feels very right to us when a behavior and an instinct are aligned.

Our instincts use our cultures to achieve their goals. That sense of "feeling right" that happens when our behavior is aligned with an instinct can be triggered when our behavior is aligned with a culture that is, itself, clearly aligned with an instinct.

At the same time, as the other side of that same "feeling right" package, our instincts can make some specific behaviors feel wrong — or at least make them feel stressful or trigger anxiety. We can feel wrong being a traitor to our group. We can feel wrong not protecting our child when protection of the child is needed.

We can feel wrong not supporting our group or our team in times when support is needed by our group or team.

Stress is a frequently used tool of instincts. We can often feel a sense of stress when we are acting in ways that are not aligned with our instincts.

Sometimes the easiest way to reduce stress is to figure out what instinct we are currently triggering in a negative way. When we figure that out, we can often either change our behavior to be aligned with our instinct, or we can simply reduce the stress level in our own mind by recognizing that the stress we are feeling is actually instinctive in its functional origin.

Knowledge can be power relative to some feelings of anxiety or stress. The book *Primal Pathways* explains those processes in more detail. Feeling right, feeling wrong, and feeling stress are all used consistently as emotional tools by our instincts to guide our lives.

Anger, Fear, Guilt, Shame, Greed, Love, and Lust All Have Links to Instincts

Several other emotions are also used by our instincts to steer our behaviors. Anger, fear, shame, guilt, greed, lust, and love all have very basic links to basic instincts. Those emotions are all used to guide us either toward the behaviors that our instincts want us to include in our lives, or away from the behaviors that our instincts want us to avoid.

That does not mean all emotions have instinctive roots or linkages. There are a number of non-instinctive and functionally situational triggers that activate our emotions.

Anger is sometimes instinctive — and it is sometimes situational. Anger can be created both by our instincts and by the facts and the circumstances of the particular situation we are in.

Fear can also be triggered in both instinctive and situational ways.

"Feeling right," however, very often means that there is an instinct in play relative to the specific behavior that makes that behavior feel right.

Understanding instincts to be a source of stress can be a very useful thing to understand. The *Primal Pathways* book explains those issues in more detail.

Instincts often use both stress and anger as tools to channel our behaviors. We feel stress and anger when our children are threatened. We feel stress and anger when our turf is invaded. We feel some level of stress when we don't have a hierarchy in place in any setting.

We can also feel stress when we do have a hierarchy in place, but when the top position in our relevant hierarchy is currently vacant.

The feeling of stress in any setting or situation can tell us that we perceive that an instinctive need is not being met in our lives in that particular setting. Satisfying the needs that are created by the instinct can often eliminate the sense of stress.

People who want to live stress-free lives can sometimes eliminate or significantly reduce some elements of stress by figuring out which package of instincts are triggering relevant stress in their lives, and then dealing with those triggers directly.

Recognizing when those instincts are relevant to our intergroup interactions — to reaching out and making connections to people from other groups, for example, can help each of us make better choices about those behaviors.

4. Instinctive Behaviors Can Be Shared by Other Living Beings

A fourth way of recognizing that a behavior pattern has a high likelihood of being instinctive is when we see parallel behaviors in other species — and when we know that the specific behavior we observe is clearly and significantly instinctive for the other species.

Having paralleled behaviors in other species is a very good piece of evidence for a behavior in us being instinctive. It's difficult to imagine a mechanism or scenario whereby other species could do something specific in a consistent way, entirely instinctively, and then have us somehow manage to do the same thing with an equivalently high level of consistency, but somehow have those same behaviors, in each setting, be based on our individual situation specific intellectual decision making processes that happen to exist for each of us, in each and every setting, where that behavior is happening.

It is unlikely that we could create those highly consistent behaviors in all of our settings for people through either intellectual invention done situationally by people in each setting, or through pure and entirely circumstantial coincidence that somehow creates parallel consequences and behavior patterns for people everywhere for that behavior.

Maternal behaviors clearly fit that pattern of behaviors, emotions, and approaches that exist everywhere in ways that could not be invented independently by each mother in each setting and in each set of circumstances. Both we and other living creatures tend to exhibit maternal instincts.

Maternal Instincts Are Clearly Shared and Clearly Not Unique to Us

Maternal instincts and the instincts to defend one's offspring are clearly not limited to humans. Mother bear and mother deer and mother sparrows all instinctively protect their young. It clearly feels instinctively right for all of those mothers to offer their offspring that support and protection.

Maternal instincts and maternal behavior tendencies clearly tend to be universal among all groups of humans. We fairly obviously also do share some patterns of those behaviors, and a number of instinctive emotions with mother bears, mother deer, and mother sparrows.

Again, if you apply the four guidelines listed above to determine whether or not a behavior is instinctive, maternal behaviors clearly satisfy the yes category for all four criteria. Those maternal behaviors are obviously universal. They are historic. They trigger very consistent emotions.

And we can see other living beings whose mothers have clearly similar instinctive maternal behaviors.

Turf Instincts Also Exist for Other Species

Turf instincts also clearly fit the pattern of being obvious motivators for the behaviors of other species. Our turf instincts are described in more detail in the next chapter of this book. They are one of the basic sets of intergroup instincts we need to understand to create intergroup Peace. We humans are not alone in having turf instincts.

A number of species also have clearly defined turf instincts and those instincts create very predictable patterns of behavior in each species.

Wolf packs and herds of wild horses tend to have instinctively supported turf alignments. Wolf packs, horse herds, and chimpanzee clans all tend to protect and defend their groups' turf.

A number of species clearly share variations of those turf instincts. Protecting our turf feels very right most of the time and — as noted earlier — it clearly feels right to wolf packs and chimpanzee clans to defend their turf as well. Turf instincts fit all four of those diagnostic definitions.

Our turf instincts are particularly relevant to the issues of creating and sustaining intergroup Peace.

Wars Are Fought Over Turf

At the intersection of our us/them instincts, our turf instincts, and our family protection instincts, we clearly have a tendency to have a sense of group turf and we have a strong tendency to collectively defend that group turf.

Wars are fought over turf. We instinctively feel great anger as a group against anyone who invades, trespasses, encroaches, or somehow takes possession of our turf.

Many levels of groups have a sense of turf. Tribes have turf. Clans have turf. Nations have turf.

The street gangs that function in our cities and the convict gangs that exist in our prisons also each have their own turf. Gang turf has a very powerful impact on gang behaviors and gang emotions.

Our turf instincts create their greatest challenges when they interact with the most important set of instincts we need to understand as we look at the core issues of InterGroup Peace — our us/them packages of instincts.

Our Us/Them Instincts Can Unite Us or Divide Us

Our us/them instincts could not be more important to us relative to the Art of InterGroup Peace and to our interactions with other groups of people. Those particular instincts affect people's thinking and behaviors in the context of groups – like communities, work places, schools, and various organizations — and they have a massive impact on interaction between groups.

If we only learn to understand one set of our instincts as a result of thinking about intergroup Peace, our us/them instincts are clearly the set of instincts we most need to understand.

It is painfully clear that we instinctively tend to divide the world into "Us" and "Them" — and then we treat people and deal with people very differently if the people are an "Us" or a "Them."

Intergroup interactions are usually defined, reinforced, structured, and actualized in the working context of those particular instincts. *The Art of InterGroup Peace* is anchored in the need to deal effectively with those instincts — both to protect ourselves from their negative consequences, and to benefit from their more positive components and consequences.

We need people to understand the basic context that those instincts create because they are relevant in every intergroup setting. Any time we have people in a setting who come from different groups, there is an extremely high likelihood that those packages of instincts will be triggered.

We React Differently to Us and Them

The patterns for those particular instincts are clear. We react very differently to us and them.

We distrust them. We tend to discriminate against them. We tend to depersonalize, dehumanize, and stereotype who ever we define to be them.

When we identify someone to be a "Them," we are suspicious, distrustful, and we tend to believe that they will deliberately act against our self-interest. We do battle with them and we feel right in defeating them. When those instincts are fully activated, we feel no guilt in doing negative things to them.

We ethnically cleanse them, drive them from their lands, and in worst-case situations, we enslave them — feeling no guilt for horrendous, cruel, and even evil behaviors done collectively and individually to them.

We see those behaviors across the planet. People attack them, bomb them, and rape and abuse them in many intergroup settings. Mass and group killings are happening today in us/them settings.

Us/Them conflicts in Iraq, Syria, Nigeria, and the Congo have resulted in mutilations and horrible deaths at the hands of people who categorized the people they were damaging as them.

Chapter Five of this book discusses those categories of conflicts. People do huge damage to people whenever those instincts are fully activated in conflict settings.

We Keep Our Word to "Us"

We do good things for "Us." That is the best side of the us/them instinct package. That part of the package is key to our future. We protect, support, nurture, aid, and help whoever we define to be us.

In our various communities, we trust us, ally with us, and we choose, when we can, to work with and live in proximity to us.

When we identify someone to be an "Us," we apply a higher ethical standard that is anchored on being "Us." We tend to keep our word to "Us." We support our laws that protect each of "Us."

We respect the roles and the rights of "Us" in the context of the communities of "Us" that we create.

So our us/them instincts have a very powerful impact on our lives. If we are going to create Peace in America — and as we become increasingly diverse at multiple levels as a nation and a society — we need to make sure that our growing diversity creates a strength and an asset to us in each setting that lets us function as an "Us" and doesn't splinter us into us/them lines by group to an even greater degree, when we are divided today.

That particular strategy needs to be used very intentionally in every setting.

We need to do that work of building a sense of us in each work setting, school, community, and organization — creating a sense of us, in each of those settings, that triggers our us-based values and our us-based behaviors. We also need to create a national sense of "Us" that can help bind us together as a country in all of those settings.

We are becoming more diverse as a country at a rapid rate. The majority of births in this country this year were to our "minority" populations. We will either need to be very good at turning our growing internal diversity into a sense of "Us" or we will find ourselves facing some very ugly and damaging instinctive behaviors.

Even Neanderthals Did Not Do Well as "Them"

The history sections of this book explain the negative consequences of creating that sense of "Them" about other groups of people that have happened in various settings in this country since we were founded. Our own history as a nation is full of people who have done very bad and often evil things to other groups of people when us/them instincts were activated in a negative way.

Even our anthropological history shows the impacts of what we do to people we define not to be us. We know that our recorded history as people on the planet is a long and consistent list of intertribal wars.

Even before recorded history, Neanderthal people lived on this planet for nearly half a million years. Neanderthals seemed to have been internally Peaceful, because they were here for a very long period of time and they didn't kill each other off over that long period of time.

And then they disappeared entirely in a relatively few years. Anthropologists tell us from the archeological records that the Neanderthals disappeared relatively quickly when our own ancestors — with our us/them instincts fully developed and activated — entered into Neanderthal lands.

Anyone who wonders why the Neanderthals disappeared entirely shortly after coming in contact with our human ancestors only has to look at human intergroup behavior for people today in Sri Lanka, or in Pakistan, or in Rwanda.

Sri Lanka has mobs of people killing and expelling other groups of people based on their tribal alignments. Germany killed millions of Jews. The Hutu and the Tutsi had mass killings.

The ISIS group in the Middle East this year is massacring entire villages full of "Them," showing no sense of guilt or shared humanity at any level as they execute people, behead "Them" and bury "Them" in mass graves.

We clearly do not do good things to other sets of people when groups of people in any setting, define themselves to each other to be a "Them." We damage "Them." We ethnically purge "Them." We kill "Them" today in too many settings.

Neanderthals clearly were a type of "Them." Human nature is not kind to "Them." Imagine ISIS coming in contact with the Neanderthals.

Ironically, from our purely human perspective — if the Neanderthals had those same kinds of deep-seated InterGroup instincts to damage whoever they perceived to be "Them," our own primal ancestors who originally migrated into long-standing Neanderthal turf probably would not have survived, and this would be a very different planet.

We Need to Create a Broad Sense of Us for Us

Our us/them instincts are very powerful. As a key component of The Art of InterGroup Peace, we need to make sure we don't continue to play out our most negative and damaging us/them instincts in this country today.

We need to take very deliberate steps at this point in our history to reach out and create a sense of us to all of us in this country. At a core level, we need to stop thinking of other people in this country as "Them." We need to end both conflict and intergroup stress relative to people we now perceive to be "Them."

We need to do that work — both intentionally and deliberately — with the clear goal of having America benefit from being an "Us" for ourselves. There are several key pieces to that strategy. We need to begin by deciding together to achieve those goals. Then we need behaviors at the interpersonal level and intergroup level that will help us achieve those goals.

CHAPTER THREE

We Need to Avoid Having Any Part of Us Be Them

IF WE WANT to succeed at The Art of InterGroup Peace — and if we really do want to create a culture of inclusion and mutual success for all groups in America, we need to be very sure not to activate any sets of instincts that cause us to perceive any segment of the population to be "Them."

We need to create an America of inclusion — with an overarching culture that appreciates, celebrates, and builds on our very real and growing diversity as a country.

We need to create alignment — based on our shared beliefs — as a values-linked American "Us."

We also need people in each community, school, worksite, and organization to have a sense of being an "Us" for each setting.

We Need Groups to Be Aligned, Collaborative, and Trusting

We need groups of people in each setting in this country to be aligned, trusting, and collaborative. We clearly need all groups acting in accord with our collectively agreed upon common goals and our shared agendas, if we want to achieve InterGroup Peace.

We need our behaviors to be aligned with positive intergroup interactions.

We need to create alignments — and we need to protect the alignments we create. It is good strategy to be very protective of any positive alignments that are created.

Any positive alignments we create can far too quickly be impaired. Groups of people who have come together to function collectively in any setting will always tend to have some levels of intergroup distrust — and intergroup division can be reactivated quickly in any setting by any actions that cause people to believe that the other group is truly a "Them."

Division in a peaceful setting can happen quickly if we insult the other groups or if we deceive or even significantly mislead the other group.

Those intergroup alignments that we create in any setting can obviously be directly damaged if we damage the other group, or if we clearly discriminate in some meaningful or visible way against the other group.

Any instances of clear discrimination against people from another group can be seen as a proof point that the people who are doing discriminatory things deserve to be regarded as a "Them."

That can be a very damaging perception.

If there seem to be instances of discrimination or damage in any setting where we are building intergroup Peace, we need to be able to talk directly with each other about those incidents and situations. We need to be able to deal in an "adult" and trusting way with the other group in that setting, instead of triggering our going to war emotions and our war instincts based on those inflammatory events or those negative behaviors.

We particularly need to avoid insulting other groups. We all instinctively react with great negative energy to insults. A positive intergroup setting can be destroyed and turned into the exact opposite of Peace — with the clear sense that the other group is a "Them" — if anyone from our group insults, demeans, or verbally attacks the other group in that setting.

Making people angry in a confrontational intergroup way is obviously not a good strategy for achieving and maintaining Peace between groups.

Mutual Respect Is a Good Foundation for Peace

We need a positive and proactive strategy for *The Art of InterGroup Peace* that can help reduce the risk of us/them emotions being triggered in us or in the other group. Mutual respect is a good place to start. We need to very intentionally create and very intentionally demonstrate mutual respect between groups and people in each setting.

We need to intentionally be respectful in dealing with other groups of people. We need to be respectful of each other at a very basic human level.

We need to see the other groups of people as also being fellow human beings. We need to respect the culture and the history of the other group of people, and learn to enjoy the diversity of our cultures as a strength for our society. We need to make learning about the other relevant groups in each setting something we do deliberately and do well.

Most groups of people tend to have relatively low levels of understanding about the cultures, history, current situation, and shared values of other groups. We need better learning processes for each of those topics.

We need to learn key information about other groups in order to understand and appreciate those groups.

We need people to get to know people from other groups, so that we can all recognize our shared values and our shared humanity. We need to reach out as individuals and as groups — in person and through various levels of social media contexts.

Trust between people needs to be anchored between people from each group actually knowing other people from other groups. We need those relationships to exist because those kinds of personal interactions can create much better levels of interpersonal understanding and interpersonal trust.

We need to create learning opportunities where we get to know members of other groups as individual human beings so that we do not just see other people only as depersonalized and conceptually objectified stereotypes for their group.

We need people to intentionally befriend and get to know other people across group lines. To make that process easier, it can be done, when possible, in the context of joint efforts that we create together to make things better for us as a community and an American people.

Our Team Instincts Can Help Us Achieve InterGroup Peace

Creating various kinds of teams and acting together as team members can be a key part of that strategy.

Our team instincts are very powerful. We can overcome some of our other basic us/them differentiation factors in almost any setting when we form teams of people from that setting. The chapter of this book that describes the six triggers we have that can create alignment, rates team instincts and team behaviors as a major tool for alignment.

It can be a very good strategy to use a team-based context in each setting to get to know one another better.

There is an ample supply of relevant and important topics for teams in various settings to focus on. We need teams to improve our education efforts and we need teams to give our infants and our children the best start in life.

We need teams that create better population health — through healthy eating and active living collective programs and strategies.

We need to create multiple ways for people to work together in an aligned way to achieve mutual goals in order to both achieve the mutual goals, and to get together and interact as people who can learn to understand and trust people as a result of their the interactions.

The tactics and the strategies for intergroup learning and context setting that are listed in this chapter of *The Art of InterGroup Peace* apply both to individuals and to groups.

Those tactics of learning and collectively creating interpersonal linkages between groups apply with particular relevance to group leaders, but they apply to all individual group members as well.

We Need Leaders from Groups to Know Leaders from Other Groups to Build Trust

Leaders are often key to any Peace effort.

In a number of cases, the strategies that are outlined in *The Art of InterGroup Peace* function in an organizational context that requires formal, deliberate, and direct action by leaders from the various groups to define, structure, and actually accomplish the targeted intergroup interaction.

To make that particular intergroup interaction process successful, it can be very useful to have leaders from our various groups get to know the leaders of other relevant groups. One-to-one understanding and 1-to-1 relationships between key leaders in key groups can be a very important step in the Peace process.

Interactions between leaders need to happen in credible ways — and they are most effective when they involve specific people in leadership positions who personally want to achieve intergroup understanding and intergroup Peace.

That same set of interpersonal linkages needs to be created at non-leadership levels as well. The whole Peace process is enhanced when people interact with people and when understanding results.

We also each need to go through our own process as individuals of personal learning and personal intergroup relationships. We need to get to know each other as people and we need groups of people to have a better sense of the common humanity of other groups of people.

We Need to Know People as People

In our various intergroup settings, we need to each seek out opportunities for direct communications, interpersonal activities, and personal interactions that we can create between individual people from various groups.

When we know another person as a person, it is much easier to move past the stereotypes that we too often use now in ways that let us understand and relate to other people in direct and personal ways.

When we get to know people as people — with shared beliefs and shared values — then intergroup conflicts can be muted because the common humanity of the various groups is understood by people in each of the groups.

Those kinds of new relationships between people from various groups can be somewhat fragile. Unfortunately, there have been too many situations where a flare-up of intergroup anger can destroy the person-to-person relationships that have been built by individual people with one another — but we need to build those relationships anyway as a key step in the Peace process.

Our likelihood of holding on to those relationships in the face of various levels of intergroup stress points can probably be enhanced if the various people involved read books from the intergroup trilogy, and understand more directly the pull away from person-to-person relationships that our instinctive reactions to intergroup interactions and stress can create.

Knowledge is, for that level of understanding, power.

We Need to Expand Our Sense of Us

Dealing effectively with and ending the negative impact of our us/them instincts is a clear objective of several of the interpersonal connectivity and person-to-person learning strategies.

We need to stop thinking of people from the other groups primarily as "Them." We need to expand our sense of "Us."

We need to create a broader sense of us so that we can extend our trust and our acceptance to the other groups, and so we can feel instinctively pleased when the other groups succeed and thrive.

We have very good and enlightened behaviors that are possible and that can happen when we perceive someone else to be a type of "Us." We can be supportive in good conscience of whoever we perceive to be an "Us."

We also act in very predictable and negative ways toward who ever we perceive to be a "Them."

So it is extremely clear that we need to perceive fewer people in each setting as "Them" and we need to perceive more people in each setting to be "Us."

We need to be careful not to activate our us/them instincts in a negative way about other groups of people, in any setting, because the individual values, emotions, and behaviors that can be triggered when a negative us/them activation happens can be so damaging and divisive — and because the group behaviors that can result from us/them instinct activation in any setting can be so destructive.

We need to be very careful not to activate a sense, in any setting, that other people in that setting are "Them." We need, in each setting, to avoid creating a sense of "Them" — and we need to respond quickly and directly when the threat that people will be perceived to be "Them" exists.

Negative Us/Them Instincts Need to Be Avoided, Minimized, Derailed, Neutralized, Negotiated, or Replaced

Leaders in any setting — community, corporate, organizational, or even national — should work very hard to be sure those negative "Them" perceptions are not triggered and activated in their setting.

The damage and division that stems from the behaviors triggered by those negative instincts should be avoided whenever possible.

When those instincts are intentionally or inadvertently triggered in any setting, then they need to be addressed.

If they continue to be activated in any setting, they will tend to grow in damage levels and power in those settings.

The Art of InterGroup Peace calls for people to deactivate, neutralize, de-energize, defuse, and where possible, simply replace those negative us/them beliefs, emotions, and behaviors with other intergroup interaction levels. Damage can be avoided or minimized with the right interactions. That basic work to keep those instincts from damaging us needs to be done well, because the consequences of having those instincts activated can be significant.

The list below offers six basic sets of responses that we can directly use in response to our more negative Us/Them instincts in any situation where those instincts are at risk of becoming the relevant and dominant responses of people to other people in any setting.

Six Steps Can Offset Those Negative Instincts

There are six parts to the basic us/them instinct risk mitigation approach.

If we want to achieve and protect Peace in a setting where our more negative Intergroup us/them instincts might be activated in ways that could destroy Peace, then we need to have our more negative Us/Them related instincts (1) Avoided, (2) Minimized, (3) Neutralized, (4) Derailed, (5) Negotiated to Truce Status, and (6), whenever possible, Replaced by a larger and more inclusive sense of "Us."

Each of those six basic response, mitigation, and minimization strategies for our negative us/them instinct activation is explained below. Each has its appropriate role and each has its appropriate time of use. Countries in Europe who are finding themselves in intense us/them instinct activation situations today should look at those six basic approaches in each relevant setting.

Work places, school systems, and various organizations that are at risk of internal us/them instinct activation should look to that list for tools to use to keep those instincts from doing destructive things to people in their setting.

1. Avoidance Is a Top Priority

The best way of dealing with those negative instincts in most settings is to avoid them entirely. Avoid activating them whenever possible. Full avoidance of having those instincts activated should be a very conscious priority for leaders in intergroup settings.

Those instincts do no damage when their activation is successfully avoided. Whenever possible, the negative side of those instincts should be simply and deliberately avoided.

Avoidance is strategy number one.

That is a very simplistic point to make, but avoidance of our most negative us/them instinct packages is often a very good strategy, and leaders should make avoidance of those instincts a priority. Avoidance is often the best approach.

The consequences of not avoiding instinct activation are usually much more negative than the consequences of avoiding instinct activation. Any thing that can be done that keeps those "Them" instincts from being triggered in a bad way, in any setting, can be both a good strategic approach, and a good tactical choice.

It is much easier to avoid those issues in many settings then it is to mitigate them. So a clear awareness of what behaviors can trigger those instincts in any setting is a good awareness to have.

Leaders, in any setting, should constantly be aware of any factors or situations that might trigger those negative instincts in their setting and activate them. In settings where there are multiple risks for issue activation, that scanning and awareness process by leaders for those instinct triggers should be constant.

We each need to understand the settings we are in and we each need to understand what us/them instinct risks exist in that setting. We clearly need to be on the alert for the intrusion of any new us/them risks in each setting as well.

We need to be on constant alert for any behaviors, actions, communications, or interactions that can trigger negative us/them instinctive responses.

We need to avoid inflammatory language and we need to avoid inflammatory situations.

We need to know from experience and judgment in each setting what situations, events, interactions, communications, and behaviors can trigger those negative instincts, and then we need to very deliberately not do those trigger things in those settings.

When someone else in a setting is acting in ways that create a high risk of the activation of those instincts — it is good for Peace to focus attention on those behaviors and on those persons in ways that can intervene with the activation process and minimize their negative impact.

2. Minimize the Impact and Relevant Issues

When those instincts actually are triggered in a negative way in any setting, then minimizing their impact is a very good thing to do. We need to minimize the damage and minimize the risk of continued damage from those instincts to the degree possible for each setting.

Speed of response is important and valuable. Doing the work quickly to minimize risk and to reduce levels of damage can be a very good thing to do. Limiting their negative impact by time, or by geography, or by creating interpersonal contact levels that can defuse negative behavior can also all be very good things to do.

Work hard to keep the activated negative instincts that are triggered from taking root in any setting.

Any direct and effective limitation strategy for those activated instincts is generally far better than letting those instinctive reactions take root in any setting, and then spread across the setting to involve growing numbers of relevant people.

The goal needs to be to not allow that package of instincts to spread beyond whatever setting and situation somehow triggered them — if that containment level is at all possible.

When those instincts are being activated in any setting, it is particularly useful to identify the specific activation triggers that are relevant in that situation, and then take steps as effectively as possible to de-activate those specific triggers.

Sometimes an event or a communication of some kind has triggered the instincts. Delineate the trigger events when possible and take steps to stop the triggers for those negative instincts from continuing to incite damage. Respond as quickly as possible to defuse the triggers.

Eternal vigilance is the price of Peace. Be perpetually aware and be quick to respond when those negative triggers are being pulled.

3. Neutralize

Neutralizing and replacing those negative instincts is also a very good strategy for dealing with that package of instincts once they are activated.

Divert attention from the trigger issues and from the actual activation when diversion is possible. People can sometimes be distracted or diverted by introducing other influencing factors that become people's new focus in that situation and setting.

Offsetting those high risk and negative instincts with other energies, other instincts, or with basic enforcement and cultural tools that keep the instincts from triggering the wrong behaviors, can be a good thing to do.

Overloading people with new issues, new interests, or new focus or factors can sometimes neutralize the negative instincts in a setting. People can't do an infinite number of things simultaneously. When negative "them" instincts are causing reactions in people, try to insert a higher priority into the situation.

Don't make a bad situation worse. Do not increase the level of negative behavior or intergroup anger into the setting to divert people from the initial negative instinct. But do steer people's thoughts whenever possible in directions that get people in that setting to put their energy down a different path.

We have a number of good tools that we can use to direct people down a different path. The six-alignment trigger pyramid that is described in detail later in this book has some good neutralization and situational alignment tools in it. Look to see which alignment tools would be most useful in that setting to offset the triggered sense of "Them" when that sense has been triggered.

Distracting the sets of people involved from the current trigger issues can be a very good thing to do. Changing the topic to a topic that captures the collective attention of the at-risk groups can be a good thing to do.

Finding a common ground topic or issue that has enough alignment power to offset a triggered "Them" perception instinct can be effective.

The alignment pyramid has a clear set of triggers that can be used to offset activated us/them thinking. The purpose of each alignment trigger is to get people to function as an aligned group.

Creating a sense of common danger or a common enemy can both take momentum away from whatever situational triggers might be creating a sense of "Them" about one of the groups in a setting.

When people perceive other people inside a setting in a dangerous way to be a "Them" — directing their energy and their thoughts to other sources of external alignment, and to other categories of "Them" can be very useful.

4. Derail or Delay the Instinct

When trigger events are creating a high risk of us/them instinct activation, it can be a very good thing to figure out the actual trigger events and re-channel the trigger events, themselves, to a safer place and to a lower degree of confrontations. Try to reduce the immediacy and relevancy of a triggering issue when possible.

As an example, it is possible to re-channel a sense of immediate turf conflict into a larger terrain turf discussion or to re-channel a current, immediate, and highly situational turf crisis into a multi-year and carefully structured process to make relevant turf related decisions for the relevant parties.

It is sometimes possible to delay a crisis or inflammatory situation by creating a future context that can move the issue at risk into a future time frame. It's hard to un-explode an explosion — but it can be possible to turn the explosion into a discussion, or into a deliberation process, or even into a new area of concern.

Derailing and delaying trigger issues can be a very useful skill set that can keep negatively activated us/them instincts from doing immediate damage in a setting.

Any delay tactic that moves the crisis to a future point in time should be combined with a strategy that involves either resolving the trigger issue at a future point or one that will make it a non-issue for future interactions. Simple delay can be a good thing — but it is even better when it is part of a strategy to keep the issue from being a danger later.

5. Create a Truce

When those negative us/them instincts have been triggered, and when they are driving behaviors, and when they are creating immediate and negative intergroup emotions or even conflict, then truces can be a necessary and extremely useful next step. Truces can stop immediate damage.

Truces are not always easy to do. But truces can stop the bleeding and put a hold on current damage being done.

Figuring out who in a given setting can actually intervene and who can negotiate a truce of some kind in that setting can often be a very good thing to do to minimize damage from that activated instinct.

Truces need to be negotiated quickly and clearly for maximum impact — but even a bad truce is usually less damaging than open conflict. Chapter Eight of this book lists nine categories of intergroup interaction options — and truces are a very useful component part of that list.

A truce is not an ultimate solution for conflicted groups, but a truce is generally better for an intergroup setting than open and destructive intergroup conflict.

In any given setting, it is important to figure out who from each group has the power and the credibility to negotiate a truce – and then it is good to work directly with those people very quickly to figure out ways of ending actual conflict and dysfunctional and destructive behaviors.

Truce is almost always far better than open and damaging conflict. An early and proactive truce can be better than a truce that is attempted after conflict in that setting has been damaging, fierce, and prolonged.

In any permanent intergroup setting, it is good to plan in advance to identify who the relevant parties should be and who the negotiators would be who could negotiate and implement a future truce if flare-ups happen and if a truce is needed.

It can be very useful to have figured those issues out in advance, so they don't need to be figured out 'under fire' in a time of crisis. This is an area where proactive thinking can be highly useful in minimizing damage.

6. Replacement of Them with Another Category of Us

Replacement of the other groups "Them" status by connecting the other group to another category of "Us" can also defuse those instincts very effectively and very directly in many settings.

That can be the best long-term strategy in some settings for dealing with negative us/them instinct activation. Replacing the us/them instinctive reactions, emotions, values, and behaviors in a setting that focus on other sets of people as "Them" with a more inclusive and accepting definition of us that includes the other relevant people, as part of our broader sense of us, is a strategy that can be extremely useful in many settings and can create long standing positive results.

The best way to eliminate "Them" flare-ups in any setting is generally simply to not have a "Them" in that setting. That is the most proactive solution. We don't trigger our "Them" instincts when there is no "Them."

We don't generate a sense of "them" when we perceive other people, in any given setting, to be "Us." We can disagree with "Us" — but we don't hate, despise, fear, and damage "Us."

So the best way of dealing with our negative "Them" instincts, for the long haul, is to minimize the sense and the perception that someone in a setting is an instinct-triggering "Them," and to expand our definition of "Us" to include all of the relevant sets and groups of people in that setting. Chapter Six of this book explains that overall strategy in more detail.

Other Instincts Can Exacerbate Our Us/Them Behaviors

The next three chapters of this book describe other sets of key instincts that we have that can compound the intergroup conflict levels that are triggered by our us/them instincts. Our turf instincts, for example, often exacerbate the emotions that are triggered by our us/them instincts.

Those packages of instincts can also each be used as a foundation for Peace — either by channeling those instincts in Peaceful directions, or by avoiding their activation with deliberate strategies that can keep those instincts from being relevant to any setting.

Both rechanneling and avoidance make sense as both strategies and tactics. To do either one, we need to know what those packages of instincts are, and we need to know what all of those instincts do to us and for us. That is the next section of this book.

Successfully Dealing With Us/Them Instincts Solves Major Problems

Successfully dealing with our us/them instincts truly is the key to almost all of our major intergroup problems. Other intergroup instincts are important as well. If we only had turf instincts as individuals, however, those turf instincts would not create intergroup wars. Those instincts might create interpersonal dislike and interpersonal conflicts, but our turf instincts that are activated at the individual level will not steer us to war.

But when our group turf instincts are tied tightly to our us/them instincts — that combined package of instinctive behaviors have created wars and shed blood all over the planet.

We need to understand our us/them instincts. We need to use them in creative ways to expand our sense of us. Intergroup Peace relies on us having a collective commitment to all groups doing well. That requires us to have some level where we perceive ourselves to be a values-linked American Us.

We also need to deeply fear the truly negative behaviors that can be triggered when we see each other as Them. Those behaviors can be horrible.

Those negative instincts are activated in far too many settings at far too intense levels. Having leaders of various groups calling for other people to be tortured, expelled, damaged, and killed is happening at multiple settings in the world we live in today. Those sets of instincts exist in us all. We need to make sure we do not activate those sets of intergroup instincts here.

Inside organizations — workplaces, schools, associations, and communities — we need to work hard to create a functioning sense of "Us" and we need to keep internal subsets of people from having their negative intergroup instincts triggered as warring "Them."

A key to The Art of InterGroup Peace for our entire country is not to have those instincts, in their worst form, ever again activated here.

To keep that from happening, we do need to understand our turf instincts, hierarchical instincts, alpha instincts, and our instincts to never be a traitor to our group.

Those instincts deserve our attention and they are described in the next chapters of this book.

CHAPTER FOUR

Turf, Traitor, Riot, and Alpha Instincts Can All Have Huge Impact on InterGroup Interactions

Our us/them instincts are not the only package of instincts that affect intergroup interactions and Peace. We have instincts to create hierarchies and to designate Alpha leaders — with their own set of instincts — to run our hierarchies.

We have instincts to form teams and we have instincts to participate in both teams and mobs.

We have instincts to create cultures and we have very strong instincts to act in accord with the guidance and the rules that are set by our cultures.

We also have a very strong package of turf-related instincts that frequently affect intergroup interactions at multiple levels. Multiple intergroup conflicts have very clear turf issues at their core.

Our traitor instincts have a huge impact on our intergroup interactions. We have a very strong set of instincts against ever being a traitor, or ever being perceived to be a traitor to our own group.

Succeeding at the Art of InterGroup Peace will require us to both recognize all of those sets of instincts, and to work with them on behalf of Peace. We need to use all of those instincts to trigger alignment for "Us" as a community and as a people.

At a very basic level, we need to take steps that allow us to have needed interactions with people from other groups without feeling like a traitor to our own group in the process.

To achieve intergroup trust, we need intergroup and direct interpersonal interactions — and it is impossible to achieve those kinds of interpersonal and intergroup interactions if we are perceived to be a traitor or feel that we are a traitor when we interact with people from other groups.

We Have Very Strong Turf Instincts

Our turf instincts can obviously have a very powerful impact on intergroup interactions, intergroup conflict, and intergroup Peace all by themselves.

We clearly have strong turf instincts.

We fight wars across the planet about issues of property, boundaries, territory, and turf.

We tend to be highly territorial. That is a very instinctive and very universal set of behaviors. Very much the same patterns of turf-linked territorial behavior exist in settings across the planet.

Tribes, clans, and nations all know exactly what they regard as their turf. Those territorial/turf related behaviors have obviously existed as long as history has been recorded because much of our written history very directly addresses issues of territorial conquest and sets of intergroup issues that directly relate to the defense and conquest of turf by various groups and sets of people.

Boundaries and property lines are everywhere on the planet. The purpose of all of those lines is to define turf at a level that supports our turf instincts in each setting.

Each nation has a clear sense of its own boundaries and nations will generally go to war relatively quickly when anyone challenges or threatens their current boundary lines.

We need to recognize the fact that our instinctive commitment to the defense of our own boundaries can easily extend to irrational and intense levels. Many very dramatic actions and even extreme behaviors in defense of our turf in various settings can feel very right to people because there is a clear turf protection instinct at the core of that commitment and those behaviors.

There are battles going on today in the Himalaya Mountains to protect a multi-nation challenged international boundary where the piece of geography at question is so isolated and so desolate that the soldiers from both countries can barely get to those boundaries and to those disputed territories to fight.

Both countries are more than willing to shed blood to protect those far distant and functionally irrelevant boundaries. However, because our turf instincts that are applied to our nations tell us to never surrender any piece of national turf, it feels very right, at a deep instinctive level, to defend every inch of our defined turf.

In a similar vein, the British reclamation, defense, and territorial recovery of the Falkland Islands was a highly emotionally energizing issue for the people of Great Britain. That war made sense to the people of that country at a purely instinctive level.

The people of Great Britain did not want any part of "their" turf taken over by another nation — even though that particular piece of turf that was being challenged by another nation is actually so far away that it is absolutely geographically irrelevant to the British homeland.

That set of distant islands was defined by Great Britain to be British Turf. It was instinctively protected by the British Military and it was protected with the full support of the British people.

The reality is that we defend turf at a very primal level — as individuals and as groups of people — once we believe turf to be our turf for one reason or another. Once we believe turf is ours, we are willing to both kill and die to defend it — and it feels very right to do whatever defending it requires us to do.

Various ethnic groups and tribes all tend to have a sense of what is, for various historic and functional reasons, their rightful turf.

The turf for each group often tends to be included as a key part of the cultural identity of the tribe. Groups in almost all tribal settings can easily identify exactly what pieces of geography are — or once were — their "rightful" turf.

Those specific turf alignments that are identified for specific groups of people can last for a very long time. Those perceived turf alignments can continue to maintain their power over our values, our behaviors, our collective and individual emotions, our ownership beliefs, and our thought processes for as long as those perceptions exist.

It Is Challenging When Two Groups Instinctively Bond with the Same Turf

Major challenges to Peace exist whenever multiple groups believe they are each the rightful owner of the same exact piece of turf.

Several of the most important border and turf control conflicts that exist today in the Middle East have obviously created, defined, and triggered conflict in that part of the world for centuries.

A major problem that exists in a number of those settings is that there is more than one group of people who absolutely believe that a piece of turf is their rightful turf.

Each group believes with deep certainty that the piece of turf in question is their own group's rightful property. There is a strong sense, for each group in those settings, that the turf belongs to them — and that the other group is a trespasser, an intruder, and a wrongful usurper of the turf.

Those turf-linked wars where multiple parties feel an inherent link to the exact same piece of turf have cost millions of lives for a very long period of time, and they continue to trigger bloodshed today. Each side in those conflicts feels, at a very visceral and instinctive level, that the contested piece of turf is their rightful ancestral turf — and that level of commitment and that definitive group alignment makes any and all behaviors that happen in defense of that turf by their group feel instinctively right.

You can't talk someone out of the energy that is triggered by a strongly solid instinctive alignment on those issues. When two or more warring groups feel that same instinctive sense of being right about the exact same and very specific piece of turf, the consequences for intergroup anger and conflict for that setting can be indefinite and almost infinite in their duration.

When the cultures and the histories of two sets of people cause them both to feel at a very deep instinctive level that they each clearly own a piece of turf, and when each group feels that the other group is trespassing, stealing, encroaching, invading, or attempting to steal that turf, the instinctive reactions for each group of people in those situations are pure and they are powerful.

People Need to Deal With the Instincts as Well as the Turf

The only possible resolution for those conflicts in those settings would need to involve having the people in each group understand the relevant instinctive reactions for both themselves and for the other group, and then addressing those instinct-related issues directly and openly — instead of simply letting their instinctive reactions and their separate sense of history dictate their beliefs and their behaviors in ways that create permanent conflict.

Those issues are addressed with more specific information about some of the countries involved in those kinds of conflicts in the sister book, *Cusp of Chaos*.

We do have our own sets of turf instincts at work in several settings in this country today. We don't have our turf instincts activated for any actual external border issue for our nation at this point in our history, but we do have those instincts activated at several points relative to pieces of group-linked turf inside our country.

We are not immune in any way from having those instincts triggered relative to our external boundaries.

We Americans would also activate those turf instincts very powerfully at an international level relative to our own external borders, if we had any functional reason to activate that international trigger relative to our borders.

We are a very powerful nation. No one is threatening to steal our turf — so those triggers relative to protecting our own national boundaries are not activated today for us as Americans.

We Americans clearly have all of our turf instincts firmly in place relative to our external national boundaries. We simply do not need to activate those instincts for our external borders at this point in time because our turf isn't being challenged at that level.

We Are Seeing Significant Ethnic Concentrations

Inside our country, however, we are seeing an increase in our ethnicity-linked turf issues. As we become more diverse, we actually are seeing significant increases in the degree of ethnic and racial concentration for groups of people in specific geographic areas.

In multiple communities, we are self-segregating by race and by ethnicity in our choices of places to live.

That has always been true to some degree and it is becoming increasingly true today as our minority groups become larger. Major areas of major communities have a very high concentration of people from specific ethnic groups.

That particular segregation of where we live by race and ethnicity tends to be both instinctive and voluntary for Americans.

Our us/them instincts cause people to feel most comfortable living with who ever we perceive to be "Us." So people tend to buy homes or rent living space in areas where the other residents feel like "Us." As our various groups grow in population, that tendency to live with "Us" is clearly having an impact on various communities.

The most recent census data shows major areas of intense ethnic and racial concentrations by neighborhood in our major cities. Many people in our cities have obviously chosen to live in the areas of our cities where other people from their own ethnic or their own racial group also lives — and those areas each tend to grow in size as each local ethnic group grows in size.

People know who lives where.

People know where Chinatown is in any city with a Chinatown. Watts and Harlem are clearly communities with a high level of African American population density. Northern L.A. or West Chicago are clearly Mexican American areas. Spanish Harlem has a major Puerto Rican population living there.

Miami has major areas of the city where Cuban Americans are the dominant population group, and other areas of the city where the population density focus is African American.

The racial and ethnic population density levels are significant enough in a growing number of our communities to the point where those high concentration levels make the likelihood of having turf instincts activated today and in the future in those areas, at a group level, predictably high. Everyone living in those areas now knows the impact and the reality of that population concentration today.

We are seeing some real intergroup anger in a number of areas where growth in the number of people from an ethnic group has caused that group's "Us" linked space-needs to expand — and that expansion can mean that the growth in population displaces people from other ethnic groups who already live in those areas.

There are several communities where the growing Hispanic groups have taken over living areas that had been primarily African American neighborhoods for many years. The growing Somali population in Minnesota cities has created similar turf issues with several groups.

Turf issues and turf instincts are triggered in any setting when any group displaces other groups in any geographic area — and the borders that exist between the various groups in those areas each create their own sets of intergroup issues.

We Americans need to understand the impact of those kinds of turf instincts on our behavior and our emotions, at both a macro level and a micro level, if we are going to achieve InterGroup Peace at this point in our history. We need people to understand those issues and we need plans to deal with those sets of issues going into the future.

Nations fight over turf. So do individual people and so do groups of people.

Gangs Create Their Own Turf Issues

Gangs in our cities create some very real turf issues for a number of people. Major parts of major cities have areas where groups feel like they control turf.

Gangs who functionally control neighborhood turf in our cities sometimes kill people from other groups who "trespass" on their turf.

That level of intergroup conflict with links to turf can become important at a very local level when local groups are armed.

The city of Oakland has major areas of the city that are now defined to be gang turf. Oakland now averages one killing every three days. Gangs in that city kill people from other gangs and they often kill people from other groups who enter their turf.

The gangs of Detroit and the gangs of Richmond have a similar significant impact on intergroup safety levels in that city. People who live in those areas are sometimes at risk if they simply enter into the areas controlled by another group.

A growing number of cities are facing major growth in the power of the gangs — and the intergroup behaviors that result are primal at a very basic instinctive level.

There are no multi-ethnic street gangs or prison gangs. To achieve full Peace in America we will need to defuse the power and impact of gangs in a number of settings.

We Need People to Be Safe Everywhere

Creating intergroup Peace for this country will require us to create intergroup safety. That issue is relevant to turf instincts because activated turf issues can damage safety. We need to be a country where people can feel safe in every setting regardless of their group and regardless of the geographic location that each person is in.

We need to make intergroup geographic violence a non-issue for our people in each of our cities.

We need people to be able to interact with people from all groups without personal safety being an issue in any setting. We need safe turf for all people. We also need people to feel safe interacting with people from other groups.

As we design our political solutions in communities going into the future, we need to recognize the fact that we have groups of people who feel group affinity to neighborhood turf — and we need to put in place an array of activities that bring people together in every setting — interacting across both group lines and group boundaries — to create a broader sense of "Us" in each setting.

We need to have a community sense of "Us" as well as a group sense of "Us" to have intergroup Peace in all settings.

We Instinctively Hate Traitors

Creating that sense of community us can be difficult to do for a number of people — for highly instinctive reasons.

We have a number of instinct-related barriers that exist in a number of areas that can make it difficult, or even impossible, for people to interact at a personal, 1-to-1 level with people from other groups. We need interpersonal interactions to happen between people from various groups for a number of important reasons, and we need to overcome those barriers where they exist.

To achieve intergroup Peace, we need healthy levels of intergroup understanding. We need people to understand and trust other groups of people. We need people to interact with one another to build that trust. Intergroup understanding at the group level is much harder to achieve if we have people from each of the relevant groups who are instinctively avoiding making contact and who are reluctant to make friends with people from each other group at the personal level.

Too often, that is exactly the situation and the problem we face today in intergroup settings. Many people do not feel comfortable or even feel safe creating the kinds of intergroup friendships we need to make to create intergroup understanding and intergroup trust.

We have those barriers because we have histories of groups doing negative things to people from other groups. Our intergroup instincts create our intergroup histories, and our histories influence our future interactions. We can be trapped in that cycle in a very self-reinforcing way.

We define people from other groups based on our intergroup history — and that history makes it hard, in many settings, to reach out to have direct relationships with people from other groups.

Our memories can be too long and too clear to make interaction at a personal level either easy or natural.

We need to be willing to look past those elements of intergroup history to create new and direct relationships with other people that are based on the new interpersonal history that those relationships create.

We need to make deliberate and intentional enlightened choices to create those kinds of relationships as a foundation for interpersonal trust and intergroup trust.

One of the major problems and challenges that we have relative to using those kinds of direct relationships, to help build a culture of intergroup Peace in any setting, is that we each have a strong set of instincts relative to being traitors. Those instincts too often keep us from interacting in needed ways with people from other groups.

We Hate and Punish Traitors

We hate traitors. We punish traitors. We have very strong internal aversions as individuals to ever personally be a traitor, and we do not personally want to be seen as a traitor to any group that we feel part of as an "Us."

We have very strong negative instinctive reactions to traitors, and those instincts can make achieving Peace difficult for several reasons.

Traitors are hated everywhere. Traitors are punished everywhere. Traitors are executed in many settings. In some countries, people who personally and voluntarily try to simply change their personal religious affiliation away from their religions of birth can be executed for being seen to be a traitor to their original specific religious sect.

In most of those cases, the original personal religious alignment of the person who is executed for converting to another religion was one they acquired at birth simply by being born. Those people did not acquire that initial link to their religion by any choice of their own at any point in their lives.

Our traitor instincts are so strong that people are burned, imprisoned, and executed in some settings, even today, for simply attempting to change the religion they were born into. The people who are executing them clearly feel right in doing the executions.

That sense that it is right to punish, and even kill traitors has great power when it is triggered. In gang settings in this country, people who try to leave their gangs are often killed for being perceived to be a traitor to their gang.

Armies often publically and visibly execute their traitors. That has been true as long as armies have existed.

Famous traitors — like Benedict Arnold, Prime Minister Quisling, or Judas Iscariot — tend to be reviled for very long periods of time for their individual behavior and for their acts as traitors.

The universality of that energy level of those anti-traitor behaviors, and of that value set, tells us clearly that our reaction to traitors is also a reaction that is instinctive at its core.

None of Us Want to Be Traitors

We tend to despise and even hate traitors. That hatred of traitors is directly relevant to *The Art of InterGroup Peace* strategy set and is included as a key point in this chapter because of the barrier that particular package of instincts, too often, creates relative to intergroup understanding. That instinct can keep us from reaching out to make links with people from other groups when and where reaching out to those people is needed to create intergroup trust.

That set of instincts and our decision to avoid those relationships is often reinforced by other people in our own groups who can became angry with us if they think we are acting as a traitor to our group. Our groups put pressure on us not to betray them — and we put pressure on ourselves not to betray our group.

At a very basic level, none of us wants to be a traitor. We each very much do not want to feel in our own hearts that we have been a traitor to our group. We don't want to be a traitor to our family, to our country, to our town, to our team, or to whatever alignment we feel is the appropriate focus and the rightful recipient of our loyalty.

That particular instinct can obviously make intergroup dialogues difficult. Those instincts can make some personal 1-to-1 intergroup friendships almost impossible.

That instinct package can keep kids at school from interacting with kids from other groups — and it can keep people in various official and leadership capacities from reaching out to people from other groups simply because reaching out to those people, might possibly, somehow either benefit the other groups or because that behavior by leaders can be perceived by their own group to be the behavior of a traitor to our own group.

People who want to depose a leader inside a group can sometimes generate significant energy against a leader who has relationships with other groups by persuading other members of the group that the behavior of a leader who creates any kind of bridges has made that leader a traitor to the group. Leaders run that risk, and that makes it hard for some leaders to reach out to create bridges to other groups.

When we perceive people in another group to be a "Them," our us/them instincts call for us to do damage to the other group — to fear, distrust, and avoid the other group —and not to create a benefit of any kind for any "Them."

It's harder to create Peace at any questionable level when we have those particular instinctive factors involved.

We Need to Create InterGroup Trust

But the truth is that we need to reach out across group lines to make Peace real and sustainable. We need to create intergroup trust — and a very useful step on the road to creating intergroup trust is to create interpersonal trust.

So we need to overcome those instinctive behaviors that are linked to traitor instincts. We need to create those kinds of intergroup linkages and those levels of interpersonal relationships at a level that will let us build understanding and create and justify trust.

When our goal is intergroup understanding, intergroup alignment, intergroup truth, and intergroup Peace, our deep-seated instincts never to be a traitor to our own group can make even the very basic intergroup and interpersonal information exchanges problematic, and it can make some basic intergroup and interpersonal problem solving impossible.

Simply giving this book as a thought resource to someone from a group that we perceive to be a "Them" could cause some people to feel like they might have aided and abetted an enemy of our "Us" by simply sharing the book.

Providing any assistance of any kind to "Them" can feel like a "Traitor" behavior to someone who hates "Them." It can feel that way even when our basic goal for reaching out to the other person actually is Peace for our own group.

Knowledge Is Power Relative to That Instinct

Knowledge very much is power relative to that instinct. We can control and diminish the direct power of our traitor instincts when we understand what those instincts are and when we know how they work.

A key Art of InterGroup Peace strategy is to teach all people that the traitor instinct exists and influences our thinking — and to teach all people how to deal with the traitor instinct at multiple levels.

Reading about that set of instincts often helps people get a sense of how they work and that can make it easier to recognize and address those instinctive reactions when they are activated.

That instinct about us never being a traitor loses a significant amount of its collective influence over us — it loses much of its power over us as individuals — once it is clearly recognized as an instinct.

It loses power over us when our direct emotions that result from the instinct are understood to be simply triggered by an instinct.

It also loses power when those specific emotions that we feel in those circumstances are not just seen or believed by us to be an actual, factual, and legitimate moral judgment about our own behavior in that situation that affirms and confirms our personal wrongdoing for interacting in some way with the other group.

When we each realize and recognize that the "traitor" instinct impact exists on our emotions and our thought process — and when we each realize that the stress aversion and the guilt emotions that we can each feel from some of our interactive behaviors relative to other people actually result purely from that particular instinct being triggered, and not from us actually doing a bad or traitorous thing – then we can individually choose not to let that instinct change our behavior on particular interactions in ways that keep us from dealing with people from the "other" group.

We can choose — when we clearly understand those issues — not to let that instinct subconsciously give us internal feelings of guilt for interacting in a person-to-person setting with people from other groups. Knowledge truly is power relative to that particular instinct.

Peace Is in the Interest of "Our" Group

In fact — when we fully understand the mutual benefit context that is created by real Peace and when we understand the win/win strategy that is the foundation for the Art of InterGroup Peace — then we can feel good about those interactions instead of feeling that they make us a traitor to our group.

The truth is — our own group actually wins when we create those relationships with people from other groups in the interest of Peace. When we have a win/win collective outcome for everyone, everyone wins. We are much stronger as a country with win/win outcomes because we benefit as a country from everyone winning. Every group wins when every group wins.

So even helping another group win isn't being a traitor to our own group — it is being an asset and a support resource for our own group.

The power of that traitor instinct to keep us from making friends with people from other groups can clearly be mitigated to a significant degree when we individually and collectively all intellectually and cognitively recognize that achieving Peace between groups actually is very much in the best interest of our own group.

Our group does very clearly win when Peace happens. That is extremely important to recognize and understand.

The truth that we all need to understand is this — our "Us" group — the group we are each most loyal to as our basic and most fundamental "Us" — can and will directly benefit from Peace and our most basic us group will benefit from a collective culture of Peace when that Peace is our shared reality.

InterGroup Friendship Can Foster Peace

When we get to know people from other groups as people and not just as depersonalized and sometimes dehumanized stereotypes, then the likelihood of

Peace improves and the likelihood of survival and success for our own group — our own "Us" — is enhanced. Enhancing Peace is a good thing to do for our core "Us."

The Art of InterGroup Peace calls for us to have people from various groups actually get to know each other as people – and not have people from each group simply stereotype each other as depersonalized symbols of the group they represent at a depersonalized level.

Intergroup friendships can solidify Peace and can create highly enriching levels of work group understanding. So not feeling like a traitor in the context of those relationships needs to be part of our strategy for achieving Peace and a key strategic component of *The Art of InterGroup Peace*.

Sun Tzu Valued Traitors

In *The Art of War*, Sun Tzu addresses traitors, spies, and informants very explicitly. He actually values traitors — in a very manipulative way — because he deliberately recruited people to be traitors on his behalf against their own group.

Sun Tzu believed that persuading people to be traitors to their own side in a war and then rewarding traitors for their treachery is a good strategy that can create major benefits. Sun Tzu believed that having very real traitors help him in treacherous ways could sometimes give his own side a significant wartime advantage over the enemy at important levels.

That benefit from treachery for a group who is supported by traitors obviously can be true in a war setting.

That means that in that us/them, win/lose war-linked negative intergroup context, as described in *The Art of War*, the worst fears that are triggered in each of us by our own traitor instincts were entirely legitimate. Those kinds of traitorous behaviors do happen to groups and those damaging behaviors done by traitors are actually why those fears exist for all of us. They are legitimate fears in war settings.

But we do not need to let those traitor-linked insights run our lives or cripple Peace today. We can't afford to let those instincts create real barriers to intergroup interactions. When our goal is to have both sides win — instead of creating a situation where one side needs to lose — then we need to all recognize that our interpersonal intergroup relationships are very useful and that they directly benefit our own side in each setting.

The Art of InterGroup Peace calls for people to reach out and to make the interpersonal linkages that will cause people to enhance success levels for their own group — not cause their group to be defeated. *The Art of InterGroup Peace* involves teaching those concepts and giving people insight that can defuse our traitor instincts and help get people focused on win/win solutions as opposed to focusing only on achieving the defeat of the other side.

Our Mob Instincts Can Also Damage Peace

Another major barrier to peaceful and positive intergroup interactions is our unfortunate sets of instincts to form mobs and to do negative things to other people in the context of a mob. Our instincts to form mobs bear a partial resemblance to our very powerful and very useful instincts to form teams.

Our team instincts tend to be very powerful and useful. The team instincts allow us to create teams in various settings and overlook other group differentiation factors for people when their team instincts are collectively achieved.

Our team instincts allow us to set aside our other dividing factors and to function together in an aligned way — with internal team loyalty — to do basic team related functions.

That is a positive set of instincts. Our team instincts and their uses are described in more detail in Chapter Seven as one of the six triggers we can use to create alignment in various positive ways.

When people function as team, the likelihood of success increases for various team activities — and the people on the team not only accomplish things together — they tend to overlook other differentiating and divisive factors and definitions, while the people are in team functions and engaged in team behaviors.

Unfortunately, we also have a much more negative set of instincts that can also trigger more damaging collective behavior.

We have much more negative instincts to form mobs and to interact with other people in the context of riot behaviors. In the interest of intergroup Peace, we need to freely use our instincts to form teams, but we need to work very hard to never activate our instincts to riot and to damage people as mobs.

Avoiding riots and mobs is not a theoretical issue or a hypothetical concern. Riots happen. Riots kill people all over the world every year. Every major police department in the world has policemen who are trained in handling both riots and mobs.

That universal police capability to deal with mobs and that consistent police force readiness level for mob behaviors across the planet isn't coincidental.

That capability exists for all of those police forces in all of those settings because there are periodic situations where people gather together in mobs, trigger riots, and then do damage in mob context to other people. When people are in mob situations, very real damage can be done.

Some mobs destroy property. Some mobs loot and burn. Some mobs rape and pillage.

Mobs in Paris burned more than 1,000 cars a couple of years ago. Mobs in Sri Lanka burned the homes and businesses of the group they collectively hated just last year — and those particular mobs killed people from other groups with the horrible suspension of ethics and elimination of moral standards that are triggered far too often by full activation of us/them instincts.

Rapes, assaults, violence, and group murders in mob settings feel justified to the people who have the depersonalized values and entirely ethics free sets of behaviors that can be triggered far too easily by our mob instincts.

Mobs are, for obvious reasons, a threat and impediment to intergroup safety and intergroup Peace.

People across the planet clearly have the destructive instincts to riot and to do evil and damaging things to other groups of people in the context of a mob.

Riot instincts are another set of instincts that we need to understand, manage, and then both avoid and suppress successfully if we intend to achieve InterGroup Peace in this country.

It can significantly undermine our collective ability to bring people together in any setting for the common good — for our children, for our health, or for our prosperity — if we create mobs and then damage people in clearly intergroup ways in the context of those mobs.

It chills and destroys intergroup trust when groups of people band together to do damage as mobs to other people from other groups.

Riots Are Unique to People

There are times when group anger in a setting is triggered by an incident or by a precipitating event.

Protests, demonstrations, and public gatherings to express unhappiness, concern, and even anger all have their place as part of our intergroup communication processes. We need to recognize the legitimacy of the group anger when various events in a setting are negative and deserve group anger. But we need to keep that anger in each setting from turning into riots and into mobs.

Forming mobs is an instinct that seems to be unique to us. There do not seem to be very many parallel behaviors that are the equivalent of riots for riots in other species. Stampedes happen — but they are not the same as riots.

Feeding frenzies and pack attacks by dogs and wolves do bear some resemblance to riots. But those behaviors seem to be more related to hunting activities, and not related to intergroup activities.

Swarms do happen in some other species. Locusts and ants both have swarming behaviors that create collective and aligned large group movements. But the collective anger that sits at the core of mob behavior for people doesn't seem relevant to a swarm of locusts or a horde of ants.

We, however, do have those instincts that have intergroup anger at their core. Our military forces in every country have training in mob control. Police departments in every significant city in the world tend to have both mob control equipment and mob control training.

History also has ample evidence of mobs at multiple times in our historic past. The reality today is that intergroup mobs can happen in a number of places and very similar behavior patterns occur when that happens.

Paris, London, Sri Lanka, Los Angeles, and Oakland, California all have had mobs and riots in recent history.

Mobs can form for a variety of reasons in a wide range of settings. There are lynching mobs that form to do damage in very evil ways to very specific targets, and there are larger street mobs that form with more of a collective intergroup target set.

When mobs do form, there is a set of very unfortunate mob behaviors that result that sometimes can do huge damage to people at multiple levels. Pillaging, burning, physical damage, rapes, beatings, and killings all happen in various settings across the planet when mob instincts are in gear.

A number of other countries have been facing some massive riots in recent history. The relatively recent riots in Paris a couple of years ago involved a million people. The recent riots in London were also large and were clearly hate-based for many people. Those riots created real intergroup fear and serious damages for very large numbers of people in that setting.

Listening to recordings of the speeches that were given during the riots by the riot leaders in London on the Internet can give an easy sense of both the anger levels and the clear intergroup targets of that anger.

The recent intergroup riots in Sri Lanka have killed significant numbers of people and the people who trigger those riots expect to kill more people before the rioting there ends.

Those riots are all relevant to *The Art of InterGroup Peace* because the riots in all of those settings tend to be triggered by intergroup issues and they tend to cause intergroup damages and long-term intergroup hatred and anger whenever they happen.

In all of those settings, the people in the mobs have been collectively and very intentionally damaging some local category of "Them." The patterns of the intergroup riots we see in all of those other countries are amazingly consistent. The mobs hurt "Them."

Only the name of the specific "Them" who is relevant to each setting and who is victimized by each riot changes from riot to riot. The behaviors and behavior patterns echo one another with depressing consistency.

Riots Destroy InterGroup Trust

We have obviously had a number of serious riots in our own country. Historically, a number of our major cities have had serious "race riots." Chicago, Boston, New York City, and L.A. all have had serious collective damage inflicted on portions of those cities by mobs.

In each of those instances, intense group anger is surfaced by a triggering event — like the Rodney King Police Trial in Los Angeles — where the collective anger of a group explodes into mob behaviors that cause people to collectively both express that anger, and do damage to whoever is perceived to be the target of the mob.

The consequences of riots tend to be functionally bad for Peace for each riot setting because the riots create such clear intergroup division, and because the people who are personally damaged by the riots tend to never forget or forgive the damages they experience from the other group who make them riot victims.

Riots leave scars. Riots can destroy intergroup trust and they can make intergroup respect disappear forever for some people who have personally been adversely affected and damaged by the power and the functions of a mob.

Riots Can Signal Underlying InterGroup Anger

The only positive impact of a mob can be that the readiness of people in a setting to participate in an event-triggered mob can be a clear barometer of the existence of intergroup anger, and tension in a particular setting that might be much less visible in that setting without the spontaneous energy exhibited by the mob.

People in a community who were unaware of the existing simmering levels of intergroup anger and stress are forced to recognize that those angers exist when they erupt through the channeling of protest — including protests that turn into riots and mobs.

When mobs do form — generally triggered by an inflammatory event — then the best outcome at that point can be to keep the mob from the levels of violence and intergroup damage that too easily can occur from those sets of instincts, and to channel the energy and the anger into a "demonstration" or "protest" rather than a "riot."

A demonstration can serve the cause of Peace. The perceptions and belief systems that exist for the people who are demonstrating in a setting deserve to be understood — because those people would not have gathered together in that way in that place without a shared sense that there was a legitimate reason to gather together.

Those issues that trigger demonstrations deserve to be understood — and for the sake of intergroup Peace, all parties in a setting need to figure out Peaceful ways of recognizing and resolving those issues.

Soccer Mobs Have Killed People in Several Cities

There is a seductive side to mob behavior that can, unfortunately, cause some people to favor and even seek out mob participation.

Mobs actually can — for a very small number of people — be addictive. Some soccer fans from some countries seem to have acquired almost a personal mob instinct addiction.

Those particular soccer fans who have that addiction go from venue to venue looking for opportunities to trigger these instinctive behaviors, emotions, and reap their neurochemical rewards.

Our team instincts are discussed in Chapter Five of this book as one of the six key tools we can use to bring people together into alignment as groups. Our team-linked group behavior instincts can function well to bring us together — but even our team instincts can also create problems when the fans of any given team exhibit riot behaviors against other fans of other teams in any setting.

Sadly, there are also a small number of people in our own country who go to mob sites when trigger-events make it likely that a mob will form to exacerbate and inflame mob behaviors, and to damage property and to literally loot at the mob site.

Some people who want to steal things or break things know that the mob setting could possibly give them a chance to break store windows, or break into homes and steal goods and property from those settings. In a couple of recent riots, the majority of people who were arrested for looting were from outside the zip codes for the site of the riot.

Having the looters in a riot coming from other zip codes is another very clear us/them behavior reality. Local people in many settings are less likely to loot "Their" own communities businesses. Outside looters see the businesses in a community purely as "Them" and feel no guilt in taking property through direct and blatant theft.

Again — as with our other negative instincts — the key challenge we need to address is that some very damaging behaviors can feel entirely justified and "right" to the people who are in each mob.

People whose normal behavior is to be civil, polite, considerate, and personally decent in their actions and behaviors relative to other people can sometimes do things under the influence of their mob instincts that are – at their core – damaging, destructive and sometimes purely evil.

We Need to Avoid and Defuse Mobs

So if we do want Peace to be our state of being in this country, we clearly do not want to activate mob behaviors in any setting.

We need to avoid setting up trigger-events that cause mobs to feel relevant to angry people in any setting. When mobs seem to be forming for any reason in any setting, we need to take the steps that are needed in that situation and in that setting to keep them from being activated or inflamed.

The intergroup residual damage that can be created by street mobs — and also by lynching mobs — should not be underestimated.

Lynch Mobs Have Done Great Evil

Lynchings have often involved mobs. There have been a large number of very damaging and very evil lynching mobs at multiple points in our history. Those pure lynching mobs in our country are not recent, but thousands of those mobs existed over the years in various settings and they still leave scars today.

Those mobs created to lynch people exemplify pure intergroup evil and pure intergroup hatred. They prove beyond any doubt that the intention of one group to damage another group exists at a very evil level and can result in truly evil behavior.

That proof is visible to anyone who might doubt how badly our us/them thinking can distort our values and influence our behaviors. The damage from those most negative instinctive behaviors is very real. Victims of lynchings tend to be dead. Their survivors are scarred.

People who are killed by other categories of mobs are equally dead, so we need to be very careful to keep all levels of mob instincts from being activated.

One of the reasons that The Art of InterGroup Peace calls for us to very intentionally avoid having mobs triggered, is that the people who have been personally victimized by mobs often have a very hard time ever forgiving the groups of people and the individual people who did the evil and damaging things that were done while those people were under that mob instinct behavioral influence.

As part of The Art of InterGroup Peace, we need leaders for all groups to be willing and able to defuse mobs when they begin to form. We need leaders who practically and functionally help to keep mobs in our settings from happening.

We need to recognize the angers and the emotions that can trigger mobs, but we need to take steps to keep those angers from degenerating into mob behaviors.

Our Groups Instinctively Create Hierarchies and Select Leaders

Our instincts to have and follow leaders are also highly relevant to the Art of InterGroup Peace. We instinctively name leaders to all of our settings. Our leaders have a major influence on our collective behaviors. We need leaders in every setting to be committed to Peace and to take steps as leaders to increase the likelihood of Peace happening.

Too many leaders prefer conflict and even war as their context for leadership. When we have leaders in any setting who are war chiefs rather than Peace leaders, creating Peaceful intergroup interactions is much more difficult.

We create hierarchies at an instinctive level in just about all settings.

Hierarchies are everywhere. Wherever we get together as a group in some way — in clans, tribes, companies, military forces, governmental units or even nations — we tend to put a hierarchy in place.

We tend to feel stress in settings where there is no hierarchy and we also tend to feel stress in those situations where the top position in the hierarchy for that setting is currently unfilled.

Chiefs and Alpha leaders of various kinds are a common component and feature of hierarchies. Almost every group ends up with a "chief" of some kind for the hierarchy. There are tribal chiefs, war chiefs, and chiefs of state.

Corporations and businesses tend to be headed by a CEO — or "Chief" Executive Officer. The "C-Suites" in companies are full of chiefs for each lead position in those hierarchies.

Our armies have levels of officers ranging up to generals and — at the top of each army — there is usually a chief. A senior general. A Commander in Chief.

We instinctively design hierarchies to have someone in charge. Captains can fill the same Alpha role and function as chiefs in many settings. Our ships have captains — as do our athletic teams and even our debate teams.

A ship without a captain can very quickly trigger feelings of both instinctive stress and functional concern for the members of any currently leaderless ship's crew.

Agreements Need to Be Reached by People with Legitimate Standing

That particular instinct to have a chief and be led by a chief is relevant for the behavioral terrain that exists for The Art of InterGroup Peace for multiple reasons.

A major goal of *The Art of InterGroup Peace* is to achieve Peace between groups. Chiefs in each setting have a major impact on group behavior. That means, at a very functional level, we are more likely to succeed if we have aligned chiefs in each setting who function as a key vehicle and supporter to help make Peace in each setting.

Groups of people tend to follow their chiefs and groups of people tend to accept the decisions that are made and the deals that are done by their chiefs.

Agreements between groups in any setting that are not blessed by the relevant chiefs for each group have less chance of succeeding. Chiefs are often needed to be the people who actually negotiate agreements and to be the people who formally reach agreements.

Chapter Six discusses the eight most common approaches we can use to bring groups of people into structured interactions. It takes leaders working with leaders to make each and any of those structured intergroup interactions function and happen.

The list of intergroup interactions in that chapter includes ceasefires, truces, agreements, confederations, mergers, consolidations, and extends all the way to full intergroup assimilation.

Each of the eight intergroup interactions requires local people from each hierarchy interacting to figure out the best alignment model for the situation and to put in place the processes for the groups in that setting to make that alignment model happen.

Agreements that are made between groups are usually made by the people who lead the relevant hierarchy of each relevant group or organization.

The Art of InterGroup Peace recognizes that some of the major intergroup agreements that need to happen in some settings, can only be accomplished and can only be done with credibility and with a sense of legitimacy for each group, if they are done by whoever is perceived to be the legitimate and authorized chief — or chiefs — of the group that is reaching the agreements.

Agreements Made by People Without the Authority to Make Them Tend to Fail

That is a key tactical point to understand in using the strategies that are included in *The Art of InterGroup Peace*. Agreements reached in any setting are vulnerable and can fail if done by people who are not perceived by their group to have the legitimate right and power to reach the agreement.

When deals that are done on key group issues are done by people who are not perceived to have the legitimate status and standing within their own group that is needed to actually do that particular deal, those agreements tend to either not be finalized or they simply fall apart over time.

Deals done by chiefs who aren't accepted by their own group as having the standing and the legitimate power to do the deal generally do not succeed in resolving the key instinctive intergroup issues that might exist about that decision for the members of those groups.

Some deals that are done by non-credible negotiators fall apart very quickly because people in the groups involved don't accept the agreements' that were done as being legitimate.

Others are simply ignored, because the people in the group don't feel that the agreements were made by someone who could legitimately represent the group, and who had the authority to do that specific deal.

So The Art of InterGroup Peace strategy calls for groups who make Peace deals with other groups to have people who have perceived leadership legitimacy for each of the parties negotiating the key deals, and then to also have those same perceived leaders explaining and selling the Peace deal that is done to the other members of their group.

Alpha Instincts Create Their Own Relevant Behaviors

As part of that entire hierarchical package of instincts, we know that when someone rises to Alpha status in any given group, achieving that status often triggers its own set of very relevant instincts and behaviors for that Alpha person.

That very basic set of chief-related instincts is directly relevant to The Art of InterGroup Peace because the chiefs in any setting — as the Alpha member of each group — tend to be very instinctively focused on a couple of key issues.

The top of that priority list for Alpha focus is often group turf. Alpha leaders in most settings have clearly activated turf instincts that relate to their own group turf. The book *Primal Pathways* has an extensive section dealing with Alpha instinct packages and their consequences for intergroup interactions.

The Alpha members of each group tend to have their own set of turf and intergroup conflict emotions and instincts fully activated, and they tend to act accordingly.

That means that the Alpha people in each group tend to be people who are often very sensitive to turf encroachment. The Alpha are often the people in a group who are personally most focused on both the intellectual turf and the physical turf issues that exist for their group.

In many cases, the person who is in the Alpha role for a group is in that position because he or she has a history of doing turf protection things at various levels for their group.

War Leaders Often Become Alpha

In many settings — the person who has been perceived by the group to be the best defender of the relevant group turf, or who has been perceived to be the best warrior in conflicted settings relative to various group protection issues, or who is perceived to be the best defender of the group belief system or ideology for any given group, ends up to be the person who is selected by that group to be their group Alpha.

The fiercest defenders of a conflicted group are often selected to be Alpha by a group to lead the group because groups tend to want to be well defended when conflict is relevant.

That selection process and those selection priorities sometimes create their own set of difficulties for intergroup Peace because those leaders who personally come to power based on their conflict response and war skills can sometimes have a very hard time either valuing Peace, or helping Peace to happen in any setting.

Power Can Be Addictive as Well

That is a key point to understand in each setting relative to the strategies embedded in *The Art of InterGroup Peace*. Intergroup alignment issues can be particularly challenging in those settings where the people who are in power and who love being in power actually personally achieved their own power by being a war chief.

The Art of InterGroup Peace also recognizes that power has its own set of instinctive reactions. Power can be addictive. Alpha people often very much want to be Alpha, and receive both strong internal rewards and strong external rewards from their Alpha status and Alpha behaviors.

Those are very instinctive behaviors and reward systems. Very consistent and very seductive neurochemicals can be triggered by Alpha status. People who achieve power in any setting tend to get the kinds of instinctive neurochemical rewards and reinforcing societal reactions that often cause them — those people with that set of rewards activated — to not want to ever lose their Alpha power.

Losing power can trigger very negative responses in people whose alpha instincts have been fully activated. The *Primal Pathways* book discusses those sets of issues in more detail.

So the reality is that the people who function as war chiefs tend to thrive in times of war — and those leaders sometimes do not like the loss of power and the loss of relative chief status that can sometimes result from the end of their war.

Some War Chiefs Make the Best Peace Chiefs

For those reasons, war-empowered or conflict-empowered Alphas can sometimes be a challenge relative to any group negotiating a Peace in any setting. It is also very true that Peace can be done very effectively in many settings with the explicit involvement of those same war leaders — and some of the best Peace deals are done by former warriors who know the horror of war and who have credibility with their people on war issues that is based on their own battle or conflict leadership experience.

But sometimes the Art of InterGroup Peace requires finding a new set of leaders for a setting who can more easily make a transition from a time of war to a time of Peace.

In any case, groups everywhere have hierarchies. Hierarchies have leaders. Leaders personally all tend to have strongly activated turf and group protection instincts.

Those patterns are normal patterns. So selecting leaders based on their commitment to intergroup Peace rather than their commitment to intergroup war is clearly a good thing to be doing at this point for us all in the process of creating Peace.

Getting leaders in place and having leaders in the process who have the personal hierarchical credibility to reach the Peace agreements is a key and important part of the Peace strategy.

Alpha, Beta, and Theta Instincts All Structure Thoughts and Behaviors

The *Primal Pathways* book also describes what that book calls Beta and Theta instincts — the instincts that people at every single hierarchical level have to be very committed to and very aware of their own relative position in any hierarchy.

We all have instincts to know our own specific relative position — to know who we expect to salute and to know who we expect to salute us in any hierarchy.

We frankly, very consistently, resist dropping levels in any hierarchy and we generally aspire to moving up levels in any hierarchy.

Those instincts and that set of thought processes create their own set of relevant behavior for people in hierarchical settings.

People tend to feel great stress and unhappiness if their relative position in a hierarchy is ever at risk. People also aspire to promotion in the context of their hierarchy.

Leaders at the Alpha level can expect to be obeyed by people who have their Beta and Theta instincts activated — but Alpha leaders can also find themselves at risk if they weaken in any way that lets the Beta people in their hierarchy depose them and take their Alpha status.

Peace can be hard to achieve if the people in Alpha roles are insecure in their internal political support and are afraid of having their aspiring Beta leaders accuse them of intergroup weakness, or of being a traitor to their group.

Those issues need to be dealt with situationally in many settings as part of The Art of InterGroup Peace in order to create both the agreements that can define the Peace, and a sense of legitimacy for each group relative to the component parts of any Peace agreement that might be achieved.

Any time we bring people together in a setting, we are well served by making sure that people have their needs met to have their relative status known and protected.

Cultures Are Everywhere, as Well

The Art of InterGroup Peace calls for cultures as well as leaders to be key tools for the Peace process. We have very powerful instincts to create cultures in each of the groups that exist. We need to use our cultures as a tool for Peace.

Today, our cultures in most settings function as the tools of our instincts, and our cultures generally help us achieve our instinctive goals in each relevant setting.

Building cultures is another highly instinctive and universal behavior. We have tribal cultures, family cultures, ethnic cultures, and organizational cultures. The groups that form even in almost spontaneous settings often tend to create their own almost spontaneous setting-specific cultures.

The next chapter of this book addresses cultures in more detail as a primary factor for intergroup interactions and as a key tool for the Art of InterGroup Peace.

We Can Use All Instincts for Peace – and for War

The basic reality that we face relative to The Art of InterGroup Peace is that nearly a dozen of our basic instinctive behavior packages can cause us to inflict damage onto people from other groups and to distrust and dislike people from other groups. Each of those instinct packages can make achieving Peace difficult in any given setting.

Our instincts to tribalize — to create and defend turf, to activate Alpha instincts against other groups of people, and to function in mob-like settings all can create barriers to Peace.

Each of those instinct packages — with the exception of mob instincts — can also be tools for Peace as well as tools for war.

We need to understand all of those instinctive behaviors and we need to channel each of them well if we want to achieve Peace. We need to understand both the thought processes that those sets of instincts trigger and we need to understand both the patterns of behavior, and the specific behaviors that they create.

Pattern delineation and discernment is an important skill we need to have. As a package, we need to collectively channel all of those instinctive behaviors toward Peace.

We can't channel those specific behaviors toward Peace with full effectiveness if we simply deal with each intergroup incident that occurs in each setting as an isolated and separate incident. We need to understand our patterns of behavior and not just focus on the pieces and incidents that are relevant to each situational activation of those instincts.

We Need Strategic Approaches to Peace

One insight from *The Art of War* that is shared by *The Art of InterGroup Peace* is the belief that if you have a good macro strategy, and if you have clear macro goals in place, your chance of success is significantly enhanced.

But if you only have situational and reactive tactics in place for each incident and for each occurrence, and if you rely on entirely situational and tactical responses to each incident and if you have no overall strategy that is guiding your overall efforts, you will very likely fail and Peace will not be achieved in your setting.

Sun Tzu said that armies who had strategies would win — and he said very clearly that the armies that were grounded only on tactics and situational reactions as their approach to war were doomed to fail.

The same is true for Peace. We need strategies and not just tactics to also achieve our Peace. That need to have an overall overarching strategy and not just rely on situational tactics to deal with intergroup issues is a very real concern for both winning a War and creating a Peace.

Peace Is More Than a Tactical, Situational Set of Responses

Wars are won by generals who understand the physical terrain. Peace can be won by leaders who understand the behavioral terrain that is created and channeled by our instincts.

A Peace strategy that takes into account all of our key instinctive issues and instinctive behaviors has the potential to use that specific terrain far more successfully than an approach that treats every problem, issue, and intergroup confrontation and conflict as though each issue is a unique problem that needs situationally tactical and incident-based responses.

Our Overall Strategy Needs to Be to Use Our Instinctive Behaviors for Peace

The basic overarching strategy of *The Art of InterGroup Peace* is to use our instincts and the behaviors and values they create to generate a collective sense of "Us" for this country that will allow us to be at Peace with ourselves. *Cusp of Chaos* and *Primal Pathways* both point out how that can be done in more detail.

We need to very explicitly address and utilize our us/them instincts as a key part of that strategy. We need to have our "Us" instincts support us in achieving Peace. We need to create an opportunity for interaction and trust between people who are not feeling intergroup trust today. We need to activate our team instincts and we need to collectively trigger a sense of "Us" at a higher level that has win/win goals as a key collective belief.

We Need to Use the Entire Set of Instincts for Peace

Cultures need to be part of the tool kit for Peace. We need to use our tendency and ability to create, impose, and use cultures to build explicit and intentional new values into each of our cultures. That will give Peace and win/win outcomes a higher likelihood of success.

We need to use hierarchies, because they inevitably exist, to achieve the agreements we need, and we need to use our hierarchies to implement them successfully. We need to have our hierarchal and Alpha leader supported behaviors and commitments that are credible to each group that will directly support our goals of intergroup Peace.

We need to deal with our turf instincts — and we need to recognize that any Peace approaches in any setting that ignore any group's basic turf instinct realties will have a much lower sense of succeeding.

We need to overcome our very powerful and often invisible instincts against being a traitor — and we need to make sure that our mob instincts are never functionally activated.

If our packages of instincts are somehow activated at the level where people are treated as "Them" in the context of a mob, we need to defuse and de-energize those behaviors and instincts very quickly before permanent damage is done in any setting. We need demonstrations — not riots — when groups are angry with other groups.

Overall, we need to put structures and processes in place to reinforce any agreements or understandings or Peaceful relationships that we might achieve. Chapter five of this book addresses those issues.

At a core level, we need to make sure that the people who are working for Peace in each setting can do that work for all of us without feeling like they are being a traitor to their initial definition of "Us."

Creating Peace Is Both a Personal and Collective Agenda

Peace cannot happen in a vacuum. Creating Peace needs to be purely intentional, very specific, and directly based on both tactics and strategies that reinforce the Peace agenda and the Peace culture.

The next chapter explains the role that culture plays in that process.

CHAPTER FIVE

Our Cultures Can Be Used as Anchors for Peace or as Triggers for Conflict

WE NEED A culture of Peace for America.

We also need a culture of inclusion and a culture of equal opportunity.

We need a culture that celebrates freedom at its most basic levels — including freedom of speech, freedom of beliefs, and freedom of religion.

We need the culture of our country — and the cultures of the various groups and communities that make up America — to be cultures of caring, compassion, and collaboration — cultures rooted in mutual achievement and shared success.

Our cultures guide our behaviors every day. They give us basic sets of standards that guide our decision-making and guide our interactions with one another.

To have the right set of cultural components be a key part of who we are as a nation, we need to understand both what our cultures do and how to get our cultures to do what we want them to do.

We need to make our cultures a tool for our beliefs — and we need to have enlightened beliefs that will create a country for us all that gives us all the best opportunity to achieve the American Dream and to achieve the enlightened values that we all share as an American "Us."

We are heavily reliant on our cultures to steer our individual and group behavior today.

We use our cultures in all settings to steer, influence, and to guide our individual and collective behaviors. Our cultures tell us what we should do and our cultures tell us what we should not do in each group context and setting.

Our Cultures Are Tools for Our Instincts

We are all creatures of instincts. We all have core sets of instincts that give us our basic patterns of behaviors and our basic goals and objectives as groups and as individuals.

Our instincts actually set our overall goals for any setting — and our cultures then tend to be used as tools in each setting to help our instincts achieve our goals.

We have hierarchical instincts, for example, so every culture creates its own rules and its own expectations for hierarchies.

We have territorial instincts, so every culture creates its rules and expectations about turf.

We have instincts to be on teams and to have loyalty to the groups we are part of. Each culture creates its own loyalty expectations and each culture creates its own basic team related behaviors and approaches.

We feel very right when our behaviors are in alignment with our instincts. Our instincts generate much of their power by making certain behaviors feel very right.

Our maternal behaviors feel very right because they are directly aligned with our maternal instincts.

Our child protection behaviors feel right because our behaviors that protect our children are clearly aligned with our child protection instincts.

Our cultures actually have some of their power over us because our cultures have the same power that our instincts have to make some behaviors feel right and to make some behaviors feel wrong. Our cultures, like our instincts, can also trigger a sense of stress and even anxiety when we behave in ways that are not instinctively or culturally aligned.

For us to succeed in creating intergroup Peace in America, we need to have behaviors that encourage and support Peace embedded in our cultures — so that we feel right when we act in ways that support and create Peace.

Rules, Guidance, and Expectations

To use our cultures effectively as tools, we need to understand what our cultures do and we need to understand how our cultures do what they do.

Rules are a key part of the culture tool kit.

Our cultures impose and enforce their guidance in large part through creating group expectations, group rules, and basic behavior guidances for each group. Our cultures often support their guidance with basic — and sometimes very explicit — instructions to group members about expected behaviors.

Cultures often enforce their guidance and functionally mandate their expected behaviors with a blend of rules, regulations, guidelines, expectations, and laws.

Cultures also often enforce and support their guidance through peer pressure — with other members of a culture putting pressure on people in various ways to comply with the expectations of their culture.

When a culture is in place in any setting, that culture tends to be taught, articulated, enforced and reinforced by other people in that culture in that setting.

People clearly can feel right acting in accord with a culture, and people can tend to feel wrong acting out of alignment with a culture.

People Can Feel Direct Loyalty to Cultures

For many group cultures, people tend to feel a level of direct and personal loyalty to the culture. Those loyalty instincts can be very powerful. Many people are willing, in a wide range of circumstances, to take various kinds of individual and collective action to loyally defend and protect their culture.

Some people have been willing to die for their cultures — perceiving their cultures to be a key part of their personal "Us" alignment and their personal identity.

Our basic instincts have used our cultures and their supporting features and functions well as a tool for a very long time.

Those relationships between instincts, behaviors, and beliefs all make our cultures extremely relevant to the Art of InterGroup Peace. We need to use our cultures in very intentional ways as a way of teaching, supporting, implementing, and reinforcing Peaceful intergroup behaviors and beliefs so that we can achieve intergroup Peace in each of our relevant settings.

We Need Enlightened Values and Behaviors Embedded in Our Cultures

To achieve the Art of InterGroup Peace, we need to make the deliberate and intentional intellectual choice as both groups and individuals at this point in our history to have this country be a country of both enlightened beliefs and enlightened behaviors.

We need to make intellectual choices about our key shared values. We then need our intellect to use our cultures as tools for our enlightenment and as a functional process for making our most enlightened ethical and moral values a functional reality for us all.

That particular process needs to be anchored on a core set of shared enlightened beliefs about who we are and about how we should all interact with one another.

We need to achieve a level of collective enlightenment that needs to be anchored in a set of clearly articulated and clearly understood core beliefs so that we all know, understand, and can commit to as a shared set of key values.

We need to become an "Us" as a values-focused country based on those core beliefs. We also need to become an "Us" in each relevant setting — so that we can achieve Peace in each relevant setting.

We need to achieve intergroup Peace, piece by piece — in each group and community — and we need to anchor the core values we create in each setting on the same core values we agree to as a country.

Those key values that we can use and embed in our cultures to anchor Peace and enlightened intergroup and interpersonal behaviors are described in the final chapter of this book.

We need to ground ourselves as a nation on that key set of shared enlightened beliefs. We all need to commit to those beliefs and we all need to act in alignment with those beliefs so that we can actually be an "Us" who is unified by our belief in those key values.

We Will Not Eliminate Our Old Categories of "Us" in the Alignment Process

We will not eliminate our other levels of basic group identification as we become a values-based "Us." No existing levels of "Us" will be erased in the process.

Our basic birth groups and our most primal personal alignment levels will continue to be real and relevant to us. We will continue to be diverse after we achieve alignment — and that is a very good thing because our diversity strengthens us and empowers us in many ways that are described by the Intergroup Trilogy of books.

What we need to do now as a key component of the Art of InterGroup Peace is to add a layer of "Us" on top of those basic alignments. That additional layer can be created by our intellect — and it can be used strategically and functionally to do what we need it to do.

Our instincts give us the ability to add overarching layers of "us," in addition to our core sets of "Us" — so we need to use that ability to be flexible that is given to us by our instincts to generate an "Us" that unifies us all as an American "Us."

We then need to use our cultures to do the things that will implement those enlightened beliefs in the context of our lives.

We need that particular unifying "Us" that creates alignment at the highest level for all of us to be based directly on our core beliefs.

Instead of being a people primarily connected with other people by our race, our tribe, or our ethnicity, we need to be a people connected at an overarching level as a people by our shared beliefs.

We need to agree on a set of shared beliefs and we need to embed those beliefs both into an overarching culture for the country and into the cultures for each of our other relevant definitions of "Us."

We need to use that strategy of forming an overarching "Us" at the largest national level — and we also need to use that strategy very intentionally and very consistently at each local group setting and community setting.

We Need to Embed Those Values and Those Behaviors in Every Culture

We need to be a values-based "Us" with ourselves in each setting. We need to do that in a way that creates both trust and shared benefits in each setting between the existing groups in each setting.

We need our various group cultures to all accept and include the overarching culture of inclusion, openness, and equal opportunity that we have set up as our overarching values for our country.

If the cultures we set up for each group in each setting go down different patterns and paths and have values that are based on distrusting the other groups or somehow doing damage to the other groups in their setting, then Intergroup Peace will obviously be extremely difficult — if not impossible — in those settings.

But if we deliberately embed values in each basic group culture in each setting that says we very much want to be at Peace with ourselves in each setting and that we want to support and celebrate each other's success, then Peace is much more likely to be the model for intergroup interaction in those settings and in the country as a whole.

We can create that set of values if we do what we need to do to make that strategy work, and if we do that work using the intergroup Peace skill set that we need to use to do that work.

Cultural issues, values, and guided behaviors are clearly extremely important for both Peace and war.

Sun Tzu Believed the Culture of an Army Is a Key to Success

Sun Tzu believed strongly in culture as a key tool for war. In *The Art of War*, Sun Tzu made the point directly and well that the culture of an army was a key factor in the success or failure of an army. He stated clearly and persuasively that the leader of each army should think of the culture of the army as a tool that can help achieve victory for the army.

Sun Tzu stated very directly that a major role for the leader of each army is to create the culture of the army.

He called for each military leader in each setting to personally exhibit specific behaviors and values as a leader, relative to issues like discipline and basic ethics, in ways that would cause the army to follow the leader and to perform and act in an effective and aligned way as a collective entity that shared a belief system about specific sets of behaviors.

He believed that an army with a unified culture was more likely to succeed.

Sun Tzu also believed that armies who had weak cultures and armies that had a divided sense of direction would be significantly more likely to fail.

The same is true for Peace.

Creating and sustaining Peace is also much more likely to fail if we don't align both our collective culture and the culture-linked behaviors of our people in ways that will cause Peace to succeed.

Clearly, if we want to see behaviors that create and sustain Peace, we need to embed those behaviors in our cultures in each setting as beliefs and as expectations. We need to agree on Peace as a goal and we need to have Peace be a shared value for the people who are part of the values-based American us.

We need to make sure that each of the other group cultures that we align with do not have values that work against Peace and steer us toward intergroup conflict.

We Tend to Have Cultural Expectations "Feel Right"

Even though there is great variation from culture to culture on a wide range of key issues — like the selection of a leader or our various ways of creating weddings and marriages — we tend to internalize whatever approach our own relevant culture uses for each of those areas. It generally feels very right for each of us to behave in alignment with the specific approach that is used by our culture.

We tend to be loyal to the solution approach that is used by our culture for each set of instinctive behaviors and we generally believe the solution used by our culture for each behavior is "right" at a basic level.

We feel the process to be "right" at a very basic instinctive level. We tend to be loyal at a very instinctive level to the approaches used by our own culture and we tend to believe that our approaches are the right approaches — at least for our own group.

Cultures Help Groups Achieve Goals

Every organization uses its cultures for the purpose of achieving its own goals. Village cultures are created to protect and enhance the success of villages. The culture of a school is set up to support the basic processes and the key goals of the school. The culture of a business is used to achieve the goals of the business.

The cultures of our communities are all set up functionally and incrementally to achieve what we perceive to be the collective goals for each community.

For each group, the culture is a tool. In some cases, the tool is very carefully designed and implemented. In other settings, the culture grows almost organically from our instinctive group need to identify expected behaviors for people in any group situation.

We have instincts to create cultures for every group — so every group builds the culture that fits its needs for behavioral guidance.

We Can Use the Culture Relevant to Each Context and Setting

We also have very flexible instincts that allow us to have layers of culture that are each relevant to a layer of our group reality and group functionality.

We can, for example, be part of a family culture and relate to that culture as though its guidances and edicts are, in fact, "right."

We also can, at that same time, relate to a clan culture that overshadows our family culture and creates its own set of behavioral expectations. In most cases, families try to build their cultures in ways that meet the expectations set by their clan or tribe for family cultures.

We can each relate to a tribal culture or to a community culture that overarches our family and clan cultures.

We can each relate at a more immediate and micro level to a team culture and we can also relate at a much more macro level to a national identity and a national culture.

We have the basic packages of instincts that lets each of us align at those multiple levels and we have the intellectual ability for each of us to situationally figure out which culture is relevant to each behavior and each decision in our life.

We Have the Ability to Relate to Multiple Cultures

We have the ability to relate to each of the relevant layers of culture in our lives — and each of those layers have the ability to shape, guide, and influence the other layers in ways that allow them to function simultaneously without giving contradictory guidance at various levels to the people in them.

We need to take advantage of that ability to have layers of instincts activated as we work to achieve intergroup Peace in each setting.

We need to set up cultures in each work-site, school, and community setting that have values embedded in the culture that support intergroup Peace.

When we have cultures in any setting that encourage conflict and that work in dysfunctional ways against intergroup Peace, then we need to change the aspects of that culture that work against Peace. We usually don't need to change entire cultures to get them to support Peace, but we sometimes need to change negative, dysfunctional, damaging, or unenlightened components of a culture.

Culture Change Can Be Difficult

Changing a culture can be difficult. Cultures themselves often have an inherent rigidity. Once they are created and once they are in place our cultures, in our most fixed group settings, tend to both enforce and reinforce themselves in perpetuity — with people in a culture who believe in the culture and who know the culture well, telling other people in that setting how to act in accord with the guidance, rules, and beliefs of the culture and even penalizing people who act in violation of the culture in some way.

Group disapproval can be a very effective penalty and enforcement tool in some settings. We instinctively do not like to have our group disapprove of us. Group disapproval can create effective cultural compliance and even — in some cases — cultural rigidity.

Under some circumstances, cultural rigidity can be an asset. In other cases, it can be dysfunctional and damaging.

Excess Flexibility Could Weaken Performance

For basic logistical reasons, we should not change the cultures that work well lightly.

Cultures would have less functional long-term value in many basic settings if the cultures used were so flexible that they could be changed, in significant ways, by minor whims or by incidental, situational, and basically circumstantial events.

When the culture of a group calls for harvesting wild rice in October every year, then deciding to skip a year of harvesting for incidental reasons could create an unintended famine for the group. Unintended famines are not good for group survival.

So we tend to be fairly rigid in following cultural practices that seem to have worked for us in the past.

Cultures that work to meet the needs of a functioning group can be major assets for the success and survival of that group. Putting a major culture guidance asset at risk in any setting by changing the asset for less than stellar reasons can have a bad outcome for a group. Culture change can sometimes put successful processes and effective approaches at risk.

So we tend not to change cultures once we create them and once we embed them in a permanent group or setting of any kind.

Once developed and once implemented, cultures tend to stay in place.

Cultures tend to become embedded as working beliefs in the minds of the people in each culture — and changing beliefs for people in a culture can be extremely difficult once those beliefs are fully embedded in the people in that culture.

Cultures Function as a Mental Model or Paradigm

Cultures often function as a category of Paradigm. We do much of our thinking about all topics in the world in the context of paradigms.

Our minds are designed to build paradigms about all major topics and to hold on to our various paradigms once we have developed them.

Paradigms are hard to change once we have them in our minds as our functioning belief system for any area of belief or behavior.

Paradigms can be changed, but paradigm change can require a careful and intentional process to make any significant changes.

Cultures follow that same pattern. We can change cultures, but we need to do it with some skill in order to achieve the most positive results.

Cultures, Strategies, and Missions Work Best When They Are Aligned

For leaders of various organizations, the functional reality is that the culture, the strategic direction, and the mission or purpose of the organization needs to be aligned for maximum organizational success.

Sun Tzu understood that reality clearly. He believed the culture and the strategy of an army worked best when they were clearly and intentionally aligned with each other.

In our times, experienced leaders knew that if the leaders in any setting attempt to implement a strategy that is out of alignment with the culture of the setting, the non-aligned strategy that they attempt to accomplish is highly likely to fail.

"Culture defeats strategy" is an adage that many experienced leaders understand. Another common management theory adage is — "Culture eats strategy for lunch."

The truth for businesses is that leaders in work settings who seek overall organizational success are often well served by working to put specific and carefully chosen cultural beliefs in place that reinforce and support their organization's strategic direction. Cultures can be used as tools by businesses who understand what cultures are and know how to use them.

The same is true for communities and for intergroup Peace.

Some Cultures Celebrate Conflict and War

Leaders who want to achieve Peace in any setting — large or small — clearly need to understand that the cultures of the groups in each setting need to value and support Peace in order to actually achieve and sustain Peace.

That is a highly relevant issue. Unfortunately, some cultures today celebrate conflict and war. Some cultures are built on a history of negative and damaging intergroup interactions.

Those cultures often celebrate the heroes who have done damage to the other group in their setting. Some cultures have rich histories of celebrating warriors and honoring the acts of war that were key factors in each warrior's life.

We need our cultures in all settings to very clearly celebrate and support Peace and to not just honor and celebrate the icons of war.

We can embed a set of beliefs about Peace into each of our relevant cultures if we do it intentionally and do it well. We need people to believe in Peace. We need to convince the people in each relevant culture and setting that Peace is a good goal and a good value in order to embed Peace in the culture itself.

We need to call for people to rise above the cultural call to be embattled and to function as warriors, and we need to ask people to choose instead to aspire as individuals to a life of mutual support and Peace.

We need individual people to help their own cultures change in favor of Peace by making personal commitments to live in Peace and to support achieve and protect Peace for their group and their settings.

We need to very intentionally include, in each culture in each setting, the specific beliefs and the specific behavioral expectations that support and achieve Peace.

Culture change is clearly needed for those settings where the current culture celebrates conflict and focuses on conflict relative to other groups of people. Some cultures pride themselves on being warrior cultures — with all of the dysfunctional intergroup behaviors that can result from warrior behaviors and priorities.

Those beliefs and values that encourage intergroup conflict obviously need to be modified for those groups by those groups in order to increase the chance of those groups succeeding at Peace.

We need to celebrate the icons of Peace — the Ghandis and Mandelas who have shown that we can reach out across groups and bring people together to mutually create and sustain Peace.

People Grant Cultures Inherent Validity

To make culture change possible, we all need to clearly understand how much power our cultures can have over each of us and over all of us relative to how we think and how we feel.

That power is significant. Even our highly situational and almost circumstantial cultures can have a major impact on our behaviors and our thoughts and feelings.

A group of people standing in a line will create a culture for the line. The culture of the line will generally have rules for who can leave the line, who can "butt in" to the line, and whether the members of the line can take a bio-break and still retain their old position in the line.

The rules and the expectations of that line culture tend to be communicated fairly efficiently in a very setting specific way for each line culture.

We give our cultures so much inherent credibility at an emotional and intellectual level that people can become angry at a very visceral level when someone violates even the situational culture of standing in a line. People can respond with significant anger if anyone violates the culture that exists for a particular line. People tend to feel right acting in accord with the culture that exists for each line.

On our highways, road rage sometimes occurs when people in cars are perceived by other people in cars to be in violation of the rules of the situational culture that is perceived by those people to exist for that particular road.

Schools, Businesses, and Communities Create Cultures

Every setting creates cultures. Schools create cultures. Businesses create culture. The very best business leaders understand the role that cultures play in running an organization and those leaders carefully script, design, communicate, endorse, and enforce the cultures of their businesses.

The best educational leaders design, implement, and enforce the cultures of their schools.

The best community leaders shape the culture of their communities.

Communities all tend to develop cultures that are self-reinforced by the communities. Community leaders typically play a major role in creating and defining community cultures — and community leaders are often the best vehicle to use if we need to change a community culture in some way.

We instinctively act in accord with our cultures. We also instinctively follow people who we perceive to be our legitimate leaders in any setting even when we are unhappy about who those leaders might be.

When those instincts to follow cultures and our instincts to follow leaders blend, and when leaders who have solid instinctive standing with us decide to change cultures, the cultures that are most relevant to the leaders can often change fairly easily.

As an architect of cultural change in any setting, one of the most effective tools for us all to use is to convert the leader of that setting to believe in and support the relevant cultural changes. Leaders can actually change many cultures, but that process requires the leaders, themselves, to be believers and advocates for the new culture.

Historically, Leaders Have Made Religious Choices for Entire Tribes

Historically, we have seen the religious conversion of leaders in various settings cause entire tribes of people to follow their leader to the new belief.

The world is full of believers whose personal religious beliefs were inherited by them as the result of a historical event where the leader of their group converted to a new sect or a new religion.

Germany had Catholic tribes and Protestant tribes — because the leaders for each local section of that country made that decision about alignment at some point in history on behalf of all of their people. Those belief alignment decisions that were made at that point in history by those leaders for their people continue to this day to determine the inherited belief system for the people in those relevant portions of that country.

Likewise, the Shiite tribes and the Sunni tribes in each multi-tribal country can all trace their allegiances to their specific sect based on a historical conversion to that belief at a point in the past by their own ancestral tribal leader.

Those tribes in those countries continue to have those same exact religious alignments as tribes to this day. Leaders made those commitments at a point in history for each of their people in all of those settings and people today inherit their personal connection to that specific alignment simply by being born.

In those settings, individual people do not make individual belief choices. Their beliefs are assigned, not ascertained, and the assignment process is so rigid that people can be executed as traitors if they choose to connect to another religion in some settings.

Leaders clearly have a major impact on cultures at historic levels. Leaders today also can have a major impact on local cultures at very situational levels. People follow leaders and that fact gives leaders an opportunity to actually lead in some key areas.

Leaders actually can change cultures today in many situations and settings.

Groups Can Change Their Own Cultures

Culture change can also happen in various settings and situations as the result of various kinds of formal culture change processes. There are a number of deliberate and legislative settings where leaders for various groups formally and officially debate the rule sets and the expected behaviors for a group of people. When legislative or governmental bodies are the vehicle for culture change, the new expectations that result from the change are often embedded in laws and regulations in ways that cause those expectations to become part of people's belief systems.

Our country made major culture changes relative to who could vote that were based on very explicit legislative changes. Once those sets of changes were actually made in the law, the new process became the new expectation and the new expectations become the new belief system for our people. We now believe in voting for all. There are no cultural pressures today for taking voting rights away from women or from minorities.

Culture change can also happen through various forms of perceived consensus where people in a culture reach a collective sense of what expectations are for people in that setting in a collective way.

Those levels of culture change all have the impact of giving people different behaviors systems for the relevant sets of issues.

Cultural behavioral expectations and belief systems can change for groups based on both following leaders and on creating some kind of collective consensus on the part of the people who are subject to the expectations.

Cultures Can Be Externally and Internally Enforced

Cultural compliance enforcement can be based on rules and laws, and culture compliance can be based on an array of group behavioral expectations.

Family members are expected to honor the culture of their family. That generally isn't an actual legal requirement — but it tends to be functional at several levels because family members put pressure on other family members to be aligned with those specific expectations for their family.

External reinforcement for each of us as individuals relative to family cultures happens when other family members enforce the family rules in one way or another. Internal reinforcement for those behaviors happen when a person in a family knows personally that it feels right to act in alignment with the family culture behavioral expectations and knows that it feels wrong to act in opposition to those expectations — and then behaves accordingly.

The culture in each setting tells us what behavior is acceptable in that setting and the culture tells us what behavior is not acceptable in that setting with that group of people — and we tend to have a sense of feeling right when our behaviors coincide with the expectations of our culture.

Our Cultures Are Embedded – Not Inherent

We need intergroup Peace to be a culturally expected behavior. We need Peace to be a culturally expected behavior so that people will feel both right and safe acting in accord with those sets of behaviors.

Feeling safety, comfort, and cultural fulfillment are all good things for people to feel. We need people to feel safety and comfort acting in ways that enhance and support intergroup Peace.

Cultural Loyalty Can Trigger Intercultural Conflict

One problem that we can face for Peace today in some settings, however, is that people sometimes feel cultural loyalty to their own culture to the point that their personal loyalty level to a culture triggers conflict in various ways with people from other cultures.

As a key part of the agenda to create Peace, we very intentionally need to take steps to not have our cultures be a source of conflict based on issues of cultural loyalty.

We need to be sure that people's perceived need to loyally defend their own culture doesn't cause conflict, anger, and division between groups at key intergroup levels.

We feel an instinctive need to defend our people and we feel an instinctive need to sustain and protect our group values — so we need to not have our various separate cultures somehow trigger behaviors in support of each culture in ways that can result in intergroup conflict, violence, division, or even death.

Some People Believe Their Culture Is Embedded in Them and Defines Them at a Core Level

Some people will die for their culture. Some people will kill to protect their culture. We see those behaviors at multiple settings in the world today. People are willing to both die and kill to support their own culture and to do damage to the people they perceive to be "Them" relative to their culture.

Some people feel personally defined by their culture.

Some people believe strongly that the specific elements of their basic culture are somehow inherent at an almost purely genetic level in them personally. Some people believe that their cultures are also inherent at a core level to the other people in their group of people who share their culture, and that any deviation from that culture by people in their group means that the person who varies from the culture is a traitor to the group.

Our loyalty instinct and our sense of cultural identity can both be very powerful.

Those are people who believe that one of their own personal highest individual priorities as a person, needs to be to both defend and perpetuate their own culture. People say they need to protect and perpetuate the Irish culture or the French culture or the Black culture in various ways — and people are often willing to do battle in support of the culture they accept as the focus for their personal allegiance and personal loyalty.

All Cultures Are Invented

That set of beliefs, thought processes, and behaviors can create significant barriers and impediments to intergroup Peace.

People who have that set of powerful feelings about defending their own cultural group at those levels can often benefit very directly from understanding more clearly what "their culture" actually is and how it originated. Knowledge is power on that issue. We need the people who love their cultures at those levels to understand that our cultures are all situationally and circumstantially invented.

Some people believe today — very strongly — that their own cultures are not simply invented but are, in fact, embedded in some very fundamental and basically genetic way in themselves.

"I am Irish," someone might say, "So I am Irish to the core of who I am. I am in synch with the basic Irish culture. I do Irish things. It is what I do. I am Irish at my most basic level. I will do battle and I will even die to defend the Irish culture because that culture is who I am at my very essence. I have Irish blood. Irish is who I am and Irish is what I am, down to the bone and the core and the center of my being."

That is an extreme example, but there are significant numbers of people who hold beliefs about their cultures at those extreme levels. There are also significant numbers of people who have those same basic loyalty patterns and those same types of feelings and beliefs about their cultures, but have those beliefs at less extreme levels.

We Have Strong Instincts to Be Loyal

We have strong instincts to be loyal. We can be loyal to our family, our group, our community, or to any other group that creates a sense of "Us" that is clear enough to trigger loyalty. Once our loyalty instincts are activated, we feel a need to defend whatever grouping that has activated those instincts.

Our cultures are often the target, object, and subject for our loyalty instinct set.

People make clear statements about the importance of their personal cultural linkage and about the intensely perceived personal inherency of their culture to them as individuals as a motivating and behavior-influencing factor for their lives.

Those kinds of culture loyalty commitments and feelings and the personal and intergroup behaviors that result from those commitments exist all over the planet.

Many people from many cultures believe that they personally need to support their culture, defend their culture, and perpetuate their culture. There are a significant number of people who believe that their culture is more important than their own lives. Some people will die to protect or defend whatever they define or perceive their culture to be.

We clearly can be significantly influenced by our instincts to be loyal. The focus of our loyalty can be our group, our family, our team, our leaders, or our culture. Those instincts can create major motivational energy in each of us when they are triggered.

Those loyalty instincts can cause us to do good, heroic, positive, and reinforcing things for our own people. Those instincts can cause us to act in ways that create value and benefit for our people. Those instincts can trigger good and productive values, beliefs, and behaviors.

That same set of loyalty-based behaviors can, however, impede Peace. They can impede Peace if we feel that our direct loyalty to specific elements and components of our culture needs to be a higher priority for us than helping both our group and other groups achieve intergroup Peace. They can also be a problem if we feel that loyalty to our culture requires us to execute negative, divisive, and damaging actions relative to people from other cultures.

Being Irish Is a Learned Behavior — Not a Genetic Functionality

We need to reduce the negative impact of those instincts as a key strategy for The Art of InterGroup Peace.

We need to begin by helping people to understand at an intellectual level that being culturally and functionally Irish at an embedded and inherent level actually isn't an accurate or true descriptor of the situationally created cultural determinants and the behavioral influences that do exist for that person.

Being Irish actually is a learned set of behaviors — not a gene. Being Irish is not a biologically defined, individually inevitable, and personally inherent set of behaviors, attributes, or beliefs for any person, regardless of their personal sense of intense cultural loyalty to being Irish.

Being Irish is behaviorally and experientially imprinted — but it is not biologically embedded or built into actual processes or behaviors of any kind.

Being Irish Is Imprinted — Not Embedded

We need people to understand the fact that if a thousand Irish children were lifted at birth and brought to Fiji and raised entirely in Fiji — and if a thousand children from Fiji were simultaneously brought to Ireland at birth and raised there — with no contact of any kind by either group of children with any part of their ancestral land or with any piece of their ancestral cultural heritage, then the likelihood of any of the Irish children who are now living in Fiji somehow inventing and implementing the specific pieces that define the current Irish culture in that new setting and completely spontaneously and collectively using either shamrocks or green beer as an icon for their group on that lovely Pacific island is pretty close to zero.

Any similarity between the details of the two cultures would be accidental.

Cultures are learned and cultures are invented. Cultures are not biologically embedded. We don't acquire them by birth. We do, however, begin to acquire them at birth. We each embed our cultures into our thought processes through our life experiences and our environmental influences.

Our key cultures do clearly feel inherent. They are not inherent. We acquire them situationally. The children from one culture who would be transplanted at birth to an initially new setting would simply and directly invent a new culture that is specific to that environment and to the actual context they are in.

There would be nothing "Irish" in the specifics of the culture that the children with Irish ancestors would invent on Fiji.

Likewise, the children who were transported to Ireland from Fiji would not build a culture in Ireland that would be anchored and tied in any way to the value patterns, belief systems, and the lifestyle factors of the Pacific Ocean Islanders. There would be no link to those cultural factors if the children from Fiji who grew up entirely in Ireland had no actual links at any behavioral or experiential level to Fiji.

Cultures would absolutely exist in each new setting. Each transplanted child would be part of a new culture in the new setting.

All of the children in each setting would definitely have, acquire, and create a new culture in their new place. The new group culture that they would collectively create as people in each setting would actually be unique and specific to the culture that they would collectively and situationally define and invent in the new place.

That new culture that the children form those old cultures built on their own in each new setting would not be echoes of an older culture that was somehow biologically scripted and sculpted in each of them by their direct ancestral, genetic tribal roots.

Cultures, However, Feel Inherent to Each of Us

Cultures are learned and cultures are invented. Every single one… All cultures are invented and all cultures are learned.

That is not how the culture linking process generally feels to us, however. We each relate very directly to our embedded culture and that embedding feels very much like it defines us at a core level.

That feeling does tend to trigger our personal loyalty instincts to our current cultures at a core feeling level, but it is only a feeling — not an inherency.

To succeed in the Art of InterGroup Peace, we need to understand both how the culture building and culture embedding process actually works and we need to remember and understand how that process almost always feels to people.

We need to understand those issues because we need to be able to modify our cultures in some important ways to achieve Peace. Cultural rigidity on key intergroup issues can easily impede Peace. We very much need to modify our cultures when any current elements of our cultures cause us to hate and harm other people, for example.

We can each make choices.

We do not actually need to hate the people our culture tells us to hate. The fact that our culture tells us to hate someone does not mean that we should or must actually hate them. We each need to rise above our cultures and we each need to make our own individual and intellectual decisions about who or what we should actually hate.

We each need to make those decisions about other people in light of the specific sets of ethical values we each choose to use to guide our lives. We need to make enlightened personal decisions — and we also need to act in enlightened ways to change the culture we are in to change the values that need to be changed. Instead of having our cultures tell us who to hate, we need to change our cultures so they don't tell us to hate anyone.

Modification of cultures is possible. We can choose to change our current cultures. Both change and choice are possible. Both change and choice are highly desirable.

We each have both the right to change negative elements of our cultures and we each have the accountability to change negative elements of our cultures when those elements of our cultures need to be changed.

We Need to Change Cultures That Cause Us to Dislike Other Groups of People

We need to understand that if our current culture causes us to detest, fear, and harm another set of people, it is entirely legitimate, appropriate, and functionally correct and right and even imperative for us to change that part of our culture.

We can choose in our own lives not to have those feelings and beliefs for ourselves — and we can do what we can to both change the beliefs of other people in our culture, and to change the culture itself.

We do not need to feel that kind of change if what would be a clearly dysfunctional, negative, damaging, and corrupt part of our old culture represents a betrayal at any level of who we are or even represents an attack at any level on the group who comprises our original culture.

Our goal is to improve the world for our group — not damage our group in any way.

Those changes to act in more positive and enlightened ways can make our culture better — and they can cause our culture to serve us all more effectively in the long run.

We need to anchor those behaviors on an enlightened set of core beliefs.

We need to be people who believe in our common humanity and who believe both in our common values and in a common commitment to real Peace.

We need true believers who shape cultures rather than being true believers who are sent down dysfunctional and evil paths by our cultures.

We Need Our Cultures

Cultures do important work. Cultures have great value. We need our cultures. We should respect our cultures and we should honor and celebrate the people who built them. We should each enjoy the creativity that is embedded in our cultures and we should simultaneously enjoy the creativity that has been built into other cultures.

We need to learn to appreciate other cultures even if we don't choose to have them run our own lives as our personal culture of choice.

The Art of InterGroup Peace calls for each of us to help our own cultures to evolve as we create better and more effective ways of having groups of people interacting Peacefully with one another.

Culture change can make new sets of behaviors and beliefs feel right. When we become more enlightened on any given set of behaviors, we can embed those new behaviors into our expectations and our laws and it will feel very right to act in those enlightened ways. That will be a positive thing for us all.

Embedding Enlightenment into Laws Can Protect Progress

We made our own culture as a nation significantly more enlightened by granting all adults the right to vote, regardless of race, ethnicity or gender. We embedded that right to vote into our laws.

Embedding that right explicitly into our laws protected that new set of values against attack by people who might want to return us all to less enlightened voting behaviors.

Making that new behavior both a cultural practice and a legal requirement helped make that behavior a new belief.

We generally each incorporate our cultural beliefs and our cultural practices directly into our personal set of beliefs. People in our country now tend to personally believe in those inclusive voting-related values of our new culture.

People no longer believe in the values of our old culture, or in the old and restrictive practices relative to who can and should vote.

We can make similar changes as needed on the other key values of enlightened interactions that are outlined in the final chapter of this book. A dozen core beliefs for us all to share are outlined in that chapter.

To achieve InterGroup Peace, we need to adopt those 12 values as our new collective set of American values.

We need each of our group and community cultures to accept those beliefs and we need to embed those beliefs in each culture to the point where we don't have dueling value systems relative to those beliefs or behaviors.

Some Cultural Labels Can Be Misleading and Even Inaccurate

We also need — in our very diverse country — to understand that our cultural labels can sometimes be confusing and even misleading.

If someone says that a person needs to be in synch with and loyal to a White culture or needs to be in synch with and loyal to a Black culture, the truth is that the world is a very complex place and those labels are often not as useful as functional labels need to be to steer our thoughts or behaviors.

That terminology relating to those kinds of groupings may feel very right to the people who say it at the point in time when people actually say it, but those statements and those aspirations are sometimes not a very good functional fit for the real world we live in.

Some of those particular broad group culture alignment goals tend to be unachievable in fact, in our country today, much of the time.

Why are they unachievable?

There is far too much variation now inside the groups of people who fit both of those labels for any sets of people with those labels to have a rigid loyalty to a specific culture that is defined in any clear way by those categories and labels.

People who make those generic group-aligning statements generally feel like they have a clear sense of what they mean by those words at the time those statements are made. Someone might say, "I feel a deep loyalty to the Black culture on those issues."

The Black culture of Mississippi, however, is not the same as the Black culture of Chicago — and both of those cultures are clearly not the same as the Black culture of London, or the Black culture of Kampala, or the Black culture of Jamaica.

Likewise, the White culture of New York City is not the White culture of San Francisco — and neither of those cultures are the White culture of either Moscow or Copenhagen.

There is actually no universal White or Black or Hispanic or Asian or Native American culture. Each Native American group has its own culture. Those cultural specifications for each of those cultures are not cloned or even interchangeable.

So people from each group do tend to feel loyalty in a generic way to their group, but the actual group we feel loyalty to in those situations is usually a specific subset of people that is relevant to our own specific situation and our own setting.

Feeling loyalty to a more generic group name like White or Black or Hispanic — that actually reflects clusters of groups rather than a simple and clear set of people with an actual shared culture and a specific value set — can be confusing and functionally hard to do.

Being loyal to a collective group culture and expecting other people to also be loyal to that same culture using those broad skin color-based or ethnicity-linked labels, is impossible.

The actual cultures that do exist in those categories are actually setting specific cultures, and the basic cultures in each setting that exist underneath those labels are very group specific.

Those cultural categories aren't universal by ethnicity, by skin color, or by race as a label for an actual existing culture.

Each culture for each group is situationally and circumstantially invented in the specific context that the people who invent the culture live in.

The Black Culture of Kampala Is Not the Black Culture of Watts

Each culture has its own specific legacy elements that reflect its historic roots, and each culture modifies its behaviors and expectations to respond to the environment and setting each culture is in.

It is a very complex set of circumstances and realities. We all want it to be simple — and we all want to know which culture we are part of — but that is often not an easy thing to do.

At a very core level, group cultures are situational and group cultures change. Using generic labels for clusters of cultures can be confusing at multiple levels. Feeling loyalty to a generic label can be difficult at best and dysfunctional at worst.

The Black culture of Chicago — to the extent that all of Chicago could be perceived to have one Black culture — clearly is very different than the Black culture of Havana, Cuba or the black culture of Kampala.

Even in Kampala, that specific label is useless, because the Black cultures that exist in that city vary significantly by the 40 clearly different ethnicities that comprise that very diverse country.

Each cultural group in Uganda takes great pride in the specific and unique aspects of their own group culture. Blending does not happen. There actually is no "Black" culture even for Kampala or for Uganda as an overall group of people.

Likewise, the White culture of London is significantly different than the White culture of San Francisco and the White culture of Mobile, Alabama. Those labels feel right in some settings to some people who use them in those settings, but they are not helpful in identifying a set of either consistent behaviors or specific beliefs for the people in those groups between and across those kinds of settings.

When we call for loyalty to our culture, and when we use those kinds of labels to call for group loyalty, it can be useful to understand exactly which specific cultures and what specific sets of expected behaviors we mean when we use those sets of generic labels for our culture.

As we look at intergroup issues in each setting, it is most useful to get a sense in each setting of which groups are relevant to each setting and to get a sense of what are the shared identity functions and the shared beliefs and realities for each relevant group in that setting.

When there are overarching reasons for groups in various settings to act in alignment with one another in response to common threats, common enemies, common beliefs, or common opportunities, those factors can be used to create alignment and collaboration in the context of those issues.

Our Instincts Defend Our Us – Our Cultures Define Our Us

Our cultures in each setting and for each group are tools that exist because they have generally served us well as a group in each setting.

We should honor the people who built the culture we are in. We should respect the values that our cultures have embedded in them.

But we also need to know that our cultures are not worth dying for as an act of pure instinctive cultural loyalty. Intense loyalty to a culture can ruin lives of people in defense of a functional behavioral artifact that was situationally invented, and that has no inherent value on its own.

All cultures are just inventions. We should not give our lives to protect those inventions. We also should re-invent our cultures in any setting when that re-invention more effectively meets the current and actual needs of our group.

We need our cultures to serve our groups. We do not want our groups to serve our cultures.

That does not mean that we should damage, disregard, or even randomly change our local group culture or our own primal group "Us"-linked cultures or identities. Cultures can be very good things. We can and should celebrate and enjoy our cultures.

The key to remember is — we invented them. They did not invent us.

We should enjoy the creativity that turned our basic package of instincts into shared rule sets used by the people whose culture we share.

We Should Celebrate the Diversity of Our Cultures

We should also celebrate and enjoy the great diversity of cultures that exist. We should learn to appreciate the great and positive impact that various cultures can have on each other when cultures interact with each other in Peaceful ways.

In the United States, our music, food, apparel, art, and thought processes are all obviously much better and richer because we are so multi-cultural in our learning and in our communities, and because we are open and flexible in our willingness to benefit from the best features of other cultures.

The blending of our cultures in a wide range of American settings has given us great diversity in our food, our clothing, our art, and our music.

Some countries have absolute rigidity and uniformity on almost every cultural point. People in some settings wear only very basic uniforms that are approved by the culture. People in some settings are only allowed to experience the art, music, and food of their own local cultures.

We are blessed with the ability in our country to share a wide range of cultural inventions and functions. Our cultural diversity makes life in this country more interesting, and the fruits of that diversity have improved life in multiple ways for all of us.

That is a very good thing. We should appreciate the value of our extensive American intercultural experience.

In each community, organization, work place, school, or group setting, we should celebrate our diversity of cultures and we should simultaneously agree to embed in each culture some key and enlightened beliefs about who we are and how we should interact with one another.

We need to use our cultures as tools for enlightened behaviors — not have our cultures push us into unenlightened behaviors and beliefs.

We should take control over our destiny by using our cultures to help us succeed.

The next chapter of this book explains how that can be done.

CHAPTER SIX

We Can Build and Shape Our Cultures to Meet Our Needs

WE CAN MAKE choices about how to use our cultures as tools to achieve our goals and to make our most enlightened beliefs and behaviors a functional reality.

Understanding that we actually invent and create our cultures gives us significant power over our cultures.

Understanding that we each invent our cultures can also allow us to interact more effectively with other cultures in more inclusive, accepting, and creative ways.

When we understand that each and every culture is invented, then we can utilize our cultures as tools and not perceive them to be either definitional, definitive, or determinative of who we are and what we do.

Understanding the role and purpose of cultures gives us the ability to modify and enhance our own cultures through a set of very intentional and strategic interactions with our cultures, without feeling disloyal or feeling traitorous to our own basic group's culture for changing the culture to make it better.

Leaders in all settings have the ability to steer, use, and modify their group's culture. Culture change can be difficult. But once people in any setting move to a different cultural expectation on key points, the new expectation in the culture on those specific points tends to be internalized in each person and the old expectation on a given issue is not only replaced — it is often even forgotten by the people who used to use that old expectation as a guide.

In the case of organizations, educational institutions, and various work settings, cultures can be designed, implemented, protected, and perpetuated by the people who lead them.

As noted earlier in this book, the very best business leaders often create, define, and use the cultures of their businesses as tools to make their businesses more successful.

Community leaders can also make changes in the cultures of the communities they serve that create better outcomes and better behaviors for their communities.

Our cultures in all of those settings are not locked into rigid manifestations that need to stay in place in their most rigid and inflexible forms. We can change our culture in every setting.

We need to use that ability in very intentional and strategic ways to have our cultures serve our beliefs. We need to use the right set of culture change tools to make our cultures better than they would have been without being changed.

Seven Steps for Improving a Culture

As we build a culture of Peace for America, we need to embed the right set of values and the right set of beliefs in that overall culture of Peace.

We also need to make enlightened decisions relative to some key choices about our cultural beliefs in each group and setting. We need to steer and embed those better beliefs into enlightened cultural expectations and positive collective behaviors in each group and setting that we are in.

Sun Tzu wrote about the five key elements that are needed to create the culture of an army. Similarly, there are seven key steps that can be used to create or shape a culture for any given organization or setting. Those same seven approaches can be used to help put a culture of any kind in place in any setting and they can be used to modify pieces of a culture that is already in place.

The final chapter of this book discusses the specific sets of values that we should all agree on that can function as the shared set of values that can help us all become an American Us.

This chapter is more structural, identifying several things we can functionally do to help change cultures or to put cultures in place in each setting that can do what we need or want the culture to do in each setting.

Those seven steps can help business leaders create better functioning businesses. They can help education leaders create better organizations for making education a more successful process.

They can help community leaders build community cultures that better meet the needs of the community.

1. Use a Clear Cultural Identity — a Name That Says Who Is Included in the Culture

A first step in the process of building or modifying a culture in any setting is to identify exactly who the culture relates to. That step involves either figuring out who we want the culture to apply to or — if the culture does not have a current name, then giving or assigning the culture relevant group in each setting a group identity and a group name.

Cultures apply to specific groups. They are not freestanding and intellectually autonomous belief systems. To build or modify a culture, we need to identify the group that the culture will apply to.

Group identity is key to our thought process for cultures. Naming the group might seem like a simple or excessively theoretical thing to do, but it is generally a useful and important part of that culture development process. We need to name and identify the group that is relevant to the culture we are building so that people in any setting know who the group culture actually affects.

That group name clearly helps people know if they are or are not members of the culture relevant group.

There is flexibility in the naming process. We can use an existing name for our group or we can create a new name for a new group. Ideally, people should feel good and positive about the name used for the group.

The group identity might say "We New Yorkers." Or it might say "We school teachers," or it could say — "We IBM employees."

Follow-up statements about the culture then might say — "We IBM employees always put the customer first," or "We IBM employees celebrate innovation."

Those kinds of statements about the beliefs of the "we" group for each culture are more effective when they identify the exact relevant group. Naming the group makes the group a tool that can trigger a sense of "Us." The group name indicates and implies the existence of both a value package and an expected behavior set for that particular identified group.

So that is a good place to start the culture enhancement process in any setting. A clear and functional label for the group can be invaluable to tee up the "Us" statements and the "We" statements for group members. "We do things in this way" statements about a culture need a defined "we" sitting at the core of that statement.

In work settings or communities, that group name can be a very specific label for a particular set of people.

As we build an overarching culture of Peace for America, we need to name the group that the culture guides and defines so we all know who the culture and beliefs apply to.

That group for our country is the Americans who became and are an "Us" based on the shared beliefs of the group.

We need to align as a values-driven "American Us" in order to have a functioning us that can be an umbrella over all of the diverse sets of "Us" groups that comprise the rich fabric of America.

2. Delineate the Culture

The second major step in the basic culture creation or culture improvement process in any setting is to identify and clearly delineate the specific key elements of the culture that we want to create, or change, or reinforce for that particular set of people.

To anchor the work of culture enhancement, we first need to know at a functional level very clearly exactly what we want that particular culture to do.

As part of the process, we need to delineate both the core beliefs that we want included in the culture and we need to define the desired behaviors that we want embedded in the culture as tools to guide people in the culture into the future.

That should not be a random process. For maximum success levels, that culture element delineation process should be deliberate, intentional, and highly strategic.

We need clarity on those cultural belief points that we use to build the culture for each setting, because those points define what we want the culture to do and they define how we want the culture to do what it does.

We need to know what behavioral guidance points we want to include in the culture and we need to do that work by understanding the context of other key points that are in place for that culture.

It is much easier to teach a culture and it is much easier to enforce and reinforce a culture when we have both specificity and clarity about the key pieces and elements of the culture.

Generically positive and vague goals about good behavior of some kind are generally not going to create the most effective culture change results in any setting. So identifying a core set of clear and functional goals for the culture is a very important and extremely useful first step.

Honesty, for example, can be chosen by the leaders of a culture to be a core value. Sharing can be a core value. Creating beauty or living in beauty can be a core value.

Continuously improving can be a core value.

The core values explain why things are done in that setting. "We are an honest people here, so we do honest things" is a "why" statement that includes a cultural belief.

"We are a hardworking people, so we work hard here," is another direct "why" statement.

"We respect one another, so sexual harassment is not allowed here," is another example of a culturally expected behavior linked to a reason explaining why we expect that specific behavior. Core values anchor that process of identifying the reasons for our behavioral expectations.

The core values of each culture are the key to actually achieving each culture in the real world.

If you are creating a culture, you need to think through the values you decide to use for that culture very carefully. If you are modifying a culture in any setting, you need to think through the core values you will want to use and also take a clear look at the current values that exist now in that culture on that specific issue.

It is often harder to replace values in an existing culture than it is to embed values into a new culture. The paradigm section of this book describes how to substitute new values for existing values in an existing paradigm. It can be done — but it takes very explicit communication about the new values and it takes a clear change in the old values.

In some areas of behavior change — for best impact — it might be necessary to make the old value and behavior illegal. A culture that has an unfortunate and negative history of allowing sexual harassment, for example, might need to make sexual harassment illegal in order to remove it as an allowed future behavior in that setting.

Once the basic and core set of goals and key values for the relevant culture is established, the implementation process can then use the steps listed below to make that culture real and to use it as a functional tool.

3. Create Expectations and Rules

Step three in putting the cultural development tool kit in place in any setting is generally to create both rules and clear expectations for the culture. Rules are very useful in many regards. Cultures tend to be rules based. Rules structure cultures.

Rules in a culture tell people in that culture what they should do and what they ought to do. Rules also explain to everyone what the people in a culture should not do.

The expectations of each culture need to clearly explain what we expect people in that culture to do and what we expect people in that culture not to do.

Values and goals for the culture need to be functionally embedded in both the rules and in the expectations. So identifying specific and explicit things that we want people in the culture to do is an important part of the culture-building and implementation process, and identifying things we do not want people to do is an equally important part of that process.

Creating rules that enforce those behaviors can be a key tool to use for many of the expected and forbidden behaviors.

Creating rules that clearly steer people to desirable behaviors and that steer people away from non-desirable behaviors is a key step in that process.

4. Clearly Communicate the "Shoulds" and "Should Nots"

Communication to people in the culture is a key part of the tool kit that needs to be used to change a culture to put a culture in place and make it a success.

People in a setting need clear communication about the culture in order to understand what the culture cherishes, honors, and values and to understand what the culture expects people to do and expects people not to do.

The likelihood of success for any culture change in any setting drops significantly if communication about those sets of issues is weak, unclear, and ineffective.

A key step in the cultural relevant process is to communicate very clearly the "shoulds" and the "oughts" of the culture and to communicate them directly, clearly, and often to the people in the culture.

People need to know what should be done as a part of each culture. People also need to know what should not be done.

That knowledge will not exist and that guidance will not influence behavior in a setting unless it is explicitly communicated.

A set of should and ought expectations can evolve for a group in any setting on its own and when that happens, sets of expectations simply emerges on its own power, in any setting, tend to be communicated informally and organically from person to person in the group.

Organic, informal, and sporadic communication of expectations is generally not an effective way to make a culture a success. A better way to create success is to have the expectation development process and the communication process both done strategically and functionally.

Functionally and systematically sharing key information about key aspects of any targeted culture is more dependable as a communication tool than hoping that the new behavior rules and expectations that are created will somehow be informally communicated to all of the relevant people.

5. Enforce the Culture

Step five in installing a culture or a culture change and making it real is enforcement of the culture. Rules need to be created for each of the key things we want people to do and for each of the key things we do not want people to do.

Those rules will only be effective and they will only have impact if they are actually enforced — by regulations, vote, law, or by collective influence.

Enforcement of the rules that relate to personal safety, property protection, harassment, or personal freedom is extremely important. Rules that protect people that are actually functionally enforced in the context of any culture very much become part of the belief system and the behavior patterns in any setting.

People tend to very efficiently and consistently internalize the rules that are actually enforced. Rules that are not enforced in any culture tend to be ignored and those unenforced rules do not become core parts of the culture or of peoples' individual belief systems.

In some settings, when rules are outlined and described, and then either ignored by the leaders of the group or violated by key members of the group, the rules that are communicated but not enforced can create both cynicism and dysfunction.

In societal cultures, a frequently used enforcement mechanism that can have significant impact on steering behavior in a group can be peer pressure — with other people in the culture expressing disapproval for specific behaviors that violate the culture. Disapproval by other people in that setting for behaviors can be a Peaceful and very effective enforcement mechanism for some critical expectations.

Actual penalties that are imposed on people for non-compliance can be very effective as a change factor — so first writing and then enforcing laws that enforce cultural expectations can give a culture the highest likelihood of success.

In a work setting, firing non-compliant workers who violate various kinds of harassment prevention rules can help cultural enforcement of those rules. In a community setting, putting people in jail or fining people for non-compliance with rules that protect other people can create new expectations in that community about the need for those particular behaviors to be followed.

6. Reinforce the Culture

Step six in the culture change roll out and the on-going operational functional agenda for cultures is reinforcement.

The leaders in each organizational setting need to reinforce the expectations, the values, and the rules of each culture by repeating them effectively and sufficiently, and by reminding people at all relevant times what the rules and the values are.

Constant reminders can be very effective to help people in that setting internalize the rules and the values.

Once the rules for any setting have been internalized by people in the culture, they do tend to reinforce themselves. People in any given culture instinctively and voluntarily tend to impose the embedded rules of each culture on other members of the culture.

That only happens when the reinforcement process embeds the rules in peoples' belief systems and values — and that takes both education and reinforcement.

7. Celebrate the Culture

The seventh step in putting a successful culture or culture change in place is to celebrate success in using the culture.

Celebration can involve formal and public recognition of people in the culture who succeed in ways that are important to the success of the culture.

Awards and public recognition can be very useful celebration tools. Rewards also can work. Promotions of people for compliance send a very powerful message about the values of the values of the culture.

Awarding key titles to people who exemplify compliance can be useful to communicate success as well.

Both icons and heroes can be good tools to use to exemplify, demonstrate, and celebrate the success of the culture. It can be very reinforcing to celebrate the heroes of the culture and to set up both hero stories and iconic teaching opportunities in various ways about cultural successes.

Heroes become models of cultural expectations and culture-linked behaviors in each culture that identifies heroes. The people leading any culture often benefit when they celebrate their heroes because that celebration of the heroes tells other people exactly what is valued, what is respected, what is expected, and what specific and explicit behaviors exemplify the culture.

Icons can be very useful as well. A particularly positive and useful way of achieving impact for tool seven is to create iconic stories about the culture. The leaders of each culture need to create, tell, and retell key stories with both persistency and consistency about the events or behaviors that help people understand what the culture is about and what the culture involves.

Stories are highly effective as teaching tools. Iconic stories help to define a culture. Telling and retelling the culture-reinforcement stories repeatedly gives them impact and credibility.

When a culture is clearly defined, communicated, enforced, and reinforced, the chance of successful use of that culture is significantly enhanced.

Cultures change very slowly and they do not change strategically when they change of their own accord. Strategic change approaches can be extremely useful to speed up the change process significantly.

Those basic culture-building and culture-enhancing tools work for a wide range of cultures.

Those basic steps can be used at a macro level to help create a Culture of Peace for America. We need to define what we want to achieve collectively with a culture of Peace for America, and we need to support that culture with expectations, rules, values, and behavior guidelines.

We need hero stories about Peace and we need an array of our iconic stories to help us understand what Peace behaviors we should celebrate and emulate.

We need to use that tool kit intentionally and well to build our culture of Peace. Chapter Ten explains how we can do exactly that.

All Groups Are Guided by Cultures

Cultures can be extremely useful in all group settings. Business cultures can be combined with business strategies to create behavior patterns that meet the functional needs of any given business. Community cultures set community expectations and values in ways that can help communities succeed as places to live and thrive.

School cultures help define the students in the school to each other as an us and can give guidance for the behaviors that are expected of the students in the school settings.

Cultures in each setting can be invented, evolve, and emerge on their own, or they can be created by someone as a tool for that setting. The more effective leaders design and reinforce their group cultures rather than having them emerge serendipitously and even haphazardly from the setting, itself.

We Need to Embed Some Key Values in the Culture of Our Country

We now need to do that same work for the entire country — setting up a culture of Peace very deliberately and collectively, and supporting it strategically — as described in Chapter Ten of this book.

We need clarity about our belief systems as Americans, identifying the key values we share — like democracy, freedom of religion, and economic inclusion — and we need to explicitly outline and describe those values and agree to share them with each other as the foundation for defining ourselves as the American "Us."

We need to embed those shared values in our overall national culture and in each of our various relevant subgroup structures.

As noted earlier, cultures, once they are well established, reinforce themselves. People in each culture tell other people in that culture what to do in synchrony with the values and with the expected behaviors of the culture.

So when we say we need a culture of Peace in America and when we say we need to link that culture to a broad and clearly defined definition of "Us," then we need to look at those tools to see which ones will work best to meet our needs.

We need to put in place a belief system for our new culture that says we are inclusive, and supportive, and that we want to see all members of our society able to achieve the American Dream.

We need a culture that believes we should have equal rights for everyone, regardless of gender or race or ethnicity. We really do want everyone to be part of the collective future of the American people.

Sun Tzu Described the Moral Influence

In *The Art of War*, Sun Tzu wrote that the culture and the belief system of an army was a key factor that would determine whether an army would be successful or whether the army would fail. He wrote that the very basic and most fundamental factor to consider relative to the likelihood of an army succeeding in a war was what he called — "moral influence."

Setting "moral influence" as a primary, foundational, and fundamental factor for winning a war doesn't seem entirely in keeping with the spirit and ethics of war until you read further and discover that what Sun Tzu primarily meant by moral influence was whether or not the soldiers in any given army would respect the personal qualities of their general and would follow the general's lead.

To be effective, Sun Tzu said, the people in an army must respect "the general's qualities of wisdom, sincerity, humanity, courage, and strictness."

He further wrote that the general, in order to succeed, must be organized, focused, and in conscious control of the operational functioning of the army — including putting in place the right hierarchy of officers to actually lead the ground operations of the troops.

Sun Tzu basically said that he could predict victory, in very large part, based on whether the officers and the general officers, "administer rewards and punishments in a more enlightened manner," to their troops.

He actually preached "enlightened" behaviors — but only for the people in his designated us — his soldiers and their leaders.

Sun Tzu urged the heads of countries, in selecting their generals, "to appraise with the utmost care" which generals possess moral influence, "as well as which commander is the most able" in a number of areas — and he said that the people choosing a general should determine which commander has an army "in which regulations and instructions are better carried out."

So *The Art of War* places moral influence, enlightened behaviors, group functioning, group structure, and the culture and the hierarchy of the army very high on the list of criteria that is functionally necessary for actual military success in times of war.

Peace Can Be the Moral Focus

We also need moral influence, enlightened behaviors, group functioning, group structure, leadership ethics, and the culture of our society to be anchors for creating Peace in this country.

The core of *The Art of InterGroup Peace* strategy is also built around the need for moral influence. We need people to collectively create a sense of moral direction and moral influence for America.

To get people aligned — and to succeed in overcoming historic stress points and long standing negative interactions between groups of people — it is essential to get the people in all relevant groups to share a sense of collective "moral influence" — believing collectively that the process and the people engaged in the process for all groups will do the right things and will do them for the right reasons.

We need to communicate both the basic values of Peace and the basic characteristics of our leaders as people who can guide us to Peace and help us sustain Peace — not go to war — when Peace is jeopardized or threatened in any real way.

We obviously need leaders with moral influence for us to succeed in Peace even more than Sun Tzu needed those qualities to succeed in War.

We Need to Understand Why So Many Countries Are Failing at Peace

One of the most important things we can do to achieve Peace in our own country is to understand why so many other countries are facing major challenges relative to either creating or sustaining Peace in their own settings.

Again, as Sun Tzu points out in *The Art of War*, knowledge is power. Observing what has succeeded or failed for other multi-ethnic countries can provide great strategic insight for us as we deal with our growing diversity here.

We need to have a sense of what is happening in other multi-ethnic countries. We need to look at what those countries are doing badly and we need to understand what they are doing well.

That topic is the focus of the next chapter of this book.

CHAPTER SEVEN

Learning About Peace and Conflict from Other Multi-Ethnic Countries

THE US/THEM INSTINCT packages that have shaped so much of the history of our country can be seen in painful clarity in every other multi-ethnic and multi-tribal country in the world.

We are not alone as a country in facing significant levels of intergroup issues — driven by instinctive behaviors, emotions, and values.

In a very large number of other settings, a significant number of countries are actually facing larger, more dangerous, and much more immediate instinct anchored intergroup problems then the ones we are facing here.

As we create our own Art of InterGgroup Peace strategies to help us build and maintain a culture of Peace in America, it is useful to get a sense of the kinds of intergroup conflicts that are creating problems relative to intergroup Peace in other parts of the world.

Intergroup problems, intergroup stress points, and open conflicts between groups are the defining factors for hundreds of settings in the world today. Conflict is widespread and conflict is growing.

Most wars in recent centuries have been between nations. Armed nation states have done battle with other armed nation states.

That is not the pattern we are seeing for the vast majority of the conflicts that are springing up in the world today.

The battles that are happening in the world today are not between nations. The battles are actually wars inside nations.

A large number of countries in the world are literally currently at war with themselves. Civil wars are happening in many settings. Very basic us/them instinct-based intergroup conflicts are happening in a significant number of settings and those wars are almost all battles between tribes of people fighting each other inside the borders of their countries.

The number and scale of those intergroup conflicts has been actually increasing for the last couple of decades.

In some of those settings where people inside countries are at war today with other people in their own country, the internal intergroup conflict that exists now has been going on for centuries.

The basic intergroup issues in settings like Barcelona, Belfast, and Belgium all extend back for centuries — with local ethnic groups seeking autonomy in each setting and with the national government in each setting opposed to any division or reduction of their overarching national turf. Those intergroup divisions in those settings with aspiring separatist groups have been going on for a very long time and those divisions continue to both simmer and burn today.

Those issues are just the tip of the inter-ethnic iceberg.

The ending of colonialism and the collapse of the Soviet Union created more than 100 new multi-ethnic countries that are now self-governing and freed from colonial or Soviet rule. Each of those multi-ethnic countries has its own levels of internal conflict — with some raging at the level of open civil war. Syria, Iraq, and Sri Lanka all fit that pattern.

Those intergroup conflicts tend to go back far into the history of the conflicted groups in each setting.

Former colonies and former satellites who now function as independent nations are almost all experiencing very clear levels of pure instinct-triggered local intergroup issues and conflicts.

For the former colonies and the former satellites, old intertribal conflicts that have existed for centuries in multiple settings have been allowed to emerge after long periods of colonial suppression.

Immigration Is Creating New InterGroup Problems in Multiple Settings

For a growing number of other countries that are not former captives or former satellites and that do not have historic separatist movements, there are additional major and entirely new levels of internal intergroup conflicts. The new levels of local conflict are the direct result of growing levels of recent immigration into those countries.

Countries that had been ethnically pure for centuries are now finding themselves with large numbers of refugees and immigrants who are from very different ethnic groups than the original inhabitants of those areas.

Those major new levels of multi-ethnic immigration are creating unexpected diversity issues and some very real and clearly instinctive intergroup backlashes in many of those increasingly diverse countries.

The combination of all of those factors — separatism, tribal conflicts, and ethnically linked immigration — has created a world at war — with countries everywhere literally at war with themselves. Our basic and universal packages of Us/Them instincts are creating intergroup stress, tension, and internal conflict in a wide range of settings. Those instinct-triggered conflicts in most settings are growing rather than stabilizing or being resolved in any effective way.

The us/them instinctive behaviors that have been activated in too many of the intertribal settings include acts of brutality, group executions, murder, rape and various levels of intentionally evil ethnic purging and ethnic cleansing. The basic intergroup instinct activation in multiple settings is creating groups of people inside countries who hate other groups of people in those countries and who do damage to other people in those countries in multiple ways.

Former Colonies and Satellites Both Have Ethnic Conflict Problems

The newly independent nations tend to be particularly active hot spots for interethnic conflicts.

In a number of the troubled countries, significant levels of conflict are happening now because the countries, themselves, are former colonies that had significant levels of internal inter-ethnic diversity, as colonies, that wasn't well handled or even officially recognized in the processes that were used to create both independent status as nations and future national governance models for those countries.

Colonial power has ebbed, faded, and disappeared in a number of African, Asian, and Middle Eastern countries. Dozens of former colonies have become separate and independent nations. Most of those newly independent countries are multi-tribal and have extensive internal levels of intergroup conflict with other groups in each setting that reach back into history to the formation of each tribe.

Those groups of people in the former colonies have multiple inter-tribal conflicts — and the very worst of them resulted in major loss of life.

More than 1 million people were killed as the tribes of India split into India and Pakistan and another million people were killed as the tribes of Pakistan split into Pakistan and Bangladesh.

Other settings that were multi-tribal have killed fewer people — but the total set of lives lost will soon exceed the lives lost in India and Bangladesh.

At roughly the same time that the colonies were freed, the dissolution of the old Soviet Union and the ending of that functional Russian-governed Empire has created a similar set of newly independent multi-ethnic countries around the periphery of Russia.

The old satellite countries and the former colonies have all achieved freedom and autonomy as nations and they each now need to figure out how to deal with their internal ethnic diversity.

In almost all cases, that new freedom for each nation has been accompanied by significant levels of internal interethnic and interracial conflict — to the point of civil war in multiple settings.

The internal ethnic conflict in those settings exists to a very large degree because each of the former colonies had functionally circumstantial and historically nonsensical external boundaries as colonies that became the official borders of the new nations — and those nation-state borders often made very little no ethnic or racial sense for the people who lived in those areas.

Those old colonial boundaries and turf ownership legacy situations that did not reflect historic ethnic or tribal realities became the new national boundaries for each new nation created by the end of colonialism.

For the former Soviet Union satellites who were freed, the current national boundaries tend to make more historical sense. But there are a number of small, multi-ethnic nations who were freed by the Russians whose long-standing internal interethnic animosities had been kept under control for long periods of time by significant levels of Soviet policing and Russian military power.

In each of those situations for each of those new countries, that external suppression of local internal ethnic conflict by the external powers is now gone.

People from Warring Ethnic Groups Have to Co-Exist as Nations

People from a variety of groups are now forced to interact with each other as separate tribes or as separate ethnic groups within each of those newly independent countries. Those separate ethnic groups in each of those new nation-states are now finding themselves in a constant state of intergroup stress, open conflict and — in too many cases — active and bloody civil war.

Syria, Sri Lanka, Iraq, Nigeria, and The Congo all have internal ethnic groups who hate other internal ethnic groups and who would rather be nations flying their own group's flag and having control over their own group's turf.

Various groups in various settings want various levels of autonomy — and those aspirations tend to be resisted or crushed — both by whoever is the local tribe in power and by a strong desire by the international community to keep all current boundaries of all nations intact.

International Law Obsessively Protects Current Borders

International law has an almost obsessive compulsion to protect current nation state boundaries. That obsession is fueled in part by our basic turf instincts that tend to make protection of current boundaries feel "right."

That obsession by other nations to keep all of the nation state boundaries intact is driven even more strongly by the fact that most nations in the world have their own internal separatist movements to some degree. So the people who run those existing countries with internal separatist aspirations very much do not want to see the precedent set anywhere of allowing ethnic separatists in any country to achieve separation as a goal.

In most cases, the central government that runs the new nations today is dominated by one of the local ethnic groups — and that group and that government tend to have their own intergroup turf instincts fully activated. The leaders of those dominant local groups resist any attempts by other local tribal groups — like the Kurds — to achieve any level of autonomy.

Those people who are currently in power in each setting tend to want the current borders to survive exactly as they exist today. Turf instincts are fully activated for both sets of people in those countries. Those turf-activated central governments in those former colonies tend to be opposed to local autonomy of any kind.

Soviet Empire Collapse Created Nations

The collapse of the Soviet Union freed two sets of countries. One set of freed countries was the former satellites — Poland, Czechoslovakia, Yugoslavia, etc. Those countries had been conquered by ideology — with communist parties in each country granting power to the Soviets as communist leaders.

Each of those countries was returned to pre-communist freedom levels.

The other set of freed countries were much smaller former captive countries that had been under Soviet and Russian domination. Each of those freed countries also had their own tribal history and their own local ethnic concentrations.

The former satellites now run their own nations. Poland and Hungary are self-governing. Czechoslovakia and Yugoslavia split into ethnic pieces that reflect their own internal ethnic alignments. Each is self-governing. Yugoslavia is now six self-governing tribal countries — and they are not at war with one another or with themselves.

That process of splitting those countries into their historic tribal pieces made ethnic sense — but even that process was not welcomed by other countries in the world.

The situation is more complicated in some of the former captive countries. Each of those former captives has its own primary ethnic group and their own ethnic language. The primary ethnic group in each setting dumped Russian as their language of government and made their own historic language the official language of each country as soon as they were freed from Russia rule.

In those countries, the formerly suppressed ethnic groups have tended to take collective revenge at some level on the local ethnic Russians who still live there. They also have tended to get control over any other local minority groups who happen to live in the national geography of those newly independent nations.

The new local majority group in each former captive country has tended to do negative things to groups they perceive to be "Them." Ethnic cleansing has been a common practice for those former captives.

They have expelled people who spoke Russian or who had Turkish ancestors from several of those countries.

In the Ukraine, the Russians have made attempts to regain control over the Russian speaking portions of that country. The local separatist movements have unified to help those Russian speaking sections of that country leave the domination of the group speaking the other language.

Russia, itself, is both a country and the lead nation in a new Russian confederation.

The new Russian confederation is made up of almost 100 ethnic groups who have each been granted some local autonomy in the context of the confederation model.

Some of the Russian confederation members — like Chechnya — have their own strong separatist movements — and people that are killing people in Chechnya in the interest of separation.

Russia faces the very challenging situation of encouraging the Ukrainian separatist movement while suppressing the Chechnyan separatists.

Countries Are at War with Themselves

The combined impact of all of those issues for all of the new countries that used to be satellites, captives, or colonies combined with significant historical ethnic conflicts that are still happening in the old multi-ethnic countries with separatist movements means that there are multiple levels and arrays of intergroup conflicts happening today in a large number of countries.

In addition to those problems, significant levels of new immigration volumes have triggered their own set of intergroup instinctive behaviors in a number of settings who used to be ethnically pure.

In total, there are more than 200 of those intergroup conflicts happening in various sites today, and the number of intergroup conflict settings is growing, rather than shrinking.

All three categories of intergroup conflict are creating major and growing problems today.

The history of those long-standing multi-ethnic countries tends to be a long legacy of serious and almost perpetual internal intergroup stress and conflict. The problems that exist between groups of people in those multi-ethnic countries are well known and they have been obvious for years.

The issues that exist for the Basque separatist in Spain and for the Irish separatists in Belfast have been known and visible to the world for a very long time.

Separatist Groups Exist in Many Settings

Separatist movements exist today in many settings across the planet as a result of those two sets of intergroup realities. In a number of countries, the separatist groups that exist are clearly defined local ethnic groups who have their own language, their own culture, and their own group identity.

Those groups have not wanted to be dominated by the larger local ethnic group or assimilated into the language or the culture of whatever ethnic group is the majority group in each setting.

Spain, Great Britain, Russia, Mexico, China, Turkey, Afghanistan, Somalia, Sri Lanka, Nigeria, and dozens of other countries all have very distinct ethnic and racial groups within their boundaries that each want to become independent and self-governing nations.

The separatist groups in each of those countries very much want to determine their own group's future through their own group's version of ethnic self-governance. Those groups who want to be separate each have their own very clear group identity. They each have their own group turf instincts fully activated.

Those separatist groups very often either want to become their own independent and self-governing countries or they want to somehow become at least semi-autonomous sections within the larger multi-ethnic countries.

Many of the Catalans of Barcelona, for example, want to stop being simply an internal portion of Spain. They want local autonomy for Barcelona.

The national Spanish government has its own turf instincts fully activated, however, and the people who run the national Spanish government have no interest in allowing the Catalans to form their own country, and remove what the Spanish leaders believe to be part of Spain from Spain.

So there is a lot of anger on that issue from both the leaders of Spain and many of the Catalan leaders and people. Those issues will never entirely disappear for that country as long as the people from that group believe that their group deserves to govern itself.

Melding into the Spanish majority group will not happen.

Similar situations exist for the Basque of Spain, the Sami of Northern Norway, and the Welsh and Scottish peoples who are currently locked into the United Kingdom as subsidiary pieces of that larger nation.

Colonial Armies Overpowered Local Instincts

The instinctive need that is very clearly felt by whoever runs the central government in each of those countries to keep their entire country intact at all costs is matched only by the equally strong instinctive need of the separatist groups in each setting to separate.

The functional reality in each setting is that the central government and dominant ethnic group has the army and runs the police — so the central government's package of instincts and goals tends to prevail in each of those divided settings.

In some countries like Pakistan, Indonesia, and Sri Lanka where the local tribal groups actually have their own significant military forces, the central government has significantly less power. Those countries tend to function more in a state of truce than a state of union.

But even those clearly problematic countries tend to follow the overall tendency of keeping any national boundary intact once it has been established as a national boundary.

As a result — conflict is happening in many places. All of those multi-ethnic, multi-tribal countries are now trying to figure out how to deal with their internal intergroup issues.

It is clear that various levels of inter-ethnic problems exist and function at a highly instinctive level on what is almost a permanent status in some of the very old multi-ethnic countries.

If local autonomy of some kind doesn't happen, the Tamil Tigers and the Basque bombers will continue their quest and will resurrect their opposition to the majority group in their countries after each defeat and setback.

Immigration Is Adding a New Ethnic Conflict Set of Crisis

Those old battles each have their ancient trajectories and their highly predictable futures.

What is new today, however, in several parts of the world is the fact that immigration is creating entirely new levels of local intergroup conflict.

A large number of countries in several parts of the world that had actually been internally conflict free for centuries because of their long-standing internal local ethnic homogeneity and even a degree of local ethnic purity, are now facing internal ethnic conflict.

Some of those formerly ethnically pure countries are now becoming much more diverse. That is happening in large part because of new internal ethnic conflict realities that exist today in all of those former colonies and satellites that have displaced over 50 million people.

Those displaced people are immigrating to other countries. Entirely new sets of instinct-driven intergroup problems are happening between groups of people in the increasingly diverse settings where the displaced immigrants are now choosing to live.

Some countries that traditionally have had almost no ethnic diversity and very little internal interethnic conflict for centuries are now becoming much more ethnically and racially diverse.

Sweden, Denmark, the Netherlands, Germany, and Austria all have significant immigrant populations that are triggering local intergroup stress in multiple settings in those countries.

Ethnically Pure Countries Are Becoming Diverse

That new stress and that new diversity are happening almost entirely due to new immigration realities for those countries. Many of those formerly Peaceful and formerly ethnically homogenous countries are currently seeing entirely new levels of intergroup pressure, internal stress, and intergroup conflict because their historic ethnic and racial homogeneity is rapidly disappearing.

Quite a few countries — particularly in Europe — who used to be relatively ethnically pure — now have growing minority populations.

In a number of highly ethnically focused Middle Eastern and Asian countries, as well, forced exiles of people from their homelands based on intergroup conflict is also creating growing local diversity in a large number of settings that used to be ethnically pure.

The new diversity comes from several categories of new immigrants into those formerly pure countries. In some cases, the new immigrants to countries are pursuing economic opportunity. Jobs create an economic pull that creates new levels of population diversity in some settings.

In other instances, the new immigrants are exiles — fleeing ethnic persecution and discrimination in their former homelands. The exiles in those settings tend to immigrate in ethnic and racial groups because the pressures that force them to immigrate are targeted at those people by those same ethnic or racial groups.

Millions of people now live in refugee camps — and those people almost all had tribal or ethnic pressure that caused them to be refugees.

Regardless of the trigger-issues for the immigration, the new people who move into each country become a new category of "Them" in that country and the old residents have very predictable intergroup responses to the new groups.

The packages of instinctive intergroup us/them reactions between groups of people that were described in Chapter Two and Three of this book are becoming internally highly relevant to the people in all of those increasingly diverse countries.

In most of those settings, the new immigration levels are generating and triggering significant levels of us/them instinctive reactions for all of the people in those countries — both for the immigrants and for the indigenous peoples in each setting.

Ethnic Diversity Is Creating Intergroup Conflict in Refugee Settings

The standard set of us/them reactions that are triggered by intergroup instincts are being generated both in the new immigrants and in the local populations who had been ethnically homogenous in those settings before the immigration began.

There is anger on all sides in each multi-ethnic refugee setting. The new immigrants feel they are discriminated against. The old residents feel like they have been involuntarily invaded.

The result is an expanding set of internal intergroup conflicts that is changing some of those countries in significant ways. So as we look at the rest of the world through the lens of us/them instinctive behaviors, we see new immigration creating new us/them issues in a number of settings, and we see old us/them stress points and conflicts continuing to create their traditional problems in a number of other countries.

Europe Has Been Purely Tribal for Centuries

Most of Europe has been fiercely tribal and ethnically pure at each local level for centuries. Tribal purity has defined Europe.

For many centuries, each area of Europe has been dominated and occupied by its own local European tribe.

Sweden is full of Swedes. Denmark is full of Danes. Holland has been full of people who are proudly Dutch. Local tribes have dominated local turf and created national identities in each nation based on the dominant local tribe.

Each ethnic tribe of Europe has tended to have its own turf — defined by its national borders.

The local European tribes fought each other as tribes across those borders for centuries. Much blood has been shed across those borders in what were clearly inter-tribal wars. For the past century or more, the individual people of Europe did very little cross-border intermingling between tribes. People tended to stay in their own tribal territories. People did not immigrate in any significant volume from Germany or Finland to France or Italy to live.

If any people from any European country did immigrate to any other European country, those immigrants were usually seen as a clearly identified outlier family in their new country and in their new setting for generations.

That static and relatively pure ethnic environment for all of those European countries is obviously no longer true.

Immigration Is Changing Europe

Immigration now has both lower barriers and reduced levels of enforcement in Europe. Significant levels of immigration are happening in increasing volumes in almost all European countries.

As a consequence, the old geographically focused local tribal purity that has existed for centuries has been rapidly eroding in many parts of Europe.

A number of urban areas in Europe now have very large local minority populations who are not from the original tribal group for that geography. That local diversity did not exist and wasn't even contemplated less than two decades ago.

The people from the old European tribes are still not moving very much from country to country. Germans and Danes still do not immigrate very often to Paris, or Madrid.

The new migration volume that is affecting major parts of Europe is from non-European sets of people. A whole new set of immigrants has now flooded into Europe from Africa, from the Middle East, and from Eastern Europe.

Non-Europeans and Eastern Europeans are both currently coming to Western Europe in large numbers.

Cities That Had Been Ethnically Pure Are Now Diverse

Cities that had changed very little in their ethnic composition for centuries are now changing rapidly as a result of that immigration. Multi-ethnic neighborhoods exist in many settings and the people in those settings clearly are forming their own communities anchored in their own ethnic group.

The religion of those areas is changing significantly as well. The major groups of immigrants into those cities tend to be from Muslim ethnic groups.

There now are Albanian enclaves in nearly every major city in Europe. People from Turkey hold jobs and live in Turkish enclaves in Germany and Austria. People from those countries tend to have Muslim religious alignments.

People from North Africa fill the suburbs of Paris. Some of the Parisian suburbs are now more clearly defined by their new residents than by their old residents. The most visible cultures in those neighborhoods are no longer "French" and are no longer based on the traditional French living approaches or the traditional French culture.

France has traditionally had one of the strongest commitments of any nation in the world to culture and to its language — with strict rules functionally enforcing language purity. There are now major areas within France where French is not the language of choice for the majority of local residents.

Many Immigrants in Europe Do Not Assimilate

So Europe is becoming significantly multi ethnic at an increasing rate. As one might expect and predict with any understanding of how instinctive behaviors work, that situation is creating some major activation of us/them instincts, values, and behaviors in a number of settings.

That activation of those us/them instincts in each of those settings is exacerbated by the fact that very large percentages of the new immigrants are deliberately, openly, and clearly choosing not to assimilate into the old European cultures in the countries they have entered and now call home.

Many of the new immigrants very deliberately continue to be and function very intentionally as a separate ethnic group inside their new country. They also tend to be Muslim in communities where the inhabitants have been primarily Christian for centuries.

The newest waves of immigrants in each setting tend to bring their own old culture into Europe — along with their own religion and their own history and cultural values. That set of changes is creating new challenges to what had long been a status of local ethnic and internal Peace in multiple areas of Europe for centuries.

In major parts of Europe, there are now significant us/them conflicts. Negative behaviors, and intergroup stress levels are increasing at an accelerated rate. All of the standard packages of instinctive behaviors and values that can be triggered by our Us/Them instincts are being activated today in various European settings by that immigration reality.

Paris relatively recently had intergroup riots where more than 100,000 cars were burned and destroyed. In that instance, a situation where French policemen shot and killed two minority students was followed by riots and some very targeted intergroup violence.

Two For Two — Completely Impersonal Intergroup Perceptions

The goal of the violence, some of the riot leaders said at the time, was to kill two French policemen. Two for two.

That was an example of completely depersonalized and purely numerical intergroup revenge. That specific two for two response is one kind of thinking that can stem from "Us/Them" instinct driven values — with people on each side stereotyped by people on the other side to the point where killing any two policemen felt symbolically right to the rioters — whether or not those two dead policemen had personally damaged anyone or whether those two policeman had any connection to any relevant issue or whether they personally were wonderful human beings.

The police of Paris were depersonalized by the rioters in that thought process and turned into a pure number. Two was the goal. Killing any two was the goal of the mob.

That is exactly how us/them instincts too often function. Us/Them instincts tend to depersonalize whoever is perceived to be "Them." Those depersonalizing thought patterns are clearly being activated in too many of those intergroup situations across Europe.

Lynchings have taken place in some European countries, and political parties that favor ethnic purity are gaining ground in a number of countries.

In another recent and very clear intergroup conflict occurrence in France, two brothers who were Muslim entered the building that housed a French publication and massacred a dozen people in an act of pure intergroup anger and revenge.

The intergroup tensions were high enough after that shooting that it was difficult again for French policemen to enter some Parisian neighborhoods.

The conflict levels and negative intergroup behaviors that are triggered by immigration are clearly being felt in multiple cities and settings.

The Internet Is Becoming a Tool for Inflammation

The Internet is fueling some of those conflicts in those European settings. This book dealt with some of the challenges and the opportunities presented by the Internet in Chapter Ten. Chapter Eleven deals in more detail with how we need to use the Internet as a key tool for The Art of InterGroup Peace to increase intergroup understanding and to support intergroup Peace.

Supporting Peace has not been the primary use of the Internet in the various European intergroup settings. The Internet has been used in many angry European settings to end local Peace and to exacerbate local anger and conflict.

Some of the most volatile and damaging intergroup conflicts in those countries are now conflicts that have been triggered, fed, informed, supported, exacerbated, incited, and inflamed by the Internet.

The Internet has a remarkable ability to transmit information and to do it broadly and quickly. That very powerful tool can be used for both good and evil.

The Internet's communication power can turn a very local and highly situational inter-ethnic negative incident in a single city — like a local police shooting of a minority student in one site — into a major explosion that reaches across multiple communities and even reaches across multiple countries very quickly.

That kind of Internet-accelerated intergroup conflict across multiple sites is happening in Europe now. The Internet is enabling various groups of people who want to inflame peoples' us/them instincts in Europe to do inflammatory things in multiple settings with a high level of success.

There are clearly growing numbers of people who use the Internet as a tool to create a strong, militant, and separatist sense of "Us" for various ethnic or religious minorities and majority groups in Europe.

Some of the Muslim extremist groups are among the most skilled users of the Internet to both recruit supporters and to inflame situations in local settings.

There are also some political parties who have strong anti-immigrant positions and there are activist groups that have very inflammatory anti-immigrant positions. Internet sites for all of those groups have clearly been set up very intentionally to give people a collective focus on a targeted set of us/them-linked issues.

Adding Religion to the Situation Exacerbates the Instinctive Impact

The current intergroup situation in Europe has been complicated and exacerbated immensely by the fact that religion was added fairly recently to the basic tribal and ethnic intergroup mix for many European settings. People are now very clearly divided along religious lines as well as ethnic lines in many settings.

The initial and original underlying intergroup conflicts and intergroup stress points that first existed in those European settings functionally tended to be between people from different ethnicities. The first set of intergroup instincts in those settings were all triggered initially by what were basically tribal differences.

But those tribal stress points were made significantly more challenging and more inflammatory by the fact that people from various ethnic groups who have been moving into the European communities also are people who have a very different religions affiliation than the traditional religion of Europe.

The original residents of those European countries overwhelmingly tended to be Christian or have Christian ancestors. The new residents are overwhelmingly Muslim and come from Muslim tribes and ethnic groups.

Different religions that exist for the people from each group in those settings definitely adds another very powerful and impactful layer of religion-linked us/them instincts and energies to the intergroup conflict mix.

Adding Religion to Ethnicity Adds a Higher Level of Disruptive Energy

That combination of religion and ethnicity has changed both the nature of the conflicts and the intergroup perceptions and intergroup interactions in most of those settings.

Most people in Europe now perceive the intergroup conflicts they are experiencing there today to be based on religion more than on tribe. Adding religion to tribe as a trigger for conflict and as a way of defining who is us and who is them has the power to significantly amplify the impact of other relevant us/them activators and us/them differentiations in any setting.

Most of the new ethnic and racial minority immigrants who are now moving to Europe are Muslim. Most of the old ethnic Europeans in those countries were either Christian or they were non-religious and basically secular people who had Christian ancestors.

Even though the initial Us/Them instinct activation that occurred relative to the new ethnic minorities by the old European majority groups in each setting tended to be functionally more tribal then religious on the part of the original Europeans, the negative intergroup Us/Them experiences that have happened for many of the new immigrants in many of those settings have fairly often been interpreted by those new immigrants, themselves, to be based very directly on their religion and not on their ethnicity, race, or tribe.

Some Group Leaders Have Pointed to Religion as the Trigger-Issue

All of those factors trigger high levels of intergroup instinct activation. Tribe, ethnicity, race, and religion can all activate us/them perceptions and reactions.

For the new immigrants to Europe who feel a sense of intergroup conflict, there tends to be a growing perception that the primary differentiation factor that makes life more different in their new settings is their religion and not their race or their tribe.

Several key religious leaders for the immigrants have very specifically made that claim of religious persecution. Those leaders attribute the discriminatory intergroup behaviors that have happened in various settings to religious causes and religious motivations rather than to ethnic issues or tribal differences.

When religious leaders speak to religious followers about religious issues, that communication tends to be singularly influential to the believers and the practitioners of that religion.

The Perception of Religious Conflict Can Be Self-Fulfilling

That perception can become a self-fulfilling belief, regardless of its original impact on people in a setting.

Because that perception of religious differentiation, religious conflict, and religious discrimination now exists for many people in those European settings — fed by multiple very clear Internet and group setting descriptions of the intergroup issues in those settings as being religious at their core — the conflicts in several settings now have a clearly religious context.

That set of perceptions about the role of religion in the intergroup stress points has currently caused some of the local intergroup conflicts in European settings to take on the context of a more generic Holy War, rather than just being another set of local, situational, intertribal, interracial, interethnic, instinctive intergroup negative us/them reactions.

A Holy War Is Hard to End

The negative and powerful energy levels that are being created in many settings by the growing perception that their intergroup conflicts represent some level of Holy War clearly will make achieving and sustaining local Peace in a number of European settings much more difficult.

Religion adds a very powerful additional energy level to us/them instinctive reactions.

People who perceive that their religion is being attacked tend to perceive the attackers as being evil and perceive their attackers as being explicitly sinful in a very theological way.

Religious Perceptions Are Self-Reinforcing

People everywhere instinctively defend their own group. People tend to defend their own group with even more energy if the people in any conflict situation feel and believe that they are also defending and protecting their faith.

The thought process and the set of experiences that results in seeing religion as a differentiator in those settings is, of course, functionally self-fulfilling and self-reinforcing.

Conflicts and local stress points that actually started out merely as cultural and inter-tribal issues that end up being labeled as religion-triggered behaviors by any of the people involved can actually cause everyone in that setting to look at religion as being the key differentiator in those situations.

Those types of conflicts can be both self-perpetuating and self-fulfilling. That perspective of a religious conflict actually becomes accurate in those settings because once that perception exists, it is at least partially self-fulfilling.

The parties in that conflicted setting who had not been thinking in religious terms can easily end up thinking in religious terms about the local conflict because the other party in the setting is defining the issue to be linked to their religion.

That can be a very a dangerous evolution for intergroup energies into an area where people are more likely to feel additional levels of real anger that is based on defending their faith.

People are more likely to believe that doing extreme and damaging behaviors relative to other groups of people are legitimate things to do when people believe those things are being done in the protection and the defense of their religion and their religious beliefs.

Leaders Who Call for Religious Conflict Can Have Impact

That blend of tribal and religious issues is incredibly difficult to deal with.

Those blended issues are particularly difficult to deal with if skillful leaders on either side very intentionally, deliberately, and skillfully use those multiple us/them triggers to further inflame their own group against the other group.

The Internet is an easy tool to use to inflame each group, and it is being used for those purposes constantly, today. The news media is also being used as a tool by people who are angry and who want intergroup inflammation to increase in a setting.

We need to understand this entire set of issues for all of those other countries who are going down those intergroup conflict paths as we look at implementing our own Art of InterGroup Peace strategy for America.

Leaders in Europe Need to Address the Underlying Patterns and Not Just the Incidents

Europe clearly has some very challenging days ahead in attempting to deal with those sets of issues. Solutions need to be found or the hatred levels and the destructive intergroup behaviors, in many settings, will continue to grow in dangerous and damaging ways.

The six group alignment-triggers that are identified in Chapter Nine of this book could be very helpful in several European settings. Many leaders in Europe seem to be dealing with most of those local intergroup issues purely situationally, and almost entirely reactively.

Those leaders have not been addressing those intergroup issues in the context of overall instinct-driven behavior patterns with the goal of creating a solution set for those conflicts that is based on defusing those very damaging and dysfunctional instincts for their settings.

Many leaders seem to be focused fully on the functional incidents to the point where the leaders are not dealing at any level with the basic patterns and the common packages of beliefs and behaviors that are the real problems underlying those conflicts.

Solutions to those levels of basic intergroup problems in those European countries will not come from incident-focused and circumstantial responses or strategies.

Leaders in those European countries need to accept the fact that their "good old days" will never return. Their old world of having local ethnic purity and cultural uniformity based on their own group is gone forever.

The leaders in those settings need to figure out how to turn their new diversity into an asset rather than a liability.

To make local diversity in those cities in Europe into an asset, the leaders in each setting need to reach out to acknowledge the pressure, the stress points, and the shared humanity of the new groups of people in their setting. Each setting then needs to make Peace with itself.

That will take clear intergroup trust in each setting — and that level of trust can only be achieved as an intentional strategy when it is led by leaders in each setting who understand the full sets of issues that are creating the local division.

Leaders need to each achieve their own understanding levels for those issues. Understanding their own thoughts, beliefs, and behaviors in the challenging days that loom ahead in the context of the new levels of us/them behavior patterns that the new diversity of their communities is creating, could help some European leaders understand those conflicts more clearly.

Leaders Need to Understand the Instinctive Underpinnings for the Conflict

All leaders need to know their own instinctive reactions and the instinctive reactions of their groups. A high level of personal understanding about instinctive intergroup issues could enable leaders in some settings in Europe to address those conflicts both more effectively and significantly more proactively.

Strategic approaches are needed rather than reactive and tactical approaches. Prevention is a far better strategic response than reaction. Prevention requires a sense of the actual behavior patterns involved and a strategy that affects the patterns themselves at a very basic level.

If the people of Europe see each of those flare-ups, riots, and intergroup explosions in each of those settings as situational and as locally incidental and individually relevant episodes of negative interaction rather than seeing each of those situations as a local and current piece of an overall pattern of instinctive intergroup behaviors, then the likelihood of dealing with those conflicts effectively and proactively diminishes significantly.

Likewise, when any of the people in those settings see those local issues and those local conflicts as being proof of an evil, overarching, sin-based conspiracy that is aimed at damaging their people based on their religion — that also will make Peace in those settings much harder to achieve.

The people in Europe from all groups need key people in each setting to understand the role that instincts are playing in creating those angers and in triggering those riots and enabling discriminatory behaviors.

Europe needs to recognize the actual intergroup instinct patterns that are being activated, and leaders in Europe need to work on the patterns as instinctive intergroup conflicts instead of either moving from crisis to crisis to put out situational fires, or instead of attacking other people en masse because of their supposed evil natures and their purported religious or anti-religious beliefs and behaviors.

Religion Wars Trigger Religious Wars

Religious wars tend to trigger religious wars. Reciprocity is a normal response to being attacked at those levels. When people feel attacked at a religious level, their responses can often cause the people who they are responding to feel their own anger in ways that can trigger their own religious challenges and threats.

Many people in Europe who had not actually identified themselves at a personal level to be Christians are beginning to use that specific definition to describe themselves because the intergroup conflicts in their communities with religion elements embedded in them are forcing that definition on them.

Others are working to create an identity as being collectively non-religious.

It will be interesting to see what definition of "Us" emerges in each setting when religion will clearly define at least one category of "Them."

Those issues are the specific topic for another book — *Cusp of Chaos*. It is entirely possible that some of *The Art of InterGroup Peace* and *Cusp of Chaos* insights, teachings, and key suggestions could functionally be useful for people from several countries in Europe as well as being useful in the U.S.

Intergroup Riots Have Instinctive Triggers

What we now know to be true is that intergroup riots have happened in a number of European cities and that those riots will clearly continue to happen. Riots damage Peace. Riots also destroy intergroup goodwill.

Riots trigger and inflame us/them instincts for all groups of people in each setting in very negative ways.

The London riots and the riots in Paris all featured intense inter-ethnic anger, intergroup conflict, and even intergroup hatred. The Internet spillover from those conflicts ended up triggering other equivalent anger levels and parallel intergroup violence in other settings.

Our ability to achieve Peace in this country will not be helped by having those kinds of events happen here. If any of the religious aspects that are now so clearly embedded in the current wave of European conflict spill over to our country, as either direct intergroup conflicts or as rebound, or negative feelings against Americans by those groups, then those negative reactions could add significantly to the challenges we already face here.

We also know that the entire list of intergroup interactions outlined in Chapter Six of this book needs to be looked at in more settings.

The multi-tribal countries who are at intergroup war with themselves may find that re-organizing into a confederation model of some kinds might relieve intergroup conflicts and promote Peace.

Leaders in all of those settings need to look at all of the options that are included in the intergroup alignment list in Chapter Seven.

The six alignment-triggers that are outlined in Chapter Nine should also be reviewed by leaders in each of those conflicted settings. Those triggers can help people in communities come together in aligned ways to prevent the continuing levels of conflict that can tear people apart.

We Have Our Own Set of Immigration Issues to Address

As Chapter Eight of this book points out, America also has its own set of immigration issues. There is now clearly a wide range of us/them instinctive reactions that are tied closely to those immigration-related issues in this country.

Us/Them thinking is being triggered here in a number of ways and in a number of settings relative to our own sets of both legal and illegal immigrants.

The vast majority of the people who are currently immigrating into the U.S. are not, however, from the same sets of people and the same ethnic groups who are immigrating into London or Paris.

Our immigrants are not from Albania or Algeria. They tend to be from Mexico and South America. We do have our own sets of immigration related instinctive behaviors to deal with — both for our new immigrants and for the people who either welcome or oppose the current sets of legal and illegal immigrants here.

We have a very different level of issues created by our immigrants, however, compared to the issues that exist in most other countries. Those immigration issues need to be addressed here and they are also discussed in more detail in the book *Cusp of Chaos*.

Our immigration issues, challenging as they are, are not creating riots like the ones in London or Paris. Our immigration issues also don't have any parallel or equivalent religious war components embedded in them.

That means that the spillover riots in London and Paris that have religion-linked triggers are not likely to trigger parallel multi-factorial riots among immigrants in Chicago, New York, Denver, or Los Angeles.

The Internet reaches easily across the Atlantic, so people in this country know now that those issues and trigger events exist in those other countries. The specific riot triggers that are at the source of the European riots generally do not, however, activate similar energy here — primarily because we have different groups of people who immigrate to our country.

People Who Are Angry Can Work to do Damage Here

We are not immune from the damage that can be done by people who have the deep-seated religion focus for intergroup anger.

We clearly do face some very real and immediate risk from people who are so angry at the various interreligious issues that they perceive themselves to face in Europe or Eastern Europe or the Middle East that they will choose to bring bombs and other weapons to this country to hurt us here. That has happened. It will happen again.

The World Trade Center disaster was one of those spillover consequences. The Boston Marathon bombing was another spillover event. People who hate us as Americans will seek to harm us as Americans in the future and we can expect those kinds of damaging events to happen in our country as a result.

This country is clearly at some risk of spillover hatred, division, anger, and even violence from these intergroup incidents in other countries — but those religion-linked conflicts are not likely to impact us here in the form of major demonstrations of Paris or London-like riots or equivalent large scale intergroup confrontations.

We do have some potential backlash against Muslim Americans that could be triggered at a simplistic level by future riots and intergroup violence in other countries or by individual acts of terrorism against people that happen here.

A major collective backlash isn't highly likely to happen — unless there are echo protests of some kind here or significant numbers of individual terrorist kinds of events that begin to undermine the sense of safety for people here.

Our primary spillover risk from all of that intergroup anger with Religion embedded in it is primarily from those terrorists from those groups who do decide to find their targets here. We know that particular set of negative reactions can happen here because it has already happened here.

Significant numbers of Americans have been drawn by Internet appeals to go to Syria, Iraq, and other Middle East combat zones to become warriors for extremist groups there.

Those recruits are killing people in those settings today for their extremist groups. Those same recruits have the potential to return to America and kill people for their extremist group here.

That is clearly happening already to sites in Europe where local people who have drawn to the various extremist groups are attempting as individuals to damage people in European settings.

We need to face that reality.

We clearly do face the risk of terrorism that is plotted against us by the people who feel those anger levels in other countries. That is a danger to us. There are people in our country who have their us/them instincts activated in very negative ways against us as Americans. Some of those people feel isolated, angry, and damaged in either direct or indirect ways and feel drawn to do damage themselves. Acts of individual terrorism here can easily result from those intergroup hatreds that are encouraged here by groups like ISIS or Al-Qaeda for people who support them in our country.

We have a high likelihood of seeing some negative incidents as a result of those pressures and processes.

Our Immigrants Don't Hate America

However, the basic fact that is that the vast majority of our immigrants don't hate America. Other than a very small subset of the immigrants who came to us from some of the settings where those extremist groups have influence, our immigrants don't despise American values or American people. France actually does have a significant number of immigrants who hate France and who both publically and privately attack French values, the French culture, and French people. London has many immigrants who hate the British. That hatred creates obvious problems for future Peace in those cultures.

We do, however, already have our own set of internal current and historic intergroup angers and trigger points and our own sets of immigration challenges that need to be addressed, and we need to deal with those issues effectively and soon because our own diversity as a country is also growing daily.

Immigration is not the major driver for our growing diversity, but it is a highly relevant factor. Our us/them instincts get triggered in different and very predictable ways about our immigrants based on the ethnic connections that exist for each group relative to each group of immigrants.

Our growing diversity is creating a new reality of who we are as a complete set of people.

We tend to have immigrants who want to join the American economy — become voters in America — and assimilate into American values. Our immigrants are drawn here by our values. They do not come here to resist or oppose our values.

That is not the situation that they face today in Europe.

Our new reality of expanding diversity for this country does not look like the challenges that are being faced by various parts of Europe that were once homogeneous and are now permanently divided and learning to deal with a future of intergroup division.

Leaders in Europe today need to understand the reality and the status of their intergroup issues. Wishful thinking or ideologically correct thinking about intergroup issues will not help Europe get to the next level of intergroup of Peace. Europe needs to make some timely interventions in their intergroup relations in multiple settings to get people there back on the road to Peace.

Europe Needs a Strategy for Internal Peace

Europe currently needs to think through all of the issues that are relevant to their growing diversity. An overall plan is needed for each of those countries. Europe needs an agenda and a strategy.

It is too late for the countries of Europe to continue to deal with each issue and each blowup situationally, and to simply try in each negative setting to avoid defeat. Too many forces are at play in Europe that now cumulatively make simply avoiding defeat impossible.

The next chapter outlines six very good approaches that can be used to create intergroup and interpersonal alignment. Those six triggers can help us create levels of alignment that can derail us/them energy and momentum in a setting. Each of the six alignment-triggers in the next chapter can be used to help us expand our sense of "us," and to bring people together into functional categories of us.

Those six alignment-triggers can work well in multiple settings – work places, communities, and even nations. Leaders in Europe should be using those triggers whenever they can be used. They work.

To be skilled in the Art of InterGroup Peace for Europe, those alignment-triggers should be in the tool kit of the people who are leading Europeans to Peace.

The leaders in Europe should also look at the list of us/them prevention or us/them alleviation strategies that were outlined in Chapter Two of this book. Avoidance can still work in a few areas and it should be used whenever it has a chance of succeeding.

Europe May Need to Create a State of Truce

In many parts of Europe, however, it is too late to avoid a wide array of very negative sets of us/them instincts. Likewise, minimization of the impact of those instincts has already generally failed in many areas.

Derailing them has also failed in most settings. Neutralizing their impact has also not been successful in too many settings.

That means that replacing the us/them alignments in those settings in creative and effective ways with a broader sense of "Us" is clearly the best long-term strategy for each conflicted European country.

That approach is probably very difficult to achieve at this point in time in most settings, however, particularly since some of the leaders of some of the new groups are heavily committed to conflict and division, and have no interest in alignment or intergroup Peace at any level.

That work of creating alignment still needs to be done — in each country — and it does need to happen at a very high level and very skillfully in those countries to have any chance of success.

It may be true that it is too late for many of the alleviation strategies at this point in many European settings. That leaves only one good tool for those settings — Truce. Truce may be the only current answer for large portions of Europe – at least for an interim period of time.

The Good Old Days Are Gone for Most of Europe

If a truce is in place in many of those European settings, then there can be an opportunity to build on the truce to figure out what might be done over time to create a new and expanded Dutch or German or French sense of Us that can create the status of long-term intergroup Peace in various settings for Europe for long periods of time.

The six alignment triggers identified in the next chapter of this book can all be used in European settings as part of that process to help create a functional and Peaceful sense of us in various settings.

That work and those alignment-triggers will need to be used very directly in each setting — and it will take skillful leaders who will need to recognize that they will never return to being the Europe of even a decade ago, to do that work well.

The leaders in each setting will need to steer each country toward a new national or European us — or they will be doomed to perpetual conflict and will suffer from destructive intergroup behaviors at multiple levels for a very long time.

Once those instincts are activated in a negative way, they tend to be self-perpetuating and they do not disappear of their accord.

Russia, China, India, Indonesia, Sri Lanka, Are Still on the List

The world is full of countries that are at war with themselves.

When we look across the planet today, we see many countries with major internal conflicts. There are literally dozens of current ethnic conflicts going on just within Russia. Multiple separatist groups in that country with their own ethnic identity and tribal language want tribal autonomy.

China is facing multiple internal ethnic conflicts as well. There is a very large Han-ethnic group, but there continues to be many additional groups with their own tribal language and identity who want to govern themselves. Uprisings are relatively frequent for some of those groups.

India has a plethora of internal ethnic groups who want some level of autonomy. Those groups in India have tribal histories and other tribal legacies that stretch back thousands of years. A desire for autonomy is festering in many of those groups.

Sri Lanka has its own internal divisions, with people killing people today based on tribe and religious affiliation. Intergroup damage is clear and growing in sections of that country.

Indonesia is a massive array of internal ethnic groups — with over a dozen tribes large and powerful enough to have their own militia and their own weaponry. The central government in that country exists at the mercy and the sufferance of those tribal alignments.

Pakistan, even today, is more a network of armed tribes than it is a single, homogenous nation. The people of Pakistan refer to themselves by their tribal identities — not their nationality — in identifying their primary loyalty levels.

Iraq is clearly a nation that has had no legitimate standing or internal group identity as a single people. The tribes of Iraq define reality for Iraq. Those tribes tend to hate one another and each needs its own turf for its own safety and prosperity going forward.

The Kurds need to run their own part of the world and to be allowed to be Kurds in the process.

Each of those countries is clearly functioning now at a very tribal level with their local us/them instinctive behaviors in full gear for each tribe.

We live in a world of tribes that have been forced circumstantially to function at least temporarily as unnaturally aggregated nations. The chapter of this book that describes the nine ways that groups of people can interact will be increasingly relevant to all of those settings.

The final intergroup status for all of those settings will need to take the tribal nature of all of those populations more directly into account in the governance process if any of them are going to have any hope of achieving ethnic Peace.

In many settings — like Russia and India — the central governments will continue to resist going in that direction. Those nations could all be better served if they look at other alignment options.

We need dysfunctional multi-tribal nations to take the lead in doing that work in responsible ways. We need nations to turn themselves into smaller nations that make ethnic and tribal 'sense' and have internal cohesion — like Yugoslavia — and we need to do that division in civilized ways that protect the safety and the rights of all people and groups of people, both in the transition process and in the long-term governance of those new and more logical nations.

The U.S. Needs to Use All Six Alignment-Triggers

For the U.S., the entire continuum of all seven possible responses to the activation of our us/them instincts is going to be an approach we should use in various settings.

We need to be using all six internal alignment-triggers that are discussed in Chapter Six of this book.

We Americans can still, if we are focused on what we do now, manage to avoid conflict, minimize conflict, derail conflict, neutralize negative behaviors, negotiate reasonable ceasefires, truces and Peace agreements, and ultimately assimilate people ideologically into a broader and more inclusive sense of being an American Us.

We need to clearly understand what the actual options and strategies are that can bring us to where we need to be — in a state of Peace — and we need to understand what tools we can and should use to create alignment in our country.

The rest of the world is a mess. We need to learn from the failures in those other countries what not to do, and we need to learn from our own successes how to create InterGroup understanding, and ultimately, InterGroup Peace.

We need to use the alignment-triggers available to us to succeed in that effort.

CHAPTER EIGHT

Six Steps and Key Triggers to Use to Create Instinct Supported Alignment

PEOPLE WHO WANT to create Peace and build internal alignment in almost any setting can use a very basic set of clearly understandable tools to do that work.

Those tools are explained here, and in more detail in the book *Primal Pathways* as useful instinct-linked manifestations of our basic patterns of intergroup thinking and behavior..

It is useful for the cause of intergroup Peace to understand and know several basic ways people can be brought, steered, helped, encouraged, incented, directed, and guided into a state of alignment in almost any setting by effectively, explicitly, intentionally, and skillfully invoking one or more of the basic alignment-triggers shown on the list below.

The Art of InterGroup Peace core strategy depends on us being able to bring people in multi-group settings into a state of alignment. We need people in each setting to feel aligned with each other and we need people to feel that they are part of an "Us" at instinct triggering levels for relevant issues in their setting in order to make Peace a success in those settings.

That is possible to do by using a basic set of alignment tools that cause people to come together, and stay together in each setting. This chapter contains a list of the six most useful tools that can be used to accomplish those goals.

The basic tools on this list can help create that sense of alignment in ways that are situationally and functionally relevant to each setting.

To create Peace, we need people in relevant settings to have a sense there is value and that there are benefits resulting from being aligned and at Peace. We need people to want to come together for mutual advantage. We want people to want Peace to happen because of the alignments that exist and the benefits that those alignments create

It is possible for skilled leaders in almost any setting who know the alignment tool options, to use one or more of the basic triggers and actions to create an instinct supported sense of value and purpose for people relative to being aligned in that setting.

Leaders often use one or more of these triggers in their leadership roles now. Leaders are usually key and central to that alignment process in most settings — but leaders are not essential to the process. Groups of informed people in a setting can also choose as groups to use any of the triggers on the list to direct and guide themselves collectively down these paths.

Groups of people in a setting who make the collective intellect-based and ethics-guided decision to want to function in an aligned way as a group can succeed in achieving that functionality by collectively invoking, and then using one or more of the triggers on the list. That can be done most effectively if the group members both understand the triggers, and agree to work together to activate one or more of the triggers in the group interest.

Six Key Tools to Trigger Alignment

These triggers are usually, however, invoked by leaders of groups who tend to use one or more of them both to direct and channel the energies and the behaviors of their groups, and to increase their own influence and their own power over their groups.

Skilled leaders generally either know these tools from experience and training, or they use them intuitively. In many settings, the triggers are taught to leaders by other leaders, or they are given to the leaders by being embedded in some ways in the cultures of their groups. In all of those cases, the six tools shown below are used by leaders in a wide range of settings because they work.

We need to use those triggers at this point in our history to facilitate Peace. We need Peace to be a collective goal, and we need people in each setting who want Peace to use these tools and take steps to build Peace into their cultures and interactions with each other. To achieve a culture of Peace, people in each setting generally need to have a strong sense that collective and Peaceful alignment in key ways makes sense and has value.

Alignment is a good thing for intergroup Peace, because Peace in any setting is very difficult to achieve if at least one of the triggers is not positively activated for people, and influencing both thoughts and behaviors in the setting.

Without some level of alignment, groups of people tend to fight with one another and too often feel that fighting is the right thing to do.

Without some level of alignment, people tend to distrust, dislike, and even damage people from other groups in any setting who are perceived to be some category of "Them" in the context of basic "Us/Them" instinct activation.

Without some level of alignment, people tend to feel stress, hostility, anger, and even fear during interactions with people from other groups in any setting.

So alignment clearly has value when Peace is the goal.

When people become aligned with each other using any of those six tools, people tend to work together. People who are aligned tend to collaborate rather than compete. People who are aligned tend to trust each other rather than fear and perpetually distrust each other.

People who are aligned try to figure out how to help each other succeed, rather than constantly trying to figure out how to make each other fail.

Each of the six alignment triggers can help create that sense of alignment for people. The triggers don't make old intergroup differences that exist in any setting disappear, but they can make those old differences situationally irrelevant, and they can allow people to act together in those settings in aligned ways.

The people in any setting who are affected by any setting relevant, and situationally specific alignment-trigger tend to be able to reduce or eliminate intergroup conflict in that setting for as long as the relevant alignment tool is activated and functioning.

The set of triggers explained in this chapter can create alignment between groups, and it can also be used to build stronger internal alignment and stronger internal support inside existing groups.

Group leaders and group members who simply want to strengthen the alignment levels that exist inside their own group can also use several of the tools — like the sense of common enemy, a sense of group identity, or a sense of group mission — to strengthen the internal identity and the basic loyalty levels for members of their own group.

The Tools Can Be Used Locally, Situationally, and Broadly — Even Nationally

Those six tools can each and all be used at the national level to help us collectively as a country — and those same six alignment trigger tools can each be used in very local and situational ways — for communities, religious groups, political parties, and even in work places, and schools. Those tools can be used in almost all settings to create locally aligned functionality as inclusive local groups of people.

Those tools can even be used in family settings to increase family member internal loyalty and alignment. Any family that wants to strengthen its internal identity and its collective effectiveness as a family, can use any of the six triggers on the list in various combinations to achieve those goals.

The Tools Can Be Used Alone and in Packages

Those six tools can each do their work very well on their own. They each have their own independent functional power to bring people in a setting or situation together.

Even though that is true, they tend to have even more impact when they are used in packages.

In fact, their effectiveness and their impact can often be enhanced significantly and their power to influence thinking and behavior can often be reinforced, and even amplified and magnified, in both effectiveness and impact if more than one of the alignment tools is used in functional alignment with another alignment tool.

The very best and most effective leaders, and the very worst and most destructive leaders, sometimes activate all six of those alignment triggers — either sequentially or simultaneously.

The *Primal Pathways* book has an addendum explaining how Adolf Hitler used the full package of six triggers to achieve his leadership strategy and to achieve power over his people. The ISIS organization, in a number of settings today, is also clearly using all six triggers now whenever they can get all six activated.

At the same time, the effectiveness of any of those tools can be weakened, diluted, or even destroyed in a setting if more than one of the alignment triggers and tools are used in direct opposition to one another inside a community or setting.

People can use those tools to bring people together, and people can also use those tools to push, or even tear people apart. People tend to act once each trigger is having an impact on their thought processes — and the actions that result from that activation can be used for either good or evil.

For *The Art of InterGroup Peace*, the goal is clearly to use those tools for good — not evil — and the belief of this book is that we are each and all more likely to use those tools for good rather than evil when we all understand clearly and explicitly what they are, and when we all understand exactly how they work.

Knowledge is power. *The Art of InterGroup Peace* book also believes we are each much more likely to have the intellectual ability to detect, discern, delineate, avoid, resist, withstand, and — in many settings — redirect, re-channel, or simply reject the negative impact of those triggers on us individually and on our group, when we understand them all clearly, and when we decide intellectually they are being used by evil, negative, and divisive leaders in our settings to move us to evil, immoral, unethical, wrong, and destructive beliefs, values, and behaviors.

Knowledge clearly is both strength and power when resisting evil and its influence is one of our goals, aspirations, and personal behavioral commitments.

Six Primary Factors Can Trigger Alignment – Individually and as a Package

So if we want to build intergroup Peace in any situations or settings, we are all often very well served at multiple levels if we clearly know and understand what each of those triggers are.

We need to clearly understand these instinct-linked group alignment and motivation influences so we can keep them from steering us into negative and evil behaviors, and so that we can use them in proactive and positive ways to do the kinds of enlightened and beneficial things that can create and support Peace in our settings and in our lives.

Their impact is very situational. They are each only relevant in the context they are in. We need to understand that fact and functionality as well.

Success in War Is Also Highly Patterned and Highly Situational

Context is extremely important. The classic, *The Art of War*, written two centuries ago by Sun Tzu, gave us very useful guidance relative to context-based strategies that fit the situation, circumstances, and settings for war. *The Art of War* celebrated the value and power of selecting and using situationally correct, complex strategies.

Knowledge is power in times of war as well as times of Peace. Sun Tzu clearly pointed out that a skillful and fully informed understanding by the generals who ran the armies of the full set of key factors that exist for war, and a full and focused understanding of the exact circumstances and facts that are situationally relevant to each setting are needed for success by armies in times of war.

He pointed out that success in war is both highly patterned and highly situational.

Sun Tzu said that military leaders should expect common patterns and should expect common situations, but he said not to expect the same exact strategy and tactics that won the last war, or the last battle, to win the next war or the next battle. Tzu stated that a skillful, specific strategy and situationally based set of tactics needs to be developed for each war and each battle that fits the circumstances of each battle and war.

That same wisdom applies to the strategies needed for Peace. Even though the six alignment triggers generate basic and understandable patterns of behaviors, the leaders in each setting need to figure out which triggers will work in each setting, and leaders need to figure out how to best utilize each trigger in the current setting and situation.

Danger, Enemies, Teams, Goals, Shared Identity, Gain, Mission, Vision, and Loyalty Bring Us Together and Keep Us Aligned

The pyramid on the following page lists the six key factors that can be activated to create alignment and common purpose for individuals and groups of people. All six factors need to be considered and understood in the context of each situation and each setting where they might be relevant to see which factors will work in that situation.

The pyramid ranks the alignment triggers in terms of their relative power in most situations. As a general rule, factors at the bottom of the pyramid tend to have the most power to sway people's emotions, thought processes, and behaviors.

That is not an absolute priority impact reality. Danger, for example, can generally overpower both greed and a desire for material gain — but the prospect of great wealth can sometimes cause people to take some risk and incur some levels of danger they would ordinarily avoid.

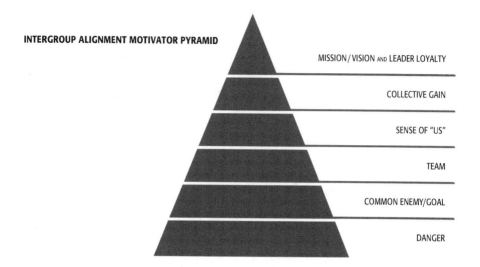

Having team instincts fully activated can usually trump a prior sense of group "Us." People often forget which group they are originally from in various Team settings, and will assign their energy and commit at a very basic level to team success and team loyalty.

That tends to be true unless and until the team setting somehow manages to involve and invoke relevant factors for individual people that actually threaten their original "Us" in some meaningful way.

When that perception of a real and valid threat to an original "Us" happens in a team setting, the original sense of "Us" tends to be reinstated for each person, and that original alignment and loyalty level often prevails over the team instincts.

People will generally not, for example, do something in a team setting to help their team win that will actually damage a member of their family.

As a general rule, however, when multiple factors are in play in any given setting and when multiple alignment factors are at odds with each other for any reason, the factors listed lower on the pyramid tend to overpower and take priority over the factors listed higher on the pyramid.

Danger Can Overpower Mission

Danger, in other words, tends to overpower both group identity and mission much of the time. When we feel a sense of real and relevant danger, we are likely to, at least momentarily, give up on our mission-based alignments and we are likely to focus directly on what we need to do to avoid or survive the danger.

That set of priorities functions very much like Abraham Maslow's famous priority pyramid for individual behavior and personal needs.

In the case of the group alignment pyramid, each factor on the pyramid has its own ability to trigger alignment and direction, and each factor has the ability to create a sense of group energy and collective activity.

They are each more effective when they are reinforced in some way by another triggering factor, and they each can be weakened by a conflicting trigger that is situationally activated.

The relative impact of each trigger is determined by the values and the situational realities for the people in each situation. All six triggers tend to work in the situations and settings where they are most relevant to people.

Each trigger has the power to cause people to become aligned with other people when the trigger is activated in a way relevant to the person who is affected by it. Groups of people who want to achieve internal alignment, and leaders of groups who want their group settings to achieve alignment, can use any and all of these tools to accomplish those goals.

1. Threat or Danger Is the Top Motivator

Danger leads the list of alignment triggers.

Danger and the potential for danger are the factors listed at the very base of this alignment-trigger pyramid. Danger is a very powerful trigger for encouraging alignment. We react very directly to danger. Danger creates instinct-related emotional, intellectual, and functional responses for both individuals and groups of people.

Danger, clearly perceived, can generate great power in motivating groups of people to achieve alignment and to join in collective behaviors that can offset, alleviate, avoid, or prevent the danger.

Collective danger is a great motivator that can help people overcome other prior levels of differentiation and prior categories of intergroup division in the cause of jointly surviving the danger.

That particular motivator is effective for both War and Peace.

As Sun Tzu said in *The Art of War* – "The Men of Wu and the Men of Yueh are enemies: yet if they are crossing a river in the same boat and they are caught by a storm, they will come to each others' assistance, just as the left hand helps the right."

Sun Tzu understood that concept of situational intergroup alignment being effectively created by a collective and very real sense of danger very well. That motivator that is triggered by facing a common danger works well for war settings and it can also work very effectively for Peace.

When people in any setting feel a sense of shared danger — and when people then actually and clearly perceive, think, and believe that coming together in cooperative and collaborative ways can help everyone survive the danger — then people are more likely to come together and be aligned to do that work.

As Sun Tzu said, the Men of Wu and the Men of Yueh overlook their prior issues, and they ignore and set aside their prior conflicts and they focus together and collectively on the top shared priority of the moment — averting the danger.

The clearly understood but unspoken point in the Sun Tzu example is that men from both of those warring armies will still be in a state of war once they reach the safety of the shore. They might situationally avoid immediate conflict upon landing, but they are still at war with one another. They did not align or merge identities or restructure core loyalties under the threat of their ship sinking — they only aligned their efforts situationally to prevent the sinking of the ship.

We actually need to use that particular motivation factor of collective danger to activate energy and to create ongoing alignment in this country in favor of Peace. The danger we face as a country if we don't create intergroup Peace is very real.

We need people to understand how much danger we will all face if we don't achieve higher levels of Peace and better levels of intergroup understanding in this country.

That same motivation tool — a sense of collective danger — can functionally be used to create internal alignment in the context of organizations, communities, businesses, and multiple other settings.

When we perceive danger of some kind to be real in any setting,

that perception of real danger is a powerful motivator and it can bring people together to do aligned things in each relevant setting.

Variations of that danger motivator can work to create alignment in schools, communities, and a wide range of work settings. Businesses who have managed to create a sense of group alignment and group loyalty with their staff and their workforce, can use the danger of going out of business as a motivator for their staff to pull together and to be internally and collectively aligned to accomplish business purposes.

Believable Is Extremely Important

For any motivator to work as a trigger in any setting, it has to be believable. Believable is very important. Believable is key.

That is true for all six alignment triggers. Each of the six motivators will only work to trigger instinctive emotions and to motivate individual and group behaviors when they are believed.

Each motivator works best when it is both real and when it is perceived to be real. Truth and honesty are both very useful — even essential — tools for that work.

People who are fooled or misled by their leaders about any of the triggers listed on this pyramid — fooled about danger or fooled about a common enemy or fooled about a mutual chance to collectively benefit in some way from being aligned — can become very skeptical, resistant, and even dysfunctional relative both to the situation at hand and to any related alignment activities or efforts for that group of people.

Performance and alignment can both deteriorate when fake threats or false promises are made by leaders, and when those untrue motivators are perceived to be false and understood not to be true by the people they lead.

As Chapter One pointed out, one of the key underlying elements that is needed to achieve success in *The Art of InterGroup Peace* is honesty. Honesty is needed within groups and honesty is needed between groups in order for those very basic motivators to drive behavior in aligned ways.

Peace is intended to be a long-term goal — not just an immediate, situational, and temporary cessation of hostilities. Peace should be more than a momentary state of being. We want Peace to last and we want Peace to survive over time.

The likelihood of Peace, in any setting, surviving over time is enhanced immeasurably if honesty is a foundation of both communications and interactions — both between groups and inside of groups in that setting.

The Art of InterGroup Peace Celebrates Honesty and Clear Intentions

As noted earlier, *The Art of War* by Sun Tzu clearly celebrates, teaches, recommends, and consistently and extensively utilizes duplicity and deception. *The Art of InterGroup Peace* — in contrast — both recommends and celebrates honesty, ethical behaviors, and very clearly communicated and well-understood collective positive intentions.

Sun Tzu believed and taught that victory in war often depends on illusion, misdirection, and pure skillful deception. In contrast — practitioners for *The Art of InterGroup Peace* need to know and understand that intergroup Peace and internal alignment between sets of people and groups can be crippled by deceit, and destroyed by deception.

So using danger as a motivator to bring people together can be a very effective thing to do — but that trigger can create backlash, distrust, and a lack of support for both leaders and for the group, if the danger is perceived to be untrue. The alignment effort and approaches based on danger will be even more effective and more likely to succeed as a functional motivator for alignment over time if the danger that is used as a trigger for alignment is real and if it is perceived by relevant people to be real.

Leaders in any setting who want to create alignment in the setting have a high likelihood of creating that alignment, if the leader can identify any factors in the setting that represent danger to be functionally relevant to the people there. That is true within groups and it is a particularly effective trigger to use to create alignment between groups when people in a setting come to believe their alignment as groups will help reduce, alleviate, or end the danger.

2. Having a Common Enemy or an Important and Relevant Common Goal Can Also Trigger Alignment

The second level up the motivation and alignment pyramid is to have either a common enemy or a highly motivating common goal. People will align in many settings around either a common enemy or an important and motivating common goal.

Having a common enemy is very similar to perceiving a threat and fearing danger— and those two factors obviously can be used in combination with each other very effectively. But they are not the same thing.

A common enemy is a very specific category of danger and it creates a very specific mind set for people that can result in a very targeted alignment against that specific enemy.

People will come together and will align around a common purpose if they perceive and believe that the alignment they create will help protect both of the aligned parties against an enemy they both share.

The Enemy of My Enemy

There is an old saying that says, "The enemy of my enemy is my friend." That thought process and that perception are shared widely by people all across the planet. Few things are more motivating as a factor for getting people to work together then the perception of a common enemy.

The perception of an enemy can directly trigger and utilize the "Us/Them" instincts that were discussed earlier. Those instincts can generate significant emotional energy.

When we perceive someone to be an enemy "Them," we tend to believe at an instinct-reinforced level that the enemy intends to do us harm

— possibly grievous harm. We generally perceive a "them" to be a threat and we tend to believe that "they" will do bad things to us if "they" actually have the opportunity to harm us.

That instinctive set of behaviors and perceptions exists because that sense that an enemy "Them" will hurt us is often an accurate assumption. It is actually a sad but valid perception about the behaviors and the intentions we can expect in far too many settings from an actual "Them," that makes that motivation factor very effective.

This is not a hypothetical concern. We have more than 200 ethnic wars and conflicts going on in various settings in the world today. "Us/Them" thought processes, values, and behaviors are being triggered in far too many of those settings and both barrel-bombs dropped on civilians, and people willing to be suicide bombers to kill their perceived "Them" are literally happening to someone in some place every day.

Common enemies deserve to be feared in many settings.

Common enemies do not just explode bombs. Common enemies create discrimination. Common enemies do negative things at multiple levels. Common enemies far too often create economic, social, and functional damage to the people they perceive in a setting to be "Them."

At a very basic and far too familiar level, discrimination, legal and social prejudice, unfair practices, and many levels of negative intergroup behaviors can be triggered in people by a response to a "Them." People suspend conscience, and actually far too often feel no guilt in doing multiple levels of damage to whomever is perceived to be "Them." The people doing that damage create a feeling of unity against a common enemy from the people who are being damaged by those behaviors.

In worst cases, massacres, mutilations, murders, and multiple levels and layers of extremely damaging and destructive behaviors can happen when one group of people takes on an enemy status relative to another group of people.

The people in the Congo last year who had their limbs cut off for speaking with the wrong tribal accent were echoed and sadly paralleled by the people in Iraq who had their homes, families, and communities blown apart at that same time because they happened to be from the wrong sect.

Those same concerns about a common enemy were reinforced by the horrible intergroup experiences of the people in Syria and the people in the Sudan whose lives were destroyed because they were from the wrong tribe and because they found themselves in dangerous proximity and under the direct power of their enemy tribal "Them."

We far too often have good reasons to fear "Them," and we far too often have legitimate cause to be aligned against a common enemy.

Enemies who function as "Them" too often do bad things to other people. That is a reality. People in many settings understand that to be true.

People also sense that to be true. Our instincts believe that common enemies exist. We all have deep instincts to dislike, distrust, and fear anyone we perceive to be an enemy "Them," and we have influential and consistent instincts to unite and align as an "Us" against any perceived "Them."

Those are powerful and aligning emotions. When those emotions and perceptions are collectively activated, they can help bring people in a setting together in their functional collective common interests to be aligned — whenever shared enemies both exist and are perceived to exist.

Skillful Leaders Point Out Common Enemies

Those perceptions trigger alignment and they create levels of aligned opposition to the common enemy. Skillful leaders can draw on and activate those instinctive reactions by pointing out who the common enemy is in any setting and by describing both why and how the perceived common enemy should be collectively responded to in an aligned way for the common good of all relevant aligned parties.

There is some irony in the fact that having a common enemy can help trigger Peace between specific groups of people. Those behaviors can be directed against people and they can be directed in favor of people. Good leaders trying to create intergroup alignment in any setting can choose how to activate appropriate energy levels about common enemies and then can direct that energy for good purposes in the cause of intergroup Peace on behalf of the groups of people who share the common enemy.

Again — the goal of using that trigger is better when it is used to direct that particular set of instincts and that energy about the shared enemy for good purposes.

Those Reactions Can Be Used for Good or Evil

We make those kinds of choices all the time. Our instincts can all be used for good and our instincts can all be used for evil. We can use the perception of a common enemy to help bring people peacefully together to resist the shared enemy. We can also use the perception of an enemy to put strategies in place that will isolate our own group of people and that will create negative and damaging reactions to other groups.

Leaders who want to increase their own power in a setting will often try to point to a common enemy as a unifying factor, and leaders in far too many settings who feel the need to increase their own power will sometimes do dishonest and even clearly unethical things to invent reasons for their people to be angry with the other group, or to be afraid of the other groups who are perceived by their own group to be "Them."

That perception has so much power to incent, motivate, and align people that some leaders who crave power in unhealthy ways use it in dishonest and unethical ways to manipulate group behavior and to gain or increase their own power.

Pointing to a common enemy is clearly a technique that is often used by group leaders — both to protect their groups and to increase their own level of support and power within their group.

Our leaders often have a major impact on how we think relative to a possible enemy. Our leaders tend to have the ability to identify enemies and then very deliberately point to enemies we should fear and even hate.

Having leaders effectively pointing to various kinds of common enemies can lead to conflict, or it can lead to alignment.

Too many leaders find their own power as leaders is increased if they can point to a common enemy, align their own group against that enemy, and make a focus on a real or perceived common enemy a key part of their leadership priorities.

We Need Leaders Whose Goal Is Peace, Not Power

We need leaders whose goal is Peace, not power. We all need to understand those patterns of leader behavior, and we each need to look carefully at leader behaviors relative to other groups of people to see what each leader's basic goals actually are.

The Art of InterGroup Peace strategy framework and tool kit recognizes the fact that we can all be saints and that we also can all be sinners. *The Art of InterGroup Peace* strategy calls for activating our collective behaviors in ways that bring us together for Peace instead of bringing us together for conquest, assault, damage, destruction, or basic retribution and revenge against another group of people, or dividing us into groups at war with other groups.

In any case, having a common enemy is one of the factors that can trigger alignment, and that alignment trigger can also be used in many settings to create intergroup Peace.

Having a common goal is another basic motivation trigger that can often achieve similar motivating results that cause people to be aligned. In many settings, if people can be pointed toward a common goal — like building a bridge across a river or educating all of our children in a community — then the people who believe in that specific goal will often work together in aligned ways to achieve the goal.

Effective leaders in various settings often find specific common goals for people to achieve — and if the goal is sufficiently motivating, it has much of the same alignment power created by having a common enemy.

When a leader wants to create alignment in a setting, identifying a common goal for the people in the setting can have great power if people believe in the value and the benefits to them and to the people they care about of the goal, and if people believe creating some level of alignment will, in fact, help them achieve that goal.

Leaders in troubled settings should always look hard to find common goals to fulfill that function of bringing people together in those settings, and should use that trigger where it is relevant to create intergroup alignment and mutual benefits for the people in the setting.

Leaders of conflicted groups who want to achieve intergroup Peace should work together to find common goals that can unite and align their people.

3. Team Instincts Also Trigger Alignment

The next step up the six-step alignment pyramid in terms of effectiveness as a motivating tool is Team Behavior.

That reality of the role and the powerful direct impact team behaviors can have as an instinct supported alignment motivator surprises some people. But people tend to become believers in the power and value of those instincts once they understand the concept of using them as a tool, and then see them in action.

We clearly have very strong team instincts, and they very effectively do the work of bringing people together very well in many settings.

Teams trigger instincts. Team instincts, team behaviors, team functionality, team loyalties, and team identity all can be triggered in the interest of creating aligned settings by having people in relevant settings very clearly function in teams.

There is actually a very powerful set of behaviors, values, emotions, and beliefs that we can activate, direct, and channel when we function in teams, and we clearly need to know how to use those behaviors and those thought processes in intentional and effective ways, if we want to create intergroup Peace.

People who are in functioning teams with fully activated team instincts generally overlook prior problematic and divisive intergroup alignments, prior intergroup difficulties, and various categories of historic and functional prior intergroup differences, and work together in a team context to create common outcomes and a common identity as a team.

Team members can often take on and feel a focused and shared loyalty to their team when their team instincts have been effectively activated.

It isn't possible to activate team instincts in anyone simply by calling a group of people a "Team." Many people have tried that approach and have failed. The label, alone and by itself, has little power to motivate people, and just using the word "Team" does not consistently trigger the right package of behaviors or basic team instincts.

To be successful in activating team instincts, the team generally has to be defined and identified as a team. It also has to function in some way as a team. It has to do real team things. It has to operationally be a team — not just be labeled, termed, named or called a team.

Simply calling a group of people a team happens in a number of settings, but the label alone generally does relatively little to create team behaviors, emotions, energies, or loyalties.

Identities are important. Teams need to have identities. They also need to have a defined membership who knows as a group they are team members.

It also needs a purpose. Teams work collectively and function as a team when it is clear they have something collectively to do as a team that requires a team to do it. Athletic teams obviously usually meet that criterion fairly easily.

Forming athletic teams is a universal behavior across the planet and people show creativity in many cultures inventing sports of various kinds to trigger those instincts.

Those athletic teams all tend to activate those instincts fairly easily. Athletic teams tend to generate team instincts inside the teams, and they often generate a sense of alliance, allegiance, and loyalty with people who perceive themselves to be fans of the team.

Fan behaviors linked to teams tend to have their own highly predictable range of instinctive patterns of behavior.

It is clearly a universal set of instincts. Again — as with other universal instinctive behaviors (like maternal instincts or hierarchical instincts) — we see the formation, presence and existence of athletic teams in every area of the world, and we see that pattern everywhere because we instinctively like to function in teams, we instinctively want to be part of teams, and we very instinctively want to support teams.

Team loyalty feels good, and direct loyalty to a team actually often feels like a higher calling to team members. People sometimes feel almost religious loyalty levels to their teams. Those team allegiances and team linked loyalty feelings both motivate, align, and give people an at least situational reason for clearly connected and aligned behaviors as groups of people.

We clearly see team behavior in military units, in hunting settings, and we often see team behavior and team instinct activation in business environments.

Business teams can achieve very solid results for businesses when the teams in a business setting are well designed, well channeled, and when they are appropriately supported and motivated.

We actually have two basic sets of team instincts — hunter/warrior teams, and gatherer teams. Both have their strengths and capabilities, and both have settings where they function well.

The book *Primal Pathways* points out that women often excel at leading our gatherer teams and men tend to lean more toward our hunter teams, but people from each gender do well across the entire team continuum when the teams are well created, and when the teams have functions that need to be done in a team context.

That set of instincts is relevant to intergroup Peace because team members — when their team behaviors and instincts are functionally engaged — will often ignore prior interpersonal and intergroup differences and will perform team tasks as a team – with focused internal loyalty to the team usually established and activated for the team as a consequence of being a team in ways that make prior differences irrelevant.

Team behaviors and team loyalties are so engrained in our set of basic instincts that we have spectator sports where large populations of people identify with a team — feel loyalty to a team — and even wear team colors and openly, enthusiastically, and proudly wave team banners in support of a team.

Fans in stadiums often feel an uplifting, collectively energizing, and sometimes synergistic, and mutually reinforcing set of team emotions and team loyalties when those sets of instincts are activated.

In worst-case athletic team settings where primal instinctive reactions are triggered, team fans have actually taken their "Us/Them" instinct activation to a level so high they do damage, and even kill, fans from other teams. Soccer stadiums in many major cities actually have chain link fences to protect fans of teams from one another.

People with team instincts fully activated can find that their team alignment creates a special category of "Us" that has its own natural internal loyalties and even its own "Team" culture.

If you are running a business or leading a community, having key parts of your organization function as true teams can create higher levels of performance for the people on those teams, and being aligned with their team instincts activated can cause people on the teams to overlook other kinds of pre-team divisions, conflicts, emotions, and issues.

People generally love being on actual teams. Team morale and team loyalty are both very mutually reinforcing emotions. Team loyalties and team behaviors "feel right." It often feels very right to be loyal to a team.

Likewise — being disloyal to your team can "feel wrong," and having a sense of being disloyal to your team can sometimes create a level of clearly instinct-fed stress. Stress, as noted earlier and as explained in both the *Primal Pathways* book and the *Cusp of Chaos* book, is also a tool that is often used by our instincts to channel and influence our behavior.

In the earliest years of human activity, team behaviors were undoubtedly useful for various hunting purposes – where collective action by multiple people from multiple families, clans, or tribes who could activate a situational team loyalty and create a functioning team agenda in the context of a hunt were often more likely to trap an elk or even capture an elephant, or a wooly mammoth, than independent and solo hunters who pursued those formidable and sometimes dangerous food sources alone.

Likewise, going back to our earliest days on the planet — there were clearly multiple settings where local groups of people were in intertribal war with other groups of people.

When those intertribal wars happened, having the people from the various families and clans inside a tribe going beyond their personal and most primal family sense of "Us" and functioning as teams of warriors fighting on behalf of their entire clan or their entire tribe clearly enhanced the likelihood of the clan or tribe having success in intergroup combat, and increased the likelihood of having higher survival rates for clan and tribe members.

The success levels for warrior teams or for hunter teams were clearly logistically higher for a number of functions than the survival or success levels of solitary warriors or solitary hunters acting purely on their own in solo activities relative to aggression, defense, or pursuing game.

Team instincts are very useful in those hunting and war-making situations. Having instincts to be able to overlook prior family differences or prior clan differences in the context of situational loyalty to a team often makes obvious logistical sense.

We Have Both Hunter and Gatherer Team Instinct Packages

In those same primal settings, a high percentage of the calorie intake needed to keep each family and each tribe alive for an entire year often came from the gathering processes. Hunting rarely provided all of the food for primal families. Gathering was also key to the survival strategies of many early families.

Gathering is actually not usually a haphazard and random process. It is almost always a team process at some level. Collecting nuts or harvesting and then preserving wild rice in sufficient quantities to keep each group alive, often took significant organizational skills at multiple levels — and those activities needed and received their own sets of team actions, functions, and instinctive behaviors.

Those topics are actually discussed in more detail in both the *Primal Pathways* and *Cusp of Chaos* books. The key point to be made here is that leaders who aspire to Peace can find the activation of team instincts that are appropriately channeled to be a way of creating levels of Peace within their own group and a way of getting things done in a multi-group setting.

It can be useful to use team processes to generate levels of collective Peaceful behavior between groups when the team members contain people from multiple groups.

That approach can be used as a tool in communities, schools, and even businesses, and it can result in the community, school, or work place building a collective identity that triggers internal levels of support.

Patient-Focused Teams Succeed

One of the largest healthcare organizations in the world has successfully managed to create and sustain an effective Labor/Management Partnership between multiple labor unions and the functional management of the care system for over a decade. Teams have been a key part of that process.

That labor/management partnership has very deliberately created a vast array of functional front level teams — with more than 100,000 workers working in the context of a wide range of small unit-based teams as this book was being written.

Those unit-level teams in that setting are each focused on improving care, creating quality improvement approaches, and improving care service levels for patients.

The work itself and its consequences are both important. Functioning as teams in each care setting is equally important.

The workers' morale and productivity, and patient care outcomes and service levels all tend to be measurably better for the workers who are in those focused team settings and who are functioning in those settings as real teams.

That same team-centered organization has improved both care delivery results and care outcomes in several categories of care to earn top quality levels and top service scores for the nation by setting up multi-disciplinary and multi-specialty care improvement teams for multiple areas of care delivery.

That team-anchored care system currently has what are probably the lowest pressure ulcer rates for hospitalized patients in the world, and one of the lowest sepsis death rates in the world because of a combination of team behaviors and a culture that focuses the teams in each setting on the care needs of each patient.

Teams do a lot of heavy and very effective lifting in that care setting. That care setting is built around one of the countries most diverse care teams, with 59 percent of the caregivers in that workforce coming from minority groups.

Teams actually can do very important work in multiple work and community settings and the people on the teams tend to enjoy and appreciate being part of the teams.

Teams can energize and teams can create synergy.

That same package of Team instincts, however, can also trigger some significant intergroup conflicts that involve competition between teams.

Like all instincts, the team instinct package can be used for good or it can be used for evil.

Taken to the extremes, team energies can create damaging behaviors. As noted earlier, many soccer arenas in the world have actual chain link fencing set up to keep the fans of opposing teams from doing damage to one another. Team loyalties in some settings have created conflicts in the spectator arenas that have been fatal for people who were damaged by the collective anger and power of opposing fans whose riot instincts were activated.

Team behavior, however, can help to create Peace and team based alignments that overcome other differences between people can be a very good set of instincts to activate in any setting that aspires to intergroup Peace.

4. Creating a Sense of "Us" Can Also Align People

The activation trigger that is one step above team behavior on the common agenda alignment pyramid is creating a sense of "us."

Creating a sense of us is one of the most effective long-term alignment tools to use in creating Peace. It can be a good thing to be an "Us" at multiple levels.

The advantages of being an "Us" and of being surrounded by "Us" were discussed more extensively in Chapter Two of this book, and fairly extensively in both *Cusp of Chaos* and *Primal Pathways*, the sister books to this book.

It is good in any setting when people are an "Us." People tend to trust "Us." People tend to feel more comfortable working with or living with or even being near "Us."

Whoever we define to be our "Us" gets the benefit of our "Us" behaviors, our "Us" values, our "Us" ethics, and our "Us" emotions. When we create a sense of "Us" — the people who are included in that sense of "Us" usually benefit in a number of ways be being an "Us."

The cause of Peace and the ability to use a sense of "Us" to help create Peace are both helped immensely by the fact that we each tend to have the ability to relate to a multiple set of "Us" categories.

We can each create levels of "Us" that can be flexible in a number of ways. Our ability to relate to multiple levels of "Us" may have a practical and functional history and value very much like the team alignment instincts mentioned above.

The second chapter of this book outlined various ways that creating various levels of us alignment can be done. It is important to the basic strategy needed to build Peace in any setting that we can relate to multiple categories of "Us."

We can be a family or a clan "Us." We can be a racial or a tribal "Us." We can be an ethnic or a cultural "Us." We can be an economic or a professional "Us." We can be an academic "Us." We can be a political or religious or ideological "Us."

We can even be a geographic "Us." Southerners in the United States can perceive themselves as being a different "Us" then Northerners in our country. Alaskans tend to have a sense of being a geographically defined Alaskan "Us."

Hawaiians of all ethnic groups tend to have — as part of their personal identity — a sense of being a "Hawaiian Us."

When we travel, we tend to look around in any setting to see who we might relate to in that setting as an "Us." If you are traveling alone in a foreign country and if you can find another American on a riverboat in Brazil or find another American in a rural village market in Uganda, it can be very easy to quickly feel part of a situational American "Us" with that particular traveler in that setting.

It can create comfort for us to find an "Us" in almost any settings. We have lower stress levels when we can relate to an "Us."

Our Sense of "Us" Can Be Created by Multiple Factors

We have a wide range of possible triggers for creating a sense of "Us." Many definable groups have the power to trigger that sense of being an "Us." Our sense of "Us" can be created by profession, it can be created by occupation, and it can even be triggered by job categories.

Doctors can be an "Us" to other doctors. Surgeons can be their own internal category of physician "Us" — as can pediatricians and psychiatrists.

Police officers have their own sense of "Us" — as do steelworkers and schoolteachers.

People who collect particular things can become an "Us" with other people who collect the same things. Stamp collectors and action figure collectors each can create their own us ... for at least some aspects of their lives.

Generally, each set of "Us" has its own natural instinctive tendency to create its own culture — with its own rules, expectations, and values. The fourth chapter of this book discussed those culture issues in significantly more depth.

The culture of each group tends to be specific to the group it supports and each culture tends to be functionally relevant to the organizing definition of each "Us." Street gangs and motorcycle gangs each have their own "Us" linked identity, definitions, rules, and a hierarchy of some kind. So do people who participate in chess tournaments — as do the people who create and run trade associations.

The point that makes that particular alignment trigger relevant and highly useful to succeeding at *The Art of InterGroup Peace* is that we are not limited to race, ethnicity, or gender for our definition of "Us" — even though those very fundamental and primal categories of "Us" tend to have great leverage and great power for each of us in defining our usual most baseline personal categories of "Us."

As a core and essential foundational strategy for *The Art of InterGroup Peace*, we need to utilize the connective power of our fundamental definitions of us and we also need to create the working context to align us across our various groups into also being a broader and more inclusive definition of "Us."

Peace is impossible and doomed to failure in any setting when people have their "Them" instincts operational and fully activated relative to other people in that setting. People do bad things to "Them."

People very often do negative things to "Them" with no guilt, conscience, ethical regret or remorse.

We need to defuse those specific instincts triggered by a sense of "Them" in each setting by giving us a broader sense of "Us" in each setting that includes whomever had been a "Them" as part of the new "Us."

It is not good to have "Them" in any setting where we want Peace. We either need to not have the people perceived to be "Them" in each setting, or we need to figure out a believable and functional sense of "Us" that includes those people in that setting who we used to perceive to be "Them."

The key strategy that we need to follow is to take advantage of our individual ability to align with other categories of "Us" in ways that help us achieve Peace in the context of a broader "Us."

We Need an "Us" Based on a Commitment to the American Dream

To create overall Peace for our country, we will need to very intentionally and very deliberately expand and reinforce our sense of American us. We need that process to be values based.

We need to create and extend a major definition of "Us" that very clearly includes the other people in this country who share our values, and who also want to create Peace, and achieve win/win results and status for us all.

We very clearly need a value based "Us" that gives us all a context for alignment that can be the underpinnings for Peace.

If we want a society that helps all of us achieve the American dream, then we need to expand our definition of us to include all of the people who very explicitly want to create Peace and who want to create that Peace for all of us by creating broad and inclusive access to the American dream.

We need to do that work of expanding our sense of "Us" in a way that is believable and credible to each of us. As noted earlier, each alignment trigger needs to feel real and each alignment factor needs to be believed in order to actually work well as an alignment trigger.

Chapters Twelve and Thirteen of this book deal with those issues and offer some strategies for achieving these goals of creating a values based sense of us. The final chapter of this book explains clearly 12 basic beliefs we can use to create a sense of being an "Us" based on sharing important beliefs.

Anyone who wants to create Peace in any setting is far more likely to succeed in creating Peace if that can be done in the context of creating an "Us" for that setting. Leaders in any conflicted setting need to figure out a pathway that causes people in that setting to achieve alignment as an "Us."

That strategy is just as true for the country as it is for any community, organization, or group.

Creating an "Us" is a major alignment strategy. Creating that sense of us in each setting and context is a key step toward achieving Peace.

Organizations Can Create an Internal Sense of "Us"

That alignment factor is relevant in multiple settings. Inside communities, schools, and businesses, there is that same opportunity to create a sense of us that reduces internal divisions, conflicts, and stress levels and increases internal alignment and collaboration.

Each of those organizational settings can find their effectiveness increased if the people in the setting have a sense of "Us" instead of people in that setting simply having a sense of just being a situational clumping of various "Us/Them" interpersonal interactions that are happening circumstantially in that location.

Chapter Four and Five discuss the steps that are needed to create a culture that can help us achieve these goals as a country and in other settings as well. As noted earlier, every group that we form in any setting ends up deliberately, consciously, and unconsciously — but always very instinctively — creating its own functionality and its own rule sets as a culture for the working purposes of the group.

We can let that culture development happen in each setting serendipitously or we can cause that culture development to happen strategically, in clear and intentional alignment with the goals we want each group to achieve and the functions we want each group to perform.

To achieve Peace strategically, we need to deliberately choose the better and more dependable route to creating a culture of us. We need to look for those opportunities for each setting, and we need to create them for each relevant situation.

The sister book *Primal Pathways* explains our various packages of culture building instincts in more detail and the sister book *Cusp of Chaos* offers strategies that can be used to turn those instincts into intergroup alignment and intergroup Peace.

The final chapter of this book very explicitly lists 12 key and foundational shared beliefs we can use to create alignment as an American "Us" — aligned by our beliefs and not divided by race, ethnicity, economic status, or any of our more primal identity groupings.

We need to create a sense of "Us" in each setting that is relevant to each setting and we need to create a national sense of "Us" that is anchored in our core beliefs. *The Art of InterGroup Peace* core strategy for Peace builds on both of those foundations.

5. Group Gain Is Also Motivating as an Alignment Tool

We can also bring people together in a wide range of settings by persuading people that they will directly benefit in a significant and relevant way by being aligned.

Potential gain can bring people together in almost any setting. People tend to aspire to acquire. Greed motivates, and property and wealth acquisition has its draw and power as a motivator for both individuals and groups.

The alignment-triggering factor that sits one step above creating a sense of us on the alignment motivation pyramid is actually simply "group gain."

In many settings, the prospect of gain can be a powerful motivator that causes people to interact and align with other people in the interest of achieving the gain.

In some earlier descriptions that were written about the six-step alignment trigger pyramid, another more direct word that was used to describe that specific stage five group gain alignment trigger was "group greed." Both are functionally legitimate. Gain and greed can both be very motivating to a number of people in many settings.

People will often come together and will align around a common agenda if the anticipated functional result, and the expected consequence of that alignment around that specific agenda is material gain of some significant kind for the people who align. Wealth is a great motivator. Money motivates. Prosperity motivates. Doing well is aspirational and motivational for many people.

You can buy collective love in some settings using those motivation triggers. If groups of people believe that their collective efforts are more likely to create both collective and individual financial gain, then alignment is more likely to happen for those groups of people.

If we can persuade people in any setting that they will be better off by doing some things as a group, then those things are more likely to be done as a group in that setting. Those mutual gain energies and their related alignment triggers can be put in play with some success in multiple settings.

Collective gain doesn't need to be actual wealth. People don't need to be tempted with riches. Simply avoiding or escaping poverty can be a highly motivational and highly relevant mutual gain. Achieving basic financial security can be a powerful motivator relative to collective gain. So can secure housing or affordable and accessible food supplies.

People who want to create alignment in any setting should be aware that property possession of many kinds can be a collective and direct motivator for aligning behaviors. Building a common alignment agenda around a collective gain goal as basic as having an actual pension plan for the people who align can be a very effective group motivator in some settings.

Unions use that particular motivator in many settings, and people will often take on strong levels of group based alignment and loyalty to create and defend that particular financial goal. Strikes to defend pension plans create alignment at one level, and can trigger a strong set of "Us/Them" energies and perceptions against the people who are being perceived as a "Them" for threatening or opposing those sets of collective benefits.

Group gain can be triggered by collective security or by shared sustenance as well as by actual wealth. Each of those goals can have significant power to motivate when they are well targeted, well channeled, and situationally appropriate.

People who want to create Peace and alignment in any setting and who use the ongoing financial well being of all group members who align as a motivator and who communicate clearly the benefits that will result from alignment can find that tool to be effective and reinforcing.

Again, leaders who want to create alignment in a given setting will often be very well served by figuring out the material gain or financial rewards that can result from that alignment.

Leaders should look hard for those motivators because they can have significant power over other levels of division and conflict. People will often overlook other color-based differences between groups in the collective pursuit of monetary Green rewards.

Leaders can sometimes also use the other types of "Green" incentives to get people to work together to achieve environmental protection goals. The environmental goals can sometimes simultaneously trigger future danger concerns and future functional aspirations for sets of people.

People who share those goals, concerns, and aspirations can work together as an aligned and mutually supportive "Us" in many settings, and people who don't have those particular triggers activated in their own thought processes can too easily perceive the people who do have them activated as a "Them."

Sad but unfortunately true.

6. The Peak Motivation Factor on the Alignment Pyramid Is Mission, Vision, Loyalty, and Deeply Held Beliefs

The final and most focused motivation tool — and the top step on the six-step alignment pyramid — is to have a sense of alignment that is triggered by a higher calling or by a commitment and level of loyalty to a belief system, a mission, a leader, or a vision. People will often do highly motivated things out of loyalty to a leader or out of deep commitment to a belief system.

Anyone trying to create alignment in any setting can trigger various versions of the mission/vision/belief system/rightful leader alignment motivator, and can often find significant numbers of people who will make that factor a major motivator for their thoughts, actions, emotions, and beliefs.

The highest level on the alignment pyramid calls for people to have a collective vision or to be collectively committed to a common mission or to a belief system, and to feel significant loyalty to either their mission or their leader.

We instinctively hate being a traitor, and we tend to feel intense dislike and even hatred toward anyone we perceive to be a traitor.

We instinctively love having our sense of mission. We love having a sense of loyalty and a sense we are doing the right things to be loyal. For many people, key aspects of our personal behaviors are anchored in what we believe is rightful loyalty to a major focus for our lives.

People want to be part of something bigger than themselves, and that aspiration and want actually motivates behavior that very often does loyal, dedicated, and respectful things in the interest of that loyalty and that belief.

For leaders who want to create alignment in any setting, a mission or a vision can be a very good alignment tool to use that can bring people in almost any setting together. People can clearly aspire to higher loyalties and higher callings. A motivating mission can be — very directly — motivating. Inspirational. Even compelling.

Mission/vision approaches that appeal to peoples' sense of a higher calling can sometimes have almost hard to believe power to motivate people, and they can be used in many settings to accomplish the very specific goal of bringing people in that setting together.

People can, will, and do obviously come together and become aligned in the interest of a collective mission, and will often make that alignment a key part of their personal sense of who they are and who they are part of.

People will often align their individual and their group efforts in very effective ways to help achieve their shared mission, shared vision, or shared fundamental and foundational collective belief.

Those loyalties are not absolute. They are sometimes set aside by other relevant factors for people. People who are working to achieve a collective common interest goal or a shared mission of some kind can sometimes be pulled away from that aspirational collective agenda if those people in that setting begin to believe that their own original and most primal "Us" group is currently in danger, or if the people believe they will personally lose material advantage instead of gain material advantage if the targeted common mission or the targeted common vision goal is actually achieved.

Some People Focus Primarily on Their Beliefs and Mission

The reality is that some people can find that other motivators on the alignment trigger chart can push them away from mission or vision as a core functional motivation factor for their own thoughts and behaviors

At the other end of that loyalty and commitment continuum, however, there are some people whose primary motivator and top priority in life is their missions, and that loyalty is almost impossible to shake based on other factors and events.

For a number of people, that commitment to their belief or their mission is so deep and so strong that it can become functionally an obsession, and that commitment or belief can become a top priority that pushes all other priorities in their lives aside.

True believers can be very motivated. Zealots exist. Zealots can be inspirational, and zealots can be destructive. Zealots often proselytize and zeolots sometimes attack or reject non-zealots. Zealots can frighten people.

At the other end of that continuum, Zealots can bring other zealots into a shared mission/shared vision alignment that can sometimes be extremely positive and beneficial to their overall group, and that is emotionally reinforcing to other people who share that belief.

That same overwhelming level of conviction can cause people to believe in a mission or belief system that can create negative consequences if the true believers collective "Us/Them" instincts, and collective and very negative instinctive behavior packages, become activated against anyone who is not a believer in their belief system.

People who are true believers sometimes feel their conviction to their own perceived truth to be so powerful that they reject anyone who doesn't share their belief and can even kill, or badly damage, people who hold other beliefs — with no sense of guilt or ethical regret or remorse for the damage they do.

Killings based on zealotry happen — and the people doing the killings have their basic "Us/Them" instincts activated and those instincts in their most dangerous level of activation cause people to feel no guilt in destroying and damaging whoever they perceive to be "Them."

Any set of triggers that invokes those instinctive "Us/Them" values at that highly intense and negative belief system level can sometimes become divisive, dysfunctional, and personally dangerous relative to anyone who is not a believer in whatever the mission or vision is for that set of people who hold that belief at the most intense levels.

Loyalty to Leaders Can Often Fill That Alignment Motivation Role

That intense level of instinct-sculpted loyalty is sometimes directed toward a belief, an organization, or societal structure of some kind. In a significant number of cases, the loyalty is directed toward a leader. In many other situations, the intense loyalty is focused on a nation, a tribe, or an ethnic group of some kind.

National loyalty is usually called patriotism. A number of people feel strong-and-motivating patriotic-loyalty to their nation, and are willing to both die for and kill for their nation. Patriotic wars have abounded throughout our history, and many people have had their relevant "Us/Them" instincts activated fully by those wars.

Large numbers of people in a growing number of countries feel their most intense loyalty to their clan or tribe, their tribal identity, and tribal leader. In countries like Syria or Iraq, almost no one has any sense of national loyalty. Their loyalty is to their tribe.

Kurds in each of those countries feel intense loyalty to their own tribe and its language, culture, history, and leadership. They have no sense they owe any loyalty to the local nation surrounding their tribe. As the books *Primal Pathways*, *Cusp of Chaos*, and *Peace In Our Time* all point out, the most relevant sets of intergroup instincts and behaviors that are activated in those settings all focus on the key Tribes as their explicit and functional loyalty commitment.

A significant number of people in a number of settings — including some areas of our country — have their personal loyalty to a leader function as their primary mission in life.

A fairly significant number of people in a number of settings have a deep commitment to a leader and make loyalty to that leader a very high priority or even their top priority.

Loyalty to a leader is clearly an instinctive thought process — and many people tend to feel very right acting out of loyalty for a leader. Gangs in our streets and prisons clearly make leader loyalty instincts a key tool for the way they structure and run gangs. Some of our political settings and religious settings also have the role of the leader elevated to a loyalty focusing process.

Countries with Kings, Emirs, or comparable royal leaders often generate strong and direct loyalty levels to those leaders — and people are often willing to die to protect and support whomever is in those roles.

In our own country, street and prison gangs, cults, some political parties, and many kinds of teams all tend to have leaders who expect to be supported, and who trigger loyalty-based instinct-supported behaviors from their followers.

Many cultures in other countries have a cult of leadership as an anchoring belief and primary motivator. That is not the most enlightened set of values and beliefs, and it clearly does not help us in our quest for intergroup Peace, if the leaders themselves in those leader focused settings do not want Peace in their settings for any combination of reasons.

This is an area where it could be good for future enlightened behavior if we get more people to understand the role of instincts in creating emotions, behaviors, and beliefs on those issues. We could benefit over the long run if we get more people in those groups, and those settings, to understand that set of loyalties, and to understand both their consequences and their implications.

Knowledge is power. We need to help people with those kinds of loyalty levels to understand how instincts structure both their thoughts and behaviors to make both future interactions more Peaceful, and to help make a shared quest for Peace a unifying factor.

Peace Can Be a Mission

In our own country, we need enlightened people who choose to make Peace, itself, a legitimate part of their mission. Peace, itself, can be both a mission and a vision in its own right. Peace can be a goal, a commitment, a strategy, a value, an expectation, and a mission. We will be far better served as a nation if we can have a growing number of people who choose to support Peace and make Peace a core part of their personal mission.

If people in our country understand the full benefits that can result from Peace for all people, then getting people collectively aligned with Peace as both the goal and the strategy can function as its own group and individual motivator. That Peace centered functionality can create its own reinforcing alignment energy and that collective commitment to achieving Peace can trigger its own self-supportive behaviors in all of our settings.

When people in our settings understand that goal and that Peace building approach clearly, and when people believe at a personal level that achieving Peace can avert danger, expand our sense of "Us," and result in a collective material gain for all groups, then our other five key motivation factors can align with and support Peace as our collective mission.

That potential role for a mission and a vision as a trigger for alignment is true for us as a nation, and it is also true in all of our other organizational settings.

The most skillful leaders in our own communities and organizational settings need to line all of the most relevant alignment factors up in favor of Peace — in support of Peace. As a nation, we need to use the full set while understanding both exactly what we are doing, and why we are doing it.

On 9/11, We Were All One People

We clearly cannot eliminate our "Us/Them" instincts. Our instincts are always with us. They are a key part of who we each are. So we need to understand that reality, and we need to work with our relevant sets of instincts. As part of that process, we need to use this set of six instinct linked triggers to help us create both alignment and the context for intergroup Peace.

As Sun Tzu said very clearly in *The Art of War* – understand and use your terrain.

That is good advice for war. We should follow it for Peace. Our basic instincts are actually the functional and relevant terrain we live in for Peace.

Those instincts are embedded in each of us. We can't erase them. We should not pretend they do not exist.

What we can do, however, is use and channel those instincts in a much better, safer and more productive ways that help us achieve Peace.

As a key part of that alignment strategy, our very best approach to achieve Peace at this point in our history is to coalesce again around being an American "Us." When the terrorists flew their airplanes into the World Trade Center on September 11, there was a time of pure American coalescence — a time where we all appreciated, celebrated, and even loved the essence of being American.

We had a clear sense of who we were in that moment. All six of the alignment triggers on that pyramid were fully activated and fully aligned. That alignment had great power, and we all felt very right having it define who we were and how we felt in that moment.

We need to recapture that alignment and that understanding. We need to recapture it and we need to channel it into strategies and approaches that will create the right opportunity and the right channels for all of us to go down for the years that are directly before us.

The best way of recapturing that sense of being us is to anchor our sense of who we are again on the values we have as an American us – values we felt that day but could not articulate that day in any way that helped us retain that strong and clear sense of us beyond those initial days after that attack.

The final chapter of this book describes the 12 basic core and foundational values that we could — and should — collectively adopt that will help us create and maintain a strongly value-based new American "Us." At a basic level, the proposed values needed to anchor *The Art of InterGroup Peace* are built on the core values that have made us great as a country, as fundamental and foundational guides for who we are, and for the best parts of what we have been.

We need to use those same beliefs in very intentional and very explicit ways as a package to guide us today. We need to use our full tool kit of interaction approaches included in this book to achieve *InterGroup Peace* as an American "Us," and we need to anchor our sense of "Us" on our most enlightened and most mutually beneficial shared beliefs.

We Can Trigger Alignment Factors in Any Setting

We can use any or all of those trigger factors and functions to create a temporary sense of "Us" in any setting. We can also use them over time as direct commitments to each other to create a long lasting, solid, internally aligned, self-perpetuating sense of us.

Sun Tzu also very clearly advocated alignment in *The Art of War*.

Sun Tzu talked about the factors that motivate an army to be aligned to achieve victory in war. Sun Tzu actually believed that alignment was key to winning a war.

The Art of InterGroup Peace believes we need alignment to win our Peace.

We Need to Activate Alignment Motivation Factors and a Sense of Common Interest

Alignment is the key.

The Art of InterGroup Peace depends — at a very basic level — on having people from all groups within an organization, community, or country aligned in spirit and ready to act together in their mutual and common interest.

Leaders should make a commitment to achieving intergroup Peace in the settings where they lead, and then should look at the alignment trigger pyramid to see which of those triggers can be used in that setting to create aligned behaviors and a sense of being aligned. The use of the pyramid in each setting depends on the actual situation in each setting.

Many successful leaders know or sense and at least partially understand most of those group alignment triggers now — either intuitively or experientially. Successful leaders generally use at least some of those factors at least somewhat effectively now. It is better to understand that specific set of triggers cognitively and intellectually instead of just intuitively — but both approaches can work.

Sun Tzu said that a great leader for war knows exactly how and when to activate the tactics that trigger victory. He compared the act of the leader to pulling the trigger on a crossbow.

He described the cocked and loaded crossbow as being the inherent energy of the people in the army and he described the selected tactical decision and the well-timed pulling of the crossbow trigger to be a key victory factor for any leader — knowing both where to direct the arrow and when to pull the trigger.

A lack of clarity for either direction or timing makes a leader in wartime unlikely to be successful.

The same is true for *The Art of InterGroup Peace*. Our leaders need to know what factors can create both alignment and Peace for each setting, and our leaders need to know how and when to activate those factors for each relevant situation.

We need to be both strategic and timely in those efforts — and we need to put together plans that will move us in aligned and intentional ways to our mutual goals.

We very much need to look at how we can align our relevant sets of instinctive behaviors and alignment factors today to help everyone both understand the value of Peace, and then we need to work collectively to help create and protect Peace.

We Have Options for InterGroup Interactions

Other chapters of this book explain our history and predict our future using the context of those instinctive behaviors and those alignment triggers. Before looking at the history of this country and at our current status relative to our intergroup interactions, it is functionally very useful to look very explicitly at the various specific options we now have as a country relative to future intergroup interactions. We do have choices. We have clear and useful options. We now need to understand our options, and we need to make choices in each setting about those options in ways that will help us down the path to Peace.

We need to understand the set of options and approaches that can be used to structure intergroup interactions and we need to select and use the approach that makes the most sense in each setting and each situation.

Choices Range from Isolation for Each Group to Full Melding into a New Group

The continuum of options that are available to us to use in creating intergroup relationships reaches from complete and isolated separation of the relevant groups at one end of the continuum, to complete assimilation, melding and full intergroup blending at the other end of the continuum.

Full blending between groups is highly unlikely to happen as the functional strategy used for most intergroup situations and settings — and

we also clearly can't afford to simply stay in separate and totally conflicted intergroup interactions if we want to achieve intergroup Peace — so the paths we now need to select for our intergroup connections at this point in our history will probably come more from the middle of that *Art Of InterGroup Peace* alignment option continuum outlined in the next chapter of this book.

If we do this process well, we should be able to choose solutions from different segments of the continuum to help us resolve different aspects of our future alignment needs for each relevant setting. The solution approach we select for our schools, for example, may be at a different point on the interaction continuum than the interaction solution set we will use for our ethnic groups.

It's a good thing to understand the full range of available organizational and alignment options as we take the next needed steps to achieve Peace.

As this chapter has described, we have six very useful alignment motivators that cause people to be aligned. We also have eight very useful alignment options.

The next chapter of this book discusses each of those eight alignment options and explains and describes ways we can use each of those structural options appropriately and well.

We need to start with a commitment to intergroup Peace, and then we need to look both at the triggers we can activate to get groups to align, and the specific organizational options we have to structure and achieve alignment.

Making the right decisions on each of those factors at this point in time will be important, but we also need to recognize that we are in a learning process, and we will not make all of the right decisions all of the time.

We also need to be in a mind-set of continuous improvement that lets us learn from our mistakes and build new approaches when approaches we try actually falter or fail. Peace will not happen unless we cause it to happen.

Let's learn how to do that and let's very intentionally make the learning process as safe and forgiving as we can along the way. Beginning with an understanding of our options as outlined in the next chapter of this book.

Look back frequently at the alignment trigger pyramid in this chapter when making those choices to see which triggers might help move people effectively to each alignment option.

CHAPTER NINE
Basic Organizational Models for InterGroup Interactions

THERE ARE A number of ways that groups can interact with one another.

People can interact in stress and conflict - and people can interact in Peaceful alignment.

People can oppose each other, and people can collaborate and help each other collectively succeed.

People can choose to be in rigid isolation — and people can choose to blend, meld, and even assimilate until there is only one group in a situation or setting.

There are a wide range of choices for intergroup interaction.

We need to understand each choice for intergroup interaction that is available to us on the functioning continuum of possible interactions.

In order to succeed at The Art of InterGroup Peace, we need to look at each intergroup situation that exists and we need to figure out what levels and what types of intergroup interaction structures, models, and approaches will give us the best chance of achieving and maintaining intergroup Peace in each intergroup setting.

There are multiple variations for interaction that are possible — but they can be distilled down for strategic purposes to eight basic ways that groups can functionally interact. Each type and each approach for interaction has its value and each has its appropriate use.

To achieve Peace in any intergroup setting, it makes sense to determine which of the eight basic approaches is the best fit for that setting.

Those eight approaches exist because they all work in the real world of intergroup interactions.

The list represents approaches that are used now in various settings.

Those commonly used approaches are commonly used and they are included on the intergroup interaction option list because they do work and because they add value to the relevant groups who use them.

Sun Tzu, in *The Art of War*, outlined a number of organizational approaches that can be used by armies as tools to help achieve victory in war settings. He based his list of approaches on models and strategies that are actually used in war. In that same vein, *The Art of InterGroup Peace* outlines and uses an organizational tool kit that contains a continuum of eight basic functional intergroup interaction approaches that can each be used by groups to have a functional relationship with one another.

Most intergroup settings end up using the approaches that their history of interactions has created for the setting. The people who arrange for the specific intergroup approaches tend to stumble into the approaches that seem to be possible in each setting.

The people involved generally don't choose their specific interaction model strategically from an interaction continuum.

They end up using models and approaches that are created by their circumstances and intergroup history of beliefs.

The Art of InterGroup Peace calls for a more deliberate and intentional thought process for choosing the specific intergroup interaction approach for each setting.

Groups should be able to make deliberate choices about the model they use.

Groups that need or want to have a powerful relationship with other groups in a setting should use the model and the interaction approach that works best in the specific context and the actual situation that exists for them as groups.

Each of the eight possible functional approaches on The Art of InterGroup Peace continuum can be used to achieve and structure a specific degree and type of intergroup interaction.

Alternative Range from Unaligned to Melded

The interaction continuum ranges from complete, unaligned, entirely separate and potentially conflicted status between the groups of people at the top of the organizational continuum to building formal and very intentionally structured intergroup alliances in the middle of the continuum and then the list extends to a complete blending and full assimilation of people from all situationally relevant groups on the bottom of the continuum.

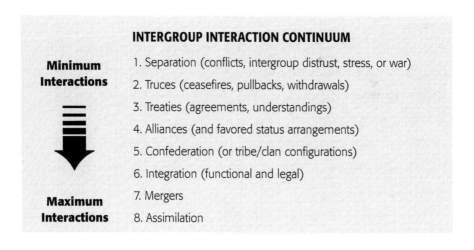

Each of the approaches included on this continuum has its own value and each has its own utility when it is used in a situation where it makes specific sense as the appropriate choice for the successful and functional interaction between the groups in that setting.

Knowing the full range of options that is available to structure those interactions can make it easier for the people who want to end conflict and create intergroup Peace to select the best option for the actual groups in each relevant setting.

Understanding the full set of potential interaction options is also very useful for looking back at the history of various intergroup interactions in a way that improves understanding about the approaches that have been used by groups in each setting in the past.

Each of the eight interaction options can functionally be used in combination with any of the 12 variable issues of instinctive terrain that were outlined in the first chapters of this book.

Those two sets of factors can be combined to design the situation specific strategies that can work effectively for intergroup alignment in each setting.

The approaches listed on the interaction continuum can obviously also be used in connection with the six approaches for defusing activated us/them instinct that were outlined in Chapter Two. In fact, a couple of the interaction options that are included on this interaction list — truces and ceasefires — also appear as major tools on that us/them instinct de-activation strategy and response list.

Those eight approaches to intergroup interaction can also all be used in strategic linkages with each of the six alignment triggers that bring people together in groups.

When people in a setting select one of the eight interaction approaches, then the six alignment-triggers can be used with the relevant people to increase the likelihood of success for the interaction approach.

Also, for obvious reasons, the choices that are made about which of the interaction options to use should be linked to the six-step culture-building tool kit that is described in the culture use chapter of this book.

For most of the interaction approaches to succeed, it will be important to put in place a culture that helps the people interact most effectively and with the highest likelihood of collective success.

Having the right culture in place can significantly enhance the probability of success.

Creating alignment as a group and basic culture building processes both have obvious relevance and use for several of the interaction options.

Separation, Truce, Treaty, Alliance, Confederation, Integration, Mergers, and Assimilation

The eight basic functional categories of organizational structure and group interaction options that can be put in place between two or more groups of people are: (1) Separation, (2) Truces, (3) Treaties, (4) Alliances, (5) Confederations, (6) Integration, (7) Mergers, and (8) Assimilation.

Separation is the first option on the list — for various somewhat obvious logistical reasons. Separation clearly involves the lowest level of intergroup interaction.

Separation can actually be a very intentional Peace strategy when it is used to keep groups from fighting by keeping the groups separate from each other.

Separation can protect and enhance intergroup Peace situations when it is a strategic choice and when it is done in the safest and least inflammatory ways.

Full assimilation is at the other extreme of the continuum. That approach also needs to be done well to succeed.

Fully assimilated groups disappear entirely as separate groups. That process also needs to be well understood and well done to give it the greatest chance of success.

Each category of intergroup interaction on the continuum has its own risks, problems, and benefits.

Each approach has its potential use in the right situation and the right setting. It is useful to recognize that even complete separation between groups — the interaction approach that is listed at the top of the continuum chart (page 243) — can add value to the lower set of groups and can be a good choice for groups to make if the separation between the groups is intentional, not hostile, and if the separation is not accompanied by some on-going levels of functioning and continuing intergroup stress or on-going intergroup conflict between the separate groups.

Full separation that results in conflict and perpetual intergroup stress is a bad choice. Full separation that results in no conflict or stress can be a useful choice.

Each option has the potential to be part of the tool kit for intergroup linkages that can be used to achieve Peace. Those approaches can each be used in a wide range of settings — and they can each have value in a number of ways when they are used.

1. Separation

The first category on the full continuum of possible intergroup interaction is — for obvious reasons — simple and basic, complete separation of groups by group. In that level of interaction status, groups in any setting are each simply separate groups — each with their own identity, culture, approaches, and agendas.

Separate groups of various kinds can functionally exist near each other with no official, formal, functional, or structured intergroup interaction.

That full separation approach can be the easiest form of interaction between groups because it doesn't require any actual interaction between the groups. Groups can decide to be Peacefully separate — with no formal and structural interaction at any level between the groups.

Being separate in a deliberate and intentional way doesn't require any structured issue-related contracts, or any structured rules of engagement or non-engagement.

Pure separate status happens for groups in many settings and that status can be a perfectly functional, normal, and Peaceful intergroup situation.

Separate Groups in Close Proximity Tend to Trigger Conflicts

Functioning as entirely separate groups works particularly well if the separate groups do not share turf of any kind, or if they are not locked into permanently adjacent geography. Proximity generally creates various intergroup issues.

The issues that exist for entirely separate groups can be more problematic and potentially troublesome when any set of separate groups find themselves at some levels of close proximity to one another or actually overlap with one another in some way.

Being entirely separate can still generate intergroup problems when the entirely separate groups actually have experienced some levels of situational InterGroup incidents and have had some negative InterGroup interactions that create negative InterGroup perceptions and reactions.

Because of our intergroup instincts, several kinds of negative intergroup interaction problems can be triggered as a consequence of close geographic proximity between separate groups that results in interactions.

Because we all have our us/them instinct packages in place, interaction between entirely separate but geographically proximate groups is unfortunately too often linked to on-going levels of intergroup distrust, intergroup dislike, or even to actual periodic intergroup conflict.

Us/Them instincts can be too easily triggered when people are constantly and personally reminded in various ways of the differences that exist between their "Us" and a particular interrelating and geographically proximate "Them."

When two groups do exist in proximity to one another and if the groups have no formal or functional relationship with one another and are not in a state of intergroup conflict at any level — the leaders of both groups can be very well served by deliberately avoiding any situations or circumstances that could trigger any of our us/them instinct packages and any related us/them behaviors for either group.

As outlined in Chapter Two, deliberate avoidance of any behavior that will trigger us/them instincts in a negative way can be a very good strategy for groups in those situations.

When any negative us/them behavior outcomes do begin to happen between separate groups, the separate groups can be well served by looking at the other interaction approaches on the continuum — often beginning with truces or even ceasefires — if the intergroup interactions have reached actual levels of conflict that require a ceasefire before the groups can move toward higher levels of intergroup Peace.

2. Truces, Ceasefires, and Pullbacks

The second category of interaction on the intergroup alignment continuum is truces, ceasefires, and functional pullbacks or withdrawals of forces.

Those approaches can each be used when groups are interacting with one another and the interaction has escalated in negative ways to actual conflict or to impending conflict.

When groups are in some level of intergroup stress, intergroup conflict, or actual war — the groups can decide to deliberately and intentionally create functional categories of intergroup interactions that are less conflicted.

Conflict at any level can be damaging, dysfunctional, destructive, and unsettling. Groups often benefit when conflict ends.

There are several standard and commonly used approaches that can end immediate conflict. Truces are a good way of ending conflicts. So are ceasefires and actual troop pullbacks or withdrawals that can be done when another group's turf has been encroached or invaded.

Those types of conflict-ending or stress-mitigating intergroup interactions are generally more formal as an intergroup interaction than simple geographically proximate co-existence.

Those specific kinds of negotiated truce-related interactions that are used in intergroup settings are usually the direct consequence of some level of active conflict between the groups. The approaches used by the groups to stop levels of immediate conflict in each setting tend to be specific to the facts and the circumstances that exist in each conflicted setting.

Truces are fairly common as a tool to use in those kinds of direct intergroup conflict situations. When two parties are in conflict, a common and useful way of ending the current bloodshed and/or reducing the immediate levels of intergroup damage is for both parties to agree to call a truce.

A truce means that open hostilities between the groups stop for the time included in the truce. Truces can be very time limited and they can also be open-ended. When a truce is in place in any setting, active fighting at least temporarily ends in that setting.

Truces often contain specific agreements about expected behavior levels during the truce. Negative interactions and behaviors that are included as banned behaviors under the terms of the truce can end while the truce is in place.

A truce can be a good thing for groups. A truce can be a particularly good thing when it keeps blood from being spilled and when it keeps conflict from escalating.

Avoiding escalation is generally a good goal to achieve. When conflict escalates in any setting, it can be much harder to end that conflict and to minimize the damage done by the conflict.

A truce can offer significant benefit to a situation when it can keep active intergroup damage from being done, and when it keeps an escalation of hostilities from occurring.

A truce is not Peace, but a truce can help groups move in the direction of Peace. A truce can be an important step on the path to Peace.

A truce can be a formal negotiated and mutually agreed upon cessation of current overt hostile action — but it's generally not a cessation of intergroup hostilities or a permanent resolution of intergroup issues. Truces are often an important tool to be used as an early step in an actual Peace making process, but a truce is usually not the end of the war or the end of conflict.

People sometimes confuse the two statuses and strategies. Peace is intended to be a permanent ending of hostilities. A truce is a delay in hostilities and a temporary halt in the processes of war and in the active manifestation of intergroup conflict.

So a truce is not the same as a permanent state of Peace, but it can create a temporary status of functional Peace that can lead to permanent Peace.

A truce can be created in times of actual armed conflict. Truces can also be created outside war settings when two groups in a setting — a community or a business or an organization of some kind — agree to stop whatever kind of intergroup fighting and negative actions are happening to create at least temporary cessation of active hostile actions between the groups.

Ceasefires are a very specific category of truce that are aimed at ending military action at a direct level.

Ceasefires can also be very good things to do. Having shooting stop is a positive outcome. It is good in conflicted settings to stop blood from being shed.

Again — a simple ceasefire in any situation is usually also not a long-term solution for any two groups of people — but it can be a hugely important step in the process.

Other steps are needed to turn a truce, or a ceasefire, into a full cessation of hostilities or into actual Peace, but having a ceasefire can significantly increase the likelihood that the warring parties can create the context where they can negotiate a higher level of Peace.

Pullbacks can also be necessary in some settings.

When any group of people has invaded, intruded, or encroached into another group's geographic or functional turf, pullbacks from that invasion status are often used to end the active hostilities, and reduce conflict levels in that specific setting. Pullbacks involve one group removing their forces and giving up physical control over another group's turf.

Groups hate having their turf invaded at a functional and instinctive level.

Pullbacks often have more positive impact on intergroup interactions than a simple ceasefire, because pullbacks can reduce the activation of very intense turf protection instincts that exist for any groups whose turf has been invaded.

Pullbacks are also not Peace, but they can also be an important step on the path to Peace in some settings if they are done in ways that enhance the likelihood of Peace being negotiated.

All pullbacks are not military. Pullbacks can also happen in various community settings, where one group of people has felt encroachment in some way by another group of people. Encroachment in a wide range of ways can set up a whole array of negative intergroup instinctive reactions.

Understanding that encroachment of one kind or another is a relevant issue in a setting and can be very important to the intergroup process. In many settings, having groups take both symbolic and functional steps to end various kinds of encroachment can significantly reduce intergroup conflict emotions and energy levels.

If the goal in a setting is to reach a higher level of Peaceful and positive intergroup interactions, then truces, ceasefires, and pullbacks can all help to create a context where other levels of agreements are more likely to be reached.

It's hard to negotiate many levels of agreements while people are still killing one another or doing active damage to the other group.

3. Agreements, Treaties, and Understandings

The next step up the alignment interaction continuum between groups is to actually reach agreements on various intergroup issues. Agreements are a widely used intergroup interactions tool.

Agreements can set up more formal intergroup interactions that can involve and include an explicit and codified understanding of some kind about future behaviors and future interactions between the relevant groups.

Agreements are a frequently used way to structure formal intergroup alignments and arrangements that are hard to achieve until the groups have achieved at least a truce or a ceasefire.

Formal agreements can also create the context and the infrastructure for a truce or ceasefire to continue to occur over periods of time.

Groups who want to end at least the current instances of conflict that are happening between themselves can reach situational agreements with one another to end the fighting, and then can use those agreements as part of longer term solutions and approaches that can help resolve issues between the relevant groups.

Basic intergroup agreements can — when they are well done — often functionally resolve some, or all, of the specific issues that have at least situationally triggered the current fighting.

Agreements between groups can be very basic and they can be very complex.

Treaties Can Create an Anchor for Future Peace

Treaties are basically a step up the interaction continuum from a basic agreement. Treaties can be a very positive step up the continuum from agreement toward Peace.

Agreements are key initial steps, however. Agreements are generally needed to start the process. Groups that have reached agreement are groups that are not at war. Ending war — even temporarily — is a major step toward Peace.

Treaties can build on the agreements that are created. Treaties can be used as a more formal and more detailed level of agreement between groups. Nations often use treaties as a tool to create specific sets of understandings between nations on particular issues.

Written treaties are a very common tool that is used in almost every culture and national setting on the planet to document the agreements that were reached between various nations and between various warring parties.

Treaties can be used to end intergroup fighting, to achieve some understanding about future intergroup interactions, and then to define and codify specific areas of agreement between the parties.

Treaties and agreements can both be very good Peacemaking tools. Really well designed treaties can have a very positive impact on all parties and the very best treaties can create their own categories of intergroup Peace.

Bad treaties, however, can simply delay or disguise the conflict, and some bad agreements can even increase and tee up future conflict levels and prolong current intergroup anger and conflict.

Punitive and revengeful agreements tend to create problems for future Peaceful interactions. Win/win treaties and win/win agreements are the best approach relative to the long-term stability of Peace — because one-sided treaties tend to have one side continue to be angry and one-sided treaties can create on-going issues that continue to motivate and incent at least one group to undermine or somehow destroy the one-sided Peace.

"Understandings" Can Be Useful in Some Settings

In some cases, where the situation that exists doesn't lend itself to a formal, written, and explicitly documented agreement or treaty, then many of that same basic set of conflict abating goals and approaches can be achieved in that setting by creating "understandings."

When two groups are in a state of conflict inside one of our cities, for example, the actual creation of a treaty might be difficult for a number of reasons, but the creation of an "understanding" that functions as treaty between the groups can have great benefit and can serve the cause of Peace in that setting.

Understandings can be reached between conflicted groups through various communication tools and approaches that can be used when the hostile actions stop and when new and mutually agreed upon intergroup behaviors replace the prior hostilities and the prior damaging behaviors.

Understandings are often more fragile than a treaty. They can be less effective and less clear than an actual written agreement — but understandings also work very well in specific situations to stop open conflict in a setting. Understandings should be used to structure and support intergroup conflict reduction when agreements and treaties are not possible.

Understandings can directly help prevent bloodshed and understandings can cause pauses, ceasefires, and even pullbacks to occur for both war and for immediate conflict in some settings where a treaty is impossible to achieve.

North and South Korea have functionally had a type of "understanding" for decades — and with both sides understanding where their current functional boundaries are, and both sides understanding what the functionally acceptable behaviors might be that can keep those two armies from clashing with each other in the battlefield with full force of weaponry and arms.

Understandings can be very useful as a tool, depending on the specific situation.

In a given community in this country, local groups might have an understanding on relevant issues like having the head of the school system or the police force, or the majority position on some appointive or elective board, rotating in some agreed upon way between the local ethnic groups who make up the population of a city, a community, or a school district.

Those kinds of intergroup understanding can have the functional effect and the impact of a treaty between those groups of people without going through the same codification and signing processes that a formal treaty or a written agreement entails.

All three of those tools — agreements, treaties, and understandings — can help move a conflicted situation in a positive path toward Peace. Each should be used when the situation in a specific setting calls for that specific tool to be used.

4. Alliances Create Mutual Support Alignments

The next step toward tighter alignment between groups on the overall interaction alignment continuum goes a step past ceasefires, truces, and even past treaties and creates formal intergroup alliances. Alliances can be a powerful tool for intergroup interactions.

In an alliance, groups agree to aligned behavior to jointly support the shared goals of the alliance.

Alliances can be very useful to create positive and productive on-going intergroup interactions in a collaborative and mutually beneficial way.

The next step up the continuum toward Peace from agreements and arms-length treaties is to create actual functioning alliances between two or more groups. Alliances can extend beyond neutrality and alliances can go far past simply ending hostilities.

The core concept of alliances is for the groups to be allies of one another. Alliances can be mutual support agreements — with the allies in any given situation agreeing to support each other in key, targeted, and generally well defined areas.

NATO – the North Atlantic Treaty Organization – functions as an Alliance that was created by treaties. NATO was originally formed in response to a common enemy and in regard to a collectively perceived shared level of danger.

Now the NATO organization has taken on its own substantial reality and functionality. It continues to give the NATO member organizations a defense tool as allies against external enemies.

Several of the six group alignment triggers that were discussed in the previous chapter are often used to incent groups of people to create alliances. Danger works well to cause people to form alliances. A sense of danger or a mutually perceived common enemy can clearly motivate the existence of alliances, and those triggers can cause alliances to be fostered, structured, and supported.

In some cases, a shared ideology or a common belief system can be a sufficient trigger to put an alliance in place. When people perceive that their groups have common goals or common missions in significant areas, an alliance can be set up to help the groups each achieve those goals.

A positive bi-product of alliances is that when they are appropriately structured, the alliances and their goals can trigger a working internal sense of "Us" on key issues for the full set of allies in the alliance.

Alliances can create collective leverage in key areas of activity — like political power or economic influence.

At a national level in this country, we see an emerging Hispanic Alliance that is being created to achieve some of those alliance functions and purposes.

The various groups of people in this country that are labeled Hispanic are actually very different from each other as cultures and ethnicities. Cuban Americans and Mexican Americans do not share the same cultures. Puerto Rican Hispanics and Chilean Hispanics are also two very different groups of people.

There is no "Hispanic" culture for this country. The various cultures that exist do, however, increasingly function as allies of one another for various political and economic purposes.

The truth is that there can be significant political leverage created for all Hispanic groups in an area or in the country when there is the creation of an alliance of Hispanic groups that can function as allies in various ways for collective and mutually supportive political purposes.

All groups in that alliance can benefit in various ways in various settings because the alliance exists and because it does its collective work to create influence.

That alliance doesn't merge those groups of people. Those separate ethnic groups don't blend into one new Hispanic group. They do become allies, however, and that approach can create significant common and collective leverage for the people who are allied under that grouping.

In local American communities, various groups often form alliances of various kinds to influence elections, appointments, and government level decision-making and to create collective economic or political advantage for the groups involved.

Agreements to extend bus lines or to extend subways into areas that serve one or more of the relevant local groups are often more likely to be made into successful projects for communities if they have some level of local multi-group Alliance support.

Community Alliances Can Achieve Community Goals

Getting local groups to collectively support healthy living agendas is a good alliance focus area. Creating significantly healthier activity level logistics for entire communities is an area where alliance thinking can have a significant impact that can bring people together and can create benefits for all groups.

Likewise, getting local groups in each of our communities to collectively support the neuron development and the neuron connectivity levels for all of the very young children from all of our groups should also be looked at as a potential coalescing and high impact agenda for future Alliance approaches, tactics, and strategies.

Those issues and those specific opportunities to do important things collectively for the common good and the mutual benefit of all groups are discussed in more detail in the next chapter of this book. It is clear that creating safe streets, convenient walking areas, and community based transportation functionality are all often made more successful by the creation of Alliances between relevant groups in each setting.

Trade Associations Are Working Alliances

In the American political and governance environment, Trade Associations are an alliance tool that has been used for many years in a specialized and very effective way in this country by a very large number of organizations to influence much of the policy level decision-making that happens in our state and national governments.

Trade Associations are one of the most common alliance format approaches in this country, today. Trade Associations have been created both nationally and in a wide range of local and state settings to bring together the collective influence of multiple entities within an industry or within an interest group in a common course of action, with a common cause for association members who associate because they collectively want to influence the laws, the rules, and the regulations that affect members of the group.

There are literally thousands of functioning and staffed Trade Associations in our states and in our national capital. Some of those Associations are massive and can be highly influential.

The American Medical Association has long been a significant power in American politics, for example. Medical practitioners who may actually compete with each other very directly for patients in their own individual daily workplace settings can use the AMA trade association's structure to function as a collective alliance to band together in Washington to speak with a common voice on issues that affect physicians at a more macro level.

Likewise, the pharmaceutical manufacturers and the airlines of America all tend to compete fiercely with one another in the marketplace and those manufacturers and industries also still find that their industry can be well served for many issues if they also function as an Alliance through their trade associations on issues of policy, law, and regulation.

Labor unions — who each have their own direct political voice in each setting — also tend to find that their collective influence can sometimes be enhanced by functioning in some ways as a national or regional coalition of unions to make their positions collectively known.

The number of trade Associations that exist in this country and that deliberately function as Alliances is very large. The skill set that is needed to successfully run and govern some of those Associations looks very much, in many ways, like the skill sets that are often needed for community leaders to achieve local Peace in diverse and complex community settings.

Political parties also sometimes function as Alliances and those parties can also achieve and exercise both power and influence through the strength of their political alliance types of efforts.

Political parties can be a very effective alliance tool — and the people who run the parties who want to personally be political successes are highly motivated to have those political party-linked alliances succeed.

Leaders of political parties often try to get their supporters and their party members collectively aligned on particular issues. That can be challenging work, but that kind of political alignment has obvious impact and influence when it succeeds.

People both join and manage political parties to function in the context of an alliance.

One challenge that can exist for political party leaders in some settings can be to figure out what levels of alliance activity and allied beliefs can give them both the highest level of support from their own party members, and also receive the broadest level of support from the general public when elections determine, through voting levels, whether or not their party will be in power.

Leadership of those political alliances is also both a skillset and an art form — because the political positions that create the most positive energy from some party members may not be the political positions that also attract a majority of total voters when elections are held.

Leading political parties can be difficult work. When the process works really well, we can end up with public policies that meet the needs of the public and that have been refined, improved, and enhanced in the context of a robust multi-level interactive political debate and feedback process.

When the process goes really badly, we can end up with confused and conflicted policy leaders who are addicted to Alpha status, but don't have a clear agenda for actual leadership and who work hard to damage one another.

When the political process goes badly, it can result in various levels of us/them intergroup conflict that can trigger and activate many of our more negative us/them instinctive reactions and behaviors, and bring levels of conflict them to the political arena.

In a very worst-case situation, the political process deteriorates from a focus on contending and competing public policy strategies into very low levels of primarily instinctive us/them values and us/them behaviors, with political leaders deliberately demonizing and even dehumanizing the other party in an effort to trigger us/them instinctive reactions with voters in ways that will win elections.

The overall political alliance process that we have invented for our country can create great government when it succeeds and it can create dysfunctional, primal, and even damaging anger and conflict when it fails. In either case, the organizational model that is used in the process is to form political party level alliances.

The trade associations who influence so much of the policy making in this country face many of the same issues. They also are subject to the same sets of instinctive behaviors.

All of the levels of alignment triggers that were described in Chapter Seven are used regularly, by the people who lead Associations, to bring the people in each association together. A sense of collective danger can create alliances and can improve support for trade associations.

Common enemies and possible collective gain both very directly enhance support for those same alliances.

A sense of shared mission can obviously trigger some alliance support. All of those alignment factors can create a sense of being an "us," who needs the support of other "Us" to survive or succeed as a trade association.

Some of the public membership groups that influence public policy in this country are also based entirely on people supporting a common cause — like environmental protection or equal rights for some segments of the population.

People who join environmental groups to have higher levels of collective influence also, very often, create a sense of "Us" with other members of their group.

Each of the various public policy community organizations ends up with its own hierarchy, its own sense of turf, and its own sense of shared mission and group identity.

People who have joined together in the context of an actual trade association tend to overlook or set aside some of the prior differences between their organizations in the interest of their common mission.

Probably the most common alignment factor that is used to bring people and organizations into Alliance membership as a trade association or as a public policy coalition group is simply the presence of a defined and perceived common enemy. That common enemy trigger functions as a high energy unifying force for political party members, public policy coalitions, and trade alliance members — giving them all a factor to be allied against.

Alliances are a good tool kit to understand and utilize selectively in the right situations as we work to create and sustain Peace.

5. Confederations Create Tighter Collective Alignment

The next step up the Interaction Alignment Continuum from alliances toward tighter intergroup interaction levels is the Confederation. That particular model has its own distinct and very useful characteristics.

The confederation approach has had very useful and significant impact in a number of settings around the world because that approach works with some of our tribal instincts and with our us/them instincts in very functional ways.

Confederation resembles alliances, but the model goes a step further because the members of a confederation typically agree to form, join, and be part of a common confederated umbrella entity of some kind.

The usual pattern is that each of the confederated parties maintains their own separate status at one level, but they generally each cede some of their own actual current power to the confederation on some relevant issues and selected functions.

Ceding actual power on selective issues to a confederation takes confederations a step past alliances. Allies almost always have the option of ending and leaving an alliance, and Allies each tend to maintain their own complete and individual autonomy.

Allies and signatories to agreements and treaties generally do not have functional power over one another at any level.

Alliances guide behavior and can structure various activities for members, but they generally can't impose behaviors on alliance members in any functional way. A confederation goes a step further — and that additional process usually creates an infrastructure and governance approach for the confederation that has some actual governance roles and functional rules that apply to all members.

A Confederation generally moves past alliance to form an overall organization of some kind that contains and involves the confederated members as functioning and at least semi-autonomous sub-units within the whole confederation.

That model has been used historically in a number of traditional tribal settings. It has been the basic model used in many settings where clans are part of the tribal structure.

One of the most common and often very successful versions of the confederation approach has been to have clearly defined clans inside each tribe who function both as clans and as confederation members. The clans each have their own turf, their own identity, and their own local governance, but they also cede some powers to the senior tribal leader and to the senior governance of the tribe.

The clans of Scotland came to mind as a good example of that approach. So do the clans of the Bogandan nation within Uganda.

In each of those tribal settings, the clans continue to exist and clans self-govern in many ways, but the clans also cede some power and some basic governance and direction setting to the confederation structure at the tribal level.

We have used the confederation model very directly in our own country.

The United States of America was originally set up to actually be a confederation of states, rather than a single nation with clear national powers. That initial confederation of states was defined to have a legal status that also kept major governance for most powers reserved to the states.

The Articles of Confederation that were developed and used after the Revolutionary War defined both the roles of the independent states and the roles and rules of the National confederation.

That original, very pure, confederation model for this country evolved relatively quickly into another confederation-like approach that now functions as the United States of America.

The term "United States" that we use as our national name implies the existence of separate states that have agreed to unite.

One reason for the evolution of our national governance model from the original Articles of Confederation into a stronger version of confederation, was that the initial member states perceived a need to be better protected against a common external enemy and the original member states believed that a more national approach to governance would help create that protection.

The original confederation model wasn't entirely abandoned when the new United States of America National Constitution was created — and it was made clear in the writing of the key founding documents that some of the functions and the powers that were originally held by the states when they were functioning as separate countries and when each state still had full local autonomy on all local issues continue to remain as governance powers that are held by the states, today.

States in this country are not allowed to secede from the new national American Union. We resolved that issue with a civil war.

But states in this country can and do clearly still set up their own laws on a wide range of legal issues. Our national government creates laws in a number of areas that apply to all citizens — and there are clear national rights that apply to the citizens in all of the states, but there are also some areas where the laws are set by the states, and laws in those areas can only be set by the states.

That makes our country a kind of confederation.

Switzerland Is a Successful Confederation

Switzerland and Canada also both function as types of confederation. Each of the provinces in Canada writes its own laws on a variety of topics. Those processes are potentially able to split off from Canada and become independent nations if the people decide in a province that the path of separation is the right path for the province.

The citizens of Quebec have held elections on that very issue. They have not voted to separate — but they do periodically make that topic of separation into a self-governing nation a subject for the local electorate to address.

The provinces of Canada each function as part of the nation of Canada — and each have major areas where they create their own laws and govern their own people.

Switzerland may be the best example of a well functioning and very long-standing confederation in the world. Switzerland is a nation that functions very clearly and very intentionally as a confederation of Cantons — or local states. Each Canton in Switzerland has its own official and preferred language. Each Canton sets its own local laws in a wide range of areas.

The National Swiss government and the Canton specific governance units are all elected by the people. The Swiss use a democratic approach for both the government of the cantons and for the national government. The elections are decided by popular votes.

Each citizen of Switzerland has the same freedom, the same protection of all Swiss laws, and the same right to vote and be heard regardless of their ethnicity, or place of residence.

There are three fundamental categories of Swiss citizens — German speaking Swiss, French speaking Swiss and Italian speaking Swiss.

Those citizens in all Cantons are all Swiss — but the reality is that those three original and separate Swiss tribes have never assimilated or merged with each other. The people in each Canton continue to exist side by side as separate ethnic groups and as separate language groups inside Switzerland.

The Cantons have equal status on selected issues and all Swiss citizens also have equal status under the law, regardless of where they are in the country.

Each area has its own clear and institutionalized preference for its own culture and its own language, and the Cantons carefully preserve and protect that specific legacy and approach for each group.

People who are German Swiss can move to the territory of French Swiss or Italian Swiss and have full rights to own property, be employed, and vote in the local elections.

Each Canton has its own identity, its own culture, and its ability to govern itself in key areas. So the Canton model in Switzerland has both retained major areas of local differences between tribal groups of people, and the Swiss have simultaneously created a functioning nation that protects all of its citizens' rights and safety, and then also does very effectively the things that a nation needs to do as a nation when National economic or National defense issues need to be addressed on behalf of the entire Swiss people.

A couple of other European countries follow a similar multi-language organizational model — with both a local ethnicity approach for governance and an overall national status for all groups of people.

Belgium is legally one country — and it is also officially, historically, and functionally split into two major self-governing populations — the Flemish and the Walloons. Each group in the Belgium confederation proudly and sometimes aggressively maintains its own culture, its own geographic base, and its own separate language.

One of the legacy languages used in Belgium is based on German and the other legacy language in the country is based on French. There seems to be little or no interest by either legacy group in Belgium in blending into a single shared national language or into a single Belgium-centered national culture.

Belgium has had and still has some significant tensions between those two groups. Those tensions have existed for a very long time.

Some people who know the country well predict that Belgium will ultimately split into two separate parts along ethnic lines and will become two separate, divided, and linguistically pure countries at some point in time.

That could happen. There are quite a few people in Belgium who believe that a split into two countries would be a good thing to do. There are others who very much want Belgium to continue to function as a single nation.

The momentum for decision-making in those situations where people in a country want to spin off a piece of the country generally favors the status quo because separation is so hard to do and because separation into two separate ethnicity defined nations is not generally supported by other countries across the planet for all of the reasons that were mentioned in Chapter Four relative to internal diversity issues in other countries.

As in Switzerland and Canada, the separate groups in Belgium have strong linkages to their separate languages. The language differences between the two groups tend to help each group identify itself to itself, and the language difference also helps each group to differentiate itself from the other group.

The Confederation Model Can Support Multi-Language Countries

That point about those nations having more than one language and still functioning as a nation is mentioned in this chapter on organizational approaches that can be used for intergroup interactions because the multi-language nations who have succeeded and survived over time and who have not destroyed themselves with internal conflict have addressed that specific key issue in ways that honor and protect the language of each group.

A tendency to split into separate parts based on each group language is a major concern in every multi-lingual setting and always needs to be addressed through the strategies that are used for intergroup interactions in each setting.

The internal tribes in any setting that have language differences obviously experience periodic flare-ups of the same patterns of instinct-driven us/them energy levels and emotions in all of the countries where those language and tribal differences exist.

Cantons Might Be Useful in Nigeria, Syria, or Pakistan

Switzerland has been the most successful user of that formal tribe-centered confederation model in the world. That separate local language model has survived in the Cantons of Switzerland for centuries. It clearly has great functional value to create local intergroup Peace. Other countries should study that model carefully.

Using that confederation model — or something very much like it — might be the only way that some other highly ethnically diverse and ethnically divided countries — like Nigeria or Pakistan — could also manage to survive as nations over extended periods of time.

If each of the major tribal groups in the Congo had its own Canton — and if the civil rights of all of the individual people of the Congo from all of the local minority tribes were carefully protected in important ways by some kind of central government oversight mechanism — and if an effective protection process for civil rights existed that would be in force for all people in the country regardless of the Congolese Canton that each person from each tribe chose to live in or visit — then that level of confederation based governance functionality could finally lay to rest some of the local intergroup bloodshed that happens far too often in far too many of these countries now.

If those multi-tribal, multi-ethnic countries moved carefully to a canton-like confederation model, those multi-tribal multi-ethnic countries could continue to function as countries at one level — but they could simultaneously use the Canton mechanism and structure to give the local tribes who are both angry and conflicted today enough self-governance and local autonomy to meet their needs as tribes and actually enable them to function as tribes without hurting other people.

Individual Safety and Rights Would Need to Be Protected

That would not be easy to do. It could be done — but there would be some real risks involved for some of the people.

Changing to a Canton-like model in those settings would require some enlightened agreement about the rights of individual people in each new Canton, and it would need to protect the rights and the security of minority tribes in all of the Cantons in each of those countries.

Those rights could all be defined. They are pretty basic. That work is possible to do. The challenge in each new Canton setting would be to enforce those rights and protections for everyone as they are defined.

That Canton-based process would take tribal leaders in each setting who are collectively committed to actual Peace, and it would probably also require some level of United Nations oversight through at least a transition time frame for each setting.

The United Nations could create a process that puts the right pieces in place in every setting that decides to become a confederation. All parties in those countries would need to agree to use the UN and the UN template to help do that work.

That work — or something like it — needs to be done in a number of settings. The current multi-tribal model is failing in far too many internally conflicted settings for us not to explore functional alternatives. People are dying every day in intertribal conflicts.

Countries with significant intertribal war today need to evolve into a win/win set of solutions that reflects Canton-like autonomy and also provides Canton-like civil rights protections and safety protections for various tribes in local settings in each country.

Dividing Multi-Tribe Nations into Separate Nations Could Create Major Negative Repercussions

That suggestion is not made lightly.

Simply splitting those nations into entirely separate countries by tribe might be possible in many of those settings. That could be the right solution for many settings. But that level of functional separation into entirely separate and autonomous tribal nations would create its own set of highly negative local issues and tee up obvious dangers for many local minority people in countries like Nigeria, Pakistan or Sri Lanka.

The United Nations could and should also play a role in both defining those protections and helping people both set them up and make them real.

Personal Safety Would Be Key

Personal safety for individual people who would find themselves in local minority status in various parts of each country after the separation process would be the key concern relative to complete separation of those countries into pure tribal states.

The ability to protect the status and safety of minority people in each of the new tribal nations and the new canton settings could be impaired significantly if each tribe ran its own turf with full local tribal power and full local tribal authority and if each tribe that gains power in a setting could simply exercise full law enforcement authority over everyone local with no civil rights screens, no personal protections, and no oversight role for the minority people who would inevitably need to live in each of those new tribal nations.

Centuries of intergroup anger and intergroup discrimination could cause people who are the new leaders of any new tribal nations to take revenge against minority people in their settings who have had a history of doing negative things to their tribe in prior years and times.

Minority people in any kinds of new ethnic majority settings can often find themselves at huge personal risk just because they are a local ethnic minority — so any division into more local tribal governance situations would need to take explicit and effective steps to reduce that risk.

The danger of revenge-focused behavior is not a hypothetical concern. There is very real ethnic cleansing going on today to a significant degree in quite a few of those settings now.

Syria has almost a million ethnic refugees today. There are major refugee camps in dozens of settings in Africa and Asia.

Some of those people who have been oppressed and damaged in that setting will want revenge if the opportunity becomes available to them. That set of intergroup, us/them motivated behaviors is likely to get significantly more dangerous for local minority people if a division of those nations into separate tribal nations creates full local tribal autonomy with police power linked to us/them instinctive behaviors.

That is why creating Swiss style Cantons with full legal protection for all local minorities in each of those multi-ethnic nations in the context of an overall national government and legal process that could enforce and administer protection when protection is needed for minority people in each Canton — like tribal state could work in many settings.

The Swiss approach works well for the Swiss because it includes and involves rules that protect people's safety, and rules that very deliberately protect people's civil rights.

That Canton model could be a much better outcome for many multi-tribal areas than the purely tribal path many of these countries are on today, but it will take a well structured transition to get to that status.

The United Nations could and should set up both a confederation model set of guidelines and a template for minority group safeguards that could be used by those Canton-based countries — with actual U.N. protection used in some places for transitional protection as the new model is put in place.

The issues of using confederation as an alignment model for people are somewhat less relevant for groups in the United States at this point in time. But that approach is not entirely irrelevant to us. As noted earlier, the power of each state in this country to perform local governance on a number of issues is actually growing right now. The U.S. Constitution and the Bill of Rights provide a national infrastructure that can be an offset and counter to any threats to American freedom from any group that achieves power at the level of each state and then has its own us/them instincts negatively activated in any state setting.

Our country has key and functional confederation components today. We need to clearly understand the areas where we function as a confederation, and we need to be sure that those areas also help us achieve intergroup Peace rather than hinder and obstruct intergroup Peace.

For other countries, confederation is a good model to use in the right settings because it recognizes the reality of intergroup divisions and it definitions and incorporates those instinct-impacted groups into an effective collaboration rather than just continuing complete division between the groups.

6. Integration

The next step up the scale on the intergroup interaction continuum from confederation is functional integration. Integration is not the same as either merger or assimilation — the next steps for intergroup interaction — but integration does create a very direct on-going level of direct interaction between people and between groups of people.

Integration keeps people in their separate group, but integrates the activities and the opportunities for all people from all groups and creates joint access to all functionality by all groups.

Integration also creates open interactions between members of each group. We have used the integration model extensively in the U.S. We decided in the second half of the last century to "integrate" America. We have had partial success.

In our broader society, we have not actually merged our legacy ethnic groups and we have not merged our racial groups — but we have consistently been putting in place a number of processes, approaches, rule sets, guideline, and functional realities that are very deliberately intended to integrate people in important ways into schools, work sites, and public settings from each and every group.

Integration at multiple levels has been a very deliberate and clear policy goal for America for the past half century. That was a change of direction from our historical approach. We moved from intentional segregation to intentional integration as our interaction strategy. Many of our older laws were used to support, endorse, and even require intergroup segregation. We have evolved over several decades to very deliberately replace mandated segregation with mandated integration.

Integration for many activities is now required by law — with people from every group given equal access to schools, equal access to jobs, equal access to public facilities, and equal rights relative to the purchase and ownership of property.

Integration functionality at the individual level means that the work sites, schools, and other functional parts of society that used to be deliberately and officially segregated by race or ethnicities are no longer segregated in those ways.

We still do some functional segregation for all of the instinctive reasons and historical realities that are described at multiple places in this book, but we no longer legally mandate and impose segregation.

Integration is now the law of the land for many clearly defined aspects of life in America. It is now illegal to discriminate in hiring people. It is also illegal when we are selling things to people to discriminate by race, gender, gender preference, age, or ethnicities in any part of the selling process.

These laws are not perfect, but they have had huge impact on intergroup behaviors and on hiring practices for many people. Deliberate and structural segregation is now illegal. Integration now happens — often imperfectly — but with great regularity and full legal support.

As we figure out how to create Peace at this point in time for our country, one of the functional tools that we now have to help us move in that direction are all of the laws and regulations that have been passed that create, require, define, and support integration.

We need to be sure that our integration and anti-discrimination laws meet our needs and we need to become extremely competent in our integration efforts and approaches, and in our application of those laws.

As this book has described in a number of places, one of the best ways of guaranteeing that newly enlightened behaviors become our new normal set of behaviors and are not lost in the backlash of periodic instinct re-activation, is to write the new behaviors into our laws.

Education is good. Teaching is good. Cultural belief enlightenment is good. Laws that stay in place are even better — when it comes to guaranteeing the survival and the continuation of the new enlightened behaviors.

The natural tendency of people from all groups to have a high level of comfort in being with other people like ourselves can skew employment practices in any setting away from integration if we simply allow instinctively natural behavior to guide our hiring actions.

Requirements to not discriminate are sometimes needed to keep discrimination from being the behavior that people return to from pure instinctive comfort. Anti-discrimination laws fit that category of strategy that offsets instinctively comfortable behaviors.

Chapter Fourteen of this book describes the instincts we have to feel comfort in being surrounded by "us," and the stress and the discomfort we can feel whenever we are surrounded by whoever we perceive to be "Them."

That package of instinctive reactions by each of us can make it very hard for anyone who is the first person from any group to integrate any setting — and it can trigger a sense of stress anytime we are in a situation of minority status for significant periods of time.

Those instinct packages all make integration more difficult.

7. Mergers and Consolidations

Mergers create even tighter levels of intergroup alignment than integration. When people want to move beyond integration into a higher level of intergroup interaction, merging the relevant groups or organizations can meet that goal.

The next step up the Interaction Alignment Continuum that goes beyond alliances and goes well past simple confederations as a way of aligning two or more groups is actual merger.

Mergers happen. Companies merge with one another. Some religious groups merge with one another. Trade Associations merge with one another — particularly in cases where the trade associations already have both overlapping membership and joint members before the merger.

Labor unions merge with one another. So do some political parties.

Mergers are a tool that groups use to direct their future relationship with other groups, with the goal of being a single group, when the merger process is complete.

Merger goes beyond confederation into forming a new single merged entity with a single hierarchy, a single chain of command and a common name for the merged organization. Newly merged entities each tend to develop their own cultures that are specific to the new merged entity and they tend to do that very soon after the mergers become a functional reality.

Corporate mergers or acquisitions often take organizations that each had their own history and their own culture and put them into a new functional reality where the culture and the structure both need to change into the new reality and into the new belief system of the merged entity.

Many kinds of mergers happen in our country today. They can be a good functional way of creating permanent alignment and a permanent sense of common agenda and common good within merged entities.

The most skilled business leaders in corporate merger settings use the sets of tools outlined in this book to create internal alignment and to build functioning post-merger cultures. The most skillful of leaders set up their own internal cultures and internal alignment approaches in ways that help each business achieve its own functional goals.

Those tools are easily diverted to that use by businesses when business leaders know how to use them. That culture-building work is particularly useful to do after a merger because the merged entities or organizations each had their own culture and there is almost always immediate confusion when a merger happens about what the new culture of the merged organization will be.

The best leaders in merger situations avoid cultural confusion, cultural ambiguity, cultural dissonance, and conflict and intercultural stress by using the kinds of culture creation and implementation tools that are listed in this book to put a new culture in place that meets the needs of the merged organization.

Mergers, as an alignment tool, are not likely to be relevant to very many of the key ethnic issues here or in any country, however.

It is hard to merge races or ethnicities. We will not use formal mergers to deal with basic racial or ethnic issues in the country because there is no practical way to officially merge multiple entire ethnic groups, as groups, into a new blended ethnic group.

As groups work together to create the new set of collaborative cultures we need to achieve Peace, we will, however, see increased alignment on key values between cultures and that will constitute a form of culture merger on some issues and behaviors.

At a personal level, obviously, the increased the levels of intermarriage that are happening between people from our various racial and ethnic groups will create its own momentum toward ethnic group blending in ways that will function like a merger for some sets of people.

Multi-ethnic, "mixed" marriages create their own level of merger. That also is an area where we need to be better as a country in helping people in a multi-ethnic situation find inclusion in an "Us" that feels right to each of the relevant people.

The book, *Cusp of Chaos*, deals with some of the intermarriage issues and the opportunities they create.

The mass media, and a wide array of blended popular culture activities, will also point us toward a shared set of culture beliefs and approaches in many areas.

It is possible that the collective momentum that is generated from weaving together multiple elements of our increasingly diverse popular culture will create some merger-like consequences — but the process of blending the blessings of our cultures will not actually merge any of our separate groups into a new ethnicity.

8. Assimilation

The interaction category listed at the bottom on the Interaction Alignment Continuum (page 243) is full assimilation — the blending of various separate groups into a single amorphous fully assimilated new group.

Assimilation does happen. Assimilation is a full step past either integration or merger — because the people who are integrated are still part of their original groups and are interacting with each other in an integrated way as individuals.

In a merger, there are usually major echoes of the former groups that continue to exist in the merged entity in various ways. But when full assimilation happens, the old separate groups basically disappear and they are functionally replaced by the assimilated group.

Assimilation happens. We have seen it happen in our country. We have done it in this country in several ways.

The various historic legacy Euro-American tribal groups all basically blended — after roughly one generation in this country — into White. White is an assimilated group. Chapter Seven of this book describes that blending process.

Likewise — the people who are descended from all of the various categories of old and very separate tribes and separate ethnic groups who lived in Africa have also basically blended in this country into Black.

The African Americans are no longer Ibo or Zulu. African Americans who share ancestry from Africa have — in this country — usually blended into a group labeled Black American.

That assimilation process has only happened to those groups of people in this country.

In each of the legacy countries that exist for all of those people from both Africa and Europe — that blending into a single new skin-color based ethnic group in the old world countries actually has not happened. That blending into a racial group doesn't exist today for the people who still live in those ancestral countries on either continent. Each country in Africa and each country in Europe still uses their local legacy tribal labels for all of their people — and the laws in some of those countries still tie political and legal rights to those very specific ancestral identities.

That blending into those two groups only happened to the people from those countries who moved to this country. That blending of multiple ethnic groups from Europe and Africa into those two macro American group categories is both true and real in the U.S. today, however.

Some people who are black and some people who are white still do hold some links to their personal ancestors specific legacy ancestral tribes from Europe or Africa. But the assimilation of both Black and White Americans into those two new blended categories of people tends to be pretty consistent and functionally complete.

Asian American and Hispanic Have Not Blended

As noted earlier, not all various legacy groups who immigrated to this country have blended or assimilated into new combined categories or into a new collective and aggregated ethnic definition in this country.

We do use some group names that can mislead people into believing that other levels of assimilation have happened for other sets of people in this country. Those labels are misleading.

Our Hispanic Americans and Asian Americans and Native Americans have not blended in the same way we have seen blending for Black and White Americans. The collective strategic choices that exist today for each of the Hispanic groups in this country that were mentioned earlier in this chapter were included under the heading of forming and using Alliances as an intergroup interaction model.

The likely future for our various Hispanic Americans does not include blending the Hispanic groups into a single new group as part of any strategy or any future that will happen for those groups.

We clearly need to understand the other major macro group labels that we use for the groups of Americans that reflect other sets of non-African and non-European legacies. For reporting purposes and for much of our media coverage and our political debate, we do label some people as Asian American and some people as Native American and we label a number of people as Hispanic.

Those specific categories represent widely used group labels. Those labels are often part of the political debate in this country at several levels.

Those labels actually do not represent any level of functional group assimilation or any real blending for the groups of people in each of those categories.

None of the legacy groups that fall under those general categories have actually merged into a single new group that uses that aggregate new label to describe themselves or to organize themselves.

Hispanic Americans, Native Americans, and Asian Americans Are Not Blended Groups

Native Americans, Hispanic Americans, and Asian Americans still tend to identify more closely with their own very specific ethnic subgroup rather than feeling as though they have somehow blended into a new composite category of people with a new aggregate group label.

As noted earlier, in the discussion of Alliances, we do use the term Hispanic or Latino to label various sets of people who speak Spanish today or who have ancestors who once spoke Spanish. We use those particular grouping names approach to collectively describe those groups of people fairly often.

But that use of the Hispanic label doesn't create or represent an assimilated set of Hispanic people. People who fit that aggregate definition sometimes find that collective labeling process useful in a number of ways, but that isn't how each subgroup included under that aggregate label actually defines itself.

Mexican Americans, Cuban Americans, Puerto Ricans, and Panamanians all tend to link their own personal identity to their specific legacy country.

The term Hispanic in Miami refers to a very different ethnic group than the term Hispanic in San Diego or the Hispanic group in East Harlem. The groups have different histories, different cultures, and different functional and economic realities.

From the perspective of the group alignment continuum choices listed above in this chapter, that particular macro ethnic alignment that does exist today for Hispanic peoples in this country is actually generally closer at this point in time to either affiliation or to alliance as a group-linking tool.

That intergroup interaction for all of the Hispanic groups functions as an alliance in some ways because the various subgroups within the Hispanic population tend to have very distinctive histories and cultures, and the people in those cultures continue to have separate identities by group.

That is true — but it is also true that there are clearly some political areas where having joint leverage under the Hispanic label can be useful for each legacy group.

Political leaders who want to influence the Hispanic vote are often more willing to be inclusive and supportive in key areas because of the sense that there actually is a relevant Hispanic vote. That vote is more of an alliance than assimilation.

Cuban Americans and Mexican Americans obviously each have their own very clear identities, histories, and internal alignments. So do Puerto Ricans. People from the various Hispanic groups are increasingly aligned on political issues, however, and that can create a reason for an alliance.

Looking at the six triggers that we can use to create alignment for people, the prospect of mutual gain is a clear and current motivator for some level of Hispanic alignment. The existence of a common enemy can also function as a powerful alignment trigger for Hispanic groups of people.

The issues of immigration reform, in particular, tend to create alignment for the various Hispanic groups against the people who are perceived to be a common enemy to various Hispanic groups on those issues.

So common enemies and shared opportunity and gain can create alignments for our Hispanic citizens at some levels — but those features do not — like Whites and Blacks in this country — create assimilation as Hispanics.

Native American Tribes Are Intact as Well

Likewise, our Native American tribal groups have not assimilated. Each of the original tribes tends to keep its own tribal identities and its own tribal geographic turf.

The distinctions between tribes continue to be both clear and clearly enforced. Members of the Cree Nation are not simultaneously Navajo, Sioux, or Cherokee. Each tribe has its own reservations, its own turf, its own hierarchy, and its own history.

Those Native American legacy tribes have not assimilated and they also have not merged. Alliances do happen. Again — as with our Hispanic groups of people, there are often a number of very valid reasons to create situational alignment as an aggregate group for Native American tribes, however.

The same sets of triggers on the alignment pyramid apply to our Native American groups.

Again, common enemies to all tribes do exist relative to some issues and the common gain potential that exists for all tribes in other areas does create levels of alliance functionality for our Native American people.

The alliances that result from that shared need tend to resemble more closely the collective functions of the Trade Associations that were also mentioned earlier in this chapter.

The label Native American has use in multiple settings, but it isn't a label that indicates any level of assimilation, and it also isn't the primary label most Native Americans use to define themselves.

Asian American Groups Are Not Merging

The same is true for the Asian Americans.

Asian Americans have also clearly not assimilated into or merged any of their specific component groups in this country. Asian American is another very specific category used by various government reporting forms, but that blended label doesn't actually represent the identity label for any group of people in any functional way in this country.

The very specific Asian American intergroup differentiations and identities that continue to exist in this country today for each Asian legacy group are equally clear and equally powerful.

Both state and federal government actions do label people from a wide range of legacy groups as Asian American. Sometimes the category used for reporting for some forms is now "Asian and Pacific Islander." That further increases the confusion levels about valid and informative use of those labels.

Anyone who thinks of Japanese American, Chinese American, and Korean American as being one new melded Asian American ethnic group, or who believes that assimilation of any kind between any of those groups is happening at any level, can quickly learn the reality of that situation by talking to actual people from any of those actual groups of people.

In many cases, the specific groups included in that blended category actually harbor historic animosities against one another in ways that make current assimilation non-existent and future assimilation highly improbable.

Alliances on some issues under that label do exist for some purposes, but the differences between the groups under that label are significant enough that the actual benefits that result from mutual effort in a formal or informal alliance under that label are not very significant.

Neither assimilation nor alliance is happening at any significant national level for Asian American groups in this country and both of those interaction levels are highly unlikely to happen at any time in the future.

Intermarriage for various Asian Americans does happen with a high level of frequency, but it is usually intermarriage with White, Black, or Hispanic Americans and it is very seldom intermarriage between the various Asian legacy groups.

Various Sets of Immigrants Are Creating Functional Identities

Likewise, the blending of people in this country who have Middle Eastern ancestry into one Middle Eastern category makes no sense as a functional label. Each of the various groups who make up that category have very clear and very separate identities.

The people from Iran, the people from Egypt, and the people from Israel all very clearly have their own legacy alignments and identity — and thinking of those groups as having somehow blended into a group that can be accurately given an accurate Middle Eastern label have very little functional use as a naming strategy.

The fact that immigrants from some of those nations tend to be Muslim does create its own set of alliances that could become increasingly relevant in a number of settings.

Those particular sets of labels are all mentioned in this chapter under the intergroup interaction category of "Assimilation" because there are some people who believe that we can think of people in all of those categories as having some degree of Assimilation in this country. That thinking would be wrong.

The Labels Trigger Checklists

Those sets of labels tend to be confusing. They are actually useful in a very simplistic and sometimes misleading way for some government record keeping.

The U.S. Government officially lists people as Asian American, Native American, Hispanic, or Middle Eastern for checklist purposes for various reporting categories.

It was better to have that information about groups of people for some purposes than it would have been not to have that particular set of information about our diversity.

Those labels give us a generic sense of how diverse some areas of our country are — but they generally tell us almost nothing about the specific realities of our diversity in those places and settings. The separate ethnic and racial groups that make up the component parts of each of those reporting categories are clearly not adequately described by those simplistic macro labels. It would be a major mistake to think that those labels point in any way to assimilation by group. Assimilation for groups included in those labels is clearly not likely to happen for any of those people beyond the point where assimilation has already been accomplished.

However, as noted earlier, White Americans and Black Americans have actually created more of a true assimilation process.

But even within those two major subgroups, there are some significant subsets of people that do not feel assimilated into the macro label for their group. There are a number of key subsets under each of those categories that are very relevant to the people in those categories.

We need to deal with that diversity even within those categories as we celebrate the overall diversity of the people of the United States.

America Is a Mosaic of Peoples

The truth is — we are a mosaic of peoples — with a variety of legacy ethnicities, cultures, and even races. We have chosen to use a mixture of all eight of the organizational models for intergroup interaction that have been described in this chapter to help our groups functionally interact.

We are actually using the entire continuum of interaction options in this country. We still have some groups who are separate and in a state of intergroup conflict. We have other people who are moving or have moved into integration, merger, and even — in a limited way — assimilation.

We need to clearly understand the full set of directions we are using now and we need to understand clearly the approaches we are headed for in the future. We need to use the tools on this continuum well to achieve The Art of InterGroup Peace for America.

Our culture of Peace that is embedded in The Art of InterGroup Peace strategy is not a culture of ethnic merger or a culture of ethnic assimilation. We need to support and celebrate our diversity and have it be a strength going forward as a country. We will not simply all assimilate into a single new American ethnicity or a new American race. We need to deal effectively with the reality of the mixture of groups we will have going forward.

We will need to build a new sense of us that incorporates all of our legacy categories of us as part of the new framework and as part of the woven fabric of America. We need to build on those categories and not making those categories disappear. We do need to blend some values and beliefs. We need to create real alliances, and we need those alliances to thrive.

One of our great strengths as a nation has been our ability to draw on the best elements from across our various legacy groups and we need to again blend that input — but not the actual groups — into an American culture, an American infrastructure, and a set of clear and enlightened American values that we all can share.

We need to build on that pathway of shared beliefs going forward to succeed in the Art of InterGroup Peace. We can do that by creating a clear sense of what directions we want to go in the future with each group of people to achieve intergroup Peace. Using the continuum of interaction options listed in this chapter, we need an alliance for intergroup Peace at this point rather than an assimilation of groups in this country into our Peace process.

We Need Win/Win Solutions for All Groups

To go to that next level of intergroup understanding — and to tee up the prospect of intergroup Peace — we need to understand across all groups how that strategy of becoming a universal mission-driven us can be a win for all groups. It is actually functionally and strategically important for each group to win as we go forward.

Since we are going to have a future in this country where our various groups are going to continue to be relevant to each other, we will need a future where all groups do individually well as component parts of the overall fabric and the overall tapestry of America. We need every group to win. We need to have all groups allied with each other to do that work.

We need our alliances to function nationally — and we need our alliances to function well in each community. Our real strength will come from local alliances — hinged on local trust and local alignment on key local issues that are important in each community.

We need to make our Peace where we live. We need our understanding to let us each function in aligned ways where we each are.

The model we need to use to achieve intergroup Peace in America isn't mergers and it isn't truces. The model we do need to use is Alliances — and to do the alliance work well, we need to have a good sense of what the key intergroup issues are today that alliances can focus on.

That is the topic of Chapter Ten.

Succeeding at the Art of InterGroup Peace will require us to clearly understand who we are as a country and to understand what issues we face at this point in time relative to achieving Peace. Chapter Eight describes who we are now and explains how our history got us to where we are today. We need to anchor our understanding of those key issues with a recognition of that historical reality and context.

We have both a very complex history and a very simple history that we need to understand and address. We need to understand that our instinctive behaviors have created much of our history. We need to remember that those same instincts continue to create current behaviors and current intergroup perceptions, energies, and emotions. We need to use that knowledge to create a better future for our society and country. We can't escape our instincts. We need to build on them to achieve the goals we need to achieve.

If we blend our instinctive terrain with our alignment opportunities, and if we do that in the clear context of our history and in the context of our current status on intergroup issues, we will be much more likely to achieve and sustain Peace.

The next chapter looks at a key commitment we need to make if we want Peace to be our future state.

CHAPTER TEN

We Need Win/Win Commitments for All Groups to Sustain InterGroup Peace in America

WE NEED TO anchor Peace for America on the concept and the goal of win/win results for all of the groups of people who make up the rich and diverse fabric of America. That commitment and that achievement will be the key to our success.

We need to have all groups win. We need to not have any groups of people who are losing and who are not being granted full access to the American Dream because of their race, ethnicity, culture, gender, gender preference, philosophical alignments, or religious beliefs.

We need to be an America where people from all of those groups can work hard, make contributions, and be fully able to benefit from the opportunities that America creates.

We need everyone to win and we need everyone to want everyone else to win as well.

Win/win should be the clearly stated goal for all groups — with each group succeeding and with each group also celebrating, endorsing, supporting, and appreciating every other group's success.

We need people from all groups to understand the value and the benefits to us all that result from a commitment to win/win results for everyone — and we need to put the processes in place to help win/win be the actual path we go down for our future as a nation.

That win/win approach can work for America as a country. It also can work in communities and in various other organizational settings.

Schools, businesses, and community organizations can all use win/win approaches as internal commitments and as guidances for thinking and behaviors. People in each of our various settings who believe in win/win as a value and a benefit can focus on the specific details and the specific realities that can create win/win outcomes for each setting.

Some people believe that someone has to lose if someone wins. That belief is commonly held — and it is wrong.

There does not need to be a loser in intergroup situations. All parties can win. It is logistically possible for all groups to win and it is actually strategically desirable and functionally preferable for all groups to win.

The Supply of Wins Is Not Finite

We need people in this country to realize at a very direct level that we don't need anyone to lose so that someone else can win.

There isn't a finite supply of wins in the world. Wins for all groups are not only possible — wins for all groups will make us all collectively stronger.

We will all be better off economically when everyone in the economy is doing well. When more people in America achieve the American Dream, their collective success will make America stronger.

The Art of InterGroup Peace is aimed at everyone winning and at everyone doing well. That goal and that outcome were very clearly and very obviously not true and not expected for Sun Tzu when he wrote *The Art of War*.

War, Sun Tzu preached, was clearly about someone winning and someone else losing. War is aimed at achieving wins for one side and at creating losses and defeats for everyone else. Sun Tzu built strategies that were designed to create losses for the other side in each war.

That win/lose approach made strategic and functional sense for Sun Tzu. Having the other party lose is the usual goal and the most commonly targeted outcome for war. War and losing are generally tied together at a very basic level.

Peace is different. Very different. Peace is tied together, perpetuated, achieved, and maintained by having everyone win.

Peace, *The Art of InterGroup Peace* preaches — when it is done well and when it is done right — is about everyone winning.

Win/Lose – Win/Win – and Lose/Lose Are the Options

There are three sets of basic outcomes that can result from intergroup interactions. One set of outcomes — the win/lose approach — has winners and losers in each setting.

Another set of possible outcomes — the win/win approach — has only winners.

And the third set of outcomes — the lose/lose approach — has everyone in a setting or a situation losing.

Lose/lose outcomes need to be on the list of options to be understood in thinking about intergroup Peace because lose/lose outcomes actually do happen. Sometimes, when groups interact, everyone loses.

Losses for all parties in a lose/lose setting can be accidental and unintended, and they can be completely intentional and the goal — of at least one relevant party.

Lose/lose strategies — the most negative possible set of outcomes that can result from groups interacting with one another — is actually not advocated or supported by either *The Art of War* or by *The Art of InterGroup Peace* — but they do happen and they need to be understood as part of the intergroup process.

Lose/lose outcomes do happen. In many cases, the lose/lose outcomes that happen in various settings are entirely unintentional. Those unintended outcomes that end up with double losses — with both parties losing — sometimes result when both sides in a setting were attempting to win and both were attempting to achieve overall wins in the context of a win/lose situation and both groups simply, purely, and unintentionally failed.

Failure happens.

Having all parties fail in a conflicted setting is a generally unintentional, but very real risk that exists as a logistical possibility in the functional context of win/lose strategies and situations.

Sometimes both groups in a conflicted or contentious setting simply and unintentionally fail to achieve wins. Both groups in the setting and situation are damaged and sustain losses.

No one on either side planned for both groups to lose in those specific lose/lose situations. In those situations, double losses are completely unintentional and both parties tend to be disappointed when both parties lose.

The leaders in both groups in those situations tend to try to figure out ways of avoiding having their side lose in the future.

In a number of other settings where lose/lose outcomes occur, those double negative results are the fully intended result and the strategic goal for at least one of the parties in that setting.

Purely intentional and very deliberate lose/lose strategies definitely do exist. Those completely intentional and entirely deliberate lose/lose strategies are generally triggered by an extremely negative intergroup context — often inspired by intense Intergroup hatred on the part of someone in that specific intergroup setting.

Intentional and deliberate lose/lose strategies and outcomes usually result from one group in a situation hating the other group so much that the strategic and tactical approach for the group who hates very deeply includes having their own group actually suffering — and having their own group take a loss of some kind themselves in various ways — so that the other group in that setting and situation suffers and loses even more.

People Who Hate Deeply Sometimes Use Lose/Lose Strategies to Do Damage to the People They Hate

In the most extreme lose/lose settings, group strategists are even sometimes willing to have their own group lose a lot so that the people who they hate very deeply will lose at least a little.

That set of outcomes and self-damaging approaches can make sense and can feel right to people who truly do have very deep-seated intergroup hate and who are willing to go to significant lengths and to sustain losses for their own group and their own people in order to damage the people they hate.

Both the books *Primal Pathways* and *Cusp of Chaos* deal with those lose/lose situations and lose/lose strategies in more detail.

It can be extremely challenging to get people in those settings and those belief systems to convert from lose/lose approaches to win/win approaches.

When people hate other people with so much intensity that it feels right to be damaged in order to inflict damage on the other group, there is clearly a major need to do significant repair work in that setting to reduce the levels of anger and hatred that drive those behaviors and thought processes.

When us/them instincts are triggered in those negative and extreme ways in any setting, people who hate can get so wrapped up in their own hatred that they aren't open to hearing or learning any other ways of thinking about, or perceiving whoever they are defining as "Them," to be anything other than an evil and inherently malevolent "Them" who deserves to be damaged.

It is very hard to create Peace in any setting where the kinds of feelings and beliefs have taken root and are bearing evil and damaging fruit.

Those sets of feelings should be resisted in each setting where possible, and avoided in all settings whenever they can be avoided. Peace in any setting depends on creating interactions that generate wins for all parties in that setting — and wins are hard to achieve when any party hates so deeply that they are willing to be damaged themselves in order to damage the other side.

Leaders Sometimes Build Power from Their Hatred

Leaders of groups who have their own personal Alpha instincts fully activated and who have their power base reinforced by the exacerbation of intergroup hatred tend to be very difficult to convert from a strategy of hatred to a strategy of mutual benefit and mutual gain.

Those kinds of conversions in the hearts and heads of Alpha leaders from hatred to Peace can sometimes happen — but those conversions can be very hard to do for many situations and settings.

It sometimes requires a leadership change in a group at a very senior level to get groups who are committed to lose/lose strategies to convert to any other model.

Groups who believe in lose/lose strategies need to be converted from both lose/lose and win/lose approaches to pure win/win commitments and strategies.

The Art of InterGroup Peace is anchored on everyone in a setting agreeing and aligning to achieve win/win outcomes for all groups.

The Art of InterGroup Peace strongly believes in winning. *The Art of InterGroup Peace* is also anchored on the belief that the safest win and the best win situation for each group is almost always one where the wins are shared and each group wins.

Most People Do Not Understand the Full Value of Win/Win Outcomes

That is an important point and concept to understand. That is not how people usually think. Win/win for all parties isn't a belief or a goal for people used by groups in very many intergroup settings today.

Most people do not know that the win/win option exists.

It can be very intellectually liberating to add win/win potential strategies to people's intergroup thought processes. Once people understand the beauty and the logistical value and functional benefits that result for all groups from win/win outcomes, then intelligent and well-intentioned people can come to support that strategy and can figure out how to achieve it in effective and creative ways in their relevant settings.

But before that understanding of the advantages of win/win strategies exists for people, win/win outcomes can seem both improbable and vaguely undesirable. We are so used to being in situations where we want the other side to lose that it can seem wrong and even alien to change to a mental model and strategic approach where we want the other side to win.

All Those Approaches Are Possible — One Is Preferable

We are used to win/lose strategies and we are used to win/lose thinking relative to other groups. To succeed at The Art of InterGroup Peace, we need to understand that all three sets of consequences are possible.

Those three alternatives are clearly three very different concepts, strategies, approaches, goals, and outcomes for intergroup interactions.

It is important to understand all three approaches — because all three have their supporters, advocates, and fans, and all three create strategies in the real world that we need to deal with as we target Peace for America.

We need wide and growing numbers of people in this country to understand why win/win solutions are functionally superior to either of the approaches that involve anyone losing. We need to use that knowledge to guide people away from win/lose and lose/lose expectations and approaches to a more positive overall intergroup strategy that is aimed at having all parties winning.

When We All Win – We All Win

When you look clearly at all of the options, win/win is obviously the most sensible, enlightened, positive, and desirable approach. That outcome of having each group win is clearly good for each and every "Us" because — by definition — each group wins. In a functional win/win outcome for all groups, our own group — our own "Us"— obviously wins.

That point of having your own group winning is key to the win/win strategy. Everyone wants to win. When everyone wins, our group wins. We win.

Having our own group do well in the areas where we want our own group to do well is clearly a good thing for our group. When we win in those areas, we win as a group.

No One Needs to Avenge a Victory

People need to understand that it isn't necessary for the other group to lose in order for our group to win. Each and every other group in a setting can also prosper. Each group can also achieve their own group goals without having their success hinder or impede or diminish our group success.

Success can be infinite and success can be simultaneous.

When winning is simultaneous and when victory is shared by all groups, then each of the other groups in our setting is less likely to want to damage, destroy, defeat, or get revenge on our group for their loss.

No one needs to avenge a victory.

We need people to understand that we can win — and we can all get our group's very real needs met — without the other group being damaged or defeated in any way.

Our Enemies Drain Us

The standard strategies that involve having the other group in a setting lose are extremely seductive to far too many people. Having "Them" lose is the way we usually think.

When we have our us/them instincts activated in a setting, we very clearly tend to want whoever we perceive to be them in that setting to lose.

When the other group loses, that loss by them can create a functional and at least temporary situational win for our group. But that win for us far too often happens at the expense of creating an enemy and at the expense of setting up a permanent adversary group for that setting.

Creating an enemy or an adversary is never a good thing.

Too often, the most expensive things we have in the world are our enemies. Our enemies drain us. Our enemies intentionally and inevitably function in various enemy ways.

Our enemies do what they can to damage us. They tend to perpetually threaten us and they very consistently try to undermine us, even when we have achieved a situational win.

If we do win in a win/lose setting, the victory we achieve is often time limited because our enemies tend to want to avenge their loss and very often want to get revenge in some way for our win.

Unless the other group disappears, we generally have to defend ourselves forever against our defeated enemies because of their permanent presence and their clear negative intentions that do not disappear. In permanent win/lose intergroup settings, we need to defend ourselves in perpetuity against the intentions of the defeated group.

We Do Not Need to Defend Ourselves When Everyone Wins

We do not have to defend ourselves at all when we all simultaneously win.

That win/win outcome can clearly be a better win for our group than a win/lose outcome for our group — because it is a less risky and much less expensive win over time for our group. The essence of the issue is that we lose the expense of having a functioning enemy in a setting when the other group in a setting simultaneously.

Everybody Wins Is the Goal — Everyone Is Inclusive

To convert people who do win/lose thinking now and who have done that kind of win/lose thinking for years into using a win/win strategy and a win/win approach, we need all people to understand that win/win outcomes are actually a very real win for their group.

This is not the way most people think about those issues today. We need to help people understand those issues.

We will only achieve intergroup harmony and intergroup Peace in a setting if we can achieve a sense on behalf of all the relevant groups that their own group is and can be part of a win/win reality and that their own group will not lose and will directly benefit from the Peace that we create.

We Need to Understand the Other Group as Well

Creating win/win outcomes in any setting is most likely to be done successfully when each of the groups in that setting very clearly understands themselves and their own goals. The win/win process works best if each group in a setting also clearly understands the goals and the wins that are needed by the other group.

Understanding the other group is part of the strategic process for both Peace and War. In that respect, *The Art of InterGroup Peace* and *The Art of War* books make almost identical recommendations about the need for understanding the other group in any setting.

The Art of War very clearly calls for each general to understand his enemy fully — to know all things about the relevant enemy. Sun Tzu calls for that level of knowledge about the other group because he believed the general in a war situation needs to use extensive and accurate knowledge about the enemy to ensure the enemies defeat.

In war, knowledge is power.

For the people who want to create lose/lose situations in any setting, a deep knowledge of people who are hated lets the lose/lose strategist identify both their strategies and the specific targets for the intergroup damage that is inspired by that hate.

So both win/lose approaches and lose/lose approaches call for understanding the enemy in each setting well.

The Art of InterGroup Peace tool kit also calls for a deep understanding of the "other" sets of people in any intergroup situation. But the goal of that deep understanding of the other party in *The Art of InterGroup Peace* is for the exact opposite reason that people need that information in war.

In Peace, we need to understand the other group so we can help the other people, in any Peace setting, achieve their group's legitimate goals. In Peace, we need to understand the other group clearly and well so that we can help the other group of people win — not cause them to lose.

Wartime winning — as described in *The Art of War* — is victory that is achieved by one party at the expense of the other party. Winning — in *The Art of InterGroup Peace* — is done by both parties simultaneously in the context of Peace.

Mutual winning is the goal and mutual winning for all parties is clearly and explicitly set up and mutually understood to be the clear and basic goal for all parties who are included in the Peace process.

The Wins Need to Be Legitimate and Beneficial Wins

The wins that are created in a win/win setting need to be legitimate wins. They need to be real. Sham wins lack stability and that instability can trigger future negative responses and intergroup difficulties for that setting.

Each of the parties in a win/win setting need to help each group in that setting achieve their own wins — including having each group able to achieve the goals and values that we need to collectively commit to in order to create a culture of enlightenment and Peace for America.

That is in stark contrast to those settings where one or both parties are attempting to create lose/lose outcomes and negative intergroup consequences. As noted earlier, a number of people feel so much anger and hatred today that they are going beyond win/lose interactions all the way to deliberate and intentional lose/lose interactions.

Lose/Lose Strategies Inherently and Intentionally Create Losses for Everyone

Lose/lose acts and activities are sometimes symbolic. Many lose/lose acts are aimed at creating a sense in the other group that their enemy hates them and that their enemy is unpredictable, dangerous, and even willing to be harmed themselves in order to create harm to the other group.

Instability is often a goal of lose/lose tactics. Revenge and retribution are generally key aspirations and goals of lose/lose strategists. We need to understand lose/lose tactics where they exist, and we need to take steps when we can to defuse the intense hatred that triggers those behaviors and those strategies.

To defuse those hatreds, we need to use all the tools at our disposal to soften the level of intergroup misunderstanding and hate.

We need to reach out broadly in Peace to the other parties — knowing that reaching out will often be rejected by leaders and group members who hate at pure and intense levels, and rejected by the people who actually do the lose/lose behaviors. But we need to reach out anyway in hopes that presenting a call for Peace as a human-to-human agenda can have a positive impact on the broader population in those conflicted groups.

Almost all people do prefer Peace when legitimate Peace is an option.

People prefer safe and Peaceful settings to conflict and war. People who want Peace in a setting need to convey that opportunity to create safe Peace for the other parties in the conflicted setting.

People in groups generally don't like being in situations of perpetual conflict. Offering honest and respectful alternatives to that conflict can create support from people on both sides of a conflict.

The alternatives need to be respectful, viable, and real to have a positive impact on people's perceptions and thoughts.

Instead of triggering intergroup hatred, the goal of the communication and teaching process from people who want Peace needs to be to trigger intergroup longing in each group for Peace and to convey a belief that real and respectful Peace is possible in that setting.

Win/Win Has to Be Mutual and Achieved in Trust

Win/Win is the right approach, but it can be very hard work.

To be successful and to work as a strategy, the win/win approach needs to be mutually understood, mutually agreed upon, and mutually supported by all of the parties in a Peace setting. Mutual support is extremely important. Everyone in a setting needs to agree that it is a good thing when everyone wins.

Old animosities can die hard. Old negative energies — levels of long-standing anger and bitterness — can linger on and can dominate people's thinking and emotions for very long periods of time. When someone has been clearly perceived to be the enemy in any setting for any period of time, all of the thought processes that have been triggered in that setting by our instinctive reactions to our enemies over all of those conflicted years need to be addressed.

That can be done. But it can be very difficult to do and it needs to be done thoughtfully and well.

Peace with Former Enemies Can Be Fragile

The reality is that any understandings about Peace, and even truces that are set up in a setting that are reached with former enemies, are particularly fragile.

Those approaches tend to be unstable because we are always on alert at both a conscious and subconscious level when we are dealing with a former enemy.

The concern that underlies those situations is the possibility that our former enemy might not really want Peace, and might possibly use the pretense of Peace as a way to damage us in some way again.

Trust can be hard. Trust is needed — and it can be very hard to achieve. Trust has to be earned in any setting and it has to be reinforced by the passage of time and by consistent good behavior.

We need people to trust each other as people. — and to do that, we need people to get to know each other as people.

We need people to reach out in our various settings and get to know other people in their setting. We need people-to-people contact and we need people-to-people trust.

The trust created in our various intergroup settings is more likely to succeed if it can be anchored on interpersonal relationships that let us interact with each other across groups as individuals and as real people and not just as categories or some level of token representations of "Them."

All Parties Need to Agree to Win/Win Strategies

All parties need to begin by understanding and agreeing to the concept of win/win in order for that strategy to fully succeed. That agreement for everyone to win needs to anchor the process.

Then we need to do real things to make that commitment real.

It's important for us generally to explicitly acknowledge that mutual commitment to win/win outcomes when the basic situation is one where all of the parties in a setting have long had their own most negative us/them instincts functionally activated.

It is hard when those energies have been activated for any significant degree for any length of time for any of us to trust the other group in that setting.

It Can Be Hard to See a Former Enemy Achieve a Win

It can be very hard for any group to accept the legitimacy, the appropriateness, and the desirability of the other group in their setting — their former enemy — suddenly having any of its key needs met by the process of Peace and by win/win outcomes.

That acceptance problem needs to be anticipated and understood. It can be very difficult for any of us in any setting to see someone you have grown to hate doing well.

We need to recognize that issue to be exactly what it is and then we need to deal directly with it.

It can be very hard to see your long time enemy happy with a situation or an outcome. That happiness for the long-term enemy will happen if our win/win approaches are successful — and that can create its own set of issues.

We need to expect those outcomes to make some people unhappy. Old hatreds can die very slowly.

For some people who have that set of negative us/them perceptions firmly embedded in their mindsets and emotions, it is sometimes easier to migrate from win/lose strategies all the way to pure lose/lose strategies than it is to migrate from win/lose interactions to win/win outcomes.

Unless both groups in a setting agree to that desired win/win outcome, however, and unless both groups end up wanting the other group to actually do well — Peace can be very difficult to achieve.

Win/Win Isn't a Passive Strategy

Ideally, each group in a win/win setting helps the other group win.

In a functional win/win situation, each group is committed both to achieving its own group goals and to either helping or allowing the other group to achieve their own group goals.

Win/win isn't a passive strategy. To be most effective, it isn't just a generic positive leaning toward doing good deeds of some kind for people. Win/win outcomes often require practical, functional, and situationally specific approaches to determine how to help each party win.

The process of communicating about specific elements of win/win outcomes for each group can help create trust and understanding for the parties who are communicating with each other.

Good intentions can be both clearly communicated and clearly demonstrated in that communication and learning process.

Practical consequences and real wins are important. Win/win isn't a theoretical or ideologically conceptual commitment to create mutually passive and neutral intergroup behaviors that provide no real benefits to either party.

Mutually passive interactions are clearly far better than mutual anger and they are significantly better than instinct activated win/lose or lose/lose interactions, but simply passive and neutral outcomes are not as good for all parties as achieving real win/win outcomes for each group.

Winning is the key word. For all parties, the win/win process can and should actually result in wins for each of the parties involved. All groups need to win to make the model work.

The next chapter of this book outlines two important collective win/win initiatives that could be used by us as a nation to demonstrate collective good will and to create true and obvious benefit for all of the groups in the country.

If those specific initiatives are successful, they will create win/win results for all groups. One initiative deals with our children. The other deals with our health. Both of those initiatives are extremely important topics that create benefit for all parties at a level that our instincts and our intellect can appreciate and value.

We All Want Our Group to Benefit

The reality is, all groups do have their own self-interests — often their own selfish self-interests. Each set of people tends to want their own group of people to benefit from any situation that exists. Benefiting is not a bad thing. Benefiting as a group is an entirely legitimate aspiration for each group.

It is good and appropriate for each of us to want good things for our own group. We all should want our own group to benefit.

To create sustaining Peace, however, it is important for each of the groups involved in a win/win strategy in any setting to know that their own group's legitimate needs are being met by the win/win process and to understand clearly that their group is actually achieving a legitimate win at the exact same time that the other group is winning.

People need to understand that no one loses when win/win is done well because each group will win when both groups win.

"Legitimate Needs" Are the Key

The term the "legitimate needs" for each group is used as part of The Art of InterGroup Peace strategy to describe each groups "win" — because the needs of each group must be "legitimate" needs for the group that do not do damage to other people or to the other group.

Wins need to be good, beneficial, and non-damaging wins. A win can't involve a group achieving some kind of problematic outcomes for a group that can do damage or undermine the collective or individual well being of the other group in a win/win setting.

At an extreme and clear level, if a particular group has racist goals or if a particular group wants to do some kind of functional racism-linked damage to other people in some way, that goal is not a "legitimate" need for that group and that outcome can't be included as a win/win outcome.

The basic win/win precept of mutual support for each group does not expand and extend to include helping any group achieve any of an array of dysfunctional, negative, or damaging goals.

Wins need to be "legitimate." The "legitimate goals" and the "legitimate needs" of each group — the need for a group to be safe and the need for a group to prosper, for example — should be included in the win/win strategies that are embedded in *The Art of InterGroup Peace*.

Those legitimate needs identified for each group should become the mutual goals of all groups.

Win/Win Involves a Commitment and a Set of Values

When win/win approaches are done well, they represent a strategy, a set of tactics, a shared commitment, and a functional set of beliefs and basic collective values.

A key value embedded in the win/win approach is that each group recognizes the validity of the goals of the other group and that each group in a win/win setting agrees to do appropriate things to help the other group achieve those goals.

As noted above, recognizing the validity and the legitimacy of the goals held by the other group of people is sometimes much more difficult than it sounds. Instinctive behaviors and emotions are highly relevant for that particular point.

We sometimes need to understand and overcome our instinctive desire to damage the other groups in some way. When any people believe that another group of people is a "Them," our instinctive value set calls for us to want "Them" to lose and to want "Them" to be damaged at multiple levels.

Our instinctive desire is for "Them" to fail and for "Them" to be defeated wherever defeat is possible.

When any of those negative us/them values have been activated for any people, the goals that are defined and desired in any setting by "Them" are usually opposed, damaged, rejected, resisted, derided, disparaged, derailed, and often attacked very directly by the other group.

As part of the win/win process, we need to overcome the desire to obstruct "Them" and we need to replace that desire with the goal and the intentional and deliberate process of helping them.

Clarity is extremely useful for that process. We need to mutually define what sets of goals will be a win for both us and them, and then we need to help each other achieve those goals in order for all of us to achieve our goals.

Equal Protection of the Law Is a Legitimate and Primary Win/Win Goal

When the needs of a group are as basic as equal protection under the law or basic voting rights for all people in the group, then the alignments and the intergroup agreements that tie to those wins can be very clear and even relatively easy to do.

When the needs of a group of people are to have all children from all groups educated — and to have all children from each group receive the stimulus in the first months and years of life that is needed to strengthen their brains to the point where education can be a functional and beneficial tool for those children — then we need all people to recognize those legitimate and very basic needs for all children and we need all people to support each group of people in achieving those basic needs for their own children.

Those specific issues are discussed in more detail in the next chapter of this book.

That collective commitment by all groups to the mutual achievement of goals for each group may seem very appropriate and basic, at one level, but that is obviously not the way most groups interact with one another in the real world today… either in our country or elsewhere in the world.

Groups generally each seek to achieve their own goals — economic, social, political, functional, and governmental goals — as wins for their groups. But groups usually do not enter into a shared commitment or engage in a process to either understand the goals of any other groups and to help any other groups achieve their goals.

"Interest Based Bargaining" Can Create Win/Win Results

In union/management negotiations, a win/win based approach that includes having each side clearly recognizing and then respecting each other's goals is often called "interest based bargaining."

That can be a very effective way of conducting a wide range of labor management negotiations.

The basic foundational approach that is used by the organizations that do "interest based bargaining" in labor negotiations is to first recognize the theoretical legitimacy of each other's goals and then to understand those goals clearly.

Once both parties' goals are clearly understood by both parties, the people doing the negotiations can work together to find sets of solutions through the negotiation process that can help both sides achieve their goals.

The alternative to "interest based bargaining" in many negotiation settings is to fall back into more basic and primal us/them behaviors, values, and emotions – with the parties involved in the negotiations too often clearly perceiving each other to be a "Them" — invoking too many of the energies, values, and perceptions that can be activated when those particular intergroup instincts are triggered in any setting.

In some parts of the world — and even in this country, earlier in our own history — those instinctive us/them reactions to union organization efforts sometimes triggered bloodshed.

Laws have been put in place to make that whole organizing process safer for all parties involved in this country — but the truth is that union organizers are still being killed in some parts of the world today. They are being killed in those settings because the people who run the companies in those countries perceive the union organizers to be a "Them" and have hired people to do those killings — feeling no guilt for killing a "Them" because the people doing the hiring have their us/them instincts fully activated.

That set of negative and conflicted intergroup behaviors in those more conflicted settings can echo the more negative win/lose activities, and values embedded in *The Art of War*.

By contrast, using *The Art of InterGroup Peace* approach, the goal is to create situations where each set of people first understands their own goals, then has their own goals clarified, and then each group learns to understand the goals of the other group.

The Process Works Best When People Have Aligned Goals

When all goals are understood, the win/win process works to help each set of people help the other sets achieve their goals. The process works particularly well when the parties involved in any setting agree on aligned goals that apply to all people — like freedom from attack, democratic selection of leaders, or the mutual and improved health of all populations.

In looking at the factors that can cause us to agree to a strategy of win/win goals, the alignment trigger pyramid that was outlined in Chapter Six of this book can be a useful reference point for the discussions.

Danger is the bottom level on that alignment trigger pyramid. We are clearly facing collective danger as a country if we don't come together to create a country that is not at war with itself.

Common enemy is another legitimate alignment motivator that is the second level on that pyramid. That is a valid trigger for us today. We do have external enemies that we can overcome and defend ourselves against if we are a unified country aspiring to win/win outcomes for all of our people.

Team behaviors are the third tier of the alignment triggers. Team actions can also help us get to win/win outcomes. Early childhood development and our collective community health are discussed in the next chapter as key goals that we should all focus on and commit to achieving. Both of those goals can benefit from team behaviors.

Creating a sense of us based on our shared beliefs leads us to a win/win set of strategies and behaviors. Seeing ourselves as an us based on our beliefs is the point of Chapter Twelve of this book.

Collective gain is at the heart of win/win behaviors. Creating collective gain is the most obvious link between the win/win strategy and the alignment pyramid. We will all do better as a country when all segments of our country have full access to the American Dream and when we have economic success across all groups.

Our country will be stronger economically when all segments of our economy are strong.

Having a collective vision that helps us all achieve the American Dream is very much a key a win/win alignment motivator. We all win if we all have access for the American Dream and we all win when our most enlightened values are embedded in our collective and individual behaviors and realities.

Peace Is Sustainable When All Parties Achieve Their Goals

Both shared goals and individual group goals can be involved in the various win/win goal sets.

When all parties in a setting achieve their goals, Peace is much more likely both to be created, and to be sustained over time in that setting.

As noted earlier, when any party in a negotiation doesn't have their key goals met, that party is likely to take steps in the future to end any truce or temporary alignment, and to undermine what appears to be a situational state of Peace. Win/lose outcomes have an inherent instability because at least one party to the situation is unhappy and wanting change.

We Need a Collective Commitment to Peace

As a first and immediate step, it would be a good thing for people in this country — collectively and individually — to decide and agree that we do both want and need Peace — both as a country and as a society.

We need individual people who are committed to Peace as a mission and a goal.

We also need to collectively agree that clear win/win commitments need to anchor that Peace. We need to all agree that we should create a win/win approach to Peace in our communities.

We also need to agree that Peace will and should involve each group of people appreciating, valuing, and supporting both the goals, and the well being of each other as groups of people. Our only path to Peace that can be sustained over time will be one that is achieved using win/win as both a baseline strategy and a foundational value set.

We are an increasingly diverse country. That is an undisputable fact. We can either celebrate and take full advantage of our diversity — growing in strength as a country — Or we can tribalize, follow the slippery and too often seductive slope presented to us by our us/them behaviors and by our us/them instincts, and we can allow our diversity to split us into us/them factions with high levels of intergroup dislike, stress, and a predictable pattern of intergroup interactions that will create sporadic, damaging, dysfunctional, and sometimes destructive episodes of pure intergroup conflict and direct and intentional intergroup damage.

That is an obvious potential danger to us all that we need to have people understand clearly so that the people who understand it are motivated to be aligned and understand the value and benefit of a win/win approach to intergroup interactions to keep us off that slippery slope to conflict and division.

We Need Several Key Goals That We Can Achieve Together

Win/win is clearly a mutual gain focused strategy. We can achieve mutual gain for all of us if we create win/win solutions that apply to all of us.

At this point in our history, we should recognize that reality and we should set some collective mutual gain goals for ourselves. To make the intergroup Peace process very real and immediate, we need to set some clear goals now that will benefit all of us and we need to work together to achieve these goals.

We need some initial sets of goals that we all share that can help bring us all together because we all believe in those goals and because we will all benefit from achieving those goals.

The end of discrimination in hiring by race, ethnicity, or gender is one obvious aligning goal that creates mutual benefit.

The end of active intergroup conflict is all by itself an obvious goal. Setting up a set of interactions that can prevent future mobs and future riots is another area where mutual goals could be set.

We should want all groups to be explicitly supportive of that goal in order to make it possible. When riots are threatened because of a triggering event, we need leaders from all groups to serve as the voices of reason to calm the situation and keep people in those settings from damaging one another.

Freedom from being damaged may seem obvious, but it isn't an actively pursued value for some people today, and riots do damage people as a result.

Peaceful demonstrations can be a very powerful and effective way of communicating key concerns and information relative to key intergroup issues. Actual riots — with damage and violence — can sometimes have a significantly more destructive impact on people's lives and intergroup good will.

We Need to Believe in the Shared Values of an American "Us"

As the final chapter of this book points out, this is a good time to agree on some very basic principles and values that benefit us all in order to function as a collective American "Us."

The rule of law is very clearly one of those common and basic mutual benefit values. Equal rights for everyone — man or woman, race or creed — is another.

Win/win commitments on issues of education, healthcare, and public safety by each group to every other group is another set of mutual benefit goals that help us all.

We need to set up collective mutual benefit goals that we all share as a country. Having collective mutual benefit goals can also help us create team behaviors and those goals can help create a functioning sense of us.

Both of those approaches are key trigger steps from the alignment pyramid. Having collective goals in those areas can obviously trigger our sense of collective gain as well as collective good will.

The next chapter of this book identifies two key goals that can both help us achieve intergroup alignment, and that can create wins for each group. If we achieve both of those goals this country will be a stronger, better, and safer place for us all.

People will be healthier. People will be more successful. Fewer people will be in jail.

Those would be win/win outcomes and can help anchor the heart and Art of InterGroup Peace.

CHAPTER ELEVEN

We Need to Support Every Child and Improve Our Health Together

FAR TOO MANY children in America can't read. The learning gaps in far too many of our schools are massive, and those gaps are not closing. Those gaps create significant negative consequences for children that last lifetimes.

The clear and consistent pattern is that the children who can't read drop out of school, and far too many high school dropouts end up in prison.

More than 60 percent of the African American males who drop out of high school end up in prison. That compares with less than 1 percent of White high school graduates and slightly fewer than 5 percent of African American graduates who end up in jail.

We have more people in prison than any country in the world by a wide margin — seven times more people in jail per capita than Canada — and 85 percent of the children in our juvenile justice system today either read poorly or cannot read at all.

We overwhelmingly imprison minority Americans. We imprison almost five times more Hispanic Americans per capita than our White Americans — and we actually have more Black males in prison in this country today than the total number of Black males who were enslaved on the first day of the Civil War.

Each of those realities tells us we are facing some major difficulties that will make it very difficult to achieve intergroup Peace in American until we deal with those key issues.

We also have major differences in economic status for groups of Americans. The financial asset base for the average adult White American family three years ago was $141,000. The average net worth for a Black family in America was $11,000 — and the average net worth for an Hispanic family was $13,700. Those financial gaps are also massive and they are actually widening.

Those are major differences. Ten times higher net worth for the families of White Americans is a number that is almost impossible to believe.

Health care disparities are following a similar pattern of adverse outcomes by group, with lower life expectancy levels and significantly higher chronic disease levels for minority Americans.

We need to address each of those issues going forward if we want a future of intergroup Peace in America — and we need to begin with our children. We need to make the learning gaps that handicap so many children today disappear.

We need to build a pathway to success for every child in America, and we need to start with helping every child in the weeks, months, and years when helping children has the highest success levels and the most effective results for each child from every group.

Those learning gaps that we see in our schools today are causing far too many children to have lives of economic deprivation and difficulty, and much higher rates of incarceration, and we need to take clear and intentional steps to make those gaps disappear.

Achieving intergroup Peace in America requires us to close those gaps and have a major, positive impact on those children.

We also need to address the major health care disparities that exist in too many communities — where minority Americans have significantly lower life expectancy levels, and much higher rates of heart disease, diabetes, asthma and stroke.

We also have some significant disparities in actual care delivery that are causing minority Americans to receive less effective care in too many settings. We need to end those care delivery differences, and we need to eliminate those health care outcomes disparities as well.

We Need Trusted and Aligned Police Forces – and Win/Win Outcomes for All Groups

We need to make a very clear and explicit collective commitment to create win/win outcomes for all groups in America.

To create an overall win/win culture for America, we need to make major improvements in each of those areas, and we also need to have some other obvious and meaningful areas in our interactions with one another where everyone wins.

We should do the right things to help all groups to do well — and we should do what needs to be done to create win/win outcomes for people from all groups in each of those areas.

There are actually a number of key areas where we can work together in our various communities to create very real win/win outcomes for all groups of people.

Our police departments give us a major opportunity to achieve win/win results. We can make our win/win commitment to each other a reality by having police departments in every community that clearly support protecting all of our people from every group in ways that create trust and support from every group.

That level of intergroup trust for our police forces does not exist today in too many communities. We should remedy that problem. We can't afford to have police departments in any settings that are in a state of on-going intergroup conflict relative to the communities they serve. Communities clearly can't create win/win outcomes for community members when the police department and members of the community distrust and dislike one another. That is the reality today in far too many communities, and we need to do the right things in each setting to make that reality change.

That level of conflict, stress and distrust between police and community members that exists in far too many communities does not need to happen — and we need to take steps in all settings to make sure it does not happen, and that our police in each setting act in ways that create both community-trust and the highest levels of community protection and safety.

Improving the basic levels of trust between community members and the police will not happen in each relevant setting on its own — but there are some proven approaches that have worked in a number of settings — and we need to extend those approaches to all relevant settings. People from every group in every setting can make building that level of trust and positive interaction a goal, and can work together in open, honest, inclusive, and aligned ways to make it real in each setting.

We need community leaders, community members, and members of the police communities in each setting to understand the "Us/Them" instinctive behavior patterns and the "Us/Them" thought processes that are explained in the *InterGroup* set of books — and we need people to use that information to make conscious and intentional decisions to build a sense of trust between police departments and community members in each setting.

We need to end the kinds of situations where discriminatory and prejudicial police activities create internal community stress and distrust, and we need to have the police departments perceived by large portions of the law abiding community in each setting to be "Us" instead of "Them."

The solutions to that problem are specific to each community because policing is a very local thing. That means the trust levels need to be built in each setting.

We need good minded people in each setting, from all groups, committed to having each community working to create and meet the interaction goals and the win/win outcomes, for all groups, outlined in the values and visions chapter of this book. We need informed and committed people working together to make community supported police functions in each setting a reality.

That will require people in each setting doing things together in joint and collaborative, fully informed and carefully structured, community and police interactions to make those goals a reality, and to create the levels of intergroup trust that can build a foundation for intergroup success in each setting.

People who understand the power and impact of our "Us/Them" instincts need to work together to make sure no one in each setting is functioning as a "Them" and to make sure people in each setting use the right sets of alignment triggers to function as an "Us."

We Need to Save Our Children and Improve Our Total Health

We also very much need to work together in every setting to save our children, and to create better health for our communities.

There are very few things we can do to provide better evidence for our mutual interest in having all groups do well in a win/win setting than helping children from every group succeed.

There are also very few things we can do that show better faith, relative to win/win outcomes for us all, than taking the steps necessary to improve health for us all, and doing what needs to be done to reduce any discrimination and disparities that might exist relative to the care we receive when people from all groups, in any setting, are receiving care.

We clearly can show good faith to one another other and we can make all of our lives better by working together in our communities to give our children better futures. We now know what needs to be done — and we need to make the clear commitment to do it.

We can also very directly make lives better for people from all groups by working together in very intentional and aligned ways to create better health and fewer disparities, in both health and care, for all of us in each setting.

Our children should be our top priority. That should be true within each group, and that should be true between groups. We all want our children to do well, and we all should want the children from all groups to have the kind of support in the first months and years of life that will give every child the best chance of doing well.

That is not happening in too many communities for too many children today. We have far too many communities where major learning gaps exist for the children in our schools. Those gaps generally run along economic lines, and they exist in far too many settings by race and ethnic group.

We have far too many communities today where roughly 70 to 80 percent of the White and Asian American children in the schools can read and perform age-level math well — but where fewer than 50 percent of the children from the major minority groups in those schools pass those same tests.

In some communities, we have fewer than 30 percent of the American Indian, African American, or Hispanic children who are able to read. In those settings, there is a high percentage of children who can't read, who drop out of school, and who end up on life paths that are economically disadvantaged and highly challenged at multiple functional levels.

We just went through the process, as an entire country, of measuring learning levels in our schools for the national Common Core education standards, and that testing process confirmed that the learning gaps between groups are large and growing, in far too many communities.

Learning Gaps Can Not Be Closed at 15 Years — They Need to Be Closed at 15 Months

Schools in many communities have been working hard, for a couple of decades, to close the learning gaps in their settings, and almost all have failed. They have failed because the scientific, biological, developmental, and functional truth is those sets of learning gaps that we see in all of those schools can't be closed at 15 years. They need to be closed at 15 months.

That is actually very possible to do — but that will only happen if we do the right things in each setting to close those gaps at 15 months.

Likewise, we have a number of communities where the health status for our minority populations is significantly poorer than the health status of White Americans. Higher rates of diabetes, hypertension, heart disease, and even stroke exist in far too many settings for minority Americans. Health problems create their own sets of problems for too many minority Americans.

The combination of learning gaps in our schools, plus health care disparities in our communities and higher levels of high school dropouts, combined with clear, discriminatory, and prejudicial patterns that we see, far too often, in hiring practices and promotions, have created major economic disparities that work in powerful ways against economic parity and functional equity in America.

We need to address all of those problems with the goal of solving them for each group as part of the basic strategy to achieve intergroup

Peace in America, which is the core purpose of this book and the goal of the Institute for InterGroup Understanding's Peace agenda.

We need to do more than solve those problems. We need to solve them in ways that prove to Americans, from all groups, that we all do believe in win/win outcomes for all people, from all groups.

That can be done, but it will only happen if we understand each of the issues, and then work together in visible and clearly intentional ways to solve each issue in each setting.

We Will Create a Sense of "Us" by Achieving Those Goals

We need leaders who understand these issues who want to help our children, and who believe in win/win outcomes for us all with enough commitment and clarity to point us and lead us in those directions.

We can and should activate every trigger on the alignment pyramid outlined in Chapter Eight of this book.

Working together to solve problems that create dangerous futures in those key areas that are important to all of us can activate our team instincts, our shared vision, our mutual trust, our sense of mutual gain for all people and our sense of being "Us" in important ways that will serve as an alignment force and as a collective motivation tool for us as a community and a people.

Win/Win Thinking Anchors That Entire Process

We will be more successful as a country when we have a culture of health for our country, and we will be more successful in each setting, and as a country, when we create a culture of continuous and successful learning for our children.

To create a culture of Peace for America, we need to all realize this is the right time to make a collective commitment to create win/win opportunities in key areas for all of our people.

We need people to know exactly what these issues, problems, and opportunities are, so we can build solutions to the problems that are appropriate for each setting and even for each family.

People are extremely creative in solving problems in a variety of innovative and functionally relevant ways — both individually and collectively — when problems of any kind are clearly understood, and when there is a clear sense of how important and relevant those problems actually are.

We Have Inconsistent Health and Children with Gaps in Their Learning

Both poor health and learning gaps are, in fact, relevant and important problems. Today, we have inconsistent levels of health, and people are being damaged as the result. We have significantly different life expectancies by group.

We also have far too many children who are being damaged because they are not being consistently well served by the levels of support for their learning abilities that we give each child in the first years of life.

We have major learning gaps between groups of children in America — and the consequences of those learning gaps are making life difficult for far too many people for their entire lives.

We are failing our children from the perspective of public health at several levels. We are currently not doing a good job of assuring that all children from all groups in America are getting the support, the mental exercise, and the education in the first three months and the first three years of life for each child that will give every child the best chance for success in life.

We actually can and should make huge improvements in those areas of development for our children.

We now know from fairly new and not widely shared new biological science exactly what needs to be done for each of our youngest children in those time frames.

Great new research that is being done and has been done at Columbia University, Harvard, The University of Washington, Stanford, UCLA, Berkeley, and a number of other child focused academic settings are all pointing us to entirely new levels of wisdom and science about the importance of the first weeks, months, and years for each child.

We now can understand that science at new and extremely important levels. As a key step for creating intergroup Peace and intergroup alignment in our country, we now need to share that science with all of the relevant people who should know that science.

We now need to make sure that people who are looking at the future of children and who are responsible for caring for — and educating — the children in this country understand both those issues and those opportunities.

The opportunities are huge.

We now know brains for all children, from all groups, develop and build neuron connections in the first three years of life, and we now know that those are the years when we need to support those processes in order to achieve maximum benefits for each child.

Every family in America should know that science and understand the impact of those processes and those time frames for every child. The opportunity and problem for each child very clearly both begin at birth, and the first weeks and months of life are actually far more important than we knew, or even suspected, for each child.

There has been a growing awareness that the first three years of life are when the neuron connectivity processes create the learning readiness levels and improve or damage brain strength levels for each child — but very few people in child development policy positions or in parenting settings have clearly understood the importance of the first weeks and months for each child.

We now know, from solid new developmental science, that even the first three months of life can be functionally important for the emotional security of our children. That is important new information. It is wonderful information to have. But it is not known by enough people.

That low level of understanding about the importance of those weeks, months, and years for each child makes sense because the people involved in leading our learning efforts and thinking about our education processes did not understand, or appreciate, what actually happens for each child in those first weeks, months, and years until fairly recently.

Some of that science is, in fact, new information.

That science about the importance and role of those first weeks and months has clearly not been part of our understanding of the development processes for children until some great researchers in some great programs at Columbia, The University of Washington, Harvard, and major California Universities did the studies that made those processes and those time frames known to us.

We now know there are epigenetic processes in place in those very first weeks and months for each child that determine key areas of wiring in children's brains.

We know when children in those first days and weeks are hungry and then fed — and when children in those weeks and months are stressed and then comforted, the brain wires itself in one generically and functionally positive direction.

But if the children in those first weeks and months are hungry and not fed, and if they are anxious and stressed, and are not comforted — then the brain tends to wire itself differently at that point in the life of each child. The results of those differences in brain wiring play out in different behavior and interaction levels for many children.

We need to share that information about the importance of those first weeks and months very clearly and effectively with every new parent, and with the families of all infants and babies in America, because knowing that those processes actually happen in that very immediate time frame can have a major impact on parenting practices for each child.

Parental Leave Policies Can Now Be Science Based

Knowledge is power. Children can benefit hugely from parents knowing that information about those first weeks of life at that key point in time.

The old science told us those were minimally important days and weeks for each child — days to get simply through on the way to more important and more pleasant days. The old science was wrong.

We now need to help parents and families who still believe the old science to know what we know now, so we can use that knowledge to help every new-born child.

The new science about those early epigenetic developments also gives us very strong evidence supporting the need for well structured and supportive parental leave policies for states, employers, and educational systems. When parental leave time overlaps directly, in real time — with the first weeks and months of life, then parental and family understanding what happens for each child in the first weeks and months can add great value to the development success for each child.

The Neuron Connectivity Levels That Happen in the First Three Years Create Brain Strength Capabilities for Life

An important sister book to *The Art of InterGroup Peace* is the book *Three Key Years*. *Three Key Years* is a sister to this book about intergroup Peace because it explains in some detail how important the first three years of life are for the brain development of our children from every ethnicity, culture, race, or economic group.

We have finally begun to understand the importance of the first three years of life for the learning readiness levels of each child.

We used to believe that education began with kindergarten. That actually is very wrong. It is, we now know, dangerously wrong. Education begins with birth and we now know the first three years of life are extremely important years for building brain strength and learning readiness levels for each child.

We now know, from excellent developmental research, the first three years of life for each child are actually the years when brains build basic functional strength for each child. It is a very biological process.

Neuron connectivity is the key. Those very first years are the years when neuron connectivity is most important for each child. Those are the years when basic brain infrastructure is put in place that serves each child for life. Children can receive great benefit from the right levels of support to build that neuron connectivity infrastructure in those key months and years.

Exercise is the tool. Physical exercise builds strong bodies. Brain exercise builds strong brains. Interaction with adults is the most important exercise for each child's brain.

If a child has significant interaction with an adult who is talking, playing, singing, and reading to the child, then rich networks of neuron connections happen in that child's brain, and the child who has that level of adult interactions is more learning ready at kindergarten, and far better able to do well in school.

But if a child does not get those levels of basic interactions that exercise and build strong brains in those key months and years, then too many of the most important and useful neuron connections do not happen, and those children tend not to be able to read when reading is a key part of their education.

The children who have fallen behind in those areas by the time they are 3 years old generally also do not do well on their mathematical computations, and in their reading related learning processes. Several universities have done very powerful research on the consequences to children of falling behind by 3 years old. Anyone who cares about our children should know what that research is telling us.

We now have a much better understanding of those brain development processes, time frames, and related biological science. It is the same process and the same time frames for children from every group. There are no differences by race, or ethnicity, or by any other kind of group.

That is important information to know. It is even more important to use that information to help children. We now understand the importance of those interactions in those key years, but the sad reality is that we don't do a good job of teaching that information in consistent ways to families and communities so that science can be used to help all children.

We are failing millions of children, and we are dooming far too many of our children to lives of challenge, functional deficits, academic difficulties, and economic deprivation and failure, because we are not providing and guaranteeing those levels of direct adult interactions for every child, from every group, in those key weeks, months, and years.

All parents love their children, and parents from every group and setting want their children to thrive — and we have done a truly horrible job of teaching that key information that can help each child thrive to every parent.

All parents and families need to know that physical exercise builds strong bodies, and that brain exercise builds strong brains.

We need every family and community to know that when children's brains are directly exercised in those first key months and years, the brains that are exercised are larger, more robust and more ready to learn.

Read, Talk, Interact, and Sing Strengthens Brains

Children who have adults exercising their brain by talking to them, reading to them, interacting with them, playing with them and singing to them in those first months and years have larger vocabularies in kindergarten. Those children with that brain exercise have better reading skills in the third grade and in high school, and those children tend to have much lower rates of both dropping out of school and going to prison.

We have more people in prison than any country on the planet by a very wide margin. We imprison far more of our minority Americans. We also imprison a much higher percentage of people who can't read.

More than 60 percent of our prisoners either read poorly or can't read at all. More than 85 percent of the children in the juvenile justice system either read badly or cannot read at all.

Small Vocabularies in Kindergarten Predict Both Dropouts and Prison

We can now predict with a high level of accuracy, by age three which children will be able to read. We can know by 18 months which children are likely to have very small vocabularies by the time they get to kindergarten.

The best predictor for who will end up in jail by age 18 is the number of words in each child's vocabulary in kindergarten.

We need direct brain exercise for each child in those first months and years of life for each child because the children who do get that exercise have larger vocabularies, read far better, and tend to stay in school and out of jail.

We need to do a far better job across all of our groups of Americans of giving all of our children the support each child needs in those first months and years to have the best chance for both better learning skills, and increased levels of functional success in key areas of life.

We Need to Help Each Child

If we want intergroup Peace for America, and if we want a future where people from all groups do well in major areas of our lives, then we need to start by making sure all children get the needed exercise to create those neuron connections in those first key months and years for the life of each child.

We also need better schools. We have opportunities to have better schools in a number of settings. We should take advantage of those opportunities as well. We can and should also improve our kindergartens and our schools. It will be particularly important to have better schools when more children are learning ready when they get to school.

We need to make sure our schools are ready to educate all children well when children who have well exercised brains come to school ready to learn.

We need better kindergartens, and we need school systems that are working to help all of the children who are learning ready actually learn. Improving the entire education system and building a well structured and comprehensive process improvement strategy for education can and should also be a collective goal for all of us.

But having better schools — by itself — will not fix the problems and will not significantly close the major learning gaps we see in our schools today. We need the children from every group who get to our schools to be learning ready. We all need to use this new science and we need to start by doing what we need to do to have each of our children learning ready when they get to school.

When all of our children have strong learning skills and when all of our children are appropriately educated, we will be stronger as a nation and all of the children will have much better chances for success in life.

We now know what needs to be done to make that happen — so this is the right time for us, as a nation and as communities across the country, to actually do what we need to do to achieve those goals.

As a nation — and as local communities — we need to take steps together now to resolve the major problems we face now in those areas. We need to collectively better support our children — to make lives better — for all children and to eliminate and prevent the learning gaps we have today where children from some groups have lower average reading and lower average math skills than other groups.

When we don't help all children in those key months and years by exercising each brain, the drop out rate goes up significantly, and the likelihood of going to prison goes up to unconscionable levels.

African American males in their 30s who dropped out of high school are 60 times more likely to go to jail than a White American male. Not 60 percent more likely or even six times more likely — 60 times more likely.

More than 50 percent of those high school dropouts are in jail today. That is a very bad thing at multiple levels.

Jail is a horrible experience for the person who is imprisoned, and the functional and economic costs to society of keeping a person in jail are extremely high as well. Everyone loses.

Making the learning levels higher for every child is very clearly a win/win set of outcomes for us all, because we will all benefit when we are all better able to succeed in all of those areas of learning.

We need everyone to understand that there is key work to be done is in the first three years of each child's life. That science and that opportunity is explained in more detail later in this chapter.

Those problems and those opportunities are each explained in some detail in the InterGroup Institute sister book *Three Key Years*. People concerned about the future of children in America should read that book. It is available and can be read on-line at The Institute for InterGroup Understanding website.

That book explains the problems and the biological science relevant to those first months and years, and identifies steps that can be taken by caregivers, communities, community leaders, families, and parents to help every child. We need to help every child in ways that show each of us cares about every child, and we need to do that because the life of each child can change significantly when that help is given in that time frame.

It happens one child at a time. Each child we save is a child we save. We each can make a major impact on the life of a child.

There are very few things anyone can do that can have a greater level of positive good than changing the life trajectory for a child. Sharing this information about those key processes with a relevant adult for each child can change those trajectories.

We also need to each think about whether or not we can individually do things that make a difference — like volunteering to read to children. That is more than just a feel good opportunity. It is a highly functional opportunity. Every time someone reads to a child in those time frames, millions of neurons connect.

It might not seem like a big thing to do — but each time you read in a caring way to a child in that brain development time frame, you help millions of neurons connect that will continue to be with that child for life. Parents, family, friends, community members, and people who just want to do good things for a child should look for opportunities to either support that reading process or to actually be the reader for a child.

As we are looking to help children in that particular area, we also all need to help ensure that actual books are available to every child. More than half of the low-income homes in this country a year ago did not have a single book. We need books in every home and books in every day care setting for low-income children.

We also very clearly need to support parental-leave programs for employers that make it possible for parents to spend key time with each child directly after each child is born.

Society needs those parental leave programs and basic interaction programs for children so we have a collective future where our children succeed and add value at multiple levels to Society, rather than having disproportionately large numbers of children who don't get that support who end up incurring major, long-term expense for the community.

We All Need to Be Healthier

We also need to do a much better job of improving population health in our communities and as a country.

We are not collectively healthy as a nation and we have significant health gaps by group that parallel and echo the learning gaps we have for our children.

We currently have significant health care disparities in this country that are based on race and ethnicity. The book *Ending Racial, Cultural, and Ethnic Disparities in American Health Care* deals with some of those issues very directly. We need to eliminate those disparities and we need to create a national culture of health to help us all avoid the need for care that too many of us have today.

The book, *Ending Racial, Ethnic, and Cultural Disparities in American Health Care*, is another sister book to this book, and can also be read chapter-by-chapter, online, at The Institute for InterGroup Understanding website.

The book, *Don't Let Health Care Bankrupt America*, explains those racial, ethnic, and cultural disparities, as well and explains why the very best things we can do to bring down the costs of care in this country is to have people be healthier, so that people actually need less care. We very much need a culture of health for America that will let us achieve those goals.

If we create a culture of health for us all, we can help define ourselves to ourselves as people who do good things collectively to functionally improve our mutual health — with everyone benefiting from our good health.

That can actually be done. Medical science tells us that there are some obvious and achievable opportunities for us to do that work. We should do that work together in each setting because we will all benefit at multiple levels from having us be healthier as a community and as individual people.

Healthy Eating — Active Living (HEAL)

To achieve that goal, we should focus our efforts on the two key and fundamental issues that will help us achieve that goal of better collective health. We need to focus on our food, and we need to focus on how extremely important it is for each of us to functionally Walk.

Healthy eating can make a huge difference in our level of health. Active living can make an even bigger difference on our health, and the active living benefit can be achieved for a high percentage of the people in our population simply by walking. We need better collective health, and we now know the science that tells us that activity and healthy food are literally the essential keys to improving population health.

In the same way we need to collectively provide support for our children to ensure their success, we should be working together in each community, and setting, to make sure people have adequate activity levels and healthy food to eat.

Too many people are significantly overweight and even obese today. Obesity is creating a wide range of ancillary diseases that damage people's lives.

Obesity is related to our eating approaches. Obesity can be reduced by both healthy eating, and by higher activity levels. We need more people to be healthy eaters and we need more overweight people to have higher levels of basic personal physical activity.

Healthy eating could be a shared and defining value, and it can also be something we work on together as a community in each setting, with a focus on having a positive, collective impact on our collective health.

For healthy eating, we can take direct and obvious steps to ban the most damaging food elements — like trans fats — from our diets. We can and should also take multiple and very clear steps to create better access to healthy foods for all Americans.

Too many of our inner-city communities do not have easy access to fruits, vegetables, and healthy protein sources. We need to make those foods available to all people everywhere.

Make the Right Thing Easy to Do

The key to improving population health is very much like the key for improving any key processes in life. The mantra and the guideline we should use to structure our thoughts and our strategies should be to Make The Right Thing Easy To Do.

Make The Right Thing Easy To Do is almost magical in its impact on achieving those kinds of goals. It is the Secret Sauce of Process Improvement.

The reason is simple and clear. In any process or any setting, when we make the right thing easy to do, it is much more likely to be done.

When the wrong thing is easy to do, we tend to do the wrong thing. When the right thing is easy to do, we tend to do the right thing.

Improving health is a key process where that thought process is extremely important. We need to make both healthy eating and active living easy to do, and we will be much more successful in getting people to be active and eat well.

We need to begin by helping all people to understand the basic strategies of healthy eating. We need to have a shared collective strategy in each community to improve the levels of healthy eating.

We can feel collectively good and mutually reinforcing in each setting when we work together as a community to collectively and individually achieve that healthy eating strategy for the community, and for individual members of the community.

We should take steps in each setting to make sure food stores have fruits and vegetables and other healthy foods, and we should encourage farmer's markets in communities to get good foods to all community members. We can do things together in communities to make that happen, and community leaders should act in visible ways to ensure healthy foods are available to community members.

We need people to understand the basic mathematical relationship between calorie intake and weight — and we need people to understand which foods are the healthiest foods, and which foods make healthy eating easiest to do.

We need people to eat moderately and well and we need people to be active to create the highest level of combined benefit for the improvement of our health.

Activity is essential as a health improvement tool. Activity is hugely important. We need to encourage people to be physically active. We should teach activity, advocate activity, support activity, enable activity, empower activity, and honor and reward activity.

Activity Levels Have a Larger Positive Impact Than Weight Control

We can actually have an even bigger collective engagement opportunity for us all, and an even bigger good health reward for all of us if we improve and sustain healthy activity levels.

People generally do not know that basic activity levels actually have huge and consistent impact on our health that can even exceed the benefit of weight control for many people. Most people do not appreciate or understand the huge positive and negative impact that activity levels and inactivity levels have on our personal well-being.

People with higher activity levels have lower levels of cancer, heart attack, diabetes, and stroke. The data is overwhelming and the science is powerful and persuasive. Walking can improve health at measurable and almost immediate levels. We can cut the risk of diabetes in half by simply walking 30 minutes each day.

That science and those results are well established. Our body needs to have some daily activity levels to have all of the circulatory systems and biological interactions function well — and simply walking for at least half an hour every day can trigger those extremely important systems into healthy functionality.

As a joint community effort, we can and should all support each other in every setting in being active by helping each other be able to walk.

Activity Levels Can Have a Massive Positive Impact on Health — Walking Can Be Almost Magical

Activity truly is key to success in improving health. The science is clear. Disease drops when we are active. Some diseases disappear when we are active. Others are significantly reduced. Activity levels help our body function better and give us basic levels of health that can truly change our lives.

We don't need to run or pedal or dance to be sufficiently active. We don't need to run marathons or compete in biathlons or triathlons. We can simply walk — and walking can be transformational.

Walking is a very powerful and effective way of achieving needed activity levels. The human body is designed to walk and the human body needs to walk to function well.

Walking can create health miracles. Walking is actually the single most useful activity level and approach that we have for health improvement. Walking can be almost magical in its positive impact on our health.

Several key chronic diseases can be significantly reduced or even prevented entirely by walking.

More than 75 percent of the health care costs in this country today come from our chronic diseases — not from our acute diseases and accidental injuries. Inactivity levels — basically from people not walking — are a major chronic disease risk factor for Americans that are creating the majority of our health care expenses.

Urbanization Has Created Chronic Disease Epidemics

That link between chronic conditions and health care costs is true in a growing number of other countries as well. Urbanization in developing countries around the world has created massive epidemics of diabetes and significantly increasing heart disease levels in many countries. That is happening because far too many of the newly urbanized people in those countries who used to walk in the rural areas every day no longer walk at all once they move to the cities.

Those health issues are relevant to intergroup Peace in all of those settings because the health status of the people from those groups is deteriorating, and the people who live in those neighborhoods, in many countries, are from the minority populations in those cities.

Major chronic disease problems are happening in some of those settings for the first time in history because people in those countries who used to live in the rural areas, and who used to walk every day as a major form of personal transportation, now live in large urban slums and most of those people do not walk at all.

When people do not walk, several damaging diseases appear. Life is shortened when walking is reduced.

The diet for those newly urbanized people also changes from their old mixture of locally grown vegetables and fruits to a new and narrow diet of processed white foods — white flour, white rice, and white sugar. Inert people whose diet has been rechanneled to over-processed and high calorie foods have much lower health levels.

Major health problems are happening for the people in those countries, and that creates some intergroup conflict issues in a number of settings because there are often ethnic differences between the original people who lived in those cities, and the new people who come to the cities from the rural areas of those countries.

Those are entirely different, but not entirely irrelevant sets of issues.

Walking Can Significantly Improve Health

In any case, the medical science is very clear.

The human body tends to be significantly healthier when people walk. Walking 30 minutes a day, five or more days a week, actually does cut the rate of diabetes in half. Diabetes is currently the fastest growing disease in America. More than 30 percent of the money spent on Medicare today is spent on diabetics.

Our minority populations in this country have particularly heavy cost burdens and health burdens for both diabetes and the adverse consequences of diabetes.

The rate of diabetes can be cut in half if people walk every day. That same daily walk can also cut strokes and heart disease by more than 40 percent.

That same daily half-hour walk can even cut prostate cancer, breast cancer and colon cancer by more than one-third.

Walking gets the body's circulatory systems and basic biological functions to perform more effectively.

That scientific information about the collective benefits of walking for all people is included in a book that deals with *The Art of InterGroup Peace*, because intergroup Peace can be enhanced if we help each other be healthier. It is also discussed extensively in the book, *Don't Let Health Care Costs Bankrupt America*.

Economic strength for all groups is enhanced if all groups have healthier people. We can be healthier if we work together and walk together to achieve important mutual gain health improvement goals.

Peace can also be enhanced if various groups consistently walk together and if the groups in each community work together and collectively create and protect safe walking environments in every setting in a common cause to make "Us" all healthier.

We Need Collective Support for Walking

It is very much a win/win for all groups if we are all healthier. It is particularly good for Peace if we walk together, and if we create safe walking environments in our communities, working together, because we are committed, together, to give us all collective good health.

Those walking environments can be and need to be very local strategies and community-based realities for purely logistical reasons.

It's hard to be more local. Walking is a very local thing to do. As a pure functional strategy, we need to create safe walking environments in our communities, our schools, our places of work — and we need to walk together in those settings as a commitment to our individual and collective health.

We need to all support creating a context where walking can be done daily by all of us.

We only need to walk a half-hour a day to achieve very high levels of benefits. That half-hour can be broken into two 15 minute segments and still provide the health benefits.

That science about only needing to walk 30 minutes to achieve major health benefits is good to know and understand when our strategic goal for that issue is to Make The Right Thing Easy to Do.

We should collectively make increasing activity for all of us at all income levels easy to do. We should make it easy to walk in all communities and settings, and we should reduce barriers to walking where those barriers exist.

As we look at ways that we can bring Americans together in a common cause with a common agenda that is clearly in our mutual best interest, creating a whole array of walking-friendly community and workplace opportunities that enable everyone who wants a daily walk to safely take a daily walk, can improve everyone's health.

Understanding that issue clearly, and then creating that collective agenda and those life-extending opportunities, in settings and communities, with the support of all of us can give groups of people in communities across the country a chance to work together in the mutual best interest of us all.

We can benefit and show our mutual commitment to each other by doing basic things that facilitate good health for us all. Walking is a good context for creating that level of health improvement opportunity, and walking together in safe ways can facilitate both a sense of community and an opportunity to enjoy and celebrate the diversity that exists in each setting.

Neuron Development for Very Young Children

Helping people be physically healthier, and facilitating both healthy eating and active living is not, however, the thing we can do collectively that will have the biggest positive impact on future intergroup interactions in our country.

Children should be our first priority.

As we look at the things we can do as a nation to give us a future of shared success and intergroup Peace, we should do what we need to do to change the futures for our children.

We all love our children. We all want our children to succeed. Helping people from other groups facilitate the success of all children is a very visible, believable, meaningful, and important area where we can create an anchor for intergroup good will and intergroup trust.

That point was outlined in some detail earlier in this chapter, and it is being repeated here in some detail again, because there are very few things more important to our future as a nation, and as a people, than understanding this set of issues, and then doing the right thing in key areas to help our children.

Helping children from all groups succeed by being learning ready when school begins is a much more important agenda than even improving our individual and collective health, and one that we ought to have as a top priority for us as a country. Almost no one in policy circles understands the importance of these issues and has a good sense of the functional fact that we have no other path that can succeed in helping us close the learning gaps we have in so many American schools.

We need success for all of our children from every group. Learning gaps should no longer be acceptable to us as a country. Learning gaps damage children, and learning gaps create futures of intergroup anger and conflict that have the ability to damage us and our future as a country.

We need to do the right things to help all children from all groups succeed. To help all of our children succeed, we need to help all of our children get the brain stimulation they need in the first months and years of life, when brain development happens for every child.

We now know the science. We now understand the functional processes. We now know that brain development for each child is a purely biological reality, and we now know the exact time frames when brain development is most important to each child from every group of children.

We now know, for purely biological reasons, we need to give every child a basic level of stimulation and adult interaction that builds strong neuron connections, and increases learning readiness in those first months and years of life.

The science of neuron development, and the neuron connectivity processes that happen for our children are now clearly understood. Brains that get exercised in the first three years of life are stronger.

It is a purely biological process. We need all Americans to understand that science and to know clearly the implications and layers of consequences that result from that science.

That opportunity that exists in each child in those key months and years for brain development is — like the consequences of both obesity and inactivity — very fundamentally and clearly biological.

We are all biological beings. Young children — from birth to roughly 3 years old — all go through a few key years where the neurons in their brains are forming their internal connections.

We now know, from very good biological science, brain development processes continue to happen throughout our lives, but the first three years of life are actually the most important time for supporting and enhancing brain development for each child. Neuron connectivity in those years is much easier to do, and the consequences of doing it well in those years are life shaping in extremely positive ways for each child.

Those first years of life are relatively brief, and we now understand much more clearly that the brain support received by each child in those first few months and years are absolutely crucial for the life pathways for each child.

Science now tells us that if individual children receive the right levels of brain exercise, external stimulation, and appropriate support from adults in those very early years, that development process and that level of stimulation can give each child the neurological foundation and the brain strength that is needed by each child for a successful and productive life.

The children who do not get that stimulation in those months and years, tend to not be learning ready when they get to kindergarten, and they tend not to catch up in their years in school. The children who only have a few words in their understood vocabulary at age three tend to have major difficulty catching up later in the education processes.

Now that we know that science, we need to apply it to every child. It is actually not that difficult to do. Providing key levels of support can be done for almost any child in almost any setting.

Reading, Talking, Interacting, and Singing Exercise Baby Brains

The needed exercise tools that functionally strengthen the brain of each child are basic and simple. Brain exercise can be done by reading, talking, interacting, and singing to each child.

Read/Talk/Play/Sing — magical and powerful tools that strengthen brains and facilitate emotional security in children.

Just 30 minutes of reading a day can have a huge positive impact on the brain of a child. Asking each child 20 questions a day — even when the child is too small to answer the questions — can also increase brain function for a child.

Simply talking to children has a major impact on neuron connecting activity. Talking is extremely important, and has a major impact on children in those key weeks, months and years.

We need all mothers to know what an incredible and wonderful gift they are giving to their children by just talking in loving, direct, and constant ways in those first months and years. We can teach new mothers, many of whom are insecure about the value they are able to give to their children, the wonderful, encouraging, and affirming knowledge that the value those simple interactions they have with their baby is a pure gift of major biological development for each child.

Children who don't get that basic brain exercise in those first early years from parents talking, reading to them, and playing with them tend to have smaller vocabularies. Children with very small understood vocabularies at 3 and 4 years old are much more likely to not be able to read, and they are much more likely to drop out of school.

(Interestingly, the spoken vocabulary is not as important for children in those first key months as the understood vocabulary for each child, so parents should not worry if their children clearly understand what adults are saying, but simply refuse to speak, themselves, in those early years.)

We now know we need to exercise the brain of every single baby and child from every group. It is very possible to do that for each child. The techniques that create positive results for children are simple and basic.

Talking Is the Most Important Brain Exercise Tool for Parents

Talking is actually the single most important brain-strengthening tool to use with children. That is particularly true in the first year of life. Children at that age need caring adults talking directly to them. Talking creates major value to children.

Talking directly to a child triggers brain strength. Neurons connect by the millions, and even billions, in those first months when adults talk directly to a child. Adults who talk constantly to children, about any topics at hand, are not just entertaining and amusing the child. They are actually triggering billions of connections in the child's brain.

We need all parents to know that science, and we need to encourage parents to talk extensively, beginning with the first weeks of life when the exact words spoken are clearly meaningless to the infant who is hearing them.

We have failed badly in teaching that reality to parents in this country, and we have some settings where children are not spoken to at all.

That, we now know, is not optimal for the infant's development or security levels.

Books and Counting Are Also Very Good for Children

Books are also very useful from a very early age. Reading clearly exercises baby brains, and reading teaches children in the first years of life the link between symbols and meaning.

Children who have been read to more extensively tend to be more learning ready when that time of learning happens in schools.

Counting also has great brain strengthening power. We tend not to teach counting to parents as a parenting tool as well. That is also a mistake for us as teachers and advisors to parents.

We should be explaining to parents that counting with a child is a good thing. Asking a child, how many apples are in the bowl, is more than just fun — it teaches quantitative thinking and basic math skills.

The counting doesn't need to be complex — but constant, fun counting for children can build stronger quantitative processes and skills. Those interactions are all extremely important to each child. The needed brain exercise stimulation to be done for each child to make sure no children actually fall behind, can simply be based on direct talking to the child, reading to the child, and singing to the child by caring and trusted adults in each child's world.

Talk, read, interact, play, and sing. Those specific activities exercise each child's brain, and those basic exercises make each brain grow.

That is a science all caregivers, day care programs, families, and communities should understand. We need learning gaps to disappear. If the neurons of those very young children are not stimulated in those crucial and key few years — the biological impact and the brain function outcomes for each child can be very damaging for their entire lives and learning gaps will continue.

We all need to understand those issues, because they affect the entire lives of people in ways that affect everyone. The consequences of not stimulating all of our children at that age are, actually, very costly for the children, and both costly and damaging at several levels for the communities where the children who have learning problems live and function.

Early Stress Levels Can Be Reduced as Well

The issues of early support for each child extend beyond learning readiness. The early interaction issues include emotional readiness and emotional stability.

We now know we can aid the emotional stability of children at important levels by feeding and comforting them in the first weeks and months after they are born — when their brains are adjusting to whatever kind of world each child seems to be in. Emotional underpinnings can be challenging, and even damaged based on those first interactions, and emotional underpinnings can be strengthened by those first encounters.

The impact of those early weeks and months can have bigger impact when children sense early stress and when the stress levels for a child are constant. When very young children are isolated or feel threatened in any way, those children tend to experience higher levels of early childhood stress.

That stress in those first years can actually, physically damage the brain. And a condition called toxic stress can result.

Specific neurochemicals in the brain that are triggered by toxic stress can actually damage some levels of functioning for the brain.

Children who have toxic stress levels in those early years are much more likely to perform poorly in school — and they are even more likely to have health problems than the children who have had the nurturing impact of being cared for and stimulated in those early years.

Many families and caregivers do not know about the very real damage that can be done to very young children by toxic stress.

Toxic stress chemicals in the brain are created when a child is either isolated and ignored, or treated badly — and those chemicals can cause children to have both physical and behavioral problems when they get to school age.

Those children who suffer from toxic stress are also much less likely to finish school and they are significantly more likely to be imprisoned.

Toxic Stress Can Be Buffered

It is possible to do very important things to prevent toxic stress and reduce and buffer its impact. Good, new research also now teaches us toxic stress and the negative impact of those neurochemicals on a child's brain can be "buffered" in each child, if the child gets at least a half-hour per day of protective attention from a loving adult.

That seems like too little time to have the impact it does, but there is good research that tells us 30 minutes of buffer time, of positive and caring interaction with a child each day, can have a major impact buffering the damage of toxic stress for a child.

That important research shows that the half-hour of positive interaction time by a child with a loving adult can help serve as a buffer time for our children that actually keeps toxic stress chemical from damaging the infants' brains.

The read, talk, and sing time that helps exercise each child's brain can also help be that needed buffer against the damage done by toxic stress.

The data is clear. Differences in behavior and differences in capacity between children are measurable. The book *Three Key Years* explains that process and outlines what we can and should do to help each child.

Children who receive less than adequate stimulation and low levels of brain exercise in those essential early years, and who don't get that buffer against toxic stress end up with smaller vocabularies, lower reading skills, and a much higher likelihood of dropping out of school.

It is a sad reality that one of the best lead indicators and key functional predictors for which children will actually end up in jail is the number of words in each child's vocabulary in kindergarten.

We have more than three times as many people in jail as any other Western country. We have seven times more people in jail than Canada. More than

60 percent of the people in our jails either read poorly or can't read at all. Studies have shown that the children who have small vocabularies in kindergarten end up having lower reading skills when they get to school.

As noted earlier, basic longitudinal studies have shown that the children who have lower reading skills in the third grade are 40 percent more likely to get pregnant during their school years — 60 percent more likely to drop out of school — and those children with low skills at that point in their lives are nearly 80 percent more likely to go to jail before age 18.

Two-Thirds of the People in Jail Come from the Set of Children with Low Neuron Stimulation

This issue is addressed at length in this book on intergroup Peace strategies because the truth today is that more than two-thirds of the children who end up in jail come from the group of children who tend to score low on their third grade reading tests or who can't read at all, and we need to have fewer people in jail if we really aspire to creating intergroup Peace in America.

We need to recognize that a majority of the children who drop out of school before graduating come from that same set of low scoring readers in those early years, and we need to change those life paths for those children.

These outcomes that happen for those particular young people who have those sets of learning issues are not a problem we can solve with better grade schools or with better high schools.

The schools for children of that age level can't solve those learning problems for the children who did not get their needed early support and brain exercise. High school is far too late for too many of our children.

So is kindergarten and grade school. The time of high opportunity neuron enrichment is in those very first months and years of life for each child. We can't close the learning gaps at 15 years old. We truly do need to close them at 15 months.

Catching up can be very hard to do — almost impossible — for purely biological reasons. The most opportune time for neuron connectivity — with billions of neuron connections happening — is in those first years.

When children miss that early neuron development opportunity, and when these children have lower reading skills by the third grade, then those children need much more support at that point from our schools. A number of the children who are behind at that very early point in their lives later can at least partially catch up — with great teaching and with great support from family, friends, and educators

We still need to help every child after those first years — and some children can, and do, benefit significantly on learning abilities and academic capabilities after that time — but the best time for that opportunity to build the highest levels of learning readiness for each child is gone after those first key years.

We need to do everything we can do to help individual and groups of children who have fallen behind, and many children who have fallen behind will benefit from those efforts.

We also can and should learn to create entirely new learning expectations for the students in their 20s and 30s who can't read, and we need to provide support for those students to guide them to settings, and to economic opportunities when they are adults, which don't require the ability to read.

Currently, the only economic infrastructures available to many high school dropouts who can't read are our gangs. Our street gangs have increasing strength in far too many communities, and they tend to be the only economic infrastructure available to high school dropouts who can't read.

If we intend to reduce the power and impact of gangs, and if we want to help more people have better lives, then we need to figure out alternative economic pathways for our most disadvantaged students.

There Is No Difference by Race or Ethnicity

Those numbers linking early learning with life success or failure are consistent for children from all racial and ethnic groups. There is no difference in the damaging functional impact of low neuron connectivity stimulation by either race or ethnicity.

There is also no difference in the benefit that children from each and every group receive from exercising their brains in those key months and years. Children from every group do well when their neurons are stimulated in those key months and years. Children from every group perform poorly when their neurons are not stimulated at that point in their lives.

A number of studies show very clearly that minority children are more likely to have low reading skills, drop out of school, and go to jail.

Those problems are not actually either racial or ethnic. They are entirely environmental.

We Have too Many Minority Americans in Jail

We have far too many of our minority population in jail. One-in-10 Black American males in their 30s are in jail today. More than half of the African American high school dropouts in their 30s are in jail. Less than 1-in-90 White American males are in jail. It is very difficult to create an ongoing culture of Peace, and to build full mutual benefit for all of us at a win/win level in our increasingly diverse communities, when Hispanic Americans are four times more likely to end up in jail, and when African Americans are six times more likely to be imprisoned.

We all need to understand clearly that there are multiple factors that explain why we have those disproportionate numbers of people in jail. Economic reasons for various groups of people are a key part of the problem. Bias in law enforcement, and bias and discrimination in judicial rulings are both part of the problem.

The "Sentencing Project" report, given to the United Nations Human Rights Committee in 2013, about discriminatory arrest rates and conviction rates in the United States is worth reading by anyone concerned about those issues — to get a sense of how much discrimination exists in those areas. It is a well-done study that truly deserves to be read by anyone concerned about those issues.

That report shows city after city where the police arrest far more minority drivers, for example, for the same levels of illegal activity. Those kinds of arrest and incarceration disparities are becoming much more visible, and that visibility gives us a chance to deal with them very directly by changing the relationships communities have with their police.

The beginning section of this chapter addresses our need to do that work.

The sister books *Cusp of Chaos*, *Primal Pathways* and *Peace In Our Time* also explain those patterns of discriminatory behaviors more completely.

Those are clearly a number of reasons why we have those major disproportionate rates of incarceration for groups of Americans. We need to understand and recognize all of those issues. We also should take explicit steps to address the factors that we can, effectively, if we want to change those realities for America.

That proportion of non-readers to imprisonment levels is true for prisoners of all races.

Those same percentages of people who can't read being incarcerated tends to hold true for other countries where we have data. Sixty percent of the people in jail in Great Britain also read poorly or do not read at all.

Not being able to read clearly creates life challenges at multiple levels that can lead to being imprisoned for some people.

Because that is true — and because we know that fewer than 10 percent of African American males in their 30s, who graduated from high school, are in jail — and we know that nearly 60 percent who did not graduate are in jail, then pure logic points us to helping people graduate as a strategy for reducing the number of people we send to jail. Ten percent is a very bad number — and 60 percent is much worse.

The pathway to prison starts very young — because we can predict with a high level of accuracy, by age three, who will be able to read, and the people who can't read are much more likely to drop out of school and end up in jail.

That points us to a basic strategy for *The Art of InterGroup Peace* applied to America today — reducing the number of people we send to prison. We can reduce the level of people in prison by giving all children from all groups the stimulation that each child needs to be able to do well in school.

Because that is possible to do, we should be doing it.

Economic Factors Both Create the Problem and Are Created by It

There are clear differences in parenting practices in America that have a direct link to the economic status of families. Many of the wealthier and higher income mothers and fathers have the time and the resources to focus their attention on their children in those first years and to constantly exercise their babies' brains. Their children tend to do well on all of those tests as a result of that support.

It can be much harder for low-income families to provide the same levels of support for their children.

Low-income mothers and fathers may have multiple part-time and low-paying jobs, poor transportation resources, very little discretionary income, and much less time to spend focused on their children. It is harder to do many things when income levels are low, and spending time and resources on children are clearly a problem when that reality exists for a family.

Having less available time for their children for low-income families is entirely understandable — but we need to figure out ways of helping each child because we know the consequences of not having that time for a child can be unfortunate for each child, and it shows up in the learning gaps we see in the schools.

The school performance gaps that exist widen when higher income parents can spend the time and resources to exercise their children's brains, and when lower income mothers need to spend their energy providing food and shelter to their kids and can't focus on getting those neuron connections to happen for their child.

Those problems are exacerbated by the fact that we have done an extremely inadequate and dysfunctional job of teaching those brain development realities and opportunities to the parents of America. Almost no parents of young children in our country today know the basic science.

Intelligence Levels Are Not Set at Birth

One survey showed the overwhelming majority of people believe the intelligence level we each have is fixed and set at birth, and most people believe we each have to play the cards we are dealt at birth for our entire lives for our individual intelligence levels.

That is entirely wrong. It is bad science, and it illustrates a poor understanding of those basic brain strength-building processes. But we have not explained the actual processes to people in ways that guide parenting decisions and practices.

When parents understand the importance of brain exercise in those first months and years, then all parents can make decisions about parenting that are better informed and more beneficial for their children.

We need to be obsessive, compulsive, persistent, and extremely effective in teaching those realities to every family in America, and we need to support parents when they make decisions intended to achieve the right sets of child development support and goals for their children.

Because we have not taught those key issues to parents, we have major portions of our parenting population who are unintentionally not making fully informed parenting decisions. We need to do far better in teaching those biological realities to all groups of parents in America.

For a whole variety of reasons, including the fact that we have not taught those biological development time frames or processes to all families, our African American children and our Hispanic children are much more likely to have heard fewer spoken words from adults in their lives before kindergarten, and each child in those groups is significantly less likely to have been read to in those essential early years where reading to a child makes the difference between a child going to college or dropping out of school.

We can correct that problem. We need to do that one child at a time. It needs to be corrected for each child in order to save each child because the process happens in those same time frames for each child.

We need to help parents from all groups understand the importance of those interactions, and we need parents and families, from all groups, talking much more to each child in those time frames, when those interactions have the most beneficial outcomes.

Talking Is the Anchor Behavior That Creates the Most Benefit

Far too many families and parents do not know talking to a child is the anchor behavior that has the most positive impact on neuron connectivity in very young children. That seems too simple to be true, but it is a functional reality. Talking adds great value to children's development, and parents have not been told how much good they can do for their children, just by talking directly, in loving ways to them.

New mothers who are feeling insecure and concerned about the level of value they can give to their children in those first weeks, months, and years need to be given reassurance by trusted and credible messengers that they are giving a wonderful gift to their baby that builds brain connections by the millions, just by talking to their baby.

That is extremely important science. Simply talking to a child literally creates millions and billions of those connections, and talking to a child can be done in any setting.

Studies have shown children from lower income homes tend to hear millions of fewer words spoken directly to them than children from higher income homes. Some of those studies about higher income children having far more words spoken to them in their first years of life are widely quoted.

The truth is, those patterns of words spoken by income levels of parents clearly exist today, but they don't need to be the reality. Talking is free. Every setting can afford spoken words. We can and should encourage people from every group, and setting, to talk constantly to their infants and babies, and to begin at birth. Each talking exchange benefits the child.

Reading Also Is a Good Brain Development Tool

Reading is also extremely useful and important for brain development for each child. Children benefit both emotionally, and in learning readiness levels, when adults read to each child. That is another area where learning gaps have group-specific differences that help create the gaps.

Several studies have shown us there are also significant differences in reading levels for children between groups of Americans as well.

Higher income Americans are much more likely to read books to their children. More than half of the low-income homes in America do not have a single book. Higher income homes average 12 books per child.

Those differences in reading levels are not dictated or mandated by the economic realities in most settings. It is possible to read books in low-income homes.

More than 30 percent of low-income mothers do read now every day to their child. We need to get that number of low-income homes that read to children to much higher levels — and we need to provide both books and reading support to low-income parents.

We need to encourage family members and other friends of families to read to our very young children — particularly in settings where parents might not be able to read, themselves. That number of non-reading adults could be up to 20 percent of the parents in some settings.

When that is true, we need to find other readers in that setting who can provide that service to each child — and we also need non-reading parents to know that simply pointing out and telling the stories from children's books to children below the age of two, can provide many of the benefits of actually reading the books to a child.

We also need to be much more effective in providing books and reading support to the day cares that take care of low-income children.

One study showed more than half of the day care settings for low-income children did not have a single book last year. We need every day care in America to have more than one book per child, and we need people in the day cares for our very young children to be both talking, and reading to their children.

We need to make sure our day care settings do a good job of helping our youngest children. Some do that well and some do it very badly.

The horror of having children in day care settings strapped into car seats, and put in front of television sets for hours on end, creates and exacerbates significant learning readiness problems for too many children. We need families, day cares, and babysitters to be reading, talking, and playing with our children, and the results will be many more learning ready children.

If we solve our early interaction problems for more children, we can at least partially decouple school failure from race and ethnicity. Shared intergroup success for us as a nation will be very difficult until we solve that problem for those children from every group.

We need to educate every single mother, every father, and every family from every single group about those issues, and we need to figure out a range of support systems for each child — grandmothers, grandfathers, aunts, community groups, day care settings, volunteers, or paid professionals — to give each child the stimulation each child needs.

Neuron Development Is Needed for Our Success as a Nation

That information about neuron development in babies is included in this book about how we can achieve intergroup Peace in America because we should now become very clear about our commitment to win/win outcomes for all groups of people if we want to be a country at Peace with ourselves. Win/win obviously should include having us all collectively doing what we need to do to give equal opportunities and equal development advantages to all children from all groups of people.

That neuron development science is important information for us all to have as we look at the collective agendas we should now set as a core goal of our new American "Us."

The Art of InterGroup Peace will depend on all of us being able to succeed. There is probably no other factor that has an equivalent impact on each child's life than neuron development in those first years and alleviating toxic stress in those same years.

If we look at the relevant logistical issues and at the overall sets of consequences, there are probably very few factors that can have a greater impact on our overall success as a nation, and as a community of successful people, than focusing on getting the right processes in place for neuron development and neuron connectivity for our very youngest children.

If we want to reduce critically important performance difficulties by group, then we need to reduce early childhood support deficits by each minority child.

We Win When All of Our Children Do Well

This is actually the epitome of a win/win issue. The potential for positive and collective impact and a win for all groups of people in America is massive.

When all children from every group have well developed neuron stimulation and connectivity levels that lead to stronger reading skills in these very early years, those children are much more likely to be successful members of the community — with the ability to get and hold jobs.

The lifetime income level difference for the children who drop out of school and the children whose early stimulation allows them to graduate from school, is roughly $1 million in personal earnings per child.

That is huge difference. We can give a $1 million gift to each child who receives that neuron development support.

From a purely financial win/win economic perspective as a government investment, the children with the right stimulation in those years are much more likely to pay employment taxes as adults — taxes that can help support all of the various programs that we have and need whose funding is based on tax support. Nobel Laureate, James J. Heckman from the University of Chicago, has pointed out eloquently the economic argument for helping those children in those key years.

Several other economists have made similar arguments and made them well.

The children with the right stimulus in those first three years of life are more likely to stay in school, avoid jail, become employed, and participate in the American Dream as full players and full participants. This is important work.

The Ethical Issues Are Clear

The ethical issues are extremely clear. Now that we clearly understand that science, those developmental processes, and time frames, the ethical issues of allowing millions of children to miss that brief and vitally important neuron connection opportunity, and to face lives of economic and functional difficulty as the result, are painfully obvious.

More than half of all births in this country this year will be into Medicaid homes. More than half is a big number.

What does that tell us about our future? We know from some studies roughly 30 percent of Medicaid homes do read every day to their children — but we also know more than half of those homes do not read at all, and more than half of the Medicaid homes do not have a single book for the children in the home.

Now that we understand the importance of those first months and years, and the value created by reading to our children, that information about the majority of births happening today in our country into settings where there are few books, or no books, should give each of us the inspiration we need to have a positive impact for those children.

That set of issues is a major topic for the long-term success of *The Art of InterGroup Peace* — both because of the long-term win/win benefits that are created by success in this area, and because of the long-term, lose/lose consequences for intergroup interactions and for intergroup trust of continual and expanded failure for that portion of our population.

The shared win/win agenda of helping all of these children from every single group achieve their full potential ought be a unifying set of activities for us all — with collaborative approaches set up, defined, supported, and operated in ways that will lend to collective alignment and success.

We need to prove our commitment to each other at this point in our history by helping everyone's children succeed.

We need to understand that many of the challenges found by children in our country relate back to the neuron development issue — and we need to take that issue on collectively and well.

We Need to Improve Activity Levels and We Need to Realize Learning Potentials

So the collective health of all of us and the biological development of our children's brains in the first months and years of life are two areas where we could jointly, collectively, and collaboratively transform America by having a shared agenda, a shared strategy, and a shared set of goals.

Both of those key collective goals can be achieved. We can do it in each community — and we can do it together.

We will be stronger as a nation at multiple levels when we achieve both goals in every setting.

We can create health and we can also create improved learning ability for children from every group in America.

If we could get people from every group to walk — just a half-hour a day, five days a week — we could cut the rate of chronic disease that is bankrupting America in half.

We could help our patient populations from all groups avoid the number one cause of blindness, amputations, kidney failure, and death from heart disease by getting people to walk.

Our minority populations today suffer the most today from those specific diseases. We need to eliminate that disparity and that burden, and we can do it by collectively getting people to walk.

At the same time, if we could put processes in place that can assure neuron development in those first weeks and months of life in very young children of every race, ethnicity, and economic status, we could cut the rate of kids dropping out of school and going to jail by more than half, and we could improve the learning ability for millions of children in ways that will change the trajectory of their lives.

Reading a half-hour a day to each child can have consequences for neuron development that are the equivalent of walking a half-hour a day and cutting the rate of diabetics in half.

We need to make those key and high value half-hours of collective commitment a reality.

Everyone loves their children. Giving great opportunities to all children is a perfect collective win/win goal. Both disease prevention and brain strengthening can be powerful and extremely effective collective mutual benefit agendas. In each setting, we can ask people to figure out what needs to be done to make those goals a success. Doing things together — as the alignment pyramid points out — can help us all relate to one another as an us.

We Need to Begin with a Sense of Where We Are Today

Putting those win/win strategies in place will have a higher likelihood of success if we have a clear sense of where we are as a nation today on our intergroup issues and interactions.

We need to start with a clear understanding of our history. Once we understand the impact of our intergroup instincts on our thinking and our behaviors, our history makes a lot more sense and our current status is also easier to understand and address.

That is the topic of the next chapter of this book. Where are we now and how did we get here?

CHAPTER TWELVE

Our Us/Them Instincts Have Created Much of Our History

To create a culture of InterGroup Peace for America, we need to begin by understanding exactly how we are doing today relative to Peace between the various groups in this country.

We need to look very clearly and very honestly at our history as a nation, and we need to look very clearly at where we are now relative to our intergroup issues and relative to our intergroup realities.

We need to use that understanding to lay the foundation for where we want to go now and for what we need to do next to create a culture of Intergroup Peace for our country.

We have had successes and we have had failures as a nation. We need to understand the areas where we have been successful and enlightened, and we need to recognize the areas where we have made progress in important ways.

We also very much need to understand the areas where we have failed. We need to understand the areas where we have committed acts of serious intergroup discrimination and where we have done major damage to various people in this country — and we need to look at those damaging behaviors across the entire course of our history.

Significant damage has been done. We need to deal with that reality today. We need to have a clear sense of how badly we have acted in some key areas, and we need to understand the very real challenges to intergroup Peace that have been created by a long series of very wrong things that we, as a nation, have committed against too many of our own people.

We need to have clear knowledge and understanding about our successes and our positive achievements. We need knowledge of our failures and our sins in order to give us a complete foundation and a full context for teeing up intergroup Peace today.

We need to begin that process by recognizing that we have both residual anger and residual damage that has been created by our long standing discriminatory intergroup behaviors.

We Have Areas of InterGroup Disparities and Damage

Today, as a nation, we continue to have significant economic differences between our major ethnic and racial groups. Our minority Americans tend to have lower average incomes and higher rates of unemployment.

We need to recognize that reality as a context for what we need to do now as a nation.

We also have some clear differences in education levels by group, and we have major differences in our likelihood of being imprisoned — based on which racial or ethnic group we are in.

Hispanic American males are three times more likely to end up in prison than White American males. African American males are roughly six times more likely to go to jail than White Americans.

We can't ignore those major differences in economic status or life patterns for our various groups. We need to close the economic and education gaps — and we need to prevent the incarceration gaps from occurring.

We need to bring all groups to the best levels in each major area of performance to ensure our long-term success as a nation.

Those differences in life patterns need to be addressed. We need to share a commitment to giving all Americans access to the American Dream.

We need to support that commitment, in part, by doing what needs to be done to have the best neuron connectivity support for each child in the first months and years of life for each child.

We need to share a commitment to helping every child from every group succeed.

There Are Wide Degrees of Success Within Groups

We can be encouraged by the fact that there is a wide range of outcomes, success levels, and economic status for people within each race and ethnic group today. There are clear patterns that show economic disparities by group and there are clear exceptions to those patterns.

Some of the wealthiest people in the country today are Hispanic or African American. Some extremely successful CEOs of major companies come from our minority groups.

Highly successful entrepreneurs and business owners have come from all groups. We have a very diverse set of artists, musicians, entertainers, and creative people in our various media venues who also come from all groups.

So those are successful exceptions to the patterns. Those exceptions prove the value of having the American Dream available to all Americans.

But the overall group-linked patterns are clear and painful and the basic data about our groups relative to performance in several areas is powerful. There are major differences today.

We need to do much better at narrowing key differences between those groups in a positive way that will help us achieve and protect intergroup Peace.

We Have Discriminated by Race, Ethnicity, Culture, and Gender

When you look at our history, it is clear that we have discriminated in major ways against very large subsets of our population. We have damaged people based on their race, culture, ethnicity, and gender. Some of the key and most discriminatory parts of our history that are described later in this chapter have given us cause for sorrow and shame as a nation.

We have enslaved people, ethnically cleansed people, and we have written very intentional and clear laws that have discriminated deliberately and shamelessly against people based very specifically and explicitly on their race, gender, and ethnicity.

We now need to create intergroup Peace in this country with that history as part of our foundation for intergroup interaction. We need to start now be recognizing where we are now — and by recognizing where we have been.

We Need to Do Deliberate Right Things to Achieve Peace

We need a strategic plan for creating intergroup equity and intergroup Peace in order to do that work successfully.

Peace between groups in our country will not happen spontaneously or serendipitously. It definitely also will not happen in a vacuum.

Peace invariably happens in a context. When it happens, Peace involves people doing deliberate right things to end stress, reduce intergroup tensions, and end intergroup conflict.

Peace involves people doing very deliberate, right things to set up the opportunity for long-term status Peace. We need the Peace we create to be protected over time by having the right things we do continue to happen and continue to exist into the future.

We Need Honesty as a Starting Point

We need to be honest with ourselves in the process, because trying to build the future on anything less than a reality-based and honesty-based foundation of facts is highly likely to fail.

There are some exceptions — and some parts of our country are significantly less safe than others — but most of us live today in a state of functional Peace. That Peace allows us to go to our schools, work places, shopping places, and places of worship almost all of the time without fear of being attacked, robbed, or otherwise damaged, threatened, or impaired in some way.

Our Laws Now Help Create Peace

We have that kind of functional Peace for our country today in large part because we have put very clear laws in place that create rules for behavior in key areas of interactions and activities. We have built an infrastructure of laws that create functional safety in most settings for most people most of the time.

We also have an intergroup culture today that is increasingly based on a clear and intentional motivational desire to not be doing damaging things to one another.

Our leaders all make at least token statements in favor of intergroup Peace. Intergroup leaders in far too many other countries openly and clearly preach intergroup hatred, division, and even violence. We have very few leaders here who are making those kinds of inflammatory and divisive admonitions to their people, and the areas who do preach hatred have relatively few followers.

We do have periodic outbreaks of intergroup violence. We have protests, demonstrations, and we even have a few mobs that periodically do angry things to the people and the property of other groups. But the mobs that do form in this country are infrequent, and they tend to be significantly less violent when they happen than the equivalent mobs we have seen in recent times in Sri Lanka, London, or Paris.

Our New Laws Codify Many Desired Behaviors

We do have some areas of major cities where gangs control much of the behavior context for communities. Those areas are less safe.

The gangs who control those areas all have strong ethnic identities and composition. The negative intergroup energy levels that are created by various mob turf issues can be very difficult for a country to overcome.

In Oakland, California, for example, significant parts of the city are functionally controlled by racially divided resident gangs and those gangs are in constant conflict with one another. Oakland has a killing, on average, every three days — and shootings actually happen daily in that city.

Detroit and Chicago also have major areas of the city where gangs create the reality for far too many people in their relevant neighborhoods. A number of other major cities in our country also have areas of the city where gang behaviors create the reality for the people who live in those areas. Everyone in those cities knows what those situations are.

But those situations where gangs create the daily living reality for people are still relatively uncommon and they are currently outlier situations for us as a total country. Most settings in this country are currently safe almost all of the time.

Laws in America Used to Mandate and Require Discrimination

We have laws that are in place to create intergroup safety. We also now have a growing number of laws that protect people against intergroup discrimination and that make some kinds of basic negative intergroup differentiation illegal.

Those anti-discrimination laws represent significant progress for us as a nation. We used to have some very negative laws that actually required and mandated intergroup discrimination. Our new laws now are intended to make those same exact basic and important levels of discrimination illegal.

Most of our anti-discrimination laws are relatively new. Those new laws clearly represent growing levels of enlightenment for us as a country.

They were not made into law without significant opposition — but they have been enacted and they create the context we use today for major areas where we have had very negative intergroup behaviors in the past.

Those anti-discrimination laws are only years or decades old instead of being centuries old. They are recent, but they are extremely important to us today because not very far back in our history, we had the exact opposite sets of laws in place.

For literally centuries, sheer and blatant discrimination was legal and encouraged. We discriminated freely and we discriminated often. Discrimination was supported by, embedded in, and even required by some of our laws.

Some laws very specifically mandated and required directly discriminatory behavior against specific sets of Americans. Laws required Black Americans, for example, to sit in the back of city buses. Those laws existed only a relatively few years ago.

Buses and public transportation were legally segregated in some cities. Other laws made it illegal for some white restaurants to feed black or other minority customers.

For long periods of our history as a nation and in large parts of the country, very intentionally racist laws separated people by race in our schools, work places, public parks, restrooms, and even in our choices of home sites.

Deed covenants that existed for homes in many communities stated that some homes could never be sold to a minority person at any future time.

Some race-related covenants on some home deeds actually said that minority people could not even be guests in those homes during evening hours. Minority people could work in those homes as cooks or as servants of some kind, but minority people could not be there after dark as guests.

The clear intent of deliberate, explicit, and entirely intentional racial discrimination was embedded openly in all of those laws. We had a wide range of discrimination laws and we had those laws for hundreds of years.

The very worst laws in our history created slavery by race. We ended slavery as the result of the Civil War — but ending slavery did not end discrimination.

The slave states did not give up their desire to enslave people lightly. When we ended slavery, we did not suddenly become a nation that extended full rights and full access to the American Dream to all of our people.

Many of the people who were willing to fight and die to keep people enslaved continued actively and deliberately to oppress the people who had been enslaved. We created an entire array of laws that were intended to damage and hinder the former slaves.

Discrimination was required by those post-slavery laws — not banned by them. Major voting barriers were created for the newly enfranchised former slaves. Education barriers and economic barriers for minority Americans were the rule rather than the exception.

Intermarriage between races was clearly illegal in much of the country for a very long time. Racial intermarriage could put people in jail for significant periods of time.

The list of laws that were created to keep both former slaves and other minority Americans in one level of inferior rights and diminished levels of inclusion and economic success were long and truly ugly in their intent and goals.

There is no way to interpret that history other than to say it was evil and it was ugly at multiple levels — and the evil was both deliberate and conscience-free. Us/them ethnics and us/them morality values were in full gear for all of those laws.

We have had a long and clear history as a nation in creating restrictions for our minority populations. The White American majority group functioned as an "Us" are treated every other minority group as a "Them."

Laws and practices discriminated against each category of "Them." Our minority Americans were prevented from voting, barred from employment, and not allowed to own property in a number of areas.

Schools, public transport, and even eating places and places of accommodation were segregated in ways that created real barriers for minority Americans.

The us/them instincts of the majority White American group discriminated with no sense of guilt, ethnical remorse, or shame — because our us/them instincts cause people to exhibit those belief systems and behaviors.

Discrimination Against Women Has Also Been a Major Problem

Discrimination against minority Americans was not the only area where major segments of our population were damaged by negative intergroup behaviors. The White males who ran the majority group "Us" for America also discriminated against women.

For most of our history, women in this country have also been discriminated against at multiple levels. The discrimination against women was also ugly and very intentional.

Women were not allowed to vote for most of our history.

Men were legally considered to be the "head of the family." There were laws in place for a very long time that made a woman's property the property of her husband with full control of the property going to the man as soon as a woman married.

Women were often legally and deliberately paid less money for doing the same jobs as men and — even more dysfunctionally — women were not allowed to even apply for a number of specific jobs that were reserved only for men.

Those levels of legal and culturally supported discrimination for hiring practices by both race and gender have been true until relatively recently.

We have now very clearly changed the legal status of those discriminatory practices and made those practices illegal, but those are very recent legal changes.

Deliberate and clearly defined discrimination against women was also a key component of our culture and our infrastructure for most of our history. The universal patterns of male discrimination against women that we still see today in so many other countries in the world were actually a major part of our own history as a country at multiple levels for a very long time.

In several parts of the world today, there are still laws in place that discriminate massively and deliberately in very direct, oppressive, and punitive ways against women.

Many other countries have become much more enlightened relative to the legal status of women, but there are still a number of countries that still make it illegal for women to do things that can be done legally by a man. Many countries continue to discriminate in major ways relative to the economic status of women.

Women in some settings are still sold as brides or even as slaves. Women are held as captives in the confines of their homes. Women who simply talk to men outside their family setting are sometimes killed by their own families in "Honor Killings."

Those packages of behavior need to be eliminated in all settings. Sexual abuse, rape, and other forms of violence against women need to be against laws that are actually enforced in far more areas of the world.

Discrimination against women has been clear and intense in far too many settings for most of human history. That is true today in many settings.

Very clear levels of discrimination against women have been part of American history as well.

The book *Primal Pathways* and the book *Peace In Our Time* both have fairly long chapters that are focused entirely on the inequality that has been embedded in those universal patterns of discrimination against women. Those chapters explain some of the reasons why that discrimination against women has existed and why that negative set of behaviors has had such discouraging consistency and such a painful and extended history across so many cultures and so many settings around the world.

We Americans have, however, managed to make significant progress on many of those specific gender-related areas in this country, and we now very explicitly outlaw discrimination against women in all legal areas rather than requiring that discrimination to happen.

Enlightenment Is Happening on Several Fronts

As we go forward to create the next levels of intergroup collaboration and intergroup Peace in this country, we can begin from a better context now than the one we had just a few years ago.

We have made major progress in multiple areas of our society. We have been slowly and steadily becoming more enlightened on many kinds of relevant intergroup issues.

In some areas — like voting laws and ending clear job discrimination — significant progress has been made. We have been working hard at multiple levels to have laws, behaviors, and belief systems that are much more enlightened on multiple sets of intergroup issues.

Enlightenment has now been embedded in our functional and legal value sets in a number of key areas, and even though we are far from perfect, there are a number of areas where the improvements in those behaviors have been significant and beneficial. Recent progress has been highly encouraging.

We now have a number of enlightened behaviors, policies, rules and laws in place today that directly reach out to create and protect many levels of intergroup and inter gender legal equality in ways that did not exist a relatively few years ago.

As noted earlier, those particular protective and inclusive laws that benefit both minority Americans and benefit women tend to be fairly recent — but they definitely now exist.

New Paradigms Change The Way We Think

As the section of this book that deals with belief systems and paradigms explains, once we adopt a new paradigm on any topic, we tend to have that paradigm and its core beliefs structure the relevant processes of our minds that deal with that topic.

We do major aspects of our individual thinking and our group thinking in the context of belief systems. We tend to place great value on our belief systems and we use them extensively to guide our thinking and our behavior.

A problem we face is that some belief systems on some intergroup topics have negative and even damaging components. To increase our level of enlightened behavior, we need to change our core belief systems to eliminate those negative components where they exist. That can be done.

Changing those negative paradigms is one of the basic strategies for The Art of InterGroup Peace.

Paradigm change can be extremely useful. It changes thinking and behavior for entire areas and tends to have long-term impact — because we tend to keep paradigms in place once we adopt them.

When we change those belief systems on any topic, our context changes for that topic and we often can't even remember the old paradigm and its key beliefs once a new belief is in place.

We need to understand how to best organize our mental processes relative to those key issues.

The functional reality is that we tend to incorporate new belief systems into our personal behaviors and into our personal thought processes once we begin to use a new paradigm on any topic. We literally change what we believe.

So when we change beliefs about a key issue, like whether or not women should be allowed to vote, then everyone who used to believe that women voting was wrong at a basic level now tends to believe that having women vote is very right at a basic level. When a paradigm, belief system, or culture changes, we each tend to embed the new values into our thought processes and our beliefs. Once that change happens we often can't even remember when we held the other opinion.

Much of the success of The Art of InterGroup Peace strategy relies on that belief-system change process. We need people changing from negative and damaging beliefs to new supportive and inclusive beliefs.

We need to facilitate that change on key points by embedding our new beliefs into our laws, into our personal expectations and into our cultures — and that all causes changes to happen in the personal values we each feel are right for our lives.

Once we have decided to act in more enlightened ways on any topic, we are more likely to actually do the enlightened things if we build them into our laws. Laws both reinforce and build paradigms. Whatever we build into our laws, and then enforce, tends to become embedded in our expectations and in our beliefs.

We Are All Stronger When More People Achieve the American Dream

It is obviously possible for us to function as people and as a country in very enlightened ways. We have proven that to be true.

We have done some very enlightened things very well. It is entirely possible for us to function for major parts of our society and for major parts of our nation in ways that embody the best features of the American Dream for us all.

For a couple of centuries, people have immigrated to this country from all over the world for a chance to participate in what they have perceived to be the Dream of America. The American Dream has offered people the opportunity to be free and to be able to work hard to create a good life for themselves and their families.

People who have been able to fully utilize the American Dream have been productive and successful. The people who have personally achieved the Dream have given us one of the best economies and the strongest nations in the world.

The functional reality is this — people can do really well when people are allowed and enabled to do really well. The American Dream —with all of its key aspects and values — has enabled people to do well. When more people are given access to that dream, we will have more people doing well, and that will strengthen us as a country.

We need all Americans to share in the key components of the American Dream.

Freedom of speech, freedom of assembly, and the freedom to pursue ones life goals have existed in this country for much of our population for a very long time in ways that have not been true for people in far too many other countries. Aristocracies and various kinds of ethnic and tribal rule and cultural discrimination levels that dictate the functional reality for people in multiple other settings have kept many people in many other settings from realizing their own personal potential.

Those constraints created in those cultures have kept people in those settings from making key choices about their own lives and they have kept people in those settings from benefiting from their own efforts.

The American Dream says that people who achieve success and who create value should be able to enjoy the value they create.

Hard work for people in other countries can too often result simply in more hard work and no reward for the hard workers.

Hard work here has traditionally resulted in owning a home, educating your children, and enjoying your portion of the shared prosperity of the American economy.

The American Dream is highly seductive — and the opportunities created by that Dream still draws people across our borders from other countries every single day.

The Dream attracts people to this country even today because it allows people to aspire and to actually achieve in ways that benefit people and their families, and the people they love.

Unfortunately — for a number of reasons that are increasingly obvious, as we understand our us/them packages on instincts — we have not allowed all of our own people full access to that American Dream. We need to understand that reality.

A wide array of discriminatory actions, prejudice and damaging intergroup behaviors have created limited access to that Dream for far too many Americans for far too many years.

Many people from our American minority groups who have aspired to achieve the American Dream have faced significant barriers that have made the Dream personally unreachable.

The frustrations felt by people who were living in this country where the Dream was visible and real for so many people, but was denied, very intentionally, to so many other people has created a reality we need to deal with and collectively understand today.

There is a significant amount of anger and some collective resentment from a number of our people about some of those clearly discriminatory and damaging behaviors, and about being denied full access to the American Dream for so long.

Us/Them Instincts Have Triggered Discrimination

Instinctive behaviors have created those key barriers to many people in this country having access to the American Dream.

Major barriers to the American Dream happened for all of those years for so many people in this country because all of the us/them instincts that were described and discussed earlier in this book have clearly played a major role in creating multiple levels of discrimination in this country for many of our people.

Instinctive behaviors have been at the root of those problems and barriers.

Those us/them instincts that were described in the earlier chapters of this book have too often worked against us in this country in some important ways. We have clearly and deliberately practiced significant discrimination against various groups of Americans.

Discrimination by group against group is obviously an "Us/Them" behavior. The patterns for those behaviors are clear. The intergroup behaviors that result from those instincts are remarkably consistent in all intergroup settings.

We Need to Understand Those Behaviors to Understand Our History

Our history is built on a foundation of those behaviors.

We need to understand those behavior patterns well in order to understand our own national history well.

The majority group in this country has tended to discriminate as an "Us" against each category of "Them." Whenever and wherever anyone perceives someone to be a "Them," we tend to discriminate against them and we tend to feel no guilt when we discriminate against a "Them."

It feels right, when those instincts and those perceptions are activated, to do negative things to them. It also feels right to favor our "Us" and to do positive things for "Us."

The damaging truth is that we can even inflict various kinds of damage on "Them" and we can often do that damage to whoever we perceive to be "Them" without regret, guilt, or remorse.

As this book pointed out earlier, each of our instinctive behaviors tend to "feel right" to us. It "felt right" to many people to deny voting rights and it felt right to deny the full protection of the laws to people they perceived to be "Them."

It "felt right" simply to keep "Them" from buying property and to keep them from being admitted to "our" schools.

It felt right to employ only "Us" and to deny employment to "Them." People making hiring decisions tended to hire "Us" and to promote "Us."

Those decisions were both conscious and unconscious — and they tended to feel right when people's us/them instincts were activated.

Far too many discriminatory and damaging behaviors "felt right" to too many people for far too many years simply because it generally "feels right" to damage "Them" when our us/them instincts are activated and when we perceive someone to be a "Them".

The American Dream Was Not Extended to "Them"

So the American Dream was not extended to Americans who were perceived to be "Them" by the people in power.

Our history on those issues is obvious and clear. Discrimination has been consistent and long standing. So have various levels of both voluntary and involuntary segregation.

Our feelings of comfort when we are surrounded by "us," and our feelings of discomfort, stress, and even anxiety when we are surrounded by "Them," has created centuries of discriminatory behavior for the people who are perceived by the majority of people in our American settings to be a "Them."

People Who Were "Us" Benefited Greatly

The people in this country who were perceived to be "Us" have been given the full benefits of the American Dream. We have become the greatest country on the planet in multiple ways because of the creativity and energy and achievements that have resulted from enabling a major segment of our population to thrive and to flourish in the very powerful, effective, and enabling economic context that is created by the American Dream.

The opportunities that have been created for the people who have been included in the American Dream have made us strong and successful as a country and made us a world leader in many ways.

At the same time, the various sets of people who have been perceived by the majority group in this country to be "Them" have had their access to that dream blocked and hindered in many ways… and those groups of people have been damaged by that blockage.

Being a "Them" is a huge disadvantage under any circumstances. The people who are "Us" instinctively distrust them, protect turf against them, and feel stress and even anger when any "Us" is in proximity to what the "Us" group feels are threatening numbers of "Them."

It is clear that we have used those sets of instinctive behaviors to shape our history — and those same packages of behaviors and perceptions are getting people damaged and even killed in many countries in the world today.

Instinctive Behaviors Can Be Brutal, Evil, and Conscience Free

It is almost painful to intellectually acknowledge the powerful impact that those instincts have on our thinking and our behaviors.

Instinctive intergroup behaviors that relate to anyone we perceive to be "Them" can be brutal, evil, and conscience free.

In our country, we had real brutality and we had high levels of sheer, blatant, and conscience free discrimination. We have had lynch mobs, Jim Crow laws, anti-miscegenation laws, and for a couple of centuries, we even had actual intergroup slavery.

We have had segregation laws that were so extreme that we even put barbed wire fences up between the graves in some cemeteries to keep "Them" from "Us" after the people in that setting were actually dead.

Each minority group has faced those issues.

We have ethnically purged and displaced entire groups of Native American people from their ancestral turf. We perceived and labeled those specific ethnic displacements to be "White Destiny" rather than "Indian Displacement."

We have embedded us/them discriminatory behaviors and us/them values deeply in the history of our country and in the laws of our country at multiple levels for whoever was perceived by the majority "Us" in each setting to be "Them."

Negative Patterns Created by Instincts or Created by Conspiracies?

It is time for us all to look openly and honestly at the impact of those us/them instincts on our own history.

We need to all openly acknowledge now that some groups of people were never allowed full access to the American Dream. Us/Them instincts made a negative difference in the opportunities that exist in this country for too many people for far too long.

That level of discrimination is so consistent and so long-standing, that it looks conspiratorial. It looks very much as though there has been a centuries long "White" conspiracy that has created that massive consistency of discriminatory behaviors against other groups of Americans.

Many people believe that an actual functional and engineered conspiracy of some kind has existed to guide all of those negative behaviors.

That belief in our overarching conspiracy is not entirely accurate. That overall consistency of behavior actually did not exist as a functioning conspiracy.

There actually was no master and macro formal conspiracy process or plan that created all of that negative intergroup behavior consistency. Those behaviors were not planned and deliberate outcomes that were created in the context and under the guidance of a functional conspiracy.

All of that extremely negative consistency of behavior was actually triggered by our instincts. The negative local intergroup conspiracies that clearly existed in so many settings also stemmed from that same set of instinctive intergroup us/them triggers, with their consequences rolling out in each local setting.

That reality about the absence of an actual overarching conspiracy gives us grounds for optimism about future behavior.

Optimism is relevant for those issues because it is much easier to discern and steer instincts than it is to uncover and crush a conspiracy.

If we believe that there is, in fact, a secret conspiracy of some level that has caused all of those behaviors to exist, then our solution strategy for improving and ending those negative behaviors would need to be aimed at uncovering and overcoming the conspiracy and somehow defeating the conspirators.

Spending time to defeat that secret conspiracy in some way is not likely to improve our country very much, because that particular macro plan actually does not exist as a macro plan.

Focusing on overcoming the power of conspirators who do not exist at a macro level isn't a strategy that is likely to make our success levels higher in resolving those intergroup issues.

There Is No Gender-Linked or Racial Conspiracy

There is not a macro gender-linked conspiracy that has created and coordinated all of that discrimination against women and there is not a macro racial conspiracy that structures all of those negative ethnic and racial discriminatory behaviors.

For better and for worse, those negative behaviors that we see in all of those settings are structured by our instincts — and our solutions to those wide ranges of problems will require us now to use our instincts and our cultures in enlightened ways to create new and better patterns of intergroup behavior.

We can do that. We need to do that, in fact. We need to keep those negative intergroup instincts from driving our future intergroup behavior. To keep those sets of instincts from doing future damage in all of our relevant settings, we need to understand what has triggered those instincts in the past. Understanding those triggers is a key part of figuring out how to deal with those issues.

We clearly activate us/them instincts based on race, tribe, ethnicity, culture, and nationality. We also clearly trigger those sets of instincts based on professional status and our employment issues.

Each and every one of multiple categories can cause us to perceive people to be us and can cause us to perceive other people to be them.

When we look back at our history as a nation, all of those us/them categories were relevant.

But those categories were the triggers that have created the major us/them problems for us as a country. Our history as a nation is anchored to a very large degree — at a very basic level — to a very primal set of factors.

Sight and Sound Trigger Those Instincts

Our basic patterns of discrimination as a nation can be traced back to the basic fact that our instincts use sight and sound to trigger a sense of us or them.

If someone looks different from us or sounds different from us, we easily perceive that person to be a "Them."

We all need to recognize the fact that the long history of discrimination against the various minority groups of people has existed in this country for so long against those specific groups who faced discrimination because of the two key personal differentiators that tend to trigger us/them conscious and subconscious alerts, and create us/them perceptions in people everywhere on the planet.

Those two key instinct focusing differentiators that trigger those instincts in all settings are sight and sound. Sight and sound.

Sight and sound are extremely important instinct triggers — and the groups that have faced discrimination in this country have been the groups who trigger those factors.

We all tend to trigger very clear and very instinctive us/them alerts and warnings in our minds if someone either looks different or sounds different than us.

Babies – before they are even one year old — have different neuron activation patterns in their brains that happen when they hear a foreign language or when they see someone who doesn't look like their familiar "Us."

We begin that differentiation between us and them at a very early age. As adults and as children, we suspect at a very instinctive level that someone who doesn't look like "Us" or someone who doesn't sound like "Us" might actually not be "Us" but might, instead, be a "Them."

That basic set of visual and audible us/them differentiation triggers creates us/them perceptions and behaviors across the planet. Those perceptions are triggered very easily — when people have a different skin color, face shape, or hair texture than the other group. Those perceptions are also triggered when people sound different than the other group in that setting.

People in Nigeria and in The Congo were killed last year because they were perceived by the sound of their voice to be of a different ethnicity than the people who killed them. In those particular settings, the people who were doing the killing and the people who were being killed all actually looked alike — but the factors that triggered the deaths of a number of people in those situations was the use of a different language in one setting and the use of a different dialect in the other setting.

The killers in each setting in those settings knew from hearing peoples' voices that the people with a different dialect were not from their own tribe. That perception triggered conscience free and guilt free us/them behaviors that resulted in killing many people in those settings without mercy in those settings merely for being "Them."

Killing "Them" based on people either looking different or sounding different than "Us" is not a new set of behaviors.

Throughout human history, tribes have often killed other tribes. Tribes each have their own languages or dialects. You can tell who is in your tribe and who is in their tribe by listening to people speak.

As noted earlier in this book in several places, tribal conflict has been part of the basic history of Europe, Asia, North America, Africa, and even Australia. The various Aborigine tribes in Australia made war on other Aborigine tribes. So did the tribes of North America, South America, Sri Lanka and Saudi Arabia.

The tribal patterns of killings that are happening in Pakistan, Syria, Iraq, Kosovo, Ceylon, Sri Lanka, and even Crimea today are all very basic and fundamental tribe versus tribe behaviors — us versus them.

Different tribal languages and dialects trigger a sense of them in each setting. The contending forces in Crimea today speak two different languages. That is, in fact, their main differentiating characteristic.

We Fear Them — and Other Tribes Are Them

That pattern of intergroup killing is a universal set of behaviors. The reality is and always has been that people can all be at actual risk even at this point in the history of the world — when people are in the presence of other tribes. That isn't just ancient history. It is behavior today.

When we look back at American history, it is clear that the people who were accepted by the White majority group who ran the country as an "Us" were people who looked White and who sounded like White Americans.

All of the European tribes melded easily into that White "Us" as soon as they sounded like that particular "Us."

But all of the groups who did not look like the White "Us" have faced centuries of clear and intentional discrimination. The patterns have been consistent and irrefutable. Looking different triggered an instinct-linked perception of "Them" — and the White American majority acted accordingly.

The majority group in this country accepted all people who looked like the majority group and who sounded like the majority group to be "Us." The next chapter of this book explains that process in more detail.

At the same time, the majority group in this country regarded all other sets of people who either looked different or sounded different to be a "Them."

That was clearly an instinctive reaction — and it was not an intellectual strategy or a conspiracy.

That differentiation process between group, based on how we look and how we sound, happens at an unconscious level for all of us on an ongoing basis. Until that entire instinct-triggered differentiation process based on sight and sound is explained to us, however, we tend not to know at an intellectual or cognitive level that those very primal triggers exist in our brains or that they have been activated.

When We Don't Know the Triggers, We Blindly Follow Their Guidance

When we don't know at an intellectual level that those instincts exist and when we don't know at an intellectual level what triggers them, then we simply allow them to be triggered and we simply define and assign the status of any person who looks or sounds differently than "Us" at a very primal level into the status of "Them."

All of the relevant negative behaviors that follow relative to how we trust "Them" can then simply emerge, originate, and stem from that differentiation.

It is not a good thing for people, in any setting, to be perceived by an "Us" who holds power to be a "Them."

Slavery and ethnic cleansing can happen in settings when we see people as them. So can denying people the right to vote or denying people the right to own property.

Ethics are affected by those perceptions. We don't instinctively feel the emotional need to be ethical relative to "Them," so we often damage them in various ways.

Ethics Tend to Be Situational — at an Instinctive Level

Ethics tend to be situational — at a very instinctive level.

That point is rarely understood or even discussed, but the reality is that our ethics generally apply fully only to "Us." People who believe they are personally deeply ethical will sometimes conduct their personal ethical behaviors at wonderful and enlightened levels relative to whoever they perceive to be "Us" and then those same people can sometimes simply lie, cheat, deceive, or even usurp possessions and steal property with no guilt if those negative behaviors are done to someone who is perceived to be a "Them."

Those highly ethical people often feel no contradiction or challenge to their self-image as an ethical person because their instincts skew their thinking and cloud their minds to the point where their normal ethics don't apply to "Them."

We fire bombed Dresden and Tokyo in World War II, killing huge numbers of women and children with those firebombs, and felt no guilt as a nation because the people in those cities were perceived at that point in our history to be "Them."

People who are loving parents, good citizens, and people of great moral character in their daily life with their own people can slip into completely immoral behavior — pillaging, raping, and deceiving whoever they perceive to be "Them" — and then those same people can slip back into their purely moral and highly ethical mindsets when they interact with us.

The stories about the concentration camp guard who did great evil to "Them" in those wartime camps, who was then captured in hiding years later and who was described by his new neighbors to be a gentle and caring person who was kind to neighborhood children, happened because that guard had his "Us" values activated in the neighborhood and that same guard had his "Them" values activated when he was in the concentration camp.

The guard wasn't hiding evil in his post-war neighborhood setting. He simply had not activated evil in that setting. Our us/them instincts steer values and thought processes to a massive degree when they are fully activated. We can feel very right being steered to any direction — negative or positive — that fits the behavior pattern for that instinct in the situation we are in.

We now need to collectively recognize the fact that we allowed those more negative us/them instincts to play out in a wide variety of very negative ways in this country over the course of our history. We need to recognize those historic behaviors and we need to understand their consequences so that we can understand where we are today and so that we can understand what we need to do now to achieve intergroup Peace.

As we build intergroup Peace for America we need to be very careful not to activate our "Them" related packages of instincts in any setting — and we need to work very hard to generate the instinctive perceptions of being "Us" in all settings.

Negative Behaviors Related to "Them" Have Damaged Many People

We need to build that entire process on where we are now. People who have been damaged in this country as a people have clear collective memories about the damages that were done to their group.

People who were not damaged individually or as a group, by those behaviors, often did not know those specific sets of damages existed. We need to bridge that awareness gap to create intergroup understanding because we need the people who were not damaged to know that damage was done.

Looking Different from the Majority Triggered the Instincts

The behavior patterns for intergroup behaviors in this country were pretty consistent and they were very clear.

Those particular us/them triggers that are activated by our appearance and by our languages have been, of course, extremely dysfunctional and they have been highly damaging to many groups of people in this country for most of American history.

The next chapter explains in more detail how those instincts played out in our history as a nation. We need to understand how painfully simple that instinct-activation process actually was.

Looking different has been the key trigger for those negative intergroup instincts in this country.

At a very core and consistent level, there has been major discrimination against anyone who either sounds different or looks different from the majority group that has been the American Us.

That majority "Us" group for this country was white in skin color and spoke English in American dialects.

Anyone who had a different skin color or a different facial appearance from the majority group who defined "Us" in this country, has faced centuries of discrimination at a very instinctive level.

We need to move past that history and build a new American "Us" based on our shared values and basic beliefs — an inclusive "Us" that can move us past that negative history into a possible future.

That will only happen if we do the right things to make it real.

CHAPTER THIRTEEN

Our History Included Inventing "White" and Using "White" to Discriminate

OUR COUNTRY HAS a long history that has been massively affected in both positive and negative ways by our us/them intergroup instincts. The impact of those instincts stretches back — without interruption — to the dawn of our history.

Basic sets of intergroup instincts were clearly relevant for local intergroup behavior in all intergroup settings long before the Europeans invaded the American continents, and those sets of instincts have continued to be relevant to our behavior in all of our settings today.

"Invaded" is the right term to use to describe what the Europeans did to the American continents.

As a first basic intergroup historical point that we should all recognize, we need to be clear about the fact that America was not "discovered" by Columbus or by any other European explorer.

There were millions of people living here when those first small ships full of explorers arrived on those shores from Europe. You can't "discover" a place that has already been populated by millions of people for thousands of years.

America was invaded — not discovered.

Tribal Behaviors Have Been Bloody in the Americas

When the first European boats reached shore on the American continents, they arrived at a place that was not only inhabited — it was inhabited by people who lived their lives and functioned every day in the context of clearly defined groups and tribes.

Each part of those continents was claimed, owned, and inhabited by people from literally hundreds of local tribes on the day that the first Europeans landed on those shores.

Every tribe had its history, culture, and clear sense of tribal territory and turf.

At the time of the European invasion, the tribes who lived here each had their own group identity and sense of group destiny — and they all tended to be in a state of at least mild conflict and historic intergroup division relative to the other tribes that were adjacent to each of them.

A look at the history of people who were living on this continent for thousands of years before the Europeans arrived tells us that there were significant and long-standing inter-tribal animosities happening in many settings. It was clear that there had been significant inter-tribal conflict and bloodshed at multiple points for very long periods of time in our pre-European collective American past.

So the Europeans did not invent tribal conflict for either North or South America. Before anyone from Europe arrived on those shores, we had many Native American tribes who lived in their own distinct tribal territories. Those territories spread across both American continents. The tribes who lived in all of those settings had at least some history of defending their territories against incursion and invasion by other tribes.

There were tribes everywhere. Tribes here did exactly what tribes do everywhere that tribes exist. Those tribes who lived on those continents all tended to have conflicted relations with the other tribes in their relevant geographic areas.

The Sioux and the Ojibwa and the Apache and the Navaho peoples each had their long-standing inter tribal wars and inter-tribal battles with the tribes that were contiguous to them. The tribal battles in North America seldom rose to genocidal levels, but the behaviors of the Aztecs and the Incas in the Southern half of the hemisphere sometimes included wide scale patterns of intertribal conflict that involved significant shedding of intergroup blood. Those local conflicts in some of those settings sometimes did achieve genocidal proportions.

The European tribes who began invading both American continents roughly 500 years ago, did not invent intergroup conflict and they did not introduce intergroup bloodshed to those continents.

But, at least in North America, the invaders from Europe significantly escalated the level of local intergroup conflict that actually existed in those settings at that point in history.

They took the intergroup conflict levels that were happening in North America from long-standing border skirmishes and small-scale intergroup battles that were happening sporadically between local Native American tribes into functional episodes of pure genocidal behavior involving very intentional ethnic cleansing processes that were very deliberately conducted by the invading European tribes against the original sets of Native American tribes.

Guilt-Free and Damaging Us/Them Behaviors Happened Across Two Continents

The intergroup behaviors that happened in those settings invoked some of the very worst functions and features of our most basic and primal us/them instinct packages. Guilt-free damage was done by the European invaders to people they perceived to be "Them" across both continents.

The European invaders attacked, abused, displaced, damaged, massacred, and sometimes literally obliterated entire groups of people. The invaders from Europe actually erased the existence of a number of original Native American tribes.

Invasion Was Called "Colonization"

There were several European countries who sent people to join in that American continent invasion and displacement process. The people from Europe referred to their invasion process as "Colonization."

Each set of Europeans created their own colonies in the Americas and then each European country populated their colonies with people from their own European tribe.

The Native American tribes who had lived for centuries in most of the invaded settings were simply forced to leave.

In some cases, the displaced peoples were given new lands to live on. Our Native American Reservation system originated from that process.

The process of intentional displacement was extremely consistent across wide areas and it was very effective as a strategy for the Europeans. The European settlers and their descendants systematically stole the original turf of the Native tribes and unilaterally forced the original tribes into limited reserved territories that functioned as their new permanent homes.

Long-Standing Battles Kept the Original Tribes from Jointly and Collectively Resisting Invasion

The fact that the original Native American tribes who were here at the time of the invasion each tended to have their own local long standing intertribal wars going on with other local tribes in each area unfortunately made those original tribes functionally vulnerable.

Those long-standing intertribal animosities made the original tribes less able to form sufficiently powerful local alliances and joint efforts of various kinds that might have had the power to collectively resist the European invaders and defeat them back in the earliest days of the invasion.

That reluctance, unwillingness, and functional inability of the original tribes to band together with their old tribal enemies to collectively face a common new tribal enemy made those legacy American tribes significantly more vulnerable to the purely intertribal aggression that was executed and implemented across all of North America by the invaders from Europe.

If the original Native American tribes had simply banded together in the early days against the European invaders, they probably could have driven the Europeans back into the sea. That unity never happened, because the original tribes were generally all at war with each other at that point in time.

Some of those Native American tribes actually helped the Europeans in various settings fight the other original tribes in their area. That tended to happen in a few settings where the legacy tribe believed it could do damage to a historical enemy by creating an alliance of some sort with the Europeans.

The European Tribes Used to Be at War with Each Other in Europe

The European invaders of those continents initially brought their own European tribal behaviors and their own traditional intertribal conflicts and intergroup animosities with them from Europe.

All of the European tribes had a long history of being at war with each other as tribes in Europe. The French, the English, the Spanish, and the Dutch settlers all initially carried their original European intertribal animosities to these shores.

Some relatively small local wars actually were fought here in several settings along those historic Euro-tribal lines.

The French and the English invaders of North America had the most significant European legacy bloody intertribal battles here. The war that Americans call the French and Indian War was fought shortly before the American Revolutionary War. The English and French did battle in several American locations. The French actually had several Native American tribes as allies in that war.

The tribes who sided with the French in those conflicts were not regarded well later by the English and fledgling American forces who won the wars and ended up in control of the territory.

In any case, those battles between the various invading Euro tribes did not continue over time in North America, because the English tribe tended to end up relatively quickly to be the dominant tribe for the eastern half of the North American continent.

The English tribe ended up with control over most of the turf that had been claimed as colonial turf by the other various tribal invasions from Europe. The descendants of the colonial invaders from the other European countries who lived in those territories almost all ended up recognizing the English victory and speaking English as their daily language.

The European Tribes in This Country Intermarried

So the original set of European intertribal behaviors and European intergroup conflicts that had created centuries of very purely intertribal war in Europe actually melted away as relevant issues in this country for all of the colonists and their descendants over a relatively brief period of time. The sets of invaders from all of European tribes functionally melded into a new American/European tribe.

Those old Euro-tribe battles faded in this country in part because the people from most of the separate European tribes actually had no separate tribal turf to defend and occupy here once England won control over that portion of the continent.

They also faded in part because the people from all of those European tribes tended to intermarry once they immigrated to America, and because people in all of the colonies began speaking English instead of Dutch or German or French as their daily language.

That process created a new "Us." Their blended descendants from those intermarriages and that shared language group identified themselves as Americans instead of continuing to perceive themselves as tribal Europeans with their primary personal legacy linkage going back to one of the European cultures.

Intermarriage tends to soften, mitigate, and even eliminate the impact and relevance of purely intertribal conflicts. That behavior pattern of making the old tribal conflicts functionally irrelevant is particularly true for the second and third generation descendants of those intermarriages.

Intermarriage and a Common Language Made Tribal Conflicts Fade

It's functionally very hard to maintain an ancestral animosity between the descendants of an historic German tribe and the descendants of an historic French tribe when people from both tribes stopped speaking their ancestral European tribal languages, gave up their tribal European cultural practices and allegiances, and started intermarrying with people from the other tribes.

It is logistically challenging – and sometimes impossible — for a child who is half French and half German to take sides with either Prussia or Paris in an intertribal dispute.

The single most important factor that supported the personal slide for those new Americans away from their old European tribal allegiances and tribal alignments was the fact that the immigrants to this country from Europe overwhelmingly tended to give up their legacy European tribal language in favor of speaking English.

With the exception of a couple of fairly well-known enclaves of French immigrants and with the exception of those people in the former Spanish colonial territories who continued to speak Spanish, the new tribal language for the new tribe of people who lived in North America — almost everywhere — became English.

The legal documents for the new country and the various governmental units were all written in English. The government was run in English. The new public school systems taught English as the only language taught in public schools.

Some of the churches that had been imported from the "old country" by the immigrants to this country continued to have their services in Swedish or Norwegian or Dutch — but even those churches tended to give up their legacy

European language in a relatively short time in order to meet the needs of their next generation of church members who needed to hear sermons in English in order to understand the services.

A New Melded Ethnic Group Emerged

A new ethnic group resulted in this country from that pattern of intermarriage and from that collective conversion of people in each setting to speaking a shared common language. That new ethnic group functionally eliminated linkages and allegiance to each of the prior European tribes when all of the people here from all of those tribes simply began speaking English.

Many of the new immigrants from European countries even very intentionally refused to teach their own children to speak their own native Italian or Norwegian or Gaelic languages. They made that decision to abandon their legacy language because the new immigrants generally each personally wanted to become American and they very much wanted their children to be seen as Americans and to be fully American as quickly as possible.

The sight and sound issues that trigger our us/them intergroup instincts were significantly reduced and mitigated when everyone in each community sounded and looked the same. The second generation and the third generation intermarried descendants of the European immigrants all looked very much alike and, once they all began to speak English, they also all sounded very much alike.

There were some — and still are some — regional variations in this country in the way English is spoken. The English speakers of Mississippi and the English speakers of Maine each have their own clear and distinctive local linguistic characteristics — and even those relatively minor differences in the language used by people can cause some sense of intergroup schisms and divisions between those particular sets of people.

But overall, the new tribal language for the people in this country was English. Only English. English became the defining language for being "American."

The New Group of People Was Called "White"

The functional result of those behaviors was that the extensively intermarried, English speaking, light-skinned descendants of all of those old European tribes created a brand new Euro-American group in this country.

The new group name that was used for those blended sets of people was either American or White. That new group was a very important historical development for this country.

The creation of that new group in specific geographic areas had a huge impact on the activation of us/them instincts in those areas — because it created a brand new "Us" and because it left the people who either looked different or sounded different out of the new "Us."

It is important for us to understand that history and the invention of "White" as an "Us" group in order for us to collectively succeed at *The Art of InterGroup Peace* today. "White" was an important invention. We need to understand "White."

White became a very useful descriptive and bonding term for the majority group in this country. White became, and soon was, the new tribal name for all of those people who lived here, spoke English, and had European ancestors.

White Is an American Invention

White was basically an American invention. White doesn't exist with any frequency as a functional group descriptor for most of the rest of the world.

People in Africa and Asia today who make reference to people who look white seldom use that specific term or label to describe any person. They almost always use each person's European tribal name to describe any Europeans — not their racial name or their skin color name.

The local people in Asia and Africa usually refer to each person with European ancestry they describe by using their actual European tribal name — describing people as being Russian or Dutch or Danish.

They use the tribal name for those people because those national names are the most relevant and functionally useful descriptors for those people in those settings.

The skin color tends to be somewhat irrelevant as a descriptor. The actual tribes and national connections for each person are, however, often important. The people in Asia or Africa or the Middle East generally find it more useful to describe someone as Irish or as Belgium than to describe them as "white."

Likewise, the people who still lived in Europe at the time of the colonization of America did not have a history of referring to themselves as white. They seldom used that term before coming to the U.S.

Europe has always been very tribal. Obsessively tribal. People from each of the European tribes in Europe always used their specific tribal names to label themselves in their old settings.

Those people from those European tribes did not blend their identity by skin color. Norwegians, Swedes, and Danes each very much insisted on being identified by their own group name and each of those groups had no reason to refer to themselves as being White — even though some Scandinavians might be physically the whitest group in Europe.

Europeans Use Their Own Tribal Names in Europe

People in most European countries today continue to tend to refer to themselves and to other Europeans by each persons individual ethnic tribal name — not by their skin color.

That purely ethnic and historic tribal-based labeling is changing to some degree in some European settings today as the new immigration realities that exist are bringing more people with other skin colors and other racial backgrounds into those European communities.

But that particular skin color diversity situation in most of Europe is a very recent development. The term "White" wasn't needed in the past and it wasn't useful for any significant functional, economic, or political issues in those countries. So white has not commonly been used in Europe as a group name to describe or differentiate anyone in any country.

But in our country, White was used as a very functional group label and White became an important term of distinction — a group differentiation label that was subsequently defined by law and then protected by statute, practice, and custom.

White became relevant as a descriptor and as a differentiating functional tribal name in America because significant numbers of people in this country were not white — and because the white majority in this country wanted — for various intergroup benefit reasons — to make a clear distinction between the white and the non-white groups of people…between us and them.

Slavery Was a Horrible, Disgusting, Evil, Sinful, Ugly, and Inhumane Way to Treat Human Beings

The primary reason for using the term "White" in a legal sense is a reason that should generate a sense of sorrow and fully substantiated shame for our country.

Slavery was the key reason this country invented the term "White."

A major reason for the people in power in the early days of this country to make that "White" distinction so clear in legal and functional contexts was to help define who could and could not be enslaved. Slavery existed, and key people in power wanted slavery to continue to exist.

The slaves who were in this country 300 years ago had almost all been brought to this country from Africa. That meant that the people who were in slavery in this country at that point in time tended to be black and not White.

White people were not enslaved. White people could be held as indentured servants for defined periods of time, but White people could not legally be enslaved.

Black people, however, could be legally enslaved.

So there was a very important legal and economic reason for the use of "White" as a differentiating term and as a definitional descriptor and group label. That term identified who could and could not be enslaved.

That label was a way of defining both "Us" and "Them" in a context where the negative behaviors that can stem from those instincts could be targeted and limited to a clearly defined "Them." Using that label was part of a deliberate process of embedding some of the most negative impacts of those intergroup instincts into our laws.

The Process Was Functional and the Intent Was Clear

It was actually possible to look very white and to still be a slave and be legally black in this country. That was obviously illogical as an approach for multiple biological reasons — but that practice and that set of definitions had very clear us/them economic, ethical, and instinctive underpinnings.

The laws that were passed to deal with those specific issues and to maintain the property status of slaves said even "one drop of black blood" was enough to define you legally as being black and therefore subject to the legal status of being a slave.

The goal was to institutionalize a specific category and definition of "Them," and there was no attempt to be fair or logical in any way relative to the treatment of "Them."

The goal was actually to facilitate negative behavior relative to that "Them."

Slavery was a horrible, despicable, cruel, disgusting, evil, sinful, ugly, absolutely inhumane way of treating human beings. It is a particularly shameful part of our American history.

People were bought and sold like cattle. People who were enslaved were abused, damaged, degraded, defiled, functionally imprisoned, and forced against their will to do demeaning, demoralizing, and sometimes dehumanizing things. That behavior happened because the laws of this country gave the people who were defined legally as being white the power to do those evil things to the people in this country who were defined legally to be black.

Some Native Americans Were Enslaved as Well

Slavery was very literally a black/white issue for our country. Slavery has existed in many countries over the course of history. It has had different definition for who could be enslaved in a wide range of settings.

In most parts of the early history of civilization, conquered people could be and were enslaved. In some settings, entire groups of people were defined to be eligible for slavery. Russia had serfs. Ancient Rome, Ancient Greece, and Ancient Persia all had large numbers of enslaved people.

Somewhat broader versions of slavery existed even in other areas of the American hemisphere. The versions of slavery that were created in the Caribbean and in some parts of South America were extended by the European invaders of those countries to legally include the local Native American tribes in those areas as slaves.

Captured Native Americans were sold in some settings by the European invaders as slaves.

Some tribes of Native Americans in some parts of South America and in the Caribbean Islands were actually destroyed entirely by being enslaved.

Columbus, himself, personally started that process. He did it for money. He used the sale of captured slaves from Native American tribes as a source of funding for his ventures. He enslaved human beings and he actually destroyed entire tribes of people in the process on some of the islands he invaded.

The role Columbus played in our history is discussed in more detail in other books in the intergroup trilogy, but there is no doubt that Christopher Columbus personified some of the worst us/them instinctive behaviors that exist. It is clear that his invasions of those lands and this hemisphere exemplified intergroup cruelty and a complete and utter lack of conscience relative to his treatment of "Them."

Columbus did truly horrible things to whoever he perceived to be "Them." Enslaving Native Americans was a key part of his legacy.

That practice of enslaving Native Americans was not, however, part of the history of the United States or of North America.

In our own country, the Native American tribes who lived here were not enslaved. Native Americans in our own country were displaced, exiled, abused, disenfranchised, and sometimes killed — but those tribes were not enslaved.

Slavery in North America Was Limited to One Group

Slavery in North America tended to be limited to those people who were legally defined to be black — and not white — and black was defined to be people who had ancestry of any degree from Africa.

So white as a group name was a differentiating term of convenience in this country that actually had legal status because it was a tool that was used for many years to help people enslave other human beings.

Our history on that issue has a lot of elements that we should be deeply ashamed of and sad about as part of our national heritage.

Our national heritage on intergroup issues gives us a very mixed legacy.

We have been saints and we have been sinners. Our total history as a nation has its wonderful and enlightened elements that we should honor and celebrate and it has elements of pure evil that we should reject and mourn.

On one hand, our ancestors created a land of wonderful opportunity for many people. The American Dream was based on enlightened principals. The American Dream was very real for very large percentages of the people who lived here and those people have benefited immensely.

On the other hand, many people who lived in that same land of opportunity and freedom have been intentionally denied access to the American Dream for hundreds of years. At our worst levels, some of our people in this country were forced in extremely evil, degrading, cruel, and unconscionable ways to be the property of other people.

Slavery was actually legal in this country. That was true for a very long time.

Slavery Was Not Unique to America

America did not invent slavery.

Slavery is not unique to America or to American history. Slavery has been happening in many settings and cultures for a very long time. The Bible refers to slaves in both Israel and Egypt.

Every country in Africa and Asia and Europe had slaves. Rome had very large numbers of slaves — many enslaved by force of arms as the result of Roman conquests and then kept as slaves for generations. The same history and that same set of enslavement practices were true for Greece, India, China, Egypt, and ancient Persia.

Slavery has been a common practice across many countries — and slavery has been an us/them ultimate behavior in every setting where it has been practiced.

The Norsemen who settled Iceland did it with slave women they purchased in Ireland on the way to Iceland. Those women on those tiny ships did not go voluntarily to that cold and inhospitable climate. They went as property.

Ireland once had thriving slave markets. So did Rome and Damascus.

So slavery happened just about everywhere on the planet. The truth is that all people have slave ancestors.

Having slave ancestors is not unique to Black Americans. The logistical facts are — as a result of that very long history of slavery that was in place in all of those settings for so many years across the entire planet — that the basic genetic truth and the shared genetic legacy is that every single one of us actually has slave ancestors from one setting or another.

There is no logistical way — given the full historical extent of slavery for so many people that extended across all of Europe, Asia, the Middle East, and Africa for so many years — for any of us Americans of any race that originated in other parts of the world not to have some ancestors who were owned as property as either serfs or slaves.

The only possible exception to people who live in those continents today who might not have at least some direct ancestors who were slaves might functionally be some people who are purely Native American.

Many of the tribes that existed on this continent before the European invasions actually did have some partial history of intergroup slavery. That early slavery was usually based on the intergroup capture of people from other tribes in times of tribal war.

But some of those original American tribes had no significant history of slavery — so it is possible that some people in this country who are purely Native American and who have no ancestors from Europe, Africa, or Asia might have that rare legacy of having no slave ancestors. It is also possible that some of the indigenous people who now live in some of the more remote areas of South America have no slave ancestors.

Slavery did exist on both American continents before the Europeans invaded, however. The Incas and the Aztecs and the other locally dominant tribes in South and Central America all tended to enslave the people from the tribes they conquered.

The slavery in some South American settings even involved using captured and enslaved people as human sacrifices at some religious events.

So, it is highly likely that even the people from those relevant areas of our two continents probably each also have some slave ancestors as well.

Slavery Is Not an Issue Where Forgiveness Is Possible

Slavery is, in any case, clearly not unique to this country nor was it invented here. But slavery was a major part of our history and the intergroup consequences of that slavery still have echoes in our intergroup perceptions and our intergroup interactions today.

Those issues are relevant to *The Art of InterGroup Peace* because the intergroup anger that has been a long-term consequence of that slavery still makes it difficult for some people to achieve unencumbered interpersonal or intergroup interactions today.

That legacy of anger about that history of slavery can create some real barriers to some of the interpersonal and intergroup interactions that we need today that can benefit us all in the cause of Peace.

We need to be able to deal with those specific issues, understand their history, acknowledge their horror, and not have them cripple us today in our interactions.

The goal is not to somehow forget or forgive slavery. Slavery is not an issue where "forgiveness" is possible. No one should forgive anyone for owning slaves.

Slavery was a sin and it isn't a sin to be forgiven.

We should not, however, blame the descendants of slave-owners today for their ancestors' sins.

The sin of owning slaves is not at all genetic. The sin of slavery, itself, is neither hereditary nor ancestral. It is a functional sin… committed by a person as a reality of their actual lives.

That sin of owning slaves is both direct and situational. It is a sin of personal and direct commission.

That sin relates to the people who owned slaves and it very directly relates situationally to those people. Slavery was very situational when it happened and it is historical now.

Slave ownership is not a current sin that is being committed today by anyone who is alive in our country today.

Some other countries on this planet still do have some slaves. There are actually large numbers of slaves in various settings in the world today. In some parts of the world, additional people are being enslaved in intergroup conflicts.

Some countries still have entire groups of people who have been enslaved for generations.

The United Nations tries to deal with those issues in the places where they are realities and has had varying levels of success. So slavery does continue to exist. Slaves by birth and slaves by capture do exist today elsewhere in the world.

There are none here now, however, and there have been no slaves here in this country since the Civil War.

Guilt Should Be Assigned to Slave Owners

We very much need to affix a sense of guilt directly and explicitly on the ancestors who actually were slave owners. But we should not assign the legacy of that guilt to any descendants of those slave owners as personal guilt today for those people with slave owning ancestors. We should not assign guilt or blame for slavery today to any living people who have not personally committed that sin.

That point is mentioned in *The Art of InterGroup Peace* because some people do believe that we should assign ancestral guilt to people, and that we should now delegate ancestral guilt in some way to the people in this country who have slave-owning ancestors.

Some people believe that if your ancestor committed a sin, you should be blamed today for that sin.

That thought process doesn't increase personal accountability. It dilutes and diminishes personal accountability. If we believe that each of us should be accountable for what each of us does — that creates a direct link between our behaviors and our accountability.

We need that link to exist. We each need to be accountable for what we do.

Any assignment of ancestral guilt to non-slave owning people who are alive today and who have slave owning ancestors doesn't actually link guilt in an accountability-based way to the specific behavior that should trigger guilt in a person who is alive today.

We Need to Set a Standard of Personal Accountability

If a major goal for our behavior today is personal accountability — and if we believe that each person today is accountable for using their intellect and values now to make enlightened and ethical choices about our own behaviors now — then we need to keep guilt at a very personal and direct level for each person, and we need to base guilt on each person's personal behaviors.

The Art of InterGroup Peace believes in personal accountability at a core level. Each one of us is affected and influenced by our instincts and by our cultures. We need to each make our own choices about our own behaviors and we each need to be accountable for the choices we make.

We each need to be personally accountable for our own personal behaviors. Ancestral guilt is not a logistical component of that context of direct personal accountability.

Assigning a level of ancestor-based link to guilt for slave owning behavior to people who never personally committed that sin could actually be a barrier to some needed relationships today. We need people to be able to interact with other people and we need to not allow the behaviors of ancestors for any of our people to impede the 1-to-1 relationships that we need to have between people living here today. Assigning ancestral guilt to people who have never owned slaves because of their direct ancestors' behavior could impede the functional levels of intergroup interactions that we need in a number of settings today.

Ancestral Guilt Is a Seductive Concept

Ancestral guilt feels like it should exist to some people. Ancestral guilt, as a concept, feels right to a number of people.

Our most basic and customary us/them thinking approaches at least partially supports that thought process.

We tend to think of people as groups and we tend to lump people in groups based on their appearance. It particularly feels like some level of guilt should exist for some people today for that set of sins because some people today look, as a group, very much like the people who owned slaves. That linkage to those old slave owners seems even more powerful if those people are, in fact, actually descended from those slave owners.

We tend to lump people together in broad groups when we do our us/them thinking. It can be easy and it can feel right to simply lump people together in a longitudinal linkage over multiple generations on that specific issue.

That is not the most appropriate way of assigning guilt to people if we want guilt to be a working tool to directly influence people's current behavior.

Guilt and blame both need to be based on actual behaviors and guilt needs to be both real and relevant to a person when specific behaviors by that person warrant that guilt.

Assigned guilt or designated guilt or ancestral guilt has less value as a motivator of actual behaviors than personal behavior-based guilt.

That sense of ancestral guilt being relevant to people today is an issue we need to successfully address now as clearly as we can, because that concept can cloud our thinking about interpersonal and intergroup relationships, and it doesn't help us solve and resolve the real intergroup issues.

Us/Them Instincts Have More Impact Today Than a Legacy of Slavery

The functional instinct packages and the basic set of instincts that allowed slavery to happen and that caused slavery to be defended when it happened in this country are more important to us, at this point in time, than our pure history of slavery.

Slavery happened. It was horrible. It was unconscionable. It was evil. And it was ended.

Our us/them instincts, however, have not ended. We still all have those same us/them instincts today that allowed our predecessors as Americans to own slaves and that allowed the tribal invaders from Europe to purge and expel our Native American tribes from their ancestral turf.

Our us/them instincts clearly have a much greater immediate impact on our intergroup behaviors and intergroup interactions today than any residue legacy impact that spills over at some level from our history of slavery.

We are each under the influence of our basic instincts to divide the world into "Us" and "Them."

When we do that dividing, we need to understand that we all tend to act and feel differently about whoever is a "Them." That set of intergroup reactions will potentially be triggered in this country as long as people in this country have the ability to differentiate between any groups of people.

As noted earlier, we build and identify us/them distinctions all the time — and we will continue to do that as long as we have the instincts we have, and as long as there are potential group instinct activation factors in any setting.

We Need a Fresh Start and to Recognize the Damage and the Pain

At one level, we need a restart — with everyone from all groups committing to the basic enlightened values of an American Us and then agreeing to do what needs to be done to make that collective approach and those shared values a success.

We need a fresh start and we need clarity about what we collectively believe in order to make that happen. We need to base that fresh start for America on a clear sense of where we are now and on a clear sense of our collective interest in creating mutual success and InterGroup Peace.

We now need to go forward as a people to build the right set of relationships and the right set of behaviors in a win/win context. But we need to recognize the reality of the damage and the pain that was created for groups of people for our entire history by many of our old, less enlightened, behaviors.

Sun Tzu said that the heads of armies need to recognize the full situation each army is in in order to create a winning strategy going forward. That need to clearly understand the full situation we are actually in today on intergroup issues is very true for Art of InterGroup Peace as well.

"White" Became a New "Us"

A basic point we do all need to understand is the undisputed historical fact that White Americans created a new blended intertribal group called White Americans. We all need to recognize the fact that White Americans have defined the majority group of people in this country for the last couple of countries.

As described earlier, the "White" group has tended, in many ways, to discriminate against each of the various other ethnic groups and racial groups that found themselves to be in minority status in this country. Us/Them instinctive behaviors have clearly massively influenced the actions of that "White" group.

The various laws and behaviors that favored white people at the expense of our other groups of people are a clear part of our collective history. We need to recognize that there has been significant prejudice and discrimination against each and all of the minority groups in this country who either look or sound different from the White American us.

There Has Been Discrimination Against All Groups Other Than White

Asian American, Hispanic Americans, and every other group of Americans with different skin colors or physical features than the majority group American White tribe have faced clear and damaging levels of discrimination.

We need to acknowledge the pain and damage created by those behaviors for all of the affected segments of the people of this country. We can't ignore those overall patterns of intergroup discrimination in our history.

We need to look clearly at how those instincts have influenced our historical behaviors. We need to understand why we have segregated and isolated so many of our minority groups in so many deliberate ways.

We need to recognize that the white invaders of this continent drove the Native Americans in almost all settings from their lands into reservations.

The first sets of Hispanic settlers and invaders in many areas of the country who had themselves often actually dispossessed earlier generations of Native Americans generally found themselves, in turn, dispossessed of their lands when the new American country founded in the English speaking colonies took control over the continent.

The Hispanic Americans who had created their own colonial-triggered communities in many parts of the country were generally politically disenfranchised when those lands that had first been invaded by Spain and by France later became part of the United States.

Later generations of Spanish speaking people who were living in those areas tended to be disenfranchised in that national expansion process by the new White Americans moved into the regions and who spoke English as their tribal language.

Us/Them behaviors and us/them values were evident everywhere in all of the settings where Hispanic Americans lived.

Several newer sets of Hispanic Americans have also immigrated to this country in relatively recent times. High percentages of the new Hispanic Americans have no historic link to those early "settlers" on this continent or to the first waves of us/them prejudicial behaviors that happened in various parts of the country.

Each Hispanic Group Has Its Own Legacy

Each current group of Hispanic Americans has its own history, legacy, and cultural alignments. As noted in the chapter about various categories of intergroup alignments, the various Hispanic groups that exist in this country are not identical and do not represent a single culture or group functionality.

Hispanic is a very broad label that includes very diverse components. It is very different to be Mexican American, Cuban American, or Puerto Rican.

All of those groups tend to be labeled today under the Hispanic group category — but each of those groups has its own culture, history, and identity as a set of people.

Each Hispanic group also has its own very real set of discriminatory stories to tell. Those painful and consistent stories of discrimination are also not identical, but they all have the same basic components of intergroup damage and major intergroup difficulties, prejudices, and problems.

That exact same history and pattern of discrimination against other groups of people has been true for the people who have immigrated here from China, India, Vietnam, and from all of the other non-White areas of the world that have given us immigrants.

We have been a nation of immigrants, and the immigrants in this country have arrived here from a wide variety of sources.

The acceptance level for the immigrants has varied widely — based on the us/them intergroup instinct packages that have been relevant to each group.

Prejudice Against New Immigrants

Each set of immigrants from every legacy country has faced its own challenges in this country in ways that could be predicted by anyone who understands how us/them instincts work. Sight and sound both trigger those intergroup instincts in all settings, and the consequences that happened for each immigrant group were heavily influenced by those trigger factors.

The same us/them instinctive behaviors that created multiple levels of discrimination against non-white Americans were also all usually activated against the first generation immigrants from each of the European tribes.

The clear prejudice that existed against the first wave of Irish immigrants was very obvious in many settings — as was the clear prejudice that existed in most areas against the new immigrants from Norway, Poland, and the new arrivals from a number of other European countries.

The same exact two key differentiation triggers — sight and sound — were activated against those first generation immigrants from each of those European countries. Sound was the major differentiation trigger factor for immigrants from those countries.

Those first generation immigrants from each of those countries tended to dress differently than the White Americans. More importantly, they clearly spoke a different language. It was easy to hear that they were not English speaking White Americans. They spoke accented English when they spoke English at all.

Both visual and audible us/them cues and triggers existed for those people and intergroup prejudices and intergroup discrimination were the norm for each group.

That intergroup prejudice generally disappeared relatively quickly for those immigrants who had European ancestors, as soon as those people and their descendants sounded like the American White "Us."

Immigrants Often Trigger the Sight and Sound Instinct Packages

Looking "different" from the majority group American White "Us" has been a main source of intergroup instinctive behaviors for all immigrants who looked "different."

People from the other non-European groups who sent immigrants to this country continue to look different from the long-standing majority group of White Americans for all of their future generations and that difference in appearance has continued to trigger those instinctive reactions from White Americans.

Immigrants from Asia, the Middle East, Africa, and South America all have increased the complexity of our diversity and all of those groups of people look different from the traditional majority "Us."

Because those people tend to not look like the White American "Us" groups, each of those groups has continued to trigger various levels of intergroup instinctive reactions within their own group and in all of the other relevant groups as well.

Those instincts cause people to feel affinity within each group as an "Us" and it causes people to have a sense that other groups of people are some level of "Them."

We need to deal successfully with that issue and with those intergroup reactions as a country. We can do that more effectively when we intellectually recognize what issues and what information consistently triggers our negative us/them instincts.

We need to recognize that our instincts to perceive anyone who looks different from us to be a "Them" create problems — and we need to recognize that we can overcome those us/them thought processes that are based on appearance when we give ourselves another way of defining ourselves as an "Us."

We haven't tended to create that high level sense of "Us" as a deliberate strategy for intergroup interaction in America. We have not realized that we could use that strategy and we have not recognized the need to use that strategy in order to keep us from tribalizing based on our more primal definitions of "Us."

We need to become a "values-based" us.

If we intellectually recognize now that we can use a shared set of values to create a new American "Us" that is based on our basic beliefs rather than on our ethnicity or our race, then we can both understand our instinctive behaviors and we can use our intellects and our basic values to make us successful as an entire people in ways that we really do need to be aligned to succeed as a people and a nation.

We Need All Groups to Recognize the Impact of Instincts

If we take Sun Tzu's advice and if we clearly understand the terrain we are on relative to these issues, it is clear that we will need to begin by recognizing all of those historical issues going forward.

We need all groups to recognize the impact of "Us" instincts on their group and the impact of "Them" instincts on their group.

It is clear that people from every group — minority and majority — will benefit significantly by recognizing the impact both of the us/them behaviors that have happened to each group in this country over time and the impact of our us/them emotions and perceptions, legacies and the intergroup challenges that we face in our increasing complexity and growing diversity today.

We need people in this country who are not part of the White group to recognize that the prejudices and the discriminatory practices that have been aimed against each set of people have had deep instinctive roots.

There was not an overall negative master-plan conspiracy that was created to do damage to each of the immigrant groups — but each group clearly triggered its own negative instinctive reactions from White Americans and it is very true that local conspiracies did exist for White Americans in each community, state, and setting in the context of those instinctive intergroup reactions.

We need to collectively understand that all of that consistently discriminatory behavior against all of those groups was less conspiratorial than behavioral — with our primal intergroup instincts sculpting our perceptions and guiding our behaviors.

We need to recognize that those old and damaging behaviors do not need to be either forgiven or forgotten — but we need to do a fresh start now that sets up a fresh context where our behavioral judgments now about how we behave from this point on will be based on our current behaviors.

We Need to Deal with Our Instincts and Make Them an Asset

Since we have no way of eliminating any of the instincts that have created our history and our culture, the functional truth is that we need to deal with them. We need to make those sets of basic instincts work for us instead of against us. That is a core strategy for *The Art of InterGroup Peace*.

The truth is, we can use our instincts to achieve our goals or we can allow our instincts to divide and possibly destroy us.

We need to recognize the dangers we face as a nation today. Destruction and impairment as a nation would be the likely outcome of letting ourselves as an increasingly diverse nation be divided in very negative us/them ways and then fall into growing levels of instinct enhanced intergroup conflict.

We need to make all of our instincts work in our favor to achieve Peace and we cannot allow our instincts to sink us into new levels of anger and future levels of conflict at this point in our history.

"White" Is No Longer a Term of Legal Privilege

As noted earlier, we have made some real progress in multiple areas. We have relatively recently managed to write an array of laws that make discrimination relative to some behaviors illegal.

Slavery, itself, has been gone for more than a century.

We now have declared formally, officially, and legally as a country as a point of national policy for us all that the American Dream and all of the opportunities of this country should extend to all of us — to people from every race or ethnicity who are part of this country.

We need to agree across all groups to now go the next step and we need to remove the key remaining intergroup barriers to progress and behaviors to Peace that still remain.

White is no longer a term of legal privilege. White, however, still differentiates a significant portion of our population. White clearly can still create its own set of positive group-linked opportunities and functional favoritism for people in that group — but White no longer creates official and automatic legal standing or legal advantage in any formal way.

That does not mean that equality has been created. It also does not mean that the old and long standing intergroup angers, tensions, or interaction challenges have disappeared.

We need to deal with our history and we need to carefully guide our intergroup behaviors — and we need to recognize both the anger and the pain that some of those behaviors have created.

We also need to make a collective commitment to having all Americans who commit to the core values of America and who support full inclusion into the American Dream to benefit from being American. We need a win/win commitment and strategy. We need everyone to win.

We Need to Start with an Honest Look at Where We Are Now – and We Should Acknowledge the Pain

That process of creating win/win solutions and win/win approaches for all groups requires clear communications between the parties involved.

Doing any win/win process well requires an understanding of each party's interests and even an understanding of each party's history and current context by the other parties.

We need to each make the personal commitment in each setting to be creative and supportive of the win/win solutions that we need to build for all groups in all settings.

At this point in time, there is a high level of misunderstanding and even confusion about some major issues that still need to be addressed. We all need to understand those issues and the stress and pain that they still create for many Americans.

White Americans Need to Recognize the Residual Pain

We need White Americans to recognize the reality created by those instinctive behaviors for so many Americans.

For white Americans to go forward today with the goal of building a new American reality of intergroup Peace without recognizing and clearly understanding the collective pain, the collective anger, and the deep unhappiness that has been created in each of the other groups in this country by centuries of discrimination against our Native American, African American, Asian American, and Hispanic peoples, would reduce our likelihood of collective success as we go forward to create that new Peace.

White Americans need to recognize and understand the anger and the stress that is created today by other groups having lower economic resources, less education, higher incarceration rules, and lower life expectancies. Some of the life expectancy issues are addressed in the book *Ending Racial, Ethnic, and Cultural Disparities in American Health Care*.

White Americans need to understand the impact of those realities. White Americans need to recognize those perceptions, those functional group based disappointments, and those negative intergroup behavior patterns.

Our intergroup patterns have created significant levels of intergroup anger that exists today for many people. That sense of anger needs to be respected for what it is, acknowledged as a real set of issues, and then explicitly addressed in the context of creating a collective future that will be better than our collective past.

There Were Saints and Sinners

We can each decide to embrace and celebrate our common humanity. We can each decide to make achieving intergroup Peace and intergroup success a personal goal that guides our beliefs and our behaviors.

We can transcend, understand, and channel our instinctive emotions to the outcomes we want to achieve — and we can use our "Us" based packages of instincts in more inclusive and accepting ways — to bring us all to levels of ethical behavior that we can feel personally proud to have as a reality for our lives.

The truth is that we will need to do that work of inclusion and acceptance intentionally and consciously in order to get us to the levels of Peace between all groups that we need to achieve as a country.

Our legacy and our reality as a very diverse country requires us to acknowledge, understand, and reflect on the historical issues of our diversity and to make decisions now to never again allow ourselves to descend to the levels of treating other people as "Them."

We need to acknowledge and celebrate our saints and we need to acknowledge, understand, and move beyond the sinners in our collective past.

We need to collectively decide right now not to allow the worst features of that history and the worst elements of that legacy to keep us from achieving Peace today.

We also need to recognize what we need to do to become more effectively inclusive in responding to our increasing diversity today.

Our History Included Some Very Negative and Damaging Us/Them Behaviors

We have put some of the basic pieces that are needed to be the groundwork for Peace in place. Now we need to go the next step and make intergroup Peace our goal.

We then need to put in place the strategic overall agenda that will help us achieve that goal.

We also need to clearly recognize the undeniable and painful fact that our history as a nation clearly has included ethnic cleansing, slavery, massive discrimination, and some very damaging and dysfunctional us/them behaviors.

We need to recognize that our exploding diversity needs to become a strength instead of a source of internal conflict and division.

We need to collectively agree on a set of enlightened values and behaviors that will keep us from reverting back to the worst behaviors in our historical legacy and will allow us to go forward to having our diversity be an asset instead of a source of behavior that generates regret and even shame.

We need to judge people from each group today based on the behaviors of each group today – and not just judge each group based on our historic intergroup behaviors.

We Need People from All Groups to Recognize the Value of Peace

We should feel regret and sorrow that our legacy has those negative elements in it, and we should do now what needs to be done to keep those truly negative behaviors from recurring.

Our basic goal at this point should be to create intergroup Peace. We need people from all groups to recognize that we will all be better off as individuals — and that we will be better off as a nation — when all groups agree to inclusion for everyone in the American Dream and when all groups support and achieve win/win outcomes for all groups.

We need a basic culture of Peace for all groups. We need to recognize the damage done by our instincts and our behaviors — and we need to agree that we now want all groups to prosper and succeed.

To do that, we need a shared commitment to the core values of America. We need a commitment to honesty and we need a commitment to clear and open communications between people.

We need commitment to use our intellect to steer our behaviors to positive consequences.

We can create a culture of Peace for America. And when we do create that culture of Peace, then we will need to defend it against all of the risks that Peace will face.

That is the next chapter of this book.

Let's create Peace and let's keep it as who we are and what we do — resisting all of the people who want Peace to fail and who would rather be in war instead of in Peace.

The risks are real. We need to see them for what they are.

CHAPTER FOURTEEN

The Art of InterGroup Peace for America Needs to Turn Our Instincts into Assets and Give Us the Tools We Need to Defeat Our Common Foes

THE GOAL FOR of The Art of InterGroup Peace strategy for our country is to make key realities about our growing diversity into assets, benefits, and pathways to prosperity, safety, and intergroup Peace.

We need to build a future for our country that turns our growing diversity into a growing strength. We need an overarching strategy that creates intergroup understanding and intergroup trust so that we can create a culture of Peace that is supported by all of the groups who make up the rich and complex fabric of our people.

We need to be on that path now.

Our diversity as a country is growing every day. The majority of births in this country this year were to our minority mothers. The majority of students in our public school system next year will be minority students.

The majority of new workers into our workforce by the end of this decade will be minority workers.

We need to become very good at being diverse because we are very quickly becoming very diverse.

Diversity in far too many settings around the world leads to intergroup conflict and intergroup dysfunctional behaviors at multiple levels. This book has outlined and described some of the major problems that are happening today in a number of multi-ethnic, multi-racial countries that are now at war with themselves.

We Do Not Want to Be Another Diverse Country at War with Itself

Civil wars are everywhere. Internal conflict abounds in multiple settings. We do not want to end up just another diverse country at war with itself. That future would damage us all badly — and it does not need to happen to us.

Every group, every segment, and every portion of our population would be damaged if we allow ourselves to tribalize to any significant degree and then activate the array of negative intergroup instincts and damaging intergroup behaviors that internal tribalization in any setting can far too easily invoke.

That would be the wrong path for us to be on. We should do what needs to be done to be sure that is not going to be the path we are on.

If we, instead, decide to become a high performing, high achievement, highly inclusive, and highly diverse American us — we can then harvest the best features of the American Dream and we can harvest the benefits of that Dream even better and more successfully than we have ever done it before.

We will benefit more now because we will now have all parties in this country finally able to participate fairly and fully in that Dream.

We Need to Utilize Our Instincts Strategically to Achieve Our Goals and Create InterGroup Peace

Our instincts will continue to guide our lives. We can't escape the emotional and mental pull of our instinctive behaviors. It is impossible for any of us to be instinct free.

Since we can't escape our instincts, we will need to utilize them very strategically to achieve the enlightened goals we want to achieve.

That, in its essence, is The Art of InterGroup Peace. Instead of being damaged, divided, and then destroyed by a growing sense of being us and them, we need to bring ourselves together to create a viable, functioning, real, self-reinforcing, and clearly enlightened shared sense of us that lets us all be at Peace with ourselves.

At this point in our history, we now need to build an American Us that is grounded on our American ideals, our highest and most honorable American values, our basic American belief system, and our very best American ethics.

We need to create a level of collective and shared enlightenment on key issues and values that will help us define ourselves to each other as an American Us and then help us all help each other succeed in a very intentionally inclusive and mutually supportive American way.

We need to very explicitly and very intentionally create an American Us as a major and foundational step in that Art of InterGroup Peace process outlined in this book, and we need to continue to focus on maintaining and protecting that sense of "Us" going into the future.

The truth is — we are only safe as a country when we are an "Us" as a country. Our safety and our success as a country depend on us creating an "Us" who is defined and guided by our key and shared beliefs.

We each have choices to make.

If we each allow ourselves to be defined primarily as an ethnic us or as a racial us or as a cultural or tribal us or as any other separately functioning and instinctively divisive and divided subset of us — and if we each allow that divisive definition of us to create and shape both our own personal functioning every day sense of us and our own individual sense of who we each are, then we can fall very easily into the dysfunctional and damaging trap of being a tribalized country at war with itself.

Becoming a Tribalized Country at War with Itself Is the Wrong Approach

We do not need to allow that to happen. But that negative outcome has a very high likelihood of happening if we do not strategically intervene in the process of becoming who we are becoming. We are more diverse than we have ever been and our diversity increases daily.

Those facts and numbers are beyond dispute. We now need to face, understand, and accept both the reality of our extensive diversity and the inherent consequences that will result from our diversity.

Our rapidly increasing diversity will inevitably force us down one of two very different paths — division into our separate pieces or alignment around our shared beliefs.

We can divide or we can unite.

We should choose the path of alignment that leads us together to Peace, safety, survival, and shared success.

Some people who look at those issues believe that level of concern about the potential consequences of our diverse future is exaggerated and overstated.

A significant number of people today believe in a very positive way that we have somehow evolved as a nation, as a people, as a world and as individuals past the point where those kinds of very basic and very primal instincts can have any significant levels of negative impacts on modern people's behavior. That is, unfortunately, not an accurate belief.

People With Modern Technology Are Acting in Very Primal Ways

Anyone who believes that people living today have reached a modern age of some kind where we have moved past and evolved beyond the direct and very real impact of those primal behaviors and those primal instincts only has to look at Sri Lanka or Syria or any of the 200 other settings on this planet where those instincts are causing modern people with full modern knowledge and full modern science and full modern technology to be damaging, torturing, abusing, killing, and cruelly uprooting, and displacing other equally modern people in very primitive, evil, and cruel ways.

Those basic and ugly packages of negative and dysfunctional intergroup instincts continue to be very real for people living today. People do very sinful and damaging things to other people with no sense of guilt or shame when those instincts are activated.

We need to be very careful to not activate those primal us/them instincts here in their most negative forms in our own country today or at any time in our future.

The likelihood of us activating those instincts here is clearly increased significantly by our growing internal diversity.

As our cities become more diverse, there is a growing risk of having neighborhoods and communities within cities that create their own intergroup conflicts at very local levels.

Instead of activating those horrible, damaging, and destructive intergroup instincts in any of our settings, we should all make the intellectual decision to come together in a higher calling to be collectively aligned and mutually bonded together around our collective sense of being a values-based us. Creating a values-based alignment as an American us can give us the safety net we want and need for our own collective success and safety.

Coming together as a mutually supportive us can give us communities that are at Peace with themselves and that function to benefit the people who live in each setting.

That coming together as a values-based us is the single most important strategic step embedded in the Art of InterGroup Peace.

We need to be bonded by a higher calling in a way that causes each of us to feel drawn to a higher collective purpose and to be motivated in a very real and functional way by a higher level of shared common good.

We can do wonderful, caring, supportive, and even loving things for other people when we know that the other people are an "Us."

We have ethical standards that are activated and relevant when we are an "Us" — and we step up in caring and supportive ways to help each other when our "Us" needs us to be there for them.

It is a very good thing to be an "Us." We need to expand our sense of who we include and who we bring together in intergroup alignment to create our American "Us."

We Face Real Danger if We Don't Become an "Us"

To start that process and to feel that it makes sense to be an "us," we now need to use the alignment trigger pyramid outlined in Chapter Seven of this book.

All of those factors on that pyramid that create alignment are relevant to us today. The alignment pyramid that needs to be used by us collectively in very intentional ways at this point in our history to be a key functional component of The Art of InterGroup Peace.

We need to use that pyramid to create a sense of "Us" in our communities and we need to use it in our various organizations. We need to use it in our work places and we need to use it in our schools.

We need to use it with the leaders of all of the groups who make up the complex set of groups that co-exist in this country today.

We need to activate those six situational alignment triggers locally and we need to activate them as a nation.

We Are Actually in Danger

Danger anchors that alignment trigger pyramid. That's a good place to start. Danger is a real issue for us all today.

We need to recognize the very real dangers we will face if we do not become an American Us. The dangers are real. A very basic set of dangers are created by our instincts any time multiple groups co-exist in any setting.

Many people in our increasingly diverse country will feel right going down that conflicted instinct-guided and fundamentally negative path to intergroup anger, intergroup stress, and intergroup conflict.

The patterns of damaging instinctive behavior that can result from groups triggering instinctive negative reactions against other groups can be extremely seductive. The negative behaviors that can spring from those instincts can be both highly persuasive and very attractive to many people at a highly emotional level.

People can be energized by negative intergroup behaviors when those negative intergroup instincts are activated in any setting.

It can feel very right and it can feel invigoratingly partisan in an instinctively, emotionally rewarding way for people to go down that us/them instinctive conflict path in too many situations and settings.

The temptation that exists today in many settings to feel those feelings and to think those thoughts is significant.

Angry demonstrations and even mobs that we see spontaneously form when those instincts are triggered tell us how much underlying intergroup anger exists in many settings today.

Chapter Fifteen deals in more detail with those issues. Intergroup anger and conflict is a path we often take and it is a path we have often taken.

We can each identify ourselves very easily with our own subset of America and we can simply identify other subsets of America as being "Them" in some highly instinct-provoking ways.

The cold and dangerous truth is that we face a very slippery slope to us/them thinking, us/them values, us/them emotions, us/them beliefs, and us/them behaviors when those packages of instincts are triggered.

Highly Partisan Behaviors Can Be Exhilarating

Highly partisan and negative intergroup behaviors can sometimes be emotionally exhilarating and collectively reinforcing when they are situationally invoked.

When we choose teams in any setting, we can commit team energy for our "Us" into wanting "our team" to win at any cost.

That can be a good thing when those team instincts bring us together — and it can be a dangerous and divisive thing when those team instincts cause us to want to defeat and damage another team.

That whole process of choosing sides can put us in danger from damage that might be done to us by another team in any setting.

We can channel emotionally absorbing and invigorating anger into our intergroup energy levels when our energy is directed against "Them." We can feel very right hating and hurting the other teams that we define as being the teams of "Them."

Protests, demonstrations, mobs, and even riots can and do happen in American settings and the people who are acting collectively in those settings can find the collective behavior to be invigorating and self-reinforcing.

Basic intergroup mobs and even intergroup riots are just the visible point of the intergroup conflict and 'anger iceberg' that exists in many settings now. We have deep-seated intergroup anger in a number of settings. That level of conflict that can spring from that anger can grow in too many settings and in too many situations if we allow ourselves to go down those very seductive and very instinctive paths into negative levels of us/them intergroup anger.

Our instincts reward those behaviors with neurochemicals that create almost addictive negative behaviors for some people. Very negative intergroup behaviors can feel very right to people at a very basic and personal level — because our instincts cause whatever behaviors are aligned with our instincts to feel very right to each of us as we do them.

So the danger is real. That entire set of risk factors presents us with a clear and present package of danger.

Collective Risk Increases in Economic Bad Times

We also will face a higher risk of collective intergroup danger at points in the future when we enter into times of economic downturn and enter those downturns as an increasingly diverse country.

That will inevitably happen. Economic downturns do occur.

We can expect as a country and as communities to need to deal with new and relevant downturns at future points in time. Some downturns can be very damaging.

People can turn against people easily and quickly when economic times are bad. Negative us/them instincts that can be activated in those time frames and difficult situations can increase the damage levels that happen to people in those intergroup settings.

If we are in a level of high intergroup stress and intergroup anger in this country and if we then face any kinds of major setbacks as a country, the consequences of the setbacks can be very damaging.

If we face an economic depression or an enemy-induced collapse of our infrastructure — or any significant challenges to our basic water supply — or even if we find ourselves facing a time of extended drought — and if we find ourselves in a time of potential panic and significant logistical deprivation as a result of any of those downturns — then the resultant instinctive intergroup behaviors that could be triggered in any of our groups relative to our other groups in that time of collective crisis could be destructive and highly damaging.

The intergroup responses that we might see for those future crisis could be negative to the point of being crippling in some communities. The responses to those threats could be negative to the level of triggering evil, dysfunctional, and highly damaging behaviors with dysfunctional and damaging intergroup consequences that are relevant to the challenges that we face.

Hard times can bring people together to find collective solutions and hard times can tear people apart — exacerbating division and increasing the level of anger that exists between groups.

We need to be so unified as a people that our future downturns and hard times will unite us rather than divide us.

Hard Times Can Bring People Together or Tear People Apart

The survival instincts that we all have for our own groups to survive in a crisis can cause us to do serious intergroup damage to each other if the entire country faces any kind of collapse and if the people in this country in the context of that collapse turn against one another in anger instead of turning to one another for protection and support.

Sun Tzu, in *The Art of War*, wrote that when the men of Wu and the men of Yueh — mortal enemies — found themselves together on a sinking boat, they all worked together to save the boat. He pointed out that survival needs for individual people can trigger collective situational cooperation instead of war.

We do need to have our own future collective dangers and our own future national economic and functional setbacks bring us together as a country instead of having them tear us apart.

We could go either way. Both paths can be triggered by the same events and by the same circumstances.

That potential for intergroup damage that will exist in a time of crisis is a real risk to us all — because negative circumstances of some kinds at future points are inevitable… whether the crises are triggered intentionally by enemy forces or triggered circumstantially and situationally by either environmental or economic forces that we can't control.

In times of crisis, we need to be together on our path to survival and to success. We need to collectively understand that very real future level of risk and we need to plan ahead to deal with it.

Some People Do Not Want Us at Peace

We also need to recognize as we go down the path to intergroup Peace that another danger we will need to face is that there are people and groups of people who want us to fail in that effort.

Peace has enemies. Outside our country, there are people who very much want America to fail. Inside our country, there are some people who want America to succeed, but want Peace to fail.

Some of those people from other countries who want us to fail as a nation flew airplanes into the World Trade Center and into the Pentagon. They set bombs off at the Boston Marathon. Those people hate us and those people very much do not want Peace in America to succeed.

There are other people who are leaders of people inside our own country who prefer to have their groups in a state of conflict with other groups in our own country instead of having their groups allied with other groups in our country.

Some people in our country and in other countries actually hate the people from other groups. That isn't speculation or theory. We know that to be true.

The Internet is full of sites that preach, teach, and attempt to incite intergroup fear, intergroup anger, intergroup conflict, and intergroup hatred.

The Internet Has Sites Hosted by People Who Hate

Those people prove their existence to us simply by proving their existence to us. We can't pretend they do not exist or hope that they will not be real.

The Internet is one of their major platforms. We can see what those people who hate believe and we can see what they want to do by going to their websites and seeing what they actually say.

What they want to do can be very ugly — evil, damaging, divisive, destructive, and ugly. There are people who want racism to be the reality for America.

There are people who are misogynistic and bigoted and ethnically hateful.

Those people who preach division inside our country clearly do not want to see an inclusive and accepting America where everyone has full access to our best values, full equality, freedom, and inclusive access to the American Dream.

Some of those people who want us to fail — both inside our country and from other countries — have enough hatred in their minds to take their own steps to create real and functional crises for America — trying to destroy various elements of our infrastructure or cripple our economy.

The next chapter of this book deals with some of those risks. When those kinds of setbacks happen, we will need to function as an American "Us" to respond successfully.

That has, in fact, been our practice. Both Pearl Harbor and 9/11 brought us together with great collective clarity and angry against our common foe at that point in time.

Common Enemies Are Also a Threat

Common enemies are the second step on the alignment pyramid.

It is clear beyond question that we actually do have common enemies who we need to resist, overcome, defuse, and defeat.

We need to defeat them by creating an America that achieves the American Dream for all of us in the most inclusive way and that responds to each crisis collectively and collaboratively instead of having our various crises dividing us into warring groups who then do damage to one another in the name of survival.

We need intergroup trust, intergroup collaboration, and intergroup alliances that bring us together and that give us the chance to celebrate and embrace our common humanity… so that we can all help each other succeed and thrive as a total and inclusive American Us.

The people who produce those websites that are so rich in hatred and so steeped in angry and evil intentions are a common enemy to all of us who want Peace.

The people who would rather lead their groups to angry division rather than to Peaceful alignment are common enemies to Peace.

The people who deliberately undermine our processes of shared understanding so they can keep us functioning as warring tribes are also all common enemies to Peace. Peace has its common enemies — and we can identify who they are by what they do and how they do it.

The common enemies of Peace can be found at the international level and they exist in each of the communities where we have people who live to keep us apart.

People in communities who hate betray their feelings and their intentions with the fruit of their hatred. We need to bring each community to feel a collective sense of "Us"— a sense that we want all of us in the community to succeed.

We need to make sure the common enemies in each setting do not divide us and trigger intergroup anger in seductive and persuasive ways.

Common enemies exist. We need to know who they are and we need to defeat what they do.

We Need Teams to Improve Safety, Health, and Our Children's Future

We also need to use our team instincts to bring us together.

To create the levels of intergroup interactions that can bring people together in the face of that opposition to Peace, we need to function now as teams at multiple levels.

Teams are the third step on that alignment trigger pyramid in Chapter Seven. This book outlines a number of areas where we can work together as teams in the common good toward common benefits and common wins.

We need to be clear on the common wins we want to achieve in each setting and then we need to use teams in each setting to help us achieve those common wins.

Health, for example, can be a common win.

We need to function in teams in various very practical ways in multiple communities and multiple settings to improve our collective health.

We need teams in place to do that good work, and we need to feel the collective mutual support that team members have for one another in the context of those teams doing that work.

To help bring us together and to support both alignment and Peace, we need teams who have real goals. Our teams need important things to do that bring team members into alignment as team members, or that alignment will not happen.

We Need All of Our Children to Get the Support They Need

Taking care of our children ranks as a top priority and an extremely important focus for our team activities.

Focusing mutually in team-based supportive ways on our children is an important shared goal that can serve that purpose of unifying us and creating trust between groups of people in multiple settings.

The science of brain development for the first months and years of life for each child points us in a clear and crucial direction.

We need to have teams in place in every community who work to maximize and optimize the neuron development in our youngest children from every single group in this country.

To succeed as a country for our collective future, we need high performing children in every group in America. We need all of our children to be able to succeed.

That will not be possible unless we make sure that our children in every setting get the biological and functional brain exercise that is needed by each child in each child's first months and years of life. The brain exercise need is specific for each child.

Every child we serve by doing the right things in those key months and years is a child we save. Every child counts. We need to help each child get the brain exercise needed in those first couple years of life so that each child has the best hope for success.

We need to function as teams to also create and support the best education system in the world. We need all of our children to have the education needed to be in great jobs.

We need great education systems to give us a work force that can prevail in the face of workforce challenges that we face now and will face in the future from the rest of the world.

We need teams of people in each setting to be doing that work of helping our children together — and we need to appreciate each other's common humanity in the context of doing all those activities in the context of teams.

We Need to Be an Inclusive, Values-Based American Us

Creating a shared sense of "Us" is a key goal and a key tool for the entire Peace process.

We need to now bring all of our collective agendas together in the context of being an American Us. We can and should each continue to identify with — and celebrate — all of the various racial, ethnic, cultural, and religious groups that make up the rich and complex fabric of America.

We also need to add another key layer to all of those identities that brings us together through our shared values and through our shared beliefs to be a functioning and very real values-aligned American Us.

We need to do that work at a very explicit and intentional level. We need to be a belief driven us.

The final chapter of this book outlines a set of 12 common values that we can all share now to help us define and align those beliefs. Other values can be added later to that list. It isn't a perfect list. But it is a highly functional and legitimate list.

That list included in the final chapter of this book is based on our current set of values that have been the bedrock belief systems for America. We use those values now — but not as a package and not in a way that lets us make a shared commitment to them in ways that can help us use them to define us as an "Us."

We need to be that "Us." We need to trigger our us instincts and our perceptions to include all of us who believe in that specific and explicit shared set of beliefs to be included in our "American Us."

We Need To Add a "Layer of Us"

In that same way that we can feel a sense of our family us and can also be part of a clan us and can also identify with each other as a tribal us — we need to continue to each identify ourselves as a racial, ethnic, cultural, gender, religious us with whatever sets of people fill those roles in our lives, but we also need to simultaneously relate to one another at another very valid and very powerful higher and more inclusive level as an American Us.

We need to add a layer of "Us."

We need to build a level of shared belief that lets us trust and support and celebrate one another as a real and functioning American Us.

When we do that, we create a context that allows us all to work together, play together, enjoy life together, and prosper and thrive together — with our America Us as the group that thrives and prospers in ways that create Peace for ourselves, and Peace for our children and Peace for our grandchildren.

We Will Leave a Legacy for Our Grandchildren

We will leave a legacy for our grandchildren. That is inevitable. Legacies happen. Grandchildren happen. That is how life works.

What isn't inevitable is exactly which legacy we will collectively leave to our grandchildren.

If we succeed in creating intergroup Peace and if we create a collective, values-based sense of "Us" and if our grandchildren inherit both that Peace and that broad and inclusive values-based sense of us, then their lives will be much better than they will be if we leave them with a legacy of destructive and dangerous intergroup conflict and damaging intergroup anger.

Our grandchildren will benefit from us expanding our us. We need to extend that inclusive sense of us to our children and to our grandchildren in very explicit ways, so their lives can be lived in the context of intergroup Peace rather than intergroup conflict.

We Need To Model "Us" Behaviors And We Each Need To Reach Out

As part of the sharing and teaching process for those values, we need to model those values-based behaviors in our own lives.

We each need to reach out across group lines to create friendships and we each need to build the kind of interpersonal interactions that build and maintain personal and group understanding and trust.

We need all of our people to be able to relate to each other as people — and we need people to not feel a sense of being a traitor in befriending people from other groups.

We need to model those reaching out behaviors for our children and for our grandchildren, because they will believe what we actually do to be more relevant than what we simply say. We need to show our offspring how intergroup friendships work and we need to show our offspring how intergroup trust begins and is sustained.

When our children aren't bound and isolated by the usual sets of divisive and separatist instinctive behaviors and feelings, then intergroup trust and interpersonal understanding can anchor intergroup Peace at a very basic and personal level for the next generations as well.

We Need Role Models for Inclusive, Interacting Behaviors

We need to teach those values in our schools and we need to teach and preach and achieve those values in our various communities.

We need to teach those values to our children and we need to teach them to each other. We need also to live those values and model them though our personal behavior in order to make them real and to give them the foundation they need to shape our future as well as shaping our world and interactions today.

We need role models for those behaviors. We each owe it to our children to model those behaviors.

We also need our community leaders, religious leaders, and even our political leaders to model the behaviors that build and support intergroup trust.

We need our various heroes from sports, entertainment, and public life to teach and model those behaviors as well.

Celebrity endorsement for intergroup trust can have a huge positive impact on embedding those values in the new American culture of Peace that we need to create and support. We need a culture of Peace that makes Peaceful behaviors our cultural expectations in each setting.

We need our most respected leaders from each group to not only model those behaviors — we need those leaders to be able to go to the crisis spots when crisis happen to help resolve the relevant issues and to calm people down in ways that people understand and trust.

Crisis and conflict situations often tend to be very local — but sometimes the solutions to local situations call for additional resources, credibility, and expertise to enter the crisis site to calm the crisis and avert the intergroup explosions that can potentially occur.

We need community, group, and religious leaders in every setting who are willing to step into that role in their communities when needed.

The Benefits to All of Us Are Significant

The benefits to us all of going down that path of inclusion are significant. The fifth step and penultimate incentive factor on the six-step alignment trigger pyramid is to offer mutual benefit and mutual gain to people in order to achieve mutual alignment in a setting or situation.

Mutual benefit is very relevant to intergroup Peace in America.

We actually have prospered as a country for hundreds of years because the American Dream has allowed people here to invent, create, produce, invest, and succeed in a wide range of areas.

We have great music, great art, and we have a very powerful economy anchored on having hardworking people creating products and services that benefit each other and also benefit the world.

The heart of our economic success and the heart of our economic engine has been to enable many people to produce and to succeed.

We have managed all of that success and all of that beneficial production in a handicapped and limited way — because we have only allowed a subset of our population full access to the American Dream.

Only White Americans have had consistent access to the American Dream and the best opportunities in this country have been primarily limited to White males.

We Will All Be Better Off When We Are All Better Off

Expanding our access to the American Dream to all groups and to all genders will give us an even more powerful engine for economic growth and success as a nation. We will be stronger, better, and more secure when everyone can bring their talents and their skills to our common good and our common goals.

The consequence to America of going down the other path — of tribalizing, splintering, and denying full Dream access to entire groups of Americans — will result in major portions of our people underperforming with many people in poverty and in major situational failure.

Major segments of our population are facing economic challenges and experiencing negative economic situations today.

We need to directly deal with those issues. Building our overall national success and protecting our national security with growing numbers of our people failing has its own obvious failure consequences as a nation and creates its own obvious, real, and dangerously high levels of risk as a strategy and as a pathway.

We can achieve those goals of mutual success and inclusion with clear laws that make discrimination in some key areas — like employment — illegal. We can also achieve those goals by helping people who want to create their own businesses and who want to set up their own economic engines succeed.

Government progress that creates access to both resources and education for all Americans needs to be part of that strategy of economic inclusion.

People will be better off economically when we are collectively in better health. Health disparities have damaged groups of Americans in very real ways — but those disparities can be eliminated if we take some key steps to make them disappear.

Healthy people are more likely to prosper in other ways.

The primary reality is this — we will experience significant mutual and collective gain when we expand the American Dream and when we create a broader set of people whose successes can strengthen us as an economy, as a nation, and as a people who want each other to succeed.

Peace does lead to prosperity if we steer it in that direction.

We Need to Commit to and Use Shared Values as a People

The final chapter of this book deals with the top step on that alignment factor pyramid that was outlined in Chapter Seven.

The top step on that alignment pyramid is to have a shared mission — a shared vision — and a shared belief system.

That particular alignment trigger also very clearly works to motivate, align, and inspire people in multiple settings. It is true that we can be unified and be united by our beliefs.

Some of the most powerful human movements that have ever existed have been based on shared beliefs.

We need to go down that path here and we need to go down that path now. We need to mutually commit to our key sets of basic values and to key sets of enlightened behaviors.

The set of shared beliefs that are explicitly outlined in the final chapter of this book are not new. Freedom, democracy, inclusion, fairness, equal rights, and all of the other shared beliefs on that list are each embedded now in various parts of our belief system and our history.

But that full set of values have not been the composite reality in the past for all of us — and they haven't been explicitly collected in the past into a functional working set of beliefs that we all to share and that we all to agree to use in an inclusive way for each and all of us as a people.

What we need to do now is to pull our various key beliefs together and weave them together as a shared package of shared beliefs — with each of us collectively agreeing to that specific package of shared beliefs and each and all of us committing to work together to make them real for all of us.

We Need to Discuss, Understand, and Enhance That List

There may be other beliefs that we can add to that values list. Adding additional key values could obviously make the list stronger.

Some people may be able to improve and enhance the list in various ways. That enhancement approach can clearly be a good thing to do.

Those are discussions that we need to have as a country and discussions that we need to have as individuals with one another.

As we expand that dialogue and those deliberations, we can use this list in the last chapter of this book as our working set of core beliefs. That can be a valid and legitimate thing to do because this is a list of a dozen key beliefs that we actually use to guide us as a country now.

The list wasn't invented. It was compiled.

The specific list outlined in Chapter Fifteen is intended both to tee up wider discussions and to also give us an explicit and functional starter set of current shared beliefs that we can all commit to use to help us go a step down the process path of becoming a values-centered American Us.

Ask Leaders if They Agree to Core Beliefs

It is a good idea to share and use this list of beliefs with other people. Ask leaders in each setting if they believe in that list and if they, as leaders, support those key beliefs.

Use the list as guidance in any intergroup setting to help structure behaviors, interactions, and decisions.

We need to go to each of our political leaders now and ask our leaders to work for a commitment to work on intergroup Peace.

We need to ask our leaders to agree to those core values and to set up open dialogue and communication about the real intergroup problems that exist in each community and setting.

Some political movements in this country have already asked our community leaders and our elected officials to sign pledges to do various things in office. Tax-related pledges exist, for example.

What we need now is a set of leaders who commit to intergroup Peace and to helping create the support needed to have our children educated, our people healthy, and to have everyone from every group given full access to the American Dream.

There is no political leaning to those issues. These are all human issues — not doctrinal or ideological issues. Each leader in each setting can use the tool kit of their own ideology and political leanings or their own religious or philosophical beliefs to create support for this set of goals.

Creativity is welcome.

We Need an Explosion of Creativity in the Internet of Peace

Creativity is more than welcome, in fact. We can be incredibly creative people.

We need to trigger our creativity now to figure out ways of both achieving those values and enhancing our success levels, insights, and behaviors in each of those areas. We need an explosion of creativity in the service of Peace.

The next chapter of this book deals with some of the risks we face in both creating and protecting Peace. We also need to trigger our creativity to figure out ways of mitigating all of those risks.

Before going to that list of risks to Peace, it makes sense to look again at some of the key strategic directions for creating Peace that have been included in this book.

Sixteen Steps to Take to Peace

The summary list below repeats sixteen of the key Art of InterGroup Peace strategies and belief points that have been included and discussed in prior chapters of this book.

Sun Tzu wrote lists of direct advice to his war leaders in *The Art of War*. This is a parallel set of advice points for Peace leaders from *The Art of InterGroup Peace*.

Each of the points on that list are guidance tools that are part of the Art of InterGroup Peace strategy. Each of the guidance points stems from specific strategy points that were outlined in various places earlier in this book.

The following advice is embedded in *The Art of InterGroup Peace*:

1) Avoid triggering and activating us/them instincts in a negative way in each setting. Make that avoidance a major priority and do it constantly and well.

2) Activate us/them instincts in a positive way.

3) Base intergroup relations and intergroup interactions on mutual winning — with win/win outcomes both a commitment and a shared value for all of the people in all of the groups.

4) Select leaders who want Peace and who believe in the 12 core values and in win/win intergroup interactions.

5) Mutually and individually commit to the 12 shared and fundamental values and core beliefs that are outlined in Chapter 16 of *The Art of InterGroup Peace*.

6) Make friends, build relationships, and create personal interactions across group lines to build intergroup trust and to create intergroup understanding at a personal level.

7) Do not insult, attack, demean, disparage, antagonize, or cast aspersions on other groups of people — and do not do things to intentionally create intergroup discomfort for other people.

8) Have open discussions about the key issues and the key beliefs that are teed up for discussion by *The Art of InterGroup Peace*. Be prepared to help resolve the situation if other people are clumsy and unintentionally offensive in their commentary and discussions. Guide people rather than condemn people when that kind of problematic communication happens. Safe discussions are needed. We all need to help to make our discussions safe.

9) Recognize that forgiveness for past sins is not the approach needed now. Some sins can never be forgiven. What is needed now is a restart — with everyone now being held personally accountable now for behaviors and for events that happen beginning now.

10) Use a blend of understandings, agreements, alliances, teams, functional integration, and cultural values interweaving with strategies to achieve the intergroup goals and intergroup interactions needed in each setting. Understand each of those intergroup interaction options and use the one in each intergroup setting that is most likely to meet the needs of the group and achieve intergroup Peace.

11) Celebrate our legacy group identities and group cultures and make them a key part of the total America — building on that whole array of cultures and group identities rather than erasing or replacing them. In building on those cultures, embed in those cultures the key beliefs that are needed to create and sustain values-based Peace.

12) Make the Internet a major tool of enlightenment, understanding, and use it as a vehicle for creating alliances and defusing anger and crisis — rather than having the Internet help to destroy intergroup Peace and function

as a tool that is only used for inciting intergroup anger and creating conflicted intergroup behaviors. Make the Internet a powerful and effective tool for Peace. *Cusp of Chaos, Primal Pathways,* and *Peace in Our Time* each have major sections explaining how the Internet can threaten and destroy Peace, and how we can use the tool kit of the Internet to support, explain, create, defend, and protect Peace.

13) Commit collectively to creating a setting of safe communities where every child from every group gets the support needed by each in their first years of life to achieve their full potential. Make that effort successful and make it clear to all groups that we all want all of our children to succeed. Do that in an honest and effective way that creates intergroup trust.

14) Avoid leaders who clearly trigger intergroup anger and intergroup conflict. Select leaders who have the status, standing, creativity, and skill set to create Peaceful intergroup interactions.

15) Be aware of the instincts we have to be very uncomfortable and to feel stress when we find ourselves in a situational minority status. Those instincts can trigger discomfort, stress, anxiety, and even anger when any of us is in a minority status — and those feelings and perceptions need to be anticipated, understood, and mitigated wherever possible.

16) Commit to include everyone in the American Dream — knowing that we will all be stronger when we each are strong — and knowing that we will be economically powerful when economic success extends to us all.

We can turn diversity into a great strength by giving everyone full paths to success and by aligning those paths in an inclusive way with the American Dream.

We Need Shared Beliefs

Those sixteen guidances from *The Art of InterGroup Peace* can all be useful if we implement them in a context that is created by having all of us with a shared set of key beliefs and a shared commitment to making those beliefs the way we function as individuals, as communities, and as a nation.

As we move forward to the point where we have a mutual agreement in place to build intergroup Peace in America, we will often need to take the steps that are necessary to actually protect the Peace we create. Defending Peace can be as critical as creating Peace.

Then next chapter of this book deals with the risks we have for Peace and what we need to do to mitigate them.

The chapter after that deals with the kinds of intergroup explosions that have created major issues in a number of American communities. We need to know why those explosions happened and we need to know how to either prevent them or effectively resolve them.

Then we need to focus on our core beliefs. That process is key to the Art of InterGroup Peace.

The final chapter of this book includes those beliefs.

CHAPTER FIFTEEN

Threats, Challenges, and Risks to Peace

IT IS IMPORTANT to protect Peace once Peace has been achieved in any setting. Peace can be fragile — and if Peace is created and lost in any setting, the events and the situations that can cause Peace to be then lost can make it much harder to regain Peace in the future in that setting.

When Peace of any meaningful kind has been created for any setting, it is important to take the steps that are necessary to protect that Peace against the array of threats that will inevitably emerge to damage, erode, or destroy it. Peace in some settings can have a self-reinforcing stability — but Peace in other settings can have an inherent fragility subject to attack, resistance, undermining, and deterioration from multiple sources and factors relevant to each setting.

Our instincts create much of that fragility.

The basic instincts we all have to divide the world into us and them and then to be suspicious and distrustful of anyone we perceive to be a them are very powerful instincts and those instincts can destroy Peace all by themselves when they are actualized, triggered, activated, or reactivated in any given intergroup setting.

Our Instincts Create a Risk to Peace

For obvious reasons, our us/them instincts serve as a constant threat, barrier, vulnerability factor, and challenge to any Peace we can create between distinctively different groups anywhere in any setting where distinctly different groups exist and where those groups interact and attempt to achieve and maintain Peace.

Those instincts cause us to have a consistent and constant underlying level of suspicion and distrust relative to any former "Them" who is now part of a Peace situation.

We can enter into those agreements and they can work well — but we tend to always have at least a low level of alert at an instinct-triggered level relative to the possibility that the former enemy is still, in secret, actually an enemy.

That low level of alert does not harm most situations that are going well, but it does make any actions by the other group that might reinforce the suspicion have more potential impact.

Peace can be undermined by those instincts to be on alert if any trigger event occurs that seems to justify the sense of not fully trusting the other people in any setting. Entirely unintentional actions that are perceived to be negative intergroup actions can cause Peace to be situationlly undermined.

Peace can also be intentionally undermined by people in a setting who simply do want Peace to be undermined. That is clearly a major risk for Peace wherever it occurs. Some people do not want Peace to happen. Those people obviously can damage, undermine, impair, or destroy Peace in any setting where they have influence.

The incidents and actions that undermine Peace can be both intentional and unintentional.

Many people do want Peace to happen but they can do things unintentionally and inadvertently to put Peace at risk.

Anger can undermine Peace. It is highly likely that various people might become angry about other groups in various situations for various reasons — and those people who become angry about an issue or event can allow their own situational anger to flare up and undermine, damage, or even destroy Peace in those settings.

Situational anger can clearly put Peace at risk. Peace can be challenged, weakened, damaged, and undermined by people who become angry and upset over various kinds of intergroup issues or intergroup problems that might naturally occur in any setting.

Knowing that to be true, people who don't want Peace to succeed in any setting can either intentionally or unintentionally do things that cause people in their own groups or in other groups to be distrustful, divisive, or angry enough to undermine Peace in that setting.

Bad Behaviors Happen

Old negative behavioral habits and old negative terminology can both undermine Peace.

People can insult or demean other groups — both intentionally and accidently — and that behavior can undermine Peace. People can simply discriminate against other people intentionally or unintentionally and can act in prejudicial ways that trigger the protective us/them instincts and emotions in the people who are demeaned or who are discriminated against.

Various kinds of unintentional, but dysfunctional and damaging intergroup behaviors can happen. Those behaviors can all create risk for Peace.

Sometimes the risk triggering behaviors done by people in a setting are deliberate and intentional. Sometimes they are entirely inadvertent and completely and entirely unintentional. In either case, Peace can be put at risk.

Behaviors that have good intentions at heart from entirely well intentioned people can create problems in a setting because people have imperfections and those behavioral imperfections can create unintentional risks for Peace.

Flare-ups Need to Be Addressed Quickly

Imperfection needs to be understood and recognized — and it needs to be addressed directly when it happens. Both unintended and intended intergroup flare-ups can easily happen — and each flare-up that occurs has the potential to damage or destroy the Peace that exists for any setting.

Flare-ups can do damage and can do it in very short periods of time.

Intergroup flare-ups that happen in any setting should be addressed quickly. Flare-ups that occur in any setting should each be handled in ways that do not exacerbate the inherent us/them instinctive reactions and perceptions that exist in any intergroup setting.

Explosions are much harder to undo once they have occurred. It is very hard to un-explode anything.

Avoidance of explosions is the better strategy. Negative intergroup interactions tend to be much harder to deal with once they build momentum and after people in any setting get us/them instincts strongly activated in their minds.

Keeping the Peace in any setting involves both averting and avoiding intergroup explosions and diminishing or defusing those explosions quickly when they occur.

Our us/them instincts can explode Peace quickly once they are triggered. It can be a short and very slippery slope to intergroup anger and to negative intergroup behavior in many intergroup settings.

So preventing intergroup anger is good and reducing or diverting that anger in any setting can be essential to long-term Peace for that setting.

We Need to Be Careful to Not Open Old Wounds

When we have an understanding between groups and when we are building good will between groups of people in any setting, we need to be careful to not do things or say things that can open old wounds or reactivate old suspicions or old angers.

It can take relatively little to undermine Peace in many settings. The wrong words can do real damage. Inflammatory language can sometimes relatively easily undermine a state of Peace.

Insults can be explosive and purely destructive for both amity and trust.

People who either intentionally or unintentionally use pejorative, insulting, or demeaning terms to describe the other groups in any setting can trigger emotional responses in the other group that can undermine Peace.

The use of pejorative terms can also cause negative instincts to be activated in the person who is using the language. Some pejorative words and thought processes create their own negative self-activation.

Doing symbolic and visible things that are insulting or offensive or damaging relative to the other groups can create obvious and overt threats to intergroup Peace.

Negative Symbols Should Be Avoided

Some people either intentionally or unintentionally display various kinds of explicit symbols that are perceived to be either insults to the other group, attacks on the other group, or insensitive reminders of prior attacks or earlier damage that had been done to the other group at some points in their past.

Those symbols should be avoided. Swastikas, for example, are obvious symbolic attacks on the groups of people who were murdered by the Nazis.

Confederate flags can be equally obvious symbolic attacks on people whose ancestors were enslaved by the soldiers who flew those flags over the Civil War battlefields where a key operational and functional goal for the soldiers who were in those battles, and who flew those flags over their own forces was to continue to enslave, oppress, degrade, damage, and actually own other human beings.

Displaying pictures of the Prophet Mohamed in settings where that display is considered to be a blasphemous thing to do also has the obvious impact of being inflammatory. People who are affected by those kinds of visual points are often deeply offended at those kinds of visual displays.

Pretending Not to Understand Is Disingenuous

Deeply offending someone in an intentional and deliberate way with any kind of visual display is obviously not a good foundation for building Peace with that person or for building Peace with the group of people that person represents.

Anyone who feels the need to do something in a public way that they know is deeply offensive to someone else should try to be very honest with themselves about their own existing motivations and about the full layers of underlying divisive intent that might exist for their own behavior.

Pretending not to understand those issues or pretending not to understand the impact of those kinds of symbols on other people is clearly disingenuous for the people who are pretending. If people feel a need to do something that they know absolutely will be perceived as a symbolic attack on other people, the person doing the attack should have the personal honesty to admit their entire goal to themselves and to be open and honest — at least to themselves — about their entire array of intentions and goals.

We can't just say — "I would not be personally offended if they said something like that to me — so therefore they should not be offended if I say that to Them."

If we want to bring people together to create a collective agenda where all groups of people do well, and where all of the groups mutually do win, and if we want to live in a setting where all groups collectively do thrive — then using any visual symbols or any symbolic actions that trigger negative us/them responses at a visual and visceral level for any of the people in that setting obviously puts any Peace that exists in that setting between those sets of people at risk.

People Who Display Offensive Material Intend to Offend

That piece of information is generally not a new insight for the people who actually do chose to display offensive materials in many settings.

The inflammatory symbolic behavior that happens is sometimes truly innocent, but more often than not, the people who display those inflammatory visual symbols do intend to put Peace at risk in that setting.

That is often their direct, clear, and purposeful functional goal for performing that negative function in that setting and in those particular ways.

The goal of anyone who displays a swastika or who wears one on his or her clothes is clearly not to bring us all together as a people. The pure act of wearing or showing or displaying those symbols is an aggressive and intensive act directed against the other group in its own right.

When those displays do happen, we need to take the time to talk to each of the people actually doing the display — with the intent of educating the people doing the display about the impact of their actions and, hopefully, converting those people to the cause of the intergroup Peace.

Conversions do happen. Some people are uninformed rather than malicious or evil. The attempt to do a conversion for the people who are uninformed is clearly worth the effort.

If conversions do not happen, however, then the other people in that setting who do want Peace to succeed need to reject those kinds of negative and damaging of behaviors and need to reject those insulting and attacking behaviors publicly and explicitly.

Clarity and speed in responding to those kinds of inflammatory symbols can be both useful for keeping the Peace and useful for restoring the Peace in any setting.

Other People from That Same Group Need to Disavow and Reject the Pejorative Action or Symbol

It is important to recognize that in the settings in our country where those negative and hate-based symbols are used, usually only a very small minority of the people in that setting from the group who is doing the insulting behaviors actually, personally and deliberately, are taking those kinds of offensive actions and intentionally displaying those kinds of negative symbols.

But because we all tend to think in terms of both group identity and group behaviors, those symbolic acts by any individuals, from any group, can easily be perceived as a symbolic attack from their entire group.

In those situations — when those kinds of inflammatory and symbolic events do happen — then other people from the group who has a disruptive person making those kinds of pejorative and offensive statements need to step forward and openly disavow and explicitly condemn that behavior by their fellow group member or members.

That public step by other and more enlightened people from that group to clearly disavow the symbols of hate and to publically reject and condemn the explicit emblems of intergroup damage can be very healing. It can put the behavior of the hateful people in that setting into context as being outlier behavior, and it can create bridges for the people who have been insulted to the people who openly and publicly reject the negative act.

Having other people for the group disavow those negative symbolic behaviors from a group member can be good for Peace in any setting.

That is an important strategy for maintaining intergroup Peace.

When people in any setting make those kinds of negative and disrespectful visual statements, then the rest of us in that setting who do respect the other group, and who do want InterGroup Peace to survive in that setting, need to explicitly disavow that specific negative symbolism and we need to reject it very directly and clearly in visible ways.

As a core Peace maintaining strategy, we need to use our collective cultural impact as reasonable and caring people to keep the most offensive symbols from being used.

In cases where those particular symbols are used, we need to make it very clear that the vast majority of people in that setting from the group who has people exhibiting the negative symbols are not in favor of slavery, concentration camps, death camps, or any kind of deliberate disparagement and intentional disrespect for anyone's deep religious beliefs.

We need to tell the people in our own groups who do chose to use inflammatory and hateful symbolism that their behavior is unacceptable to us as their "Us"— and we need to make that collective opinion very real to the people who are being attacked and insulted by those symbols.

Our negative us/them instincts tend to trigger seductive negative group behavior when those kinds of symbols and inflammatory language is in play. We need to resist the temptation to be sucked into that behavior and we need to signal clearly that we reject both the intent and the behavior.

We Need Freedom of Speech Without Direct Attacks

Some people who display those symbols say that they are not being symbolic and that they only display those symbols as a personal linkage to their own ancestors who actually were soldiers who fought under the Nazi symbol or under the Confederate banners.

Those people sometimes say they are simply honoring their own ancestors by sharing those symbols externally and they say that they do not intend to be attacking any other people by those symbol displays.

There is a useful way to test that contention and see those people are telling the truth about that issue. Once the full symbolism of those flags or those emblems as symbols of evil to entire groups of people is explained to those people in a clear and thoughtful way, then the decisions that are made by those people who are displaying the symbols about their personal future display and about their own personal future use of the offending symbol, tells us fairly clearly what their actual motives are and what their real intentions are.

There are obviously many other very effective ways of displaying respect for one's own grandparents and for one's own ancestors that do not involve celebrating death camps or human bondage.

Freedom of Speech Needs to Be Protected

Peace can be at risk if we don't reject those kinds of negative symbolism and if we don't make that collective belief and our collective rejection of those behaviors both obvious and real when those kinds of events happen.

That is not to say that freedom of speech should be attacked or undermined in any way.

Freedom of speech is an extremely important part of our culture, our values, and our functionality and our survival as a people. Freedom of speech helps keep us free and it keeps us functioning as a nation that governs itself in a democratic way.

We need to protect freedom of speech.

Our strength as a nation is heavily dependent on the fact that we do have freedom of speech and the fact that each of us can express our beliefs and our values openly and clearly without the kinds of retribution and negative consequences that happen in so many settings in other places in the world where freedom of speech doesn't exist.

It is a blessing to have free speech. It is also a strength and an asset. That benefit of that freedom for us all is obviously very true.

Freedom of speech is included in the 12 basic beliefs that are outlined in the last chapter of this book that give us a set of shared beliefs we can collectively commit to together as a key part of being an American "Us." We need to support freedom of speech.

At the same time, we need to be sensitive to using that freedom in ways that are offensive or painful to other people or groups of people.

We can have both free speech and respectful speech. Maintaining Peace involves making respectful choices not to insult or attack or demean other people.

Clear expression of opinion is a good thing. That clear expression can be done without attacking the beliefs or the dignity of other people.

Hate speech that is clearly and intentionally intended to do damage and to inspire hatred and anger can be outlawed without undermining our overall freedom of speech.

We Need a Larger Sense of "Us"

The fact that the last issue needed to be addressed points out another reason why Peace can be at risk and explains why Peace needs to be protected.

There are constant levels of intergroup risk that exist anytime we have more than one group in a setting. Every multi-group setting is at risk for having some kind of trigger issue or trigger event divide the groups in ways that could activate those sets of us/them instincts. We need to be aware of those risks and we need to be sensitive to them.

We need to create intergroup harmony and then we need to protect that harmony from the instinctive challenges it will inevitably face.

We can't afford to let ourselves slip backward into increasing levels of intergroup tribal behaviors at the exact point in our history where we should be turning our growing diversity into a national strength.

We need to come together at this point rather than pull apart. We need to protect the collective sense of being an American us against its inevitable challenges.

The primary key to maintaining Peace at this point in our history is to create, protect, nourish, and maintain a larger sense of "Us" that involves all of the various groups that make up America as the component parts of our functioning Peace coalition.

Having a collective sense of American Us is a powerful and effective way of creating and protecting the context we need to anchor an American culture of Peace.

Converting Enemies of Peace to Peace Is a Good Strategy

As noted earlier, the Peace coalition that we create will always be at risk from people who don't want Peace. It will always be at risk from people who will deliberately trigger a sense of them and who will deliberately and intentionally activate various behaviors and communications approaches that are aimed at damaging or angering them.

We need to understand that those people exist. We need to try to convert those people to the side of Peace wherever we can. The best response to a former foe can often be to convert them to be an enlightened and sincere friend. That can be done.

Many people who do negative intergroup things today do those negative intergroup things to be loyal to their own group. They aren't necessarily doing negative things for the sake of being negative. They want to help their "Us" succeed.

We Need to Convert War Chiefs to Leaders for Peace

We need to expand the sense of "Us" and we need to have those people understand the benefits of win/win outcomes in a way that makes wins for all groups something we can all support.

In a best-case outcome, we should try to make the current intergroup war leaders in any setting an asset for Peace rather than a liability for Peace.

If we can't convert those people to the cause of Peace, then we need to minimize their impact and we need to offset their damage when that is the best option available to us.

A key part of The Art of InterGroup Peace strategy is to help those people who want their own group to win to appreciate the value of connecting to a win/win strategy for all groups as part of our Peace agenda.

If conversion is impossible and fails, then we need to be very aware of the threats those people can create. We need to deal with each of those threats effectively and well when they happen.

We need to know who is working to destroy and undermine Peace and we need to deal with their behaviors in ways that keep the worst set of instincts from damaging us in any setting.

Common Danger, Shared Values, Collective Gain Can Unify Us and Protect Peace

A major strategy we need to use to protect Peace is to build on the commonalities that bring us together.

Some of the key alignment factors that were described earlier in the pyramid that was outlined in chapter three of this book — a sense of common danger, shared values, shared concerns, common enemies, and a collective agreement about shared strategies — are all good and functional tools to use to both trigger and protect Peace.

Those six alignment triggers that are outlined and described in Chapter Seven can help tie and link people together in ways that allow for the creation and the existence of additional levels of intergroup alignment and intergroup Peace.

Those same six triggers can also be used to protect that Peace once it is in place. We can achieve that Peace in particular settings, and for significant periods of time. We can aim to create a national agenda of Peace for the entire country by using that set of functional alignment tools clearly and well.

Tools Can Be Used for Good or Evil

At the same time, we need to be aware and cautious that those same alignment instincts and that same set of tools that are described in Chapter Seven to bring people together can also be used in a negative way by skilled and divisive leaders to pull some parts of our coalition for Peace away from our collective "Us" to become a separate and conflicted divided segment of internal "Them."

That is a very real risk. Those basic alignment tools can align all of us, but they can also be used to split us and to align and realign subsets of us into isolation and separation from the rest of us.

Creating a sense of a common enemy for a specific subset of our Peace coalition can be very easy for someone who opposes Peace to do, for example.

The subset of people in any setting who then begin to perceive that common enemy to exist will often decide to group together and to align as a separate subgroup to resist that enemy in ways that functionally pull those internally aligned people away from our collective us.

Skillful and negatively motivated leaders for various groups who want division to happen in any setting can use each and all of those basic six alignment triggers to make division of some sets of people into their own militant and internally aligned "Us" happen.

We Need People to Understand Current Stress Points

We need to be very aware of the risks to Peace that will always continue to exist based on any of the component groups in the Peace coalition having their own us/them instincts activated in a negative way that creates separatist behavior.

There are significant levels of intergroup stress in our country today. Those stress levels can become anger levels based on incidents and on behaviors and those stress levels can cause real division and separation in various settings and communities.

We need to understand that intergroup stress risk and we need to know why it exists.

To preserve the most effective levels of our common agendas and to create mutual understanding, over time, we need to collectively be aware of how differently various groups of people in this country look at issues of race and ethnicity today.

To create intergroup Peace in our settings and to protect the Peace we create, we need to be very honest about those differences.

We need to do what needs to be done — when necessary — to keep a combination of old divisions, bad history, and new trigger events from segmenting our new Peace coalition into conflicted and angry Us and Them subsets in the future.

We need to clearly understand what our old patterns of behavior have been in order to build a new pattern that can achieve Peace.

White Advantages Are Often Invisible to White People

White Americans often significantly underestimate the impact of both race and racial prejudices on key pieces of our history, our society, and our economy. That is an area where education can be very useful relative to creating the next set of strategies that can be used to attain Peace.

Peace is actually at risk if White people in America don't have a clear sense of that history and a clear understanding of those continuing intergroup perceptions held by the rest of America.

We need education for White Americans on those basic intergroup issues and we need other groups to have a sense that those education efforts have been successful.

It will not be easy to have some groups of people in this country believe that White Americans are now ready for the next level of intergroup equality and intergroup benefit without some conscious recognition by White Americans of the long history of discrimination that we have had as a country and without open recognition of the clear patterns of intergroup inequality that have favored White Americans over other groups for our entire history as a nation.

The point of achieving this understanding on those issues at this point in time is not to blame or attack White Americans.

The personal advantages that have existed for White Americans that are part of the current and historic American experience were not created, invented, designed, architected, or implemented by each and all of the White Americans who are alive in America today as a strategy of deliberate positive differentiation in multiple areas for people who are White.

Those advantages of being White do exist — but they have stemmed from a societal and cultural implementation of key behavioral elements and basic thought processes that are anchored directly in our us/them instinct packages.

That implementation of those various advantages for their own group was not done deliberately or consciously by White Americans functioning today as a conspiracy strategy.

The behavior patterns that have created those advantages for White Americans are instinctive. The benefits that exist are personal, but they are not intentional — and those beliefs were not created by people at a personal level and then somehow implemented as part of any actual plan or strategy.

White Americans often do not have a clear perception of the various personal advantages in multiple areas that accrue to being White — because the reality is that those advantages functionally tend to be visible clearly only to people who do not have those advantages in their own lives.

The advantages of being White often have the lowest visibility to people who are actually White — and they tend to be most visible to the people who haven't had the benefits that those advantages entail and create for White people.

We Have Made Major Areas of Discrimination Illegal

Overall, we are far more enlightened today across all of America on various intergroup issues than we have ever been. We now have laws that make many kinds of discrimination illegal.

Those laws have emerged in a positive way from a growing sense, by the White Americans who have been making the laws of this country, that the old intergroup approaches were ethically, morally, and functionally inappropriate and often entirely wrong.

That enlightenment on those specific sets of issues is relatively recent, but it is very real for many people. The majority of Americans now believes in those new values. Those new intergroup interaction values are far superior to the values we held as a nation just a few decades ago.

We have laws that now make discrimination illegal — and those are very enlightened laws. We should celebrate and protect those laws and we should respect and honor the fact that White Americans who were in positions of power when those laws passed have made the ethical decisions to share that power in inclusive ways through passing those laws.

Majority Tribes in Other Countries Are Often Less Enlightened

We are not seeing the majority tribes in many other countries in the world voluntarily making those same kinds of enlightened choices about inclusion of their minority people.

Minority people in Saudi Arabia or Japan or Fiji or the Dominican Republic are still second-class citizens at a very fundamental, direct, and intentional level and that isn't likely to change in any time soon.

For our White Americans, those new sets of more enlightened laws didn't create a new access to some entirely new level of personal opportunity — because the old level of access to opportunity was already very effective and available for White Americans.

That opportunity change that is resulting from those new laws is most obvious to the people who were denied opportunity in the past. The full impact of that change has been less visible to the White Americans who have always had those particular opportunity levels as a fact of life.

So our collective progress as a nation is clearly real and clearly significant — but we still do need White Americans to understand why significant resentment levels still exist and we need White Americans to know what the old behaviors and the old advantages actually have been for their group.

One way of dealing with that specific set of issues very directly with people from all groups could be to share this book and its sister books with other people who read and to point out those issues of our long history of discrimination explicitly and directly as facts of life for many people in this country.

This book was written in part to function as a tool that gives people both a mechanism and an intellectual context to use to explicitly discuss those historical intergroup issues, to recognize that reality, and to sympathize and empathize with the people who have felt pain as the result of those historic behaviors and realities.

We Need to Understand the Powerful and Negative Input of Us/Them Instincts on Our History

It is a significant risk to intergroup Peace not to understand that our history has given us an unfortunate context where significant intergroup damages have clearly occurred over long periods of time for many people in our country. For Americans from our minority groups, the memory of those wrong doings continues to make that history relevant and real today.

That is very true in those settings where discriminatory situations are still happening today and it is true even in those settings where there are no current traces of either intergroup conflict or wrong and discriminating behaviors.

Each painful category of historic discrimination still leaves some scars and angry memories.

The fact that people of all races and all ethnic groups — and both genders — can vote today does not erase the memory that getting that vote was a painful experience for many people and that there were multiple occurrences of very ugly, painful, and powerful intergroup interactions that occurred as that more enlightened voting rights process unfolded.

Even today, there are settings in our country where voting rights still can be impeded by new laws that create various barriers to voting for some people.

The new laws that focus on voter identification issues don't create explicit barriers to voting by group or race, but the functional impact of those laws can have that same potential effect in some settings.

Minority Americans who could not vote at all a relatively few years ago, can clearly see echoes of those clear patterns of historic vote-denying behavior that are embedded again in the new voting laws.

The impact of restricting voting access is obviously not a new pattern of behavior. Those current voting concerns and issues are tied to the intergroup memory of absolute voting discrimination for many people.

So the new approaches that make voter identification rules more stringent can easily look and feel like a linear extension of the old practices and the old approaches to people who were unable to vote in the past. Those memories have not faded.

Likewise, the collective memories for Black Americans about the Civil Rights protests just a few decades ago, when White people in police uniforms brutalized them with batons, unleashed dogs on them, or sprayed water from their fire hoses into the crowds of black people who were seeking to vote, or to ride on the front section of a city bus, or who were just trying to sit and eat at a public lunch counter have not faded for many African Americans.

Those memories are regularly reinforced by the old news film that was taken of those events and that is increasingly being replayed when there is a reason to replay it.

We also have had those memories collectively jogged recently by the powerful Ken Burns specials on racial issues in America and by intergroup issues movies, like *Selma*, that retell those stories with clarity and skill.

All of that history is good to understand — and the replay of those events through all of those communication approaches has the inevitable impact of resurrecting group anger that is justified by those behaviors.

The Films Re-Trigger InterGroup Anger

It is easy to both trigger and renew intergroup anger when those news films and those movies about racial issues and injustices are shown. Evil and cruel things were done in this country by people to other people because of their race.

The truth is that the white people who held those fire hoses or who wielded those baseball bats in those settings look just like other white people look today. As noted earlier in this book, we tend to link our us/them emotions to how people look and we tie them to how people sound and we do both linkages at a very basic and instinctive level.

White people today do not have those particular fire hoses in hand today — but the memories of those hoses exist today for Black and minority Americans and white people who look just like those 'hose holders' exist today as well.

It is easy to link those facts and those perceptions at an instinctive level. The anger that is and was directed at the first set of real people who actually had those damaging hoses in their hands can fairly easily spill over to be directed against the other sets of people who look just like those people — white people today.

There are multiple areas where our values and our behavioral expectations are significantly more enlightened today — but our memory of prior enlightened behaviors has not gone away and we need White Americans today to understand why the scars and the angers from those particular events have not disappeared and are still relevant today.

Shootings of Unarmed Teenagers Trigger Protests

That set of issues is made even more relevant by more current events — like the shooting of an unarmed Black teenager in Ferguson, Missouri by a White policeman, or the shooting of an unarmed Black teenager by a White policeman in Oakland, California — that triggered protests and street demonstrations by angry and saddened people in both settings.

There have been a number of highly visible similar incidents recently where a police officer, who is not Black, has killed an unarmed person who is Black. Those incidents are serving as catalysts for collective intergroup anger in a number of settings.

The "Black Lives Matter" movement is gaining strength and has resulted in protests and demonstrations in multiple cities and on a number of college campuses.

The existence of intergroup Peace in this country is put at risk by each of those trigger events. People who are angry because unemployment levels for minority Americans are high and who are angry because incarceration rates for minority Americans are even higher look at those incidents as absolute proof for intentional patterns of intergroup damage in those settings.

There are enough current and very real disadvantages that still exist, at least situationally, for many minority Americans today to have that entire set of historical and current experiences feel like a complete package.

Any clearly discriminatory event that happens today has the ability to trigger longitudinal memory recall for all of the discriminatory things that are part of our history.

Overall, as a country, African Americans are six times more likely to be arrested than White Americans. We have more people in jail than any country in the world by a large margin — and the majority of our prisoners come from our minority populations.

Each incident that happens today in this country has the ability to unleash the collective impact of those negative behaviors and those negative realities.

The recent widely publicized demonstrations in Ferguson, Missouri were about a shooting at one level — but they were more about the pent up anger of a local Black population regarding the high unemployment levels, high levels of incarcerations, and a strong sense of on-going discrimination at multiple levels.

Those issues are discussed in the next chapter of this book. They do put Peace at risk. They also create opportunities to make Peace happen.

Those issues also give us a very public context that we should use to build better levels of intergroup Peace. We need to look at what each of those incidents teach us about our reality today — and we should use that learning to help us solve the key issues rather than have them drive us farther apart.

Win/Win Requires Clarity About the Actual Win by Each Group

We have some major stress points directly in front of us that each put Peace at risk. We clearly need to deal with immigration as an issue. We need immigration laws that meet the needs of Americans to achieve the American Dream — and we need immigration laws that do not inflame intergroup anger levels.

We need immigration laws that protect Americans from being damaged by issues relating to immigration. All groups who have an interest in immigration as a key topic need to look for win/win solutions for that issue. Win/win is the key.

Win/win solutions can fail and can cause Peace to fail if the solutions used in any setting are weak and if each group in a win/win strategy does not actually have its own core needs met. For win/win success to happen, each group actually needs to understand its own core needs, so that it can know when they are being met.

Each group also needs to understand and respect the legitimate core needs of the other group. That understanding needs to be part of the Peace process.

This chapter of this book is about the various sets of things that can put Peace at risk or can cause Peace to fail.

The risk of failure increases when people in any setting are not clearly benefiting from an intergroup situation. The likelihood of achieving Peace, in any setting, is much higher if groups in that setting do clearly understand their own needs and if the groups who understand their needs can achieve them in the context of a win/win strategy.

The Mixture of Relevant Groups Is Changing in Many Settings

In each setting where we want to achieve intergroup Peace, we need to know who the relevant groups actually are for the setting.

The set of relevant groups is changing in many settings as we become more diverse. We now have a wide range of relevant intergroup interactions in our various settings.

The old dynamic and the historic context of having local intergroup situations that were almost always defined and structured as involving a White majority group, and one or more local minority groups, who deal collectively in various ways with the White majority group on community power issues is fading.

We now have multiple groups in many settings. Each group is relevant.

The situation of determining which groups should be included in our win/win strategies in each setting is now much more complex in many settings. Settings are more complex — and each local group needs to be relevant to the process and included in the strategy in order for the intergroup Peace process to succeed in any setting.

In any local area, the relevant groups, in addition to the White group, might be local concentrations of immigrants from a particular country — like Japan, Vietnam, China, or Russia — or the relevant groups might be the traditional Hispanic and African American minority groups.

We Need to Understand Which Groups and Which Leaders Are Relevant for Each Setting

Different settings have different intergroup mixtures and realities.

Peace can be at risk if we don't involve the right groups in each setting in the Peace process.

Peace is also at risk if we don't have the Peace that we create in each setting negotiated by people who their group accepts and recognizes as the leaders in that setting who have the legitimate standing and the personal power to actually negotiate the deal.

The issues of who should be doing the deal for each group in each setting are not always obvious. We need to determine in each situation which leaders have the standing needed to negotiate and lead Peace.

Our increasing diversity can make that a challenge. Some settings have entirely new majority groups. Others have no majority and are a combination of various minority groups.

The new sets of intergroup relationships that will increasingly drive and dominate both the political and economic agendas in a number of areas will now need to be new relationships between the various minority groups who have grown to be the major players in each setting.

In a number of settings — like Los Angeles or Oakland — the key intergroup relations and the new intergroup competition is now black and brown rather than black and white or brown and white.

Chinese American communities are also growing rapidly and are increasingly relevant to the political process in many settings. Vietnamese, Hmong, Scandinavian, and Korean populations hold majority status in some communities.

The African American, Asian American, and Hispanic battles for control of school boards, county boards, and city councils are now the most relevant local political power issues in a growing number of settings.

In those increasingly complex settings, we can either come to a situation where we strive in positive ways for intergroup understanding and alignment — or we can deteriorate into us/them instinctive behaviors with us and them in a setting now being black and brown or multiple other intergroup interactions between the relevant local groups.

In a number of cities, the fastest growing local group is now from one ore more of our Asian American populations. The Asian American populations each tend to maintain their separate identities. Japanese Americans and Chinese Americans and Vietnamese Americans who each have population concentrations in various cities are not melding into a generic Asian group. Each of those ethnic groups tends to keep its separate identity and to create its own local cultural reality.

So we have an increasing number of settings where the new intergroup reality is that there are multiple groups — each with its own relevance and each with its own power base.

In each setting, our goal for overall local intergroup relations should be community synergy rather than intergroup division. Understanding how to do win/win negotiating among all relevant groups in each setting can be key to the basic Peace process we need for each setting.

We need the people from each group who are coming to the community discussions and negotiating situations with the goal of creating win/win results for the whole community in ways that also achieve wins for each group.

That can take real creativity — and it takes a very clear recognition of how local most intergroup solutions now need to be.

The Best Negotiators Help the Other Side Win as Well

We need people who lead all groups who want their own group to do well and who also support having all other groups to do well as well.

We need leaders who understand that their groups win when all groups win.

As noted earlier in the win/win chapter of this book, the very best negotiators in any setting not only help their own side figure out their winning issues — they also very often help the other side figure out their own winning set of goals and objectives. Doing that entire win/win approach well very directly minimizes the risks to Peace.

Really good negotiators in any setting can help the people on both sides of the negotiations be able to understand and articulate their own clear definition of a win.

The best negotiators do that work for both sides very intentionally because negotiations in any setting that result in mutual wins, that are clearly perceived by all parties to be mutual wins, are much more likely to be perpetuated and much more likely to survive over time than negotiations that end up with either one-sided results, or with outcomes that are so bad and so unfortunate that neither side achieves a win and both sides end up with a loss of some kind.

Peace is at risk when any of those results involving losses happen.

One-sided deals tend to be killed at the first available opportunity — often with a significant amount of ill will and even anger involved. Actual lose/lose situations often simply collapse of their own accord.

Those kinds of agreement collapses can easily damage one or both parties, particularly if they collapse in unfortunate ways.

Parties who negotiate a deal in good faith in any setting can become angry and can feel betrayed if the other party collapses the deal and reneges on the agreements after the deal is negotiated.

That scenario of having a deal fail can make relevant people extremely angry and — when us/them instincts are activated by the collapsed deal — vindictive.

Vindictive is a dangerous motivation for any intergroup setting.

Lose/Lose Strategies Clearly Put Peace at Risk

The worst results in many settings — and the highest risks to Peace in almost any setting — are not the win/lose results but the lose/lose strategies and results. Lose/lose situations sometimes emerge accidently when win/lose efforts fail.

Lose/lose situations can also happen in far too many instances when one of the parties in a setting deliberately aims for a lose/lose outcome for all parties.

When people really hate other people in any setting, then lose/lose situations that create a loss for one side so that one can inflict a larger loss on their side are far too common.

Those behaviors obviously create risks for Peace. They are not a hypothetical concern. People strapping bombs to their own body so they can kill "Them" by dying themselves as a 'suicide-bomber' actually happen every day somewhere in the world.

Groups of people in multiple settings who are driven by hatred often create lose/lose situations as their intergroup strategy. That is a particularly sad, destructive, dysfunctional, and damaging set of strategic choices, but it is clearly one that motivates some people, and it is a reality that needs to be addressed.

When Peace deteriorates in any given setting — triggered by an incident or an insult or any kind of clearly perceived negative intergroup behavior — anger can be triggered and that anger can take people from win/win strategies past win/lose strategies all the way to the levels of hate and anger that inspires lose/lose strategies and vindictive and mutually destructive thinking.

Revenge, rather than wins, can become a key motivator. That is a very bad path to be on. Peace is very much at risk when that happens. Peace can be destroyed. People can be hurt badly.

Peace Is at Risk if Wins Are Not Wins

So win/win is obviously the best set of strategies to pursue to reduce the risk for Peace — and it is an approach worth achieving and defending for multiple reasons. Win/win needs to be not only a philosophy and a commitment — it needs to be a skill set.

Negotiated terms and mutual agreements that can achieve win/win outcomes in any setting can do wonderful things for everyone involved in the process.

The likelihood of Peace surviving over time is diminished, however, if people do not feel that their own group is having its key and important needs met. That perception of not winning can turn into the source of real conflict if one party withdraws or breaks the deal and if the other party feels betrayed by the change in status.

Lose/lose situations need to be avoided. Members of any group whose leaders are choosing lose/lose strategies need to look hard at the leaders who they have in place to see if the leadership needs to be replaced in order to return to win/win approaches to intergroup interactions.

When any party in any setting becomes committed to lose/lose results, great energy needs to be diverted in helping those people understand the range of alternatives to those strategies.

Defusing hatred is hard – but it is not impossible. Taking steps to defuse hatred needs to be part of the goals and strategies for the other party in those lose/lose settings, because the consequences of double losing can be so devastating to everyone.

The Negotiators Need to Be Accepted and Have Authority

Community leaders who bring people together to create a sense of inter-ethnic Peace need to be people who have the perceived legitimacy and the standing with their own people to have credibility on those issues and to speak with authority on behalf of their own people.

Having credible negotiations for each side is essential for having the people in any setting accept the deals done by their negotiators. The Art of InterGroup Peace can be best implemented when people believe their leaders have the standing and the legitimacy to negotiate for Peace.

It is often a good tactic for leaders who aspire to achieve Peace to support the credibility of the leaders of the other group who are involved in designing and creating intergroup Peace.

Taking steps to give credibility to the leaders on the other side in a situation can be a very good thing to do when that credibility gives those leaders on the other side the support they need to put Peace in place.

It is a risk to create Peace that isn't built on the work of credible leaders for either side.

The next chapter of this book deals with some basic and fundamental intergroup stress points and realities we need to understand before we can put a credible Peace in place in most settings.

Success is possible — but, it won't happen because of either magical thinking, wishful thinking, or strategies based on optimism and good will, rather than reality and practical decision-making.

We need to understand issues for Peace to happen and survive.

CHAPTER SIXTEEN
Multiple Issues Create the Stress and Anger That Triggers the Explosions

ANYONE WHO WANTS to either believe or pretend to believe that significant, meaningful, and relevant racial and intergroup stress points do not exist in this country today, is having that belief crushed by very visible and clear instances of collective intergroup anger that have happened recently in several American cities.

We have recently seen fairly major and very public explosions of intergroup anger in a number of our communities. Those explosions have generally been triggered by an intergroup death. In each case, large numbers of people from specific communities have gone to the streets in protests and demonstrations that have, in the heat of intergroup anger, sometimes turned from demonstrations and protests into mobs and actual riots.

Intergroup anger was clear in each setting. Each of those sets of protests was triggered by a killing, but the killings were not, on their own merit, the cause of the collective anger in those communities.

The killings in each case actually unleashed the anger that existed in those settings rather than creating it.

The Killings Unleashed the Anger Rather Than Creating It

Those community explosions in those cities each happened because there was a significant level of intergroup tension and intergroup anger in those settings that existed before the trigger events actually occurred.

When people in a community go to the streets in large numbers immediately after a trigger event or incident, it is fairly clear, most of the time, that the actual trigger event did not create that collective anger as much as it uncovered, exposed, and released basic levels of collective anger that already existed in that setting.

The anger in the most recent instances that created national visibility in our news media had a channel for release as intergroup anger for Black Americans, because the person who died in several of those settings was Black and the person in each setting who did the killing was White.

An African American youth was shot and killed by a White policeman in one case. An African American youth was shot and killed by a White neighborhood-watch person in another case. An African American youth was shot and killed by a White police reserve officer in a third case.

In another recent case that also triggered demonstrations and protests, an adult African American was choked to death, on the street by a White policeman.

The communities in each setting where a death occurred reacted to the death immediately with protests and demonstrations.

People were angry in each of those settings. There have also been sympathy marches in multiple other settings around the country that tied back to each of those events. A movement called "Black Lives Matter" is gaining ground in a number of settings as a way to express concern and anger about those events and about what the events, themselves, say about issues relating to police behavior and intergroup stress points in America.

The recent street protests in Oakland, California; Ferguson, Missouri; Miami, Florida and New York City, all showed that those towns have significant numbers of angry people whose anger became evident and visible in those settings in the direct context of those life-ending events.

To understand why those explosions happened and to deal with a wide range of relevant intergroup issues and intergroup behaviors more effectively and well, we need to better understand the overall situation and the functional and perceptual reality that creates those angry and sometimes volatile reactions in those communities.

To create intergroup Peace for communities in America, we need to do a better job of understanding and anticipating those explosions. We also need to do a much better job of preventing those blow-ups. We need to keep the worst aspects of those events from happening and we need much better approaches for dealing with those kinds of events when they do happen.

Multiple Issues Caused the Explosions

Those are multiple issues at play in each of the communities where those riots and protests happened. Minority citizens who went to the streets in each of those settings clearly felt that they have been damaged in various ways. The demonstrations in those cities gave the people in those settings a mechanism to display their anger.

The demonstrations also gave the people in each setting a way to feel the sense of solidarity and the levels of mutual comfort that can be created by group activity when the group activity is done for a "righteous" cause on behalf of a clear "Us."

When the facts of any particular case seem to be clear relative to the intergroup nature of an event, then the people whose group has been wronged can feel a sense of affirming solidarity as an "Us" by publically demonstrating as an "Us" against whoever damaged a member of their group.

People who are feeling individual anger about intergroup issues for any number of reasons can find it to be affirming and reinforcing to be able to exhibit that anger collectively with other angry people. People who have felt isolated, alone, and unheard as individuals with underlying levels of anger can find the experience of being in a mass demonstration with other angry people to be a reinforcing and reaffirming experience.

Several sets of instinctive behaviors are relevant to those settings.

Feeling Wronged Triggers Collective Responses

Feeling wronged by "Them" triggers entire packages of behaviors.

Getting together in a collective group setting with people who directly trigger a sense of "Us" and a sense that "our us" has been damaged in a way that deserves our collective anger can be an energizing experience. People with those behaviors activated can find the experience of being angry together to be instinctively energizing and even, to some degree, sometimes rewarding.

That anger for the people who are angry existed in each setting before each killing. The killing in each setting gave the anger a focus and the demonstrations in each setting gave the anger a forum.

There are clear reasons why people in those communities feel that on-going collective underlying level of stress and group anger. There are significant problems for large numbers of people in those settings. Those cities tend to have very high percentages of minority youth going to jail for various offences.

High school drop out rates are high. Unemployment levels are high. Learning gaps between groups are significant, and they are not being reduced.

Both the economic issues and the criminal justice issues in those communities create settings and situations where minority group members feel both disempowered and angry.

Police Force Relations Tend to Be Strained

There are strong feelings and strong beliefs in those communities that high levels of discrimination exist and are very real. The relationships of those communities with their police forces tend to range from strained and tense in the better sites, to active conflict, on-going anger, intense distrust, and both dysfunctional and intentionally negative interpersonal and intergroup interactions at multiple levels in the most problematic sites.

Instead of the police force being seen as a protective "Us" in those communities, there is a general perception from many residents that the police in their community are a category of "Them" and that the police need to be both distrusted and feared.

When the police are distrusted and when the police are feared by any significant percentage of the residents in an area, any visible police action that seems racist validates that distrust, and any police action that damages or kills someone from another racial group validates that fear.

That can be remedied. There are things that the best police departments do to reach out to communities to create alignment and trust. We need those "best practices" to happen in all of our communities where intergroup challenges exist.

The very best police forces reach out to create community trust. That makes communities safer for all people who live there — and has the police support as "Us" rather than being perceived to be a "Them."

We need those approaches everywhere.

We Have Instincts to Feel Stress When We Are Surrounded by Them

Those concerns, issues, and local intergroup realities and challenges are all reinforced by a powerful set of instincts that we have that are activated whenever we find ourselves in a minority status in a setting or a situation.

We tend not to be aware that those instincts exist, but they do exist. They have an impact on our thinking and behavior at multiple levels that we usually do not understand or appreciate.

We need to understand the reality that is created by those instincts as well as understanding the other relevant issues and situations that also trigger negative group perceptions and behaviors.

We need to recognize the simple fact and reality of any of us being in situational minority status far too often creates its own very stress provoking links to our own instinctive us/them mind set.

Some Instincts Are Triggered by Minority Status

We need to recognize the fact that we have relevant and important instinctive intergroup reactions that are triggered purely by our situational minority status.

Any time any of us find ourselves situationally in a minority setting, some basic instincts tend to be triggered in our own heads purely by our own situational minority status.

We each tend to feel stress whenever we are surrounded by "Them."

The simple fact of being in a minority status creates its own level of instinctive stress. That level of stress can create a negative context that we use to interpret other intergroup behaviors or events in our lives.

Simply being in a minority status in any setting generally creates its own set of instinctive reactions for each person who is in that current minority situation.

Those reactions tend not to be pleasant. We instinctively feel personal discomfort and we feel personal stress — usually at a subconscious level — whenever personally surrounded by people who might be "Them."

We Are All Uncomfortable Surrounded by Them

That is an important point to understand because being surrounded by "Them" is a very common occurrence for many people.

As we work to integrate our work places and our schools, the people who are at the front line of that integration — the minority people in any setting — tend to have those particular protective instincts situationally activated on a daily basis.

That stress level is triggered often by various integrated situations or integrated settings — and we very often do not understand the discomfort and the stress that we often feel in those settings.

When any of us from any group is in a setting where everyone around us is different in some common way from us as an individual — different race, different ethnicity, different religion, different gender, different culture, etc., — the mere fact us of being clearly different from the other people in any setting creates its own emotional and instinctive activation context in each of us for that situation and for that setting. We feel stress. Instinctive stress.

We tend to become basically uncomfortable as individuals in those settings and we often don't know exactly why we feel that way. That stress can cause us to have negative feelings about the situational majority group in that setting that often feels like it is being an intentional trigger for that stress.

Integration Creates Multiple Instances of Subconscious InterGroup Stress

The fact that we have made a conscious and well-intentioned decision as a country to integrate our society at multiple levels means that those negative feelings of being a situational minority are being triggered for a growing number of people in a growing number of settings.

We all need to understand the reality that if you are one of the first people to integrate a workplace, or if you are one of the first people to integrate a school, you are likely to feel constant levels of purely instinctive stress that is triggered at a perceptive level by your situational minority status.

Those feelings can make the experience of being the first person of any category to be included in a group of other people in any setting definitely unpleasant.

Those feelings create a complex set of interactions and behaviors.

People who feel situational minority stress often seek out any other people in that setting who might be an "Us" in that setting.

People who are the only White face in a room look instinctively for other white faces. People who are the only Hispanic person in a room look for other people with Hispanic heritage.

We feel comfort when we find another "Us" in any setting.

People Are Drawn to Us in Those Settings

Once we understand the impact of those instinctive reactions on our thinking and our emotions, it can be much easier to be a situational minority. It can also be much easier to make decisions to be with an "Us" in a work or a school setting.

It can very directly help reduce the stress levels for each of us when we recognize that the stress we are feeling is caused by an instinct and not by any truly negative aspect of a situation.

The book *Primal Pathways* explains those issues and those choices in more detail.

Those instincts for each of us to be uncomfortable when we are surrounded by any category of "Them" explain why we tend to live in such self-segregated communities and it explains why we pray in such segregated congregations.

We definitely prefer to pray with our "Us." Our religious sites tend to be highly concentrated by ethnic or racial group.

Learning to pray together in more ethnically and racially diverse settings might be a good way for many people to begin to create better and richer levels of interpersonal alignment and understanding.

The Majority People In a Setting Can Be Oblivious to the Stress

Because we don't understand the actual source and the cause of our sense of stress in those intergroup situations, it often feels that the stress is somehow being intentionally created by whoever is the situational majority in the setting.

Some people who feel that particular level of stress in a setting believe that the other people in that setting are being deliberate and intentional in creating the unpleasant aspects of the situation, and that those people are somehow at fault for creating that level of discomfort and stress.

In reality, most of the time, the majority people in the room or in the setting are actually almost completely oblivious to those stress points. The majority people are often totally unaware at any level of the stress being felt by whoever is the situational minority person in that setting. That lack of awareness tends to be the reality for those majority group people because the majority set of people in that setting are personally feeling no intergroup stress at any level in their own minds.

The majority group in most of those situations perceives itself to be in a safe group environment and people from that group generally have no sense that the minority person in the room has their own personal intergroup stress instincts activated.

So a situation that feels like a clear intergroup encounter of some kind to whoever is the situational minority in a setting might trigger almost zero levels of intergroup perceptions of any kind for the majority group people in that same room.

The exact same meeting and setting can feel very different for each set of people. The meeting can feel like it has rich and deep racial and ethnic undertones for some people and it can create absolutely no active sense of either ethnic or racial context for other people in the same room.

Feeling Constant Low Level Stress Is Stressful

That whole set of instincts is important to understand because the discomfort created for people by those situations can be very real and that discomfort creates a context for other intergroup interactions.

The instinctive alarms that can go off for each of us when we are in a minority situation create very real levels of discomfort and stress. Those feelings can be unpleasant. Creating discomfort is both their function and their goal.

The discomfort is intended to guide our behavior. We need to remember why those instincts exist.

They exist to save our lives.

Stress is created in those settings by our instincts to cause us and steer us each to avoid being surrounded by Them. The instinct that is being triggered in each of us by those situations wants us not to be near "Them" and not to ever be by "Them."

The goal is safety — our personal safety. That set of instincts tries to guide us to safe situations and to safe settings. Safe is a good thing to be.

Those instincts are ancient, but they are unfortunately relevant for large numbers of people today. Sadly, those sets of those instincts to feel stress when we are surrounded by "Them" actually do make very real sense much of the time in far too many settings in the world.

Many people live in parts of the world where "Them" is often dangerous. Entire villages have been massacred every year for the past several years by people who perceived those villages to be a category of "Them." The people in those villages would have been well served had their instincts somehow kept them from the presence of "Them."

We don't massacre entire villages in this country — but we do still have our thinking influenced in significant ways by the activation of those instincts, and being aware of who in a setting might be "Them" can be highly relevant for us today.

That set of instincts can cause us to become very apprehensive about the behavior of others when we find ourselves in any "Them" linked settings. We tend to become very aware of potential intergroup risk and we become very sensitive to issues of functional intergroup risk whenever those instincts are activated.

We Go On Full Innuendo Alert

When we are in a situational minority setting, we often go on full innuendo alert — looking for any words or any behaviors by the other people that might indicate the possibility that a threat or an attack or an insult might exist.

That innuendo alert can be triggered on each of us whenever we are surrounded by anyone that isn't "Us."

That can be a useful awareness to have in settings where real threats do exist — but the negative consequence of having those interactions activated is that it causes us to sometimes interpret both behaviors and language of other people in negative ways when the actual intent for both the words and the behaviors of the other people was not actually negative.

Being on perpetual subconscious alert and feeling constant low-level situational stress is not an easy or pleasant place to be.

For obvious logistical reasons, that feeling of stress and of being reminded cognitively of our status of being "other" than the rest of the group in a given setting can happen often for minority Americans.

Those same instincts can be triggered for majority Americans who find themselves in a setting where they are situationally a minority.

We all have that same package of instincts. The level of intergroup stress can be unpleasant for anyone who has it activated.

Integration Can Trigger That Stress at an Instinctive Level

We need to understand the practical impact in our society of those instincts.

That set of instincts can create constant stress for the minority students in a school when a school is integrated. The new students from any group in a school can feel an instinctive discomfort that runs constantly in their minds.

It can happen when anyone from any group is hired into a work setting where that person is a situational minority. The work setting can trigger instinctive stress for that employee.

Those issues and those perceptions need to be understood more directly as we succeed in integrating more work settings and schools, so that we can help people overcome the negative consequences that those situational minority feelings can create.

We need everyone in each work or school setting — minority or majority — to know that those instincts exist and we need new people from the existing group in each setting to reach out to make new people feel safe and included.

When people in any setting are inclusive and build interpersonal and intergroup trust, those particular sets of instincts and stress points can disappear entirely for that setting.

Those stress levels can be erased — and life is better for people from every group when they are gone.

Algerians in Paris Feel the Same Stress

That set of feelings relative to being a situational minority is clearly absolutely not unique to us as Americans. Those same feelings happen when people are in a minority status in other countries. The stress levels that are instinctively triggered for a situational minority person in Dublin or in Prague can be almost constant for some people in some settings in those cities.

The stress levels for an Irish Catholic in Ulster who is standing on the grounds of a Protestant church can also be unceasing and can create real levels of negative feelings as long as the Catholic person is physically in that specific church setting.

An Algerian Muslim in Paris who is working in a site where all of the co-workers are White Parisians would have those same instincts activated. That Algerian worker is likely to find some situations in that integrated work setting far more stress-provoking than the White workers in that same setting perceive the same incidents and situation to be.

Minority situations everywhere create that stress and that stress adds pressure in a real way to peoples' lives when it occurs.

Those feelings can create a negative context for peoples' lives that make being a situational minority person a constant stress-invoking experience and that can make it significantly more difficult to create intergroup interactions at a level that generates friendship and trust.

We need both personal friendship and intergroup trust for intergroup Peace, and both are hard to create when intergroup stress levels are situationally active and relevant.

We do need all people in intergroup settings to understand that those levels of anxiety can easily exist. We need people to accept people as people and to reach out in ways that generate a sense of safety and trust to other people in those settings.

We can do the right things to make the situations much better for all parties.

White Americans Can Go for Long Periods Not Thinking of Race

For White Americans, that particular intergroup instinctive stress level is a much less common experience. The truth is, for obvious reasons, that White Americans in most of this country are much less likely to face those levels of situational minority-status instinct-triggered stress in their daily lives.

Many White Americans in many settings can actually go for very long periods of time without even thinking of race or ethnicity in any direct or relevant way. When White Americans live in basically White communities and when White Americans tend to work in basically White work settings, the instinctive reactions of perceived minority status are not triggered in those White Americans very often for any of those settings.

Also, the layers and incidents of functional discrimination that happen with some frequency for minority Americans in a number of settings are not happening in any setting for most White Americans — so those more negative intergroup realities are also not perceived or functionally relevant to the lives of White Americans.

People in a situational minority status are often aware of those issues almost all of the time. Majority people in that same setting can be completely unaware of those issues almost all of the time. People who are in an overwhelming permanent situational majority status may be completely unaware that those issues or those stress points exist at any level.

Each Real Negative Event Confirms the Suspicions and Fears

The level of intergroup stress that is created by those instinctive reactions can be periodically reinforced in very negative ways by any active and actual experiences of discrimination, prejudice or intergroup animosity that do occur.

Negative intergroup experiences do happen. Prejudicial decisions are made. Bigoted or negative comments are made.

Each real incident of racism — even if those incidents actually very seldom occur in a given setting — reinforces the validity of the on-going sense of intergroup stress for people who are affected by those incidents.

The truth is that we look instinctively for behavior patterns in intergroup settings and we use each piece of evidence as a proof point for the patterns.

Even if most policemen do not act in racist ways in each setting, each policeman who does a racist thing can be seen as a proof point for many people that the police, generally, are racist or are at least somewhat likely to do racist things.

Non-racist, but negative behaviors can also be perceived to be racist when those intergroup stress levels and underlying perceptions exist. A rude or unpleasant or even discourteous police officer behavior that might be interpreted by a White person in this country as being rude and jerky behavior can be perceived by a Black or Brown or Native American person to be racist and intentional rather than just rude and jerky.

Expectations clearly color perceptions. The expectations in that case that a situation or a police behavior might be racist are not unreasonable to hold because, the truth is, sometimes those rude behaviors by police officers are, in fact, racist.

So it is legitimate and intellectually sound to suspect racism for a negative behavior when we know for an absolute fact that some negative behaviors do have racist roots and when we don't know for an absolute fact that racism isn't relevant for that particular rude behavior.

We need all police departments to recognize that reality. We need all police departments to explicitly reject racism and reach out to the communities they serve to both commit to non-racist behavior and to prove, through good and non-racist behavior, that the motivations of the department and the officers are not racist.

Improving that situation is a benefit to the community and to the police.

Police departments in any setting are handicapped and even crippled when the people in that setting perceive the police to be "Them."

Real crime doesn't get solved because the community will not help a police "Them" solve crimes.

More than 70 percent of murders in Detroit were unsolved a year ago because the community did not help the police solve those crimes.

That kind of situation is very bad for the community and for the police.

An Incident Can Be an Anomaly or It Can Be Positive Proof

For many minority Americans, the issue of race or ethnic difference creates multiple daily reminders. Those differences can generate frequent and daily trigger points and relevant behaviors in work settings, schools, and various community and public settings.

The perception and the belief that the issue of race is functionally relevant to people all of the time is constantly in place for many minority group members, and that creates a context for understanding a wide range of behaviors.

Those very consistent on-going levels of instinct-triggered of stress for minority Americans means that when a negative intergroup incident of some kind — like an interracial shooting — actually does occur, the groups of people interpret the event very differently. That specific negative incident can be seen as an anomaly and perceived to be an infrequent and even rare aberration from normal reality by a person from the White majority.

That exact same incident can be seen and interpreted as an absolute, clear, and affirming proof point for the ongoing sense of intergroup stress intergroup prejudice and intergroup damage. That event can be a proof point for discrimination by a person in any relevant minority status who has been continuously feeling ongoing and continuing instinctive levels of intergroup stress.

Any actual intergroup incidents — like a White policeman killing a Black child — that make the race or the ethnicity of the relevant people clearly visible to everyone in that setting can very directly reinforce, confirm, and affirm that continuous alert level for the people who have been instinctively feeling that intergroup stress.

Those specific events that have obvious and clear race links are seen as both affirming the legitimacy of the on-going general concern and confirming the validity of the on-going intergroup stress level for the people who have been feeling that daily level of stress.

An Interracial Murder Can Be a Trigger Event

That set of perceptions explains why large numbers of people can go to the streets in collective anger and collective alignment when those incidents happen.

In the macro context for that community — with both a very long history of intergroup negative experiences and extended periods of perceived stress for many of the people in minority status in that community — the kind of incident where a minority student is shot and killed by a white policeman isn't seen as a rare, outlier, solo incident by the specific minority group that the student is from.

That occurrence is often seen by people from that particular group and by people in that community to be a proof point for intergroup fears.

Each shooting creates a clear, highly visible, and immediate reinforcement for the constant intergroup stress levels that exist in those settings and each shooting is seen as another very current, egregious, and particularly unforgiveable incident of intergroup oppression, intergroup damage, intergroup discrimination, and deliberate and targeted intergroup violence.

We have seen a number of very public recent occurrences that prove that set of very diverse reactions to those kinds of events is very real and robust. The recent issues in Ferguson — with a shooting of an 18-year-old Black youth by a White policeman — triggered an extended period of protests, demonstrations, and even some mob behavior.

The Ferguson Police Department Had Instincts Clearly Activated

The tendency to see those events as intergroup confrontations were exacerbated in Ferguson by a local police department that clearly had its own us/them instincts activated and guiding their thinking and behavior.

That particular police department took multiple visible and symbolic public positions of pure, clear, and intentional intergroup confrontation.

Us/Them behaviors and us/them perceptions were the clearly visible police response pattern at several important levels in Ferguson.

The police lined up as a direct confrontational wall of heavily armed police "Us" in clear contrast to the community "Them." The police public and highly visible positions of pure intergroup confrontation in the streets of Ferguson could only be interpreted by other people in that community as being created by an us/them mindset and as an us/them intergroup reaction.

Those behaviors all feed on themselves — reinforcing themselves in a group. Those behaviors also activate the same instincts in the other group in any setting.

Those processes for both groups are reciprocal and can even lead to escalation if the cycles are not broken.

When the Police Communicate as a "Them," the Consequences Are Predictable

Whether a less confrontational set of behaviors by the police in those particular streets would have improved that situation in that setting is not something that can be proven, but it is hard to come up with a more public statement of negative us/them alignment behaviors, and negative us/them perceptions than the ones that were initially chosen by the local police in Ferguson.

The riot gear and the combat zone automatic weapons, alone, said that the police perceived that their "Us" was ready, willing, and even eager to do battle with the local "Them."

It also said — symbolically — "we" feel good about our alignment and our position and "we" have in solidarity as a police unit to resist whatever relevant "Them" decides to do.

Ferguson gave the country a highly visible and very valuable lesson in a wide range of intergroup issues.

As the Ferguson situation fully unfolds, the reasons for the community anger that triggered the demonstrations are becoming increasingly clear. The police department had a long record of clearly racist patterns of arrests for minor offences. Many minority people in Ferguson were functionally damaged badly by the fines and by losing their license to drive when they could not pay their fines.

People who could not pay fines and who could not drive lost their jobs. So a horrible employment situation that already existed for minority residents of Ferguson was actually exacerbated by people losing employment as the result of police traffic arrests.

The shooting, itself, just unleashed the anger created by all of those other issues.

Two Hundred Killings in Oakland Did Not Trigger Riots

In a fairly similar recent case in Oakland, an unarmed black student was shot and killed by a white policeman on a subway. Demonstrations, mobs, and riots also resulted in Oakland. People were damaged. Businesses were closed, and property was destroyed in the riots.

Again — the killing of an unarmed youth and having a person die was not the major reason all of those people were on the Oakland streets.

The issue and incident that caused people in that particular California community to riot, and to do it so fairly quickly, clearly was not purely the fact that a person in Oakland had been murdered.

Oakland actually often leads the country in the number of people who are murdered each year.

Oakland has drug violence, gang violence, and intragroup violence levels that literally result in daily shootings, daily stabbings, and nearly 200 deaths of Oakland residents just by murder each year.

None of these 200 killings trigger any riots.

All of the people who are shot and killed each year in Oakland are equally dead. But most of their deaths barely rate a mention in the local paper — much less triggering riots that first shut down the business and the commercial districts of Oakland, and then did damage to both people and property in a couple of Oakland settings.

Why did that particular killing trigger those reactions and generate those particular riots? Again — as in Ferguson — Us/Them instincts were triggered by that killing.

It was obviously and clearly an intergroup killing. That specific shooting was done by a White policeman. The young man who died was African American.

That act created a symbol of intergroup conflict and that event brought the existing intergroup anger realities that exist in Oakland into the situation. Many people were already angry in Oakland — for a wide range of reasons.

Oakland Is a Troubled Community

Oakland is an economically troubled community. It has school systems that do not meet the needs of Oakland students. Unemployment levels are high. Many minority kids in Oakland are being set to jail.

Oakland is an unhappy and angry community. That particular killing was a situational tipping point that made that existing anger visible.

Like the situation in Ferguson, the shooting was a release factor for a significant level of very real on-going intergroup anger that has existed for a very long time in that community — anger that is fed daily by both small and large acts of discrimination that either happen or are perceived to be happening in that community.

That anger and the context that created the protests and riots in Oakland and Ferguson were also fed, in part, by the on-going stress levels we all feel when we are in minority situations.

The anger in each of those settings had been visible and visceral. Some of the people protesting each shooting death were situationally violent.

Businesses closed. The city of Oakland basically advised people who were White to avoid the sections of the city where the demonstrations were happening. Intergroup and interracial anger was clear and that anger was shaping behaviors.

Some businesses and government buildings were damaged in the process. Much of the damage was done by people who do not live in Oakland.

People actually came to Oakland from a number of other communities to participate in the demonstrations and some of those people who came from other communities used the Oakland protests as cover to loot and destroy things.

Many people came to Oakland from other communities to support the protests and demonstrations. Some came simply to loot and do damage. There were a number of local places where looting was possible to do under the cover of the group activities and the group anger.

That same problem happened in Ferguson. A number of people came to town in both communities in ways that demeaned the legitimacy of the actual protests and the group causes just to steal things from businesses that they could loot.

Significant intergroup anger exists in Oakland and the people who were demonstrating wanted the world and the rest of Oakland to know how much anger exists.

That same kind of on-going intergroup anger exists at a constant level in many settings in this country. Where it exists, it can be triggered by symbolic events like an intergroup shooting and it can be turned into real intergroup violence and intergroup damage. The Trayvon Martin shooting and the jury decision for that case also triggered intergroup demonstrations in a number of communities. People in many settings were angry about a wide range of issues and were ready to collectively make their anger visible to the world.

The protests created a pathway for that anger.

Sun Tzu, in *The Art of War*, likens group collective energy to a cocked and loaded crossbow — ready to fire. Specific triggers actually turn that group energy into action and release the arrow and that energy from the cocked and loaded bow of intergroup anger.

Pent Up and Simmering Anger Is Unleashed

That is obviously the same sort of energy release that can happen in response to intergroup killings in our country today. The existence of that pent up and simmering anger is fed by actual centuries of dysfunctional and very real and very damaging intergroup history.

It is fed as well by the day-to-day actions, emotions, and experiences that are created currently by intergroup negative perceptions.

All of those factors combine to create the local energy release into the collective anger that we see as riots and demonstrations with some regularity across the country.

For the reasons that are outlined above, those riots and that level of collective anger often tend to completely surprise the White Americans in this country. The White Americans who are surprised by the riots and who are taken aback by the anger are not experiencing the daily personal stress of minority status in their own lives.

Those significant collective responses to that event, however, do not surprise the minority populations who are relevant to those communities and to the rioting groups.

Many of the people in that set of people are already feeling simmering anger and constant unhappiness. The event is just a spark that provides flame for the simmering set of beliefs and emotions constantly being felt and perceived in those settings.

Differences by Group Are Clear

Public surveys that were taken about each of those trigger situations showed very different reactions to those events from each of the surveyed groups.

For the Ferguson situation, surveys taken in the midst of the event showed that more than 80 percent of Black survey respondents felt the police responses in that community were wrong — and a majority of White survey respondents at that same point in time felt that the police responses — at that stage of the process — had been appropriate.

For both the Trayvon Martin shooting in Florida and the subway train shooting in Oakland, there was a similar opinion and perception split by groups in the public surveys taken about the results of the jury action for each case.

Again, significantly higher percentages of the black people who were surveyed — at the 80 percent level — felt that the courts had not done their job well relative to convicting or punishing the defendants in those cases.

The White people surveyed tended to be split about evenly in their opinion and the decisions by the courts.

The perspectives that are used to judge and evaluate the trial results in each case of intergroup killing were clearly significantly different perspectives for each group of people surveyed.

Racist Experiences Create a Context and Expectations

About half of the White people who were surveyed about each of those trials seemed to have a pre-trial predisposition and belief that said the young person who was killed in each situation may well have been doing something wrong or might have been doing something inappropriate, that may have justified the police action in some way.

The minority group members who were surveyed about those cases tended to believe that the policeman with the gun who killed the youth was very likely acting in a racially prejudicial way, and believed that the policeman had clearly committed a punishable criminal act.

Racism Is Real — Racist Things Happen

That particular interpretation of the facts in those intergroup-linked shooting cases involving policemen is clearly influenced by the fact that many of the minority people who were surveyed may have personally had at least one discriminatory and negative encounter with a racist law enforcement officer.

Racist policemen do exist. Racism is real. Racist encounters do happen.

All policemen are not racist. Only some policemen are racist. Large numbers of policemen from all groups and settings actually want to serve and protect the public. Most police officers try to do good things for people from all ethnic groups and from other races.

There are very well meaning and motivated policeman who make police work a calling and a mission of service, and who spend their lives creating safety for people in their communities.

But the truth is, that some police officers are racist. Some policemen do at least some racist things. Some police departments have patterns of racist behavior.

When Black drivers make up 20 percent of the drivers on a particular Florida highway and when Black drivers make up 60 percent of the drivers who are stopped and searched by police on that highway, it's hard to interpret that data in any way that doesn't have racism involved.

The set of facts create a reality. The functional reality is that each individual racist policeman who actually exists, and each racist policeman who does actually do racist things to people can leave a lot of scars and have a very broad impact.

The facts that some police departments have patterns of racist behavior are also known and visible to the group of people who are the targets and victims of those behaviors.

People from each affected group who have those clearly racist experiences with those racist police officers tell those stories about those racist experiences to family and to friends and to the relevant community for a very long time. That telling and retelling of those experiences extends the scars over time to more people and it creates an overall context and a set of expectations for perceiving and interpreting the next racist act by any police officer.

Those incidents, experiences, and scars can cause very different responses to survey questions by groups of people about the guilt or the innocence of the shooter and the victim in those cases.

"Stand Your Ground" Trial Results Were Evaluated Differently by Race

White people have not had to face significant levels of prejudice and discrimination in their own lives. White people did not have friends who had been arrested for "Driving While White." So White people have had a different context to use to interpret each of the public incidents of intergroup violence involving the police.

No one makes jokes about being arrested as a driver for being White because those incidents are not part of the shared and communicated group experience for White drivers.

Most Black Americans do at least know someone who was clearly stopped by police for "driving while being Black."

Real issues of prejudice and discrimination do happen. The book *Ending Racial, Ethnic, and Cultural Disparities in American Health Care* has very real examples of bias in health care delivery that creates bad health outcomes for minority Americans.

That health care focused book explains the disparities that exist in the context of three B's — Bias, Biology, and Behavior. The net and total impacts of those care disparities and care differences creates several years of lower life expectancy for far too many minority Americans.

Those are very real and legitimate issues.

That particular set of information and those data points about group perceptions are all highly relevant to *The Art of InterGroup Peace* because that information tells us that there will be significant challenges and some real intergroup trust issues to address as we go forward to create Peace among various groups in our society today.

It tells us that we will need to look at issues that result from events with a strong sense of context and a strong sense of relevancy.

We Need a Sense of Us in Each Community

We need to keep various intergroup flash points in specific settings from creating significant damage to intergroup Peace in those settings.

We need each community to have a sense of "Us" that includes White Americans as one of the groups committed to intergroup success and values.

A primary goal of the people in each community should be to create a clear and deliberate sense of community "Us." We need that commitment from all of us in each community — and we particularly need it from our leaders.

We need the people in local government roles to clearly support intergroup Peace and we need our police forces to be openly and clearly and honestly on the side of the community "Us" that we create in each setting.

We need leaders who both preach and practice inclusion at key levels. When intergroup incidents do occur, we need to respond to those incidents and events from a community perspective that is inclusive of all people.

We need leaders in each setting from each group who value protecting and extending that community sense of "Us" as one of their personal leadership goals.

We all need to be true believers in those values and goals.

The values and commitments that tie us together as an "Us" in each community need to be real or they will not have the impact they need to have. We need community specific actions that lead each setting to have a legitimate sense of "Us."

We need people in each community both creatively and consistently doing the work that earns a sense of local "Us."

Some Current Leaders Also Have Patterns of Divisive and Inflammatory Responses

The challenge of achieving intergroup Peace in various settings is increased by the fact that a number of people who are in leadership positions for each of the relevant groups of people are actually leaders who rose to power in their own group on the strength of their personal negative reactions to earlier intergroup issues and based on their personal prior militant positions as conflict leaders of their group for earlier confrontations.

Some leaders prefer conflict — and some leaders find that continuing conflict increases the personal power with the group.

It can potentially create a real risk to some leader's personal power as war leaders in some settings if Peace exists in their settings. The Alpha instinct chapters of this book describe those behaviors and those motives in more detail.

A problem we can face is that people who have been at the microphone in past intergroup incidents as the people who were preaching anger, extending negative perceptions and advocating antagonistic behaviors relative to the other group are often very ready and even eager to continue to interact with the other group in attack and conflict mode whenever new incidents occur.

That perspective and that personal readiness, and even eagerness to be conflicted can create a low likelihood of those particular leaders coming into any new intergroup situation as a calming influence.

As noted earlier, it is best at several levels when those former war leaders can become the new Peace chiefs. Former warriors can make great leaders for Peace.

War Chiefs Tend to Be War Chiefs When Incidents Happen

It is also true that people whose personal rhetoric has inflamed and informed prior situations are often not the people who are most likely to offer calming advice to their groups when new inflammatory incidents occur.

War chiefs tend to be war chiefs — and the war chiefs in various kinds of tribal and intergroup settings tend to be most relevant, most effective, and have the most personal power in times of war.

So when a triggering event happens, the people who have been war chiefs during prior events tend to take on those same war chief roles and they tend to use the same intergroup language and the same conflict-oriented approaches that they had used as leaders in the prior events.

That pattern is understandable. Those particular people who function as war chiefs are often very angry — sometimes for very good reasons — and they can easily extend and embed that anger into the people they lead and into the situations they face.

That common behavior pattern for those leaders makes perfect sense — and it is entirely understandable as a standard pattern of human leader behavior.

But it can obviously create real barriers to intergroup Peace when incidents occur that inflame our emotions and trigger those us/them instincts in us, and when those particular war chief leaders lead our response in ways that increase the conflict and add to the negative intergroup group energy.

We Need to Convert War Chiefs to Peace Chiefs

We need our leaders at this point in time to be able to set aside their prior anger and to work together to defuse and de-energize those kinds of situations when they occur rather than inflame them.

Each set of people in every American setting needs to look for Peace chiefs rather than war chiefs when trigger events occur.

Converting war chiefs to Peace chiefs is a great strategy when that conversion process is possible.

Or we need to do what needs to be done to have a different set of Peace chiefs in place if the war chiefs refuse to convert.

The Mohawk Indians — for intertribal conflicts — actually had a tradition of naming specific people to be Peace chiefs to achieve exactly that purpose and to perform exactly that function. That was a wise thing to do.

We may need to do similar things in multiple settings to keep our budding Peace in any setting from being destroyed by incidents of intergroup anger and conflict.

We need leaders who are committed to Peace and who are willing and committed to resolving incidents rather than inflaming them.

We Need Inclusive Leaders Who Value Peace

As groups of people look for the next generation of leaders in various settings, identifying people whose goal is to create a win/win outcome for everyone rather than creating situational inflammation and win/win outcomes is the right thing to do.

We should ask each of our leaders what their own strategies are for achieving win/win results rather than their strategies for winning conflicts, defeating the enemy, and avoiding losses for our side in intergroup win/lose interactions.

We Need Police Who Generate Community Trust

We also need to do what needs to be done to create trust and a common commitment to community safety on behalf of the police departments and the various groups who make up our neighborhoods.

Some crimes damage people badly and some crimes can only be successfully addressed by police action.

If the police are not trusted or liked by the people in a community, then the relevant laws that are needed to protect people will generally not be well enforced. People who do not have good police protection can be deeply damaged badly at several levels because they have no safety net or security against violence or danger.

That is why more than 70 percent of the killings in Detroit were not solved a year ago. That failure to solve those murders happened in part because the people in too many neighborhoods in that city perceived the police to be "Them" and the people in those neighborhoods did not trust the police enough to help "Them" solve those crimes.

The obvious problem that is created by that lack of trust is a growing number of murders and a huge increase in thefts in those settings.

Murder is clearly not a good thing. It is bad for all groups in a setting to have both the number of murders, and the number of property thefts in any setting growing.

Police Need to Be "Us" — Not "Them"

Police departments need to be an "Us" — not a "Them" — in the communities they serve. That approach is a basic need that we need to achieve if we want our communities to be safe and if we want the people in our communities to succeed and thrive.

It is very good for each community when the police in that setting can be an "Us." Our personal safety levels in each setting improve when we have the key laws that directly protect our personal safety both enforced and followed.

Communities each need to have their community police function well to protect the people in each community. Where the police in a setting are perceived to be "them," then key trust issues need to be resolved and protection levels drop for all people in the community.

Multiple levels of crimes will grow in the areas where the police are not perceived to be the communities' tool for preventing crime, creating safety, and for ensuring adequate protection for all groups.

Basic distrust of the police creates a real threat to Peace. We need to eliminate suchthat distrust by having the police function as an "Us" in the service of the people that they protect.

A key goal for the leaders in each community needs to be to create mechanisms that protect the safety and the possessions of the people who live in each community.

Lawless settings and a lack of basic protection can very easily trigger truly evil and dangerous behaviors.

We need to create a clear and shared sense in each community that safety for everyone is a goal. We need our police departments to be enough of an "Us" in each community that people call on their police without hesitation or fear to protect the people against people who assault, damage, or steal from other people in the community.

We Need Each Community to Be an "Us"

The principals are pretty basic and fundamental. The specific solutions need to be specific to each setting because trust and safety are both setting specific.

We need each community in America to very deliberately create a sense of community "Us."

We need the people in each community to share support for community schools, community transportation, community safety, and community health.

We need people in each community to create processes and approaches that improve the futures for our children and improve the health for all of the people who are being damaged by the diseases that do not need to be allowed to do that damage to so many people.

We need leaders in each setting who react immediately when negative us/them situations occur — with the goal of restoring a sense of functioning, beneficial, and legitimate sense of "Us" to that setting as quickly as it can be restored.

We need political processes that give us leaders who might differ on their pathways and who might differ on their ideology, but who concur entirely on their goal of having us all succeed by becoming an inclusive America where the American Dream is available to us all and where we all have the safety and protection of being an "Us."

The set of beliefs and rules that we need to create alignment and bring us together is outlined in the final chapter of this book. For all to succeed, we need a common path to success.

The time to be on that path is now.

We each need to make the personal commitment to Peace that will make that path possible for us all.

CHAPTER SEVENTEEN

The American Dream and Our Core Values Can and Should Unite Us All and Create Peace

WE CAN ACHIEVE a culture of Peace for America.

We can — if we come together to be a people united by our values and our core beliefs — create an America that succeeds and thrives going into the challenging years that lie ahead.

We can help all Americans have the opportunity that we all should have to achieve the American Dream.

We can build a future where we all do well and where our country is strong, safe, and successful because we are all doing well.

To succeed in creating Peace for our country, we need to very intentionally build and use a shared set of values as a country that can bring us together as a people. We need an explicit set of shared values and shared beliefs that can both help guide our collective behavior and shape our collective sense of right and wrong going forward, so that we can work together in aligned ways to create a new culture of Peace and inclusion for America.

To succeed as a nation and as a people, we need to agree to be united as an American people by our shared values and by our shared beliefs and we need to commit as individuals, and collectively, to act in accordance with those beliefs.

We need to recognize that when we are aligned as a people by an enlightened belief system, and by a clear intergroup mutual support commitment, that we can be the greatest country on the planet, and we can continue to be the country on the planet that is most likely to succeed.

We need to understand that we will all benefit from being on that path, united by those behaviors and aligned by those beliefs.

We Will All Do Well When We All Do Well

We are all in this together. We need to recognize that fact to be true.

In very practical and important ways, we will all do well when everyone does well. We will do badly collectively as a society and as an economy, and we will do badly as a country if major subsets of our population do badly or fail.

We need to understand and recognize the fact that failures by any significant subsets of our population will not have a neutral, irrelevant, or insignificant impact on our overall economy and on our individual and collective safety.

Significant failures for any group in this country will create a purely functional economic and societal drag at multiple levels that will ultimately pull the whole country into economic and functional distress and failure.

A significant failure by any major portion of our people can put us all at collective risk of intergroup anger, intergroup division, and highly dysfunctional negative and damaging intergroup behaviors at multiple levels that will and can continue to damage us in increasingly significant ways for a very long time.

The anger levels, alone, that can be triggered in groups and individuals when any group feels it is being damaged by other groups, can result in unsafe neighborhoods, physical violence at intergroup levels, and even shootings and bombings of various kinds.

We are very clearly not immune from the kinds of behaviors those sets of instincts trigger in people who feel their group is being threatened or actually damaged. Those kinds of actions create both direct damage and backlash damage — and those actions and reactions can far too easily put us on a very dangerous road to intergroup division and to the clear failure of intergroup Peace as our future as a country.

We need to understand that reality, and we need to act accordingly. We need to succeed in our collective alignment as a values-driven American "Us."

We should make success for all groups a goal for all groups, and we should understand our real problems and real challenges at levels that will help us succeed in creating the future we need for our collective success.

We need to very openly and very publicly align to do the key things we need to do relative to education, early childhood development, good health, safe communities, full access to jobs, and clear and inclusive functional and economic opportunities for all groups of people in ways that will make us strong across our entire population.

We can't afford to have some subsets of our nation doing well and prospering while other segments of our population are damaged, disproportionately disadvantaged, dangerously dysfunctional, angrily and deliberately divisive, and increasingly and intentionally damaging and dangerous to other people and to our communities because that damaged portion of our people is fueled by a collective and functionally justified sense of basic intergroup anger that creates, and then amplifies and exacerbates intergroup hate.

Anger is the wrong status and the wrong outcome for any portion of people of America. Collective success is the outcome we need for all of us at this point in our lives and history.

We All Gain When We All Gain

There is great group gain to be had from having everyone being able to gain. When all parts of our country prosper, that full and shared national success obviously will create prosperity for all of us.

If we bring all of our people into the full benefits of the American Dream, the positive consequences of including everyone in the American Dream will make us richer, stronger, and safer as a country.

We need to do that work. We need to achieve those benefits. We need to all succeed, because the consequences of failure for any of us will damage all of us.

There is no future possibility for us as an extremely and increasingly diverse country where an insulated subset of our population continues to be successful while the communities they are in fail around them.

Walled cities and armed enclaves for subsets of our population are the wrong future for us as a country, and the people who would live in those enclaves will have lives that are hugely inferior to the lives we all can live when all groups in this country succeed and those walls are not needed.

We need to choose future paths where we all succeed — and we need to anchor those futures on a clear understanding of the issues we face and an absolutely clear intent to have success extend to all of us.

To anchor our key strategies of full inclusion and mutual success, we need to begin with a very clear sense of what we believe in as a country.

We need to be united in our shared beliefs and in our shared vision of who we are.

We should know, from the beginning, what we hate.

We should all hate discrimination, hate prejudice, hate behaviors that damage other groups of people, and we should all hate, reject, and oppose any behaviors that undermine the dignity, freedom, and personal value of each of us.

We Need to Know Exactly What We All Collectively Believe in as an American "Us"

Those core beliefs about what we hate should be clear. They should be explicit and they should be shared by all of us.

It is not, however, enough for us to be just against racism, and against ethnic, cultural or gender-based discrimination. We need to know more than what we oppose. We need to know exactly what we endorse and support, and we need to know clearly and explicitly what we will work together to create and defend.

We all very much need to know very specifically what we are for — what we support — and we all need to know exactly and explicitly what we collectively believe in as the core beliefs of our shared and collectively supported American "Us."

It is not enough to have a generic, collective, or individual commitment to vague and basically positive American values. Generic, positive aspirations and undefined, but definitely positive, collective good will are all very good things, but they are insufficient, and functionally and operationally inadequate to give us the tools and approaches we actually need to truly align and succeed as a people.

We need to go beyond good will and generically-positive patriotic leanings. We need a clear and explicit set of shared and universally supported core values we can use in a number of important and functional ways to anchor who we are as a country and as a people.

We need to all agree that we each believe in our clearly understood basic sets of core values and we all need to agree both that we are each individually committed, and that we are all collectively committed to having those core values define what we do, and shape both how and why we do it.

To get that process to the next step, this chapter lists the basic set of values we use as a country now. This list is based on our history, on our structures, and our agreements of various kinds that we have in place today — and it pulls exactly a dozen key values into a single set of shared beliefs to give us a starting point for making our explicit collective commitments as a people to one another going forward into our immediate future.

The basic list of key values proposed and outlined below isn't a long list. But it is a very familiar list. This list includes a dozen key beliefs that we all share, and that we use now in various ways to govern our country and guide our lives.

We all know each of these values, because we use them in various ways now, but we have not set those values up as a package, or used them as an intentional collective alignment-structuring tool. We did not need that kind of explicit aligning tool in the past, but we do need it now, and so we do need to build it now.

At this point of rapidly increasing diversity as a country along racial, cultural, ethnic, religious, and even economic lines, we need to basically commit very clearly and very explicitly to collectively and individually use a very specific set of core beliefs now, to guide us into our future — because to build trust and in order, to build and maintain a collective sense of being Us, we now need a clear commitment from all of us to each of us about how we will live, and how we will collectively and individually act in key ways in our communities and our lives.

We need to be united by our beliefs. In order for that to happen, we need to know what beliefs unite us.

We Believe in These Values Now

The list outlined below to help tee up that collective alignment process is not, in fact, a new list of values and core beliefs. These are our current and existing basic core beliefs compiled into a single working list so that we can use them to guide us in understood and mutually agreed ways in each of our communities and settings.

This is basically what we believe in now. This list is a compilation of basic and foundational core beliefs that have anchored "Us" as a nation in the past and that should have the ability to continue to guide us and anchor us in the future.

These individual beliefs have each guided us in various ways for a very long time — but they have not officially and explicitly committed us as a structured and organized package of values and beliefs.

We need to go the next step now. We need explicit, clear, and understood agreements, and we need direct and clear commitment statements that exist as a single set of shared beliefs. We need, at this point in time, to be very explicit about each of those values and we need to be explicit about our individual and collective support for, and commitment to, all of those core values as a package in order to create alignment, intergroup, and interpersonal trust about future behaviors and expectations.

The reason to be explicit and intentional about these commitments as a package at this point in time, is that we currently have a generic set of shared beliefs that we use now in various non-specific ways to define what we believe in, but we don't each know for a fact if other people who believe in American values actually believe in the same list of values that we believe in.

We can't use the current array and the generically understood list of shared beliefs to unify us in a clear way if we don't actually have a clear list.

So this book proposes we agree to use this explicit set of beliefs and values at this point in time as a package to commit to as a full and explicit package, because we clearly have been using each of these 12 values on their own power to guide who we are, and to structure and guide what we have believed in the past. This is a compilation — not a new list.

You can make up your own mind as you read the list whether or not it is, in fact, simply the compilation of the core beliefs we already use, and you can think about whether there might be other values and beliefs that should be added.

We can and should create a process to use in the future to enhance this list. We clearly can improve on this list — and we should work in a wide variety of participative and inclusive ways to make this list better.

But starting with a broad process instead of a proposed list isn't practical as the starting point for this particular alignment approach, because any of the kinds of group involvement approaches that could create an initial list from scratch might take years. We need a list now. We have too many conflicts and divisions, in very real and damaging settings, today to spend years building an initial official list of shared beliefs to be our alignment focus.

To build a first list with any kind of group process based "starting from scratch" approach would take a very long time, and we could easily find ourselves spending more time, simply figuring out and setting up the process, than we might want to take at a time in our history when we really need a tool to identify our core beliefs now.

Because this list is actually a compilation of prior and current beliefs, the functional truth is that we actually have already gone through centuries of participative processes to build this specific list.

As a result of those realities, until we figure out a better process for enhancing the list, the suggestion is that we use this list until we get something better — and that we do, in fact, agree with each other that these are, in fact, the basic values and beliefs we share, and will commit to as a people and as individual people.

Read the actual proposed list and think about the contents before deciding whether or not that approach can work for you.

So what are the core beliefs that we have developed over the centuries as a nation and a people?

Democracy Leads Our List of Beliefs

Democracy absolutely needs to be at the top of the list of our core and foundational beliefs. Democracy is key. Democracy defines us.

We need to anchor our shared belief system for all Americans on a belief in democracy as a shared value and as a shared and collective commitment that we all make to one another.

We need to be fully committed to the democratic process — to having each and all of us with the full rights and the responsibilities that are embedded in using the democratic approach to running our country and running our various political leadership settings and infrastructures.

People have died to defend democracy, and those deaths reflect how extremely important democracy is as a value and a defining principal.

Those of us who collectively believe in the American "Us" need to have democracy as a shared core belief. We can and should all agree that we will use democracy as the foundation for the new American "Us" belief system and commitment to one another.

We Need to Believe in Equality

That belief needs to be accompanied by an equally strong commitment to equality.

Equality is absolutely foundational to our belief system. No one is higher in any way than any of the rest of us. We need to be equal under the law. We need to be equal in our political status, and we need to all be equal in our ability to participate in the democratic processes that govern us.

Our nation was founded on democratic principals. The people who founded our country were not, unfortunately, all full believers in full equality back in the very first days of this country.

Some people limited their use of equality as a value and a practice to a subset of our population. Equality did not functionally apply to everyone when this country began. White males ran the country, and there was significant discrimination against both women and all people from groups that were not White males.

That inconsistent support for equality in our founding days was a problem for many people at a number of levels.

We had multiple layers of inequality in those early years, and those layers of inequality were built into our cultures, our behaviors, and our laws. We have since grown in our wisdom and in our enlightenment, and we now have reached the levels of believing in legally defined and explicitly inclusive equality for all of us, regardless of ethnicity, race, gender, culture, or beliefs.

That commitment to full and inclusive equality for all of us needs to define us going forward, and it needs to be a foundation for all of the values we share and mutually support. We all need to commit to equality as a core and foundational belief, and as a guide for our laws and our behaviors.

We Believe in Inclusion

That value is directly linked to our commitment to inclusion. We need to believe in the value of being inclusive to all groups of people who are part of the great and diverse fabric of this country.

Inclusion should be our commitment, our practice, our philosophy, and our reality.

Inclusion can't be sporadic or inconsistent or provisional or situational.

We need to be deliberately, absolutely, intentionally, functionally, successfully, and universally inclusive — and that approach of being inclusive needs to be a key component and anchor for our shared beliefs. We need to include people from all groups who believe in our American ideals to be full members of the American "Us" — and we need to reach out to make inclusion a thing we do well in all settings.

We Believe in Freedom

We also need to believe in freedom.

America is "the land of the free and the brave." Freedom is also an anchor attribute.

We are not owned by — or subject to subjugation by — any other people or any other groups of people.

Slavery doesn't exist. It did exist — and it ended.

We are all free people, each able to think freely, act freely, and to believe freely in whatever beliefs we choose to believe in — with no one telling us how to act, how to think, or what we should believe. We need to be free in our thoughts and beliefs, and we need to be able to pursue life, liberty, and happiness in ways that we each choose for our own lives.

We don't have the freedom to harm other people, or take the property or possessions of other people. We don't have the freedom to order other people to do what we want them to do, or to tell other people how to think. Our freedom is not unlimited.

We have very appropriate constraints on some aspects of our behavior that relate to other people.

But other than those constraints, we are each free people, and we each can and should enjoy the blessings of freedom as a key part of who we are and what we do.

Freedom is a core belief and it needs to be defended and supported by us all.

We Believe in Religious Freedom

We particularly need to support and protect our religious freedom. We treasure our freedom of religion.

In far too many settings in the world, people with religious beliefs have imposed those beliefs on other people in those settings against their will.

At the other extreme, in some settings, some governments in power have actually made all religions illegal.

Both of those approaches are wrong.

We need freedom of religion. We believe in our religious freedom at a very basic level.

We respect religious beliefs. We honor religious beliefs. We are all allowed to celebrate whatever religious beliefs we each choose to hold.

We each need to protect the right for each of us to have and to hold religious beliefs or to choose not to have religious beliefs — and we absolutely do not allow anyone to impose his or her religious beliefs, or his or her lack of religious beliefs on any other person against the will of that other person.

Religion, itself, benefits from that approach to the legal status of religion.

Religion, itself, is better protected when that clear approach to religious freedom is used — because each religion has the full protection of the law, and each religion is not subjected to the whims, dictates, edicts, or beliefs of any government official, government body, or of any proponents or advocates for any other set of either religious or anti-religious beliefs.

We Believe in Justice

Justice is another core belief that needs to anchor the shared belief system for the American "Us".

We need to collectively agree that justice is our value, our commitment, and our foundational approach for each of our people.

We need full justice under the law for all of us — with full protection of the law, and with objective justice used to interpret the law and our accountability under the law.

Freedom and justice for all both need to be anchor beliefs.

We Believe in Accountability

Accountability at a personal level needs to be another core belief. We each need to be accountable for our own behaviors and for our lives.

Our first ethical responsibility to the others in America is to be personally accountable for doing our share of what needs to be done, and for accepting accountability as individuals for what we have each individually done.

It is a good, ethical, and even noble thing to be accountable at a personal level.

At the same time, we need to provide each other with a safety net so that if any of us are in need at a basic level, we are collectively accountable for making sure those needs are met.

We have a shared accountability for putting out fires, saving other people's lives when action is needed to save lives, and for creating the infrastructure that is needed so that the people who need our collective support can and will receive our collective support when that support is needed.

We Believe in Merit

We also believe in merit as a core value.

When people work hard and achieve success and build things and do things that create value for others, we believe in being a culture and a society where the person who has achieved and who has created that value then merits, benefits, and can receive both recognition, and reward for that achievement.

In too many settings around the world, various levels of discrimination and functionally and intentionally unfair processes undermine, erode, and damage merit as a consequence for doing well.

That damage to merit in those settings cripples future progress and weakens each country's overall success levels as a country and as a people. Countries that follow the kinds of approaches that undermine merit are much less successful as a country than we are as Americans — where merit is recognized and accepted.

We need to acknowledge both merit and relevant reward if and when reward is appropriate to the success and the accomplishment of our people.

We can build a society anchored on success when we reward and encourage success.

We Believe in Creativity, Invention, Innovation, and Continuous Improvement

In that same vein, we need to be a country, a culture, and a society that celebrates, encourages, empowers, and enables creativity and innovation. We want our world to get continuously better.

The world we live in can only get continuously better if we have people in it who are continuously making it better.

That is a basic fact of life. We need innovation to be a defining part of who we are and what we do.

Far too many settings in the world make various elements of innovation illegal and some settings penalize various levels of creativity. Some countries make change and improvement illegal.

We have been one of the most successful countries on the planet for many years because we have been innovative and creative in multiple ways, and because we both allow, encourage, and reward innovation in a wide range of areas.

Yankee Ingenuity was a foundational skill set and highly acclaimed virtue for our Founders. The rest of the world has respected and envied Yankee Ingenuity.

We need to build on that strength and that capability. We need to make our endorsement and our support for those areas to be a key part of our collective commitment to each other, and to the new and continuously improving American "Us."

We Believe in Honesty

Honesty also needs to be a key value and a core belief for us as a people and as a culture. That value needs to be stated because it is not automatically included in behavioral expectations in all settings. Some cultures enable and allow dishonesty, and expect and even enable varying and inconsistent levels of honesty.

For us to successfully bring all of our groups together, we need to have intergroup trust, and we need positive, beneficial, and trustworthy intergroup and interpersonal interactions.

Our basic intergroup interactions need to be anchored on trust or they will deteriorate in dysfunctional ways. Situations and interactions can far too easily explode, implode, or erode when trust is violated in any real or perceived way.

We need interpersonal honesty to be a core behavior that we both expect and celebrate. Honesty needs to be a standard behavior and a source of individual and collective pride.

We need honesty to build intergroup and interpersonal trust.

We need to be a culture where we can rely on the truth of our key interactions and where we can trust that the agreements we make are the agreements we honor.

We Believe in Human Dignity

We also need to clearly support human dignity. Each of us needs to respect each of us.

Doing demeaning things to people needs to be something that does not happen to people in our society or in our nation.

We need to celebrate each other's personal worth, and we need to support and show respect for each of us as human beings.

The protection of our dignity in various interactions should be an expectation held by each of us at a fundamental level.

We Believe in Win/Win Outcomes for All People

Our overall agenda — to succeed in *The Art of InterGroup Peace* — needs to be anchored on win/win outcomes and on win/win belief systems.

We need win/win behaviors for all groups and we need to commit to win/win approaches and outcomes for all groups. We have been moving very directly but slowly to that shared belief over the past century, and we need to take that belief and commitment to the next level now in order to succeed as a country and as a people.

We all need to support each other. We all need to be pleased when we each and all win. We need to make having everyone win a strategy, a commitment, a skill set and a goal.

When we all win, everyone benefits. When we all win, we each end up with the outcomes we need.

When we all win, no one is on the outside looking in, wanting to upset the Peace in a setting in order to get revenge, to avenge a set of intergroup wrong doings, or to do damage to another group in order to keep them from winning in some way in the future.

This book and its sister *InterGroup* books explain and demonstrate how to achieve win/win outcomes. Those outcomes are central to *The Art of InterGroup Peace*. We need to be a country where everybody wins … And that will only happen if we make that commitment to one another and then do the right things to make it happen.

As the win/win chapter of this book explains, we all need to be good at defining our own desired wins, and we all need to be good at understanding, supporting, encouraging, and facilitating wins for all groups.

All Groups Should Benefit from and Use the Core Values

A highly foundational and highly functional part of that win/win process is to use the 12 core values and shared beliefs outlined in this chapter to help every group succeed and win.

Those basic, positive, time-honored, enlightened, wise, ethical, inspirational, and highly inclusive values create benefit for us all. We need every group to be able to participate receiving the full benefits of each value.

Those values give us a clear context for our commitment to one another as Americans. Those values articulate clearly what we believe, and they state clearly what our expectations are for each other as a country and an American People.

Those values give us a functional, visible, inspirational, and credible safety net for our interactions with each other and they give us a clear direction to steer our country in the most enlightened ways into the increasingly challenging years that lie ahead.

We need those values to be actualized, and we need those values to be real — and we need those values to be shared, understood, clearly articulated, supported, defended, honored, treasured, and celebrated as our expected behaviors and as our collective core beliefs.

We Need to Build on Our Wonderful Diversity — Not Eliminate It

The Art of InterGroup Peace does not call for people from all of the diverse groups who make up the fabric of America to abandon their old group affiliations, or to give up or eliminate their old group allegiances or identities.

We need to build on our diversity — not erase it. It is a strength and an asset to be diverse. We need to appreciate and collectively relate to each of the diverse levels of who we are.

We all need to appreciate the fact that diversity creates major strengths at multiple levels. Diversity gives us wide ranges of options, approaches, and problem-solution tools to both solve our problems and to take advantage of our opportunities.

Our lives are more interesting and our communities have layers of additional value and layers of additional choices and opportunities when our communities are more diverse. Diversity in art, music, apparel, food choices, skill sets, and thought processes make us both stronger and more interesting.

There are other countries in the world where variety is banned and where diversity is oppressed. We perform better at every level than those countries, we are a much better place to live, and we are more successful as a country and a people as a result of all of those diverse factors coming together to shape who we are.

We need to celebrate and utilize all of the diversity in creativity, functionality, and thought processes that result from our diversity as a people in order to give us the highest levels of shared success as a nation and a people. The intergroup books have multiple examples of the success that diversity can create when inclusion is used as an asset and a strength.

We need to have the cultures of our communities enjoying and appreciating the choices, options, and variations that our diversity creates in each setting. We need to enjoy being diverse at the same time we find comfort, collective strength, and support in being aligned, united, and functionally protected by our key values and our shared beliefs.

We Need a Shared Sense Of "Us"

That overarching level of alignment is crucial to our future success, and to our future state of intergroup and interpersonal Peace.

The Art of Intergroup Peace calls very directly and specifically for each of us, and all of us, to bring each and all of our old alignments consciously and intentionally into a new and additive, intellectually enlightened, philosophically and ethically unifying, intentionally and deliberately overarching, large scale intergroup and interpersonal belief based alignment levels that give us all an aligned path forward together.

We need to maintain and enjoy our old group identities, and we need to simultaneously come together to also very intentionally form a new group that is defined, united, and unified by our key shared beliefs.

We need to form a new and powerful additional level of "Us" that we create, build, support, and enjoy with the other people whose shared values and whose clear and direct commitment to intergroup Peace can create and sustain that new additive American "Us" level of us for all of us here.

We need to have that specific sense of being a values-driven "Us" sense guide our interactions with one another in every relevant aspect of our lives.

Being a values-based "Us" is the basic strategic goal of *The Art of InterGroup Peace*. That approach is, in fact, key to Peace itself.

We each need to make the individual choice to go down that path. We each need to want Peace — to value Peace — and we each need to take several key aligning steps together to create and protect Peace.

We need to use the cultures for each of our groups and communities as part of that Peace strategy. This book explains how that can be done. When we understand both cultures and instincts, we can choose to control our cultures, rather than having our cultures control us.

As a key part of that process, we need to both celebrate and honor our cultures, and we need to very intentionally and carefully add elements of Peace to the value sets and expectations of each culture.

We need to put in place a very deliberate and very enlightened American culture of Peace. We need to be united by our beliefs in pursuit of Peace.

This approach needs to include all of us. We need to be intentionally inclusive. We need all groups to be included and part of the process and commitment to each other.

We need to solve our intergroup problems together as a people, and we need to understand, honor, appreciate, and celebrate those solutions.

We need heroes and leaders who exemplify and model those behaviors for "Us." We need to celebrate our heroes who solve intergroup problems, and we need to honor and support our heroes and leaders who exemplify and protect Peace.

We need to avoid inflammatory situations wherever possible. When intergroup inflammations of any kind in any setting occur, we need to resolve them quickly, and we need to resolve them well.

That is an extremely important thing to do. Our basic intergroup instincts make dividing into angry groups, in various settings when trigger events occur in those settings, very easy to do.

We know from events that are happening in our world today, that we can, and do, respond quickly at very primal levels when our intergroup anger levels are triggered by any situation, event, or circumstance that reaches, touches, and activates those instincts at a fully reactive level.

We all need to recognize how vulnerable and even fragile our intergroup Peace building processes can be in a setting. We can be inflamed in deeply instinct linked ways very quickly and very deeply by both words and deeds. We tend to be on full alert for various intergroup infractions, even when we are currently in a state of Peace in any setting.

The sad truth is that we can move from Peaceful and enlightened, mutually supportive intergroup interactions, to pure anger — and to high and powerful levels of defensiveness and protectiveness for our group based on relatively low levels of provocation ... And it too often feels very right for us to defend our group, and to obstruct or damage the other group when that happens.

We each need to know and understand at a purely intellectual level how vulnerable and susceptible we each are to having those thought processes, values, emotions, and behaviors take over our lives in very damaging ways whenever they are situationally activated. We are all at risk. We need to understand that risk clearly.

We each need to understand and know with great clarity of understanding that those divisive and instinctive thought processes and responses can far too easily create risk for each of us.

We need to use our intellectual powers and our most enlightened understandings of ourselves and of those instinctive influences — and we each need to use that knowledge, and that insight about those processes, to make wisdom based and insightful life choices for ourselves when we feel those instincts being activated.

We need our carefully learned and intentionally developed levels of enlightenment to come to the rescue and offset those negative and inflammatory instincts whenever they are triggered — in us — in ways that put us at risk of having them run our lives in damaging and destructive ways.

To give ourselves the strength and the emotional support to withstand those powerful and highly seductive and negative instinctive influences, we need to be very successful in being diverse. We need to make being diverse a strength, and we need to make being diverse an asset in very intentional and influential ways.

We need to make the intellectual choice to create an overarching alignment level of shared beliefs that includes us all, and we need to embrace, celebrate, and benefit from our growing diversity as we simultaneously embrace and celebrate all of the factors and all of the shared and enlightened beliefs that make us an American "Us."

We Have Achieved That Sense of Us Before

We can go down that path of being an American "Us." It can be done. It has been done. We were there in a very powerful way for a couple of weeks after the terrorists flew their planes into the World Trade Center.

We all saw, collectively, how much we appreciated and valued the best parts and the best components of who we collectively are as Americans.

At that moment, when those planes crashed into those buildings, we felt that sense of "Us" very clearly. We knew exactly who we were in that moment, and we very much liked being who we were. It was good to be American in the light of those enlightening events.

But we did not know how to turn that brief and shining coalescing time for us all into an ongoing collective sense of "Us."

As a result, much of that coalescing energy naturally faded. The underlying value set that directly and clearly bonded us together in that moment is still there, however, and we need to use it now to give us the shining future we all should have.

To realize Peace in our time, we now need to be very intentionally clear and more explicit about what those actual shared values that bind us together are.

We need an intentional and values-based culture of Peace and we need functional processes of Peace that can make those values accessible to us all in each of the settings where we need those values to be real.

Those processes are each explained in more details in the four sister books to this book. The books *Cusp of Chaos*, *Primal Pathways*, and *Peace In Our Time* all explain our instinctive behaviors and the problems and opportunities they create.

The fifth sister book to the four *InterGroup* books — *Three Key Years* — explains in practical and functional ways what we need to do, and what we clearly should do, to create success for the children from every group in America. A major chapter of this book explains those processes, needs, and opportunities for our children.

Please use these books to help us achieve all of those goals. Each of those books is intended to be used to help build understanding, and to help create and defend Peace in America.

We Need Leaders Who Want Peace

Leaders will very obviously be key to that Peace building process. To build the future we want and need, we need to select and support leaders who are committed to achieving intergroup Peace as a major part of their leadership agenda. That support for leaders who support Peace is a key component of *The Art of InterGroup Peace* strategy.

We need our leaders to be explicit in their support for InterGroup Peace, and to be clear in their support of win/win outcomes for us all. We need leaders who embrace the values that are outlined and listed above in this chapter.

We need leaders who see their mission and role to be the makers and defenders of Peace — and not instigators of intergroup anger and violence — and we need to support our leaders in their Peacemaker functions and roles.

We also need laws and a culture that all make that level of mutual benefit a reality. We need expectations supported by both enforcement and reinforcement, and we need the basic celebrations and the hero recognitions for all of the successes that will occur as we go down this path to be part of the way we communicate with each other about our shared commitment to *The Art of InterGroup Peace*.

The chapter of this book that describes the tool kit for building and reinforcing our cultures describes those tools in more detail. We need to use those culture-building tools now for us all to benefit.

All of the *InterGroup* books make the point that we need Peace to be embedded in each of our cultures.

The books also state that we need collective and individual understanding of the value of Peace.

To anchor that process, we need both individual and group self-awareness about our own behaviors and thoughts relative to Peace.

We Need to Persuade People to Give Peace a Chance

A key step in getting support for the overall *Art of InterGroup Peace* goal set and strategy is to help other people understand and believe that creating and defending Peace is the right thing to do, and that this is the right time to do exactly that. Each of us who believes in Peace as a higher calling needs to help persuade other people that Peace should be a goal and a commitment for us all.

We each need to persuade people in our own groups to give Peace a chance — and we all need to reach out to people from other groups to create relationships, understanding, and trust at levels that will support and facilitate intergroup Peace.

We need all of us to commit to comply with the key values, the shared commitments, and the preferred and enlightened behaviors that are outlined in *The Art of InterGroup Peace* strategies in order to make those values real, and to have them shape our lives together in ways that create security, trust, and mutual support at multiple levels.

Success in creating the needed levels of Peace will only happen if we take the time to understand what those commitments that we make to each other are, and if we take the time and make the effort to understand what we need to do individually and collectively to make those commitments real.

This book is intended to help with that process. This book is intended to both explain and help people understand the key issues in a very basic way — to help create a sense that Peace is possible and desirable, and to help create a shared sense that Peace should be collectively and individually supported.

We Need Honesty, Understanding, Insight, Courage, Wisdom, Conviction and Commitment to Make Peace Real

We need to do several very important things as part of that process. We each need to understand our instinctive behavior and we all need to be very honest with ourselves and with each other about how those instincts have shaped our thinking, our behaviors, and our lives.

We need to recognize that we each have the mental and emotional components, and instinct linked functions, that can make us saints — and we each also very definitely have the fully wired ability to be sinners — and we all need to clearly understand that our instincts can cause each of those very positive and very negative behavior packages to feel very right in the settings, situations, and contexts where they are each activated, and when they are each guiding our lives.

As part of that understanding, we need to see, acknowledge, recognize and, where appropriate, admit to the sins of our past — and we need to all acknowledge the damage that has been done in sinful ways to people in the places, times, and settings where those instincts have been activated.

We need to regret and condemn our past sins — and we need to act now in ways that will keep those sins from reoccurring and from running and potentially damaging and even ruining our lives in the future. We need honesty — painful honesty — about all of those factors and actions, and we need a new beginning that is anchored in that honesty because we clearly need to begin again in some key areas if we want to get to where we need to go.

We need to commit to one another that we understand what we have done and why we have done it — and we need to commit now to each other and to ourselves that we will do the right things for the right reasons in the right ways to shape our future.

One of our highest levels of ethical achievement is when we commit to ourselves to act in enlightened ways, and then keep that commitment to ourselves. Keeping an explicit and enlightened commitment to ourselves is one of the most effective and solid foundations for self respect, and it is an extremely reinforcing behavior and life choice relative to meeting and honoring the expectations of other people who have also been the recipient of that commitment.

We need to do exactly that with this set of shared beliefs.

The values listed at the beginning of this chapter are intended to function as compass points, guidelines, personal and group commitments, and functional keys and anchors for that process of doing the right things in the right ways for the right reasons. We clearly now need values and beliefs that we trust and understand, and even love, to bring us together and keep us together — and that list is intended to fill that need.

We either need to use the values listed in this chapter — or we need to build another list very much like it — in order to functionally anchor the process of creating a new "Us" here in America.

The list embedded in this chapter isn't perfect, but it is perfectly functional, and it is historically accurate and correct — and that level of collective correctness and practical and operational functionality should be sufficient to meet the needs we have today for a specific and explicit set of aligning beliefs..

We should and can improve that list over time. Other values and beliefs can be added to make the set of core beliefs even more robust and useful. Ideally, we can create a process and develop an ongoing open dialogue for all of us about our core values and foundational beliefs that will help us to enhance, and even expand, this list over time.

Until we have that enhancement process in place, however, this list is available now and it should be functionally good enough to do what it needs to do. Good enough is not perfect — but good enough literally can be good enough.

Other countries that want to use a similar values and core belief alignment process to build internal Peace between their own people who are internally divided in each of their settings should take the time to create their own basic set of core beliefs to use in their settings for that purpose.

They obviously could borrow and study and even use our list as a starter set, but each setting and each country should figure out what the values and beliefs are that will make them good and functional as a country ,and should use the values and beliefs that meet their specific needs.

This particular list of values and core beliefs outlined in this chapter is an anchor list for "Us" in America. It is very American — built from the actual core values that we have expressed and used in various ways as Americans since our country was founded. We are blessed as Americans with very good and fundamentally and foundationally enlightened core values, and it is a functionally appropriate thing to use them now as a package to guide us to a new and extended sense of who we are and who we need to be to succeed in the times we now face.

We Need to Be a Nation of People Who Believe in Peace

It will be important for us as a people to truly be a people who want Peace. It will be important for us as individuals to want and commit to Peace and to have both the insight and the personal courage to do the things that need to be done to make Peace possible.

We need a strong sense of our shared humanity. We need our sense of shared humanity to be a higher calling, respected in every culture and setting, and believed with enough conviction and energy to use that sense of shared humanity to offset and neutralize the seductive primal pull of our powerful instincts that have the constant power to divide us, and to have people in various settings feel great energy doing divisive and damaging things to other people.

To make Peace real, we need all of our people to accept, endorse, agree to, and embrace the highest callings of our common humanity — and we need to commit individually, through our hearts and our heads to Peace.

We need to build Peace everywhere.

Each setting and each community in this country needs to build its own Peace. This book is written to help in every setting—and to be a culture-building and culture enhancement and group support tool for people who believe in those values and those beliefs, and who want to build and protect Peace wherever they are.

We need to make individual commitments to share these values and beliefs, and then we need to act in very clearly focused ways to achieve intergroup understanding and Peace in the settings and situations we are each in.

We need to be able to count on each other to make Peace real. We need the other people who join us in our path to Peace to know that we can each count on each other at a core, fully dependable, full-hearted, highly principled, and explicitly ethical level to support inclusion, democracy, equality, freedom, human dignity, continuous improvement, personal accountability, ethical and intellectual enlightenment, and win/win outcomes for all of us — beginning with creating needed support for all of our children on their paths to personal and collective success.

We Do Need Peace

We do need Peace. It will not happen if we don't do what needs to be done to make it a reality.

Our growing diversity — coupled with our very basic sets of instinctive behaviors that turn intergroup settings far too easily and far too often into intergroup conflict, intergroup anger, intergroup damaging behaviors, and intergroup war — make it very clear to us that we need to keep ourselves from going down that very slippery slope of damaging, negative, sometimes evil instinct guided us/them behaviors, emotions, thought processes and beliefs to a very bad place for all of us in this country.

Knowledge is power.

That is never more true than it is today on this set of issues, challenges, dangers, and opportunities.

We need knowledge. We need collective good will.

We need a commitment to help create win/win outcomes for us all.

We need Peace.

This is the time to be doing that work. We who understand those issues, and we who want Peace are the people who need to do it.

No one else on the planet will somehow do this work for us — and no one else can actually do this work — other than us.

Peace.

In our time.

With each and all of us making it happen.

Is there anything that we could be doing that is more important to the future we want for our children and our grandchildren, and for the people we love than to make Peace a reality now?

Made in the USA
Middletown, DE
24 September 2017